HIP HOP
AT EUROPE'S EDGE

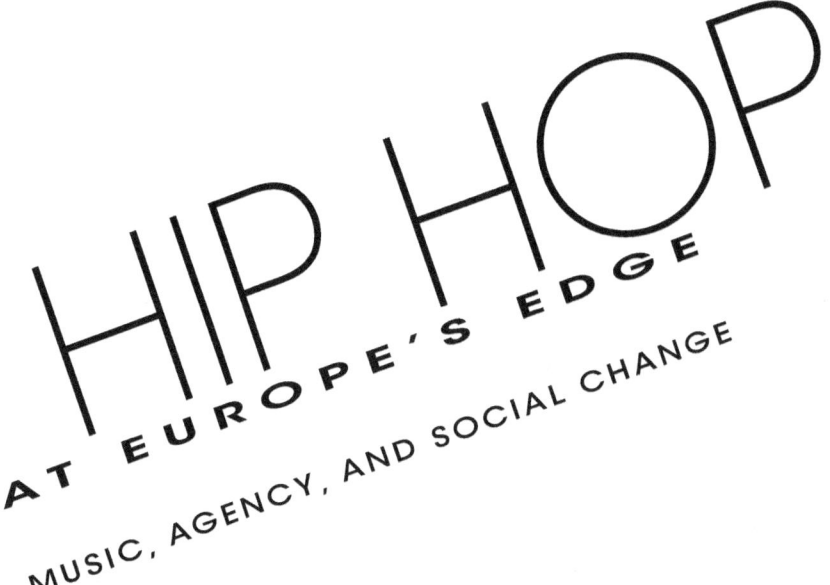

HIP HOP

AT EUROPE'S EDGE

MUSIC, AGENCY, AND SOCIAL CHANGE

Edited by

MILOSZ MISZCZYNSKI AND ADRIANA HELBIG

Indiana University Press

Bloomington and Indianapolis

This book is a publication of

Indiana University Press
Office of Scholarly Publishing
Herman B Wells Library 350
1320 East 10th Street
Bloomington, Indiana 47405 USA

iupress.indiana.edu

Manufactured in the United States of America

Library of Congress Cataloging-in-Publication Data

Names: Miszczynski, Milosz, editor. | Helbig, Adriana, editor.
Title: Hip hop at Europe's edge : music, agency, and social change /
    edited by Milosz Miszczynski and Adriana Helbig.
Description: Bloomington ; Indianapolis : Indiana University Press,
    2017. | Includes bibliographical references and index.
Identifiers: LCCN 2016043843 (print) | LCCN 2016048153 (ebook) |
    ISBN 9780253022738 (cloth : alk. paper) | ISBN 9780253023049
    (pbk. : alk. paper) | ISBN 9780253023216 (e-book)
Subjects: LCSH: Rap (Music)—Europe, Eastern—History and
    criticism. | Rap (Music)—Europe, Central—History and criticism. |
    Rap (Music)—Social aspects—Europe, Eastern. | Rap (Music)—
    Social aspects—Europe, Central.
Classification: LCC ML3531 .H567 2017 (print) | LCC ML3531 (ebook) |
    DDC 782.4216490947—dc23
LC record available at https://lccn.loc.gov/2016043843

1 2 3 4 5   21 20 19 18 17 16

In loving memory of Urszula Miszczynska.

CONTENTS

ACKNOWLEDGMENTS

THIS VOLUME SEEKS to define hip hop, popular culture, and systemic transition. It explores an experience of a generation treating hip hop as an important element of its life. It shows multiple meanings and dimensions of popular culture. It also reflects complexity of experiences of westernization, globalization, and capitalism on the edge of Europe. It has been a very fruitful and valuable experience to work on this project.

I am grateful to Indiana University Press and Raina Polivka for their interest in the project from the initial call for papers. It has been an excellent collaboration. I would like to also thank all of the authors and reviewers for their work and valuable advice in shaping the final vision of this volume.

I am much obliged to all the institutions that helped me while editing this volume. The work was realized during my doctoral studies at the Institute of Sociology at the Jagiellonian University, Poland. I worked on this project while affiliated with the University of California, San Diego, Columbia University, New York, and the University of Oxford.

Thanks to my colleagues who supported the development of ideas and provided insightful feedback about the book. I would like to thank Jacek Nowak, my friend and academic mentor who provided valuable practical advice on the process of editing and always encouraged new developments. Important roles in supporting me at various stages of this project were also played by Marek Kucia, Janusz Mucha, Martha Lampland, David FitzGerald, Christina Turner, Akos Rona-Tas, and Saskia Sassen. I thank them kindly for their friendly advice, openness, support, and faith in the project.

Without the support of my friends and family, this project would probably not have happened. Emma Greeson has been the best partner I could imagine, supporting the volume's idea from the very beginning. My wonderful parents, Urszula Miszczynska and Jan Miszczynski, were always there for me, ready to listen and providing valuable directions. I would like to thank all of my friends who helped me through all the stages of my work: Przemek Tomaszewski, Maciej Zacharewicz, Andrzej Kuta, Charlotte Lercel, and Erwin Tarczyn.

Finally, I would like to thank Adriana Helbig, who joined me as a coeditor and was an invaluable asset in shaping the contents to the book and leading to the final stages of its publication.

Milosz Miszczynski

HIP HOP
AT EUROPE'S EDGE

INTRODUCTION

Milosz Miszczynski and Adriana Helbig

VLADIMIR PUTIN MADE headlines when he appeared on the televised 2009 "Battle for Respect" music contest run by Muz TV (Russia's MTV) to deliver an antidrug message to young people. Putin's decision to engage with hip hop, while admittedly awkward, hints at the powerful cultural and political role that the genre plays in former socialist contexts. From the most marginalized to the most influential, people engage with hip hop to shape and make credible their economic, political, and social realities. However, if even the president of a country as influential in global politics as Russia is participating in televised rap events, then why is scholarship on hip hop in former socialist countries so scarce?

Hip hop in Eastern Europe has been stigmatized as inauthentic, due to its apparent lack of historical connection to the genre's African American roots and alleged lack of connection to black identity. Strongly influenced by aesthetics from the United States since the early the 1990s when hip hop first traveled across post-socialist borders, hip hop has since developed unique trajectories in each locale. The degree of access to music from the United States in the post-socialist era depended on a country's political relationship with the West prior to the break-up of the Eastern Bloc. The state of the music industries following socialist collapse also determined how musical genres were introduced, circulated, and appropriated, post-1989. Networks of corruption that took root in the collapsed Eastern economies in the 1990s determined the type of technologies to which people had access. Illegally dubbed cassettes and compact discs sold at bazaars shaped post-socialist aesthetics and relationships to music from the West, which in certain aspects of the everyday seemed just as inaccessible for the majority as it had during the socialist era. Social, economic, and political attitudes toward digital

1

piracy were shaped by the degrees to which copyright laws pertaining to digital media were introduced and the varying ways they were enforced. Digital piracy rates continue to be very high, and in certain contexts are still on the rise as access to digital technology and the internet increases. As post-socialist consumers traverse digital borders, varying abilities to physically move across borders have also shaped musical consumer culture. New borders, reshaped territories, the expansion of the European Union, the Schengen Zone, economic migration, educational and professional opportunities, and foreign language skills shape new realities for the young generation of consumers born in the post-socialist era.

To say that hip hop was merely yet another genre appropriated from the West in Central and Eastern Europe is to gloss over the complex ways that certain genres marked listeners as cosmopolitan and reconstituted power dynamics in social systems where Western cultural products were imbued with high degrees of social capital. Complex social networks among family, friends, and friends of friends facilitated access to currency, food, and everyday items needed to survive the transitions of the 1990s. Hip hop, with its roots in impoverished urban landscapes, reverberated strongly among a generation whose opportunities for safety, stability, and success seemed to shift and close at a moment's notice. The generation growing up in the chaos of post-socialist transitions found footing and solace in experiences expressed by musicians in the United States giving voice to the marginalized. In a post-socialist society marred by violence, police corruption, poverty, and instability, hip hop offered not only a language to voice these experiences, but also a sense of strength that such realities could, in some way, be transcended.

More than 20 years after socialist collapse, the former Eastern Bloc countries are as dissimilar as ever. There has been a war in the Balkans. Czechoslovakia has split into two countries—the Czech Republic and Slovakia. Poland, Hungary, Bulgaria, and Romania have entered the European Union. Russia has used military might against Georgia and Ukraine. Pre-socialist histories are shaping post-socialist narratives. Thus, while this book offers country-based analyses of hip hop histories in Eastern Europe, it does so in relation to the complex historical, economic, social, and political realities that determined how hip hop has been appropriated, and where, why, and by whom it is deemed a source of agency and identity.

Contributions to the volume elucidate a wide range of theoretical issues relevant to the study of global hip hop. First, they address issues connected to the social tensions and political rhetoric embodied in and reflected in hip hop performance, consumption, and circulation. They analyze the political nature of hip hop and its inherent power in post-socialist society through its historic association with African American civil rights struggles. Second, they place hip hop in new, post-socialist commercial spaces that position music as a commodity to be circulated, purchased, and sold. The market's engagements with music shed light on individual relationships to music in post-socialist societies, where music production once was controlled by the state. The growing access to technology and social media has positioned the internet as an inclusive music-making sphere. Drawing on a variety of methodological orientations, including participant observation and interviewing, archival-historical research, critical textual analysis of the mass-mediated texts of public culture, and content analysis of lyrics, contributors from a variety of disciplines including sociology, ethnomusicology, and anthropology analyze the seen and unseen globalizing forces that continue to shape the relationships youth have with hip hop. Third, they offer interdisciplinary perspectives on the processes through which global hip hop forms have shaped and are shaped by local social conditions, offering case study analyses that elucidate how local actors infuse hip hop with context-significant meanings and position hip hop as a viable form of local expression. Fourth, they contextualize black hip hop's influence within post-socialist hip hop culture. The authors theorize how issues of race, class, gender, and sexuality shape discourses of authenticity and influence notions of identity among hip hop musicians and audiences.

HIP HOP, POST-SOCIALISM, AND DEMOCRACY

Musical genres from the West are widely perceived as having played instrumental roles in offering alternative spaces of expression within musical spheres perceived as censored. Jazz, perceived as protest music by musicians in socialist society, was cast as an expression of freedom and individuality. Scholars in the West imbue rock music with the power of having brought the Cold War to an end. These genres are positioned in scholarly literature of the 1980s and 1990s as products that hold the promise of freedom, capitalist dreams, and individualism. Not analyzed within these texts, however, are the cultural, racial, class, and gender constraints that shaped the musical products of the United States before these products came across socialist borders. Constraints in the music industries regarding expressions of sexuality, censorship regarding lyrics, augmented by industry-wide glass ceilings for women and minorities, are never part of the picture. The idealized notion of rock as freedom clouds scholarly understandings of how people in socialist countries actually engaged with these musical genres, many of which were banned, albeit not always because they were from the West. Where an analysis of hip hop differs is that it is a genre that gained broader popularity in the United States at the time of the socialist collapse in the late 1980s. It hit public awareness in the United States with a sharp turn among African American hip hop musicians toward the political, critiquing police brutality, racism, and economic marginalization. These ideas coincided with broader sentiments in societies transitioning from socialist systems to market economies. Widespread corruption, violence, social insecurity, and a change in values augmented anxieties that were expressed in African American hip hop of the time. Hip hop becomes the genre of choice for young men and women because it gives voice to their present-day experiences. This argument is strengthened by the drastic decline of jazz in post-socialist countries in the 1990s. Once the voice of antigovernment protest, jazz lost its political salience as the state collapsed and struggled to define itself. Hip hop, with its visual and aural messages of marginalization, took its place.

As Elezi and Toska point out, hip hop in Albania has played an important role in politics, giving voice to alternative identities of political candidates and the Albanian electorate. The politicization of hip hop is no surprise in Albania, where music has been used as a tool for ideological control and political promotion, especially during the highly repressive communist regime. Nevertheless, hip hop has also emerged as a genre of the everyday—apolitical and underground. These diverging yet overlapping and mutually engaging scenes remind us of the complexities in researching popular music, deemed by some as political and by others as apolitical. As Balandina (this volume) notes in her analysis of hip hop in Macedonia, rap has been used as a platform to express ethnic and cultural difference while at the same time serving as a cultural mediator to bridge ethnic divides.

Mujanović reminds us that hip hop is best understood in the historical context of the music scenes from which it emerged. The antichauvinistic and antiauthoritarian character of Yugoslav popular culture that had begun in the 1980s and was cut short by violence in Bosnia-Herzegovina found a renewed voice in hip hop after the war. Ewell makes a similar argument regarding the emergence of Russian rap as an expression that finds parallels in Russia's rich literary tradition. Through an array of hip hop examples, he shows that hip hop has offered an avenue for artists to promote dissent and question power in a country where freedom of speech continues to be suppressed.

Hip Hop and Emerging Market Economies

Hip hop emerged on the post-socialist scenes just as the state-owned music industries spiraled into collapse. The drastic decline in state sponsorship for music production, performance, reproduction, and training forced the reconstitution of relationships between the artist and the public. With the arts no longer subsidized, musicians of all genres had to find alternative ways of supporting themselves and their work. Many classical musicians moved abroad, seeking performance opportunities in the West. Folk and traditional musicians were usurped into nation-building efforts, often sponsored by political parties eager to build on socialist associations of folk with "the nation," establishing post-socialist political agendas within ethnic frameworks made audible through folk music and dance. Popular musicians, especially those in earlier stages of their career, faced extreme difficulties in launching their careers with no national or international network of distribution in place. Emerging independent labels emerged alongside Western majors including EMI, Sony BMG, Universal Music Group, and Warner Music Group, which shaped the development of post-socialist music industries. While the majors flooded the markets with music from the West, relatively few locally known musicians gained international recognition in the first decade of transition. Local genres such as turbo-folk (Serbia), disco polo (Poland), chalga (Bulgaria), manele (Romania), and arabesk (Turkey) were widely disseminated through informal bazaar sales and high revenues based on relatively low musical production values.

In this era of collapse and drastic change, musicians with limited access to technology and minimal funds for recording studio time took to hip hop as a way to make music within their economic means. Often with nothing more than a home computer, musicians created beats and samples, replicating sounds they heard on hip hop albums from the United States. Many hip hop concerts were held outside, accompanying break dancing in public parks, similar to how hip hop emerged on the streets of the South Bronx, as public parties. With a high unemployment rate, especially among young men, hip hop offered an outlet for social connection, a safe space amid surrounding violence, and an improvised form of expression that allowed for an immediacy in sharing one's feelings and ideas.

Whereas hip hop's origins are associated with lower-income musicians in impoverished neighborhoods, Musić and Vukčević point out that, throughout the 1990s, the hip hop community in Serbia was composed mostly of middle-class youth who used the genre to stress their cosmopolitan identities. They adopted moralistic views toward lower-class youngsters and their culture. By the late 1990s, however, hip hop in Serbia was claimed by a variety of subcultures, among them dizelaši associated with street crime. The opening up of hip hop to *dizel* culture has helped Serbian hip hop shed its association with top-down, middle-class morals and find new forms of expression among socially mixed crowds.

Hip hop's association with emerging post-socialist class identities is made clear in the contribution of Barrer as well, who argues that Slovak rap in the mainstream is characterized by a masculine narrative of capitalism that champions upward social mobility through financial enrichment and celebrates practices of conspicuous consumption. Similarly, Miszczynski and Tomaszewski, in their chapter on hip hop in Poland, identify the role of branding in rap. While Polish rap nurtures the idea of classlessness and collective solidarity, it constructs a new sense of self in reference to Polish neoliberal reality. The theme of capitalist mobility, couched in a rhetoric of modernization and globalization, is picked up in the contribution on hip hop in Estonia by Vallaste, who points to the contradictory nature of nation-building and globalization that is at the heart of numerous political, economic, and artistic projects in Estonia.

HIP HOP ON THE MARGINS

Hip hop, as a genre of individualized expression and as a genre of social critique, has become romanticized in global hip hop scholarship as the voice of the marginalized. Indeed, marginalized groups have turned to hip hop expression not only in the United States but worldwide. But to simply state that people turn to hip hop to express discontent, anger, and social critique is to limit not only the genre's broader meanings but also the multivalent ways that people have engaged with hip hop on a global scale. Throughout Eastern Europe, hip hop, through its association with US popular culture, has been perceived as a genre of status. People familiar with hip hop mark themselves as cosmopolitan, as being aware and able to engage with cultural products from the West that cost money to produce and consume. They separate themselves from those who do not understand or don't want to engage with hip hop, claiming a level of cultural capital in a society that in fact may dismiss them because they differ in physical appearance from the majority. Hip hop practitioners set themselves apart through the types of clothes they wear, oftentimes purchased in hip hop specialty stores that carry styles not available at bazaars that carry more affordable clothing. Hip hop practitioners also set themselves apart through the ways they move their bodies. Many are physically fit through their participation in break dancing—a visible difference, especially in the early years of transition, when alcoholism was widespread. Women participating in hip hop embrace the option of a more unisex appearance that sets them apart from the hypersexualized gender representations of the transition years. Because the economic transitions affected everyone across the board, hip hop scenes emerged as inclusive of anyone who could help facilitate the scenes in their development. Though some hip hop scenes have divided along ethnic lines as they have become more commercial in nature, it is significant to note that ethnicity has not been a major factor of disunity, which is significant when considering that violence in Eastern Europe has historically erupted along ethnic lines.

Tochka's contribution to the volume touches on themes of social, economic, and political exclusion among Albanian migrants living in Greece. He contrasts this group's experiences with participants in Tirana's emerging entertainment economy, arguing that while hip hop creates spaces of inclusion for some, it reinscribes long-standing hierarchies of difference in the other. Işik and Basaran delve deeper into hip hop's role in creating as well as forming divides among communities. Focusing on economically differentiated youth in Turkey, the authors analyze how an arabesk-influenced hip hop has given voice to an unemployed, uneducated segment of the population and has spurred the development of a genre known as "arabesk rap." The genre offers a glimpse into the ways in which the modernization process in Turkey has created exclusionary cultural and economic spheres.

The contribution on Romani rap in the Czech Republic by Ruzicka, Kajanova, Zvánovcová, and Mrhalek shows how Roma use rap to give voice to their experiences of marginalization and discrimination. Gontchar, in his analysis of rap in Russia, offers a similar analysis of how hip hop shapes but also normalizes excessive consumption and violence. In contrast, Ventsel and Peers, in their analysis of hip hop in Sakha, point to the absence of resistance and protest in Sakha rap and its strong emphasis on good, clean fun.

Hip Hop and Global Circulations of Blackness

Eastern and Central Europe has a relatively limited history of contact with the African continent, having no colonial history to speak of, unlike Western powers such as the United Kingdom and France. Thus, unlike in Western European countries, the number of African migrants is relatively lower and can be attributed more to a socialist relationship built on educational exchange between countries such as the former Yugoslavia and the former Soviet Union with socialist-leaning countries on the African continent. Cultural engagements with blackness are mediated through a socialist rhetoric of racial equality that now engages with predominantly US-mediated representations of blackness through movies, sport, and music, including hip hop. Through its indexical association with the United States in the post-socialist era, blackness is celebrated, (mis)appropriated, reified, and engaged with as a concept, an identity, an expressive medium, and as an ideology. It is simultaneously a symbol of power, strength, and endurance as it is one of marginalization. Hip hop gave voice to the anxiety experienced as a result of shifting degrees of power in post-socialist society. Initially a genre that sought legitimacy through degrees of appropriation of African American aesthetics, it quickly gave rise to localized styles through language choice, lyrical content, and other performance aesthetics.

Šentevska analyzes the appropriations of "ghetto" imagery and rhetoric in Serbia hip hop videos. Looking closely at local concepts of "ghetto," she argues that the ghetto can refer to a disadvantaged neighborhood, a whole city, or it can point to Serbia as the ultimate ghetto. Pointing to tropes that characterize hip hop in the United States, Oravcová analyzes the notion of "realness" in Czech hip hop. Drawing on her long-term involvement as an active member of Czech hip hop scenes, she offers insider perspectives on notions of realness in commercial and underground hip hop. Craig, in his analysis of hip hop in Croatia, analyzes the notion of "keeping it real" from the perspective of DJ culture. Focusing on DJ Phat Phillie, who founded the first chapter of the Zulu Nation in Croatia, Craig argues that the tenets of hip hop shaped by the genre's circulation through time and place are based on the positionality of the DJ. His chapter rounds off the volume by focusing on the agency of the individual in formulating global circulations of hip hop.

New Trajectories

Hip Hop at Europe's Edge joins the growing number of volumes dedicated to global hip hop analysis in a variety of disciplines. Its unique perspective, focusing primarily on hip hop in post-socialist contexts, permits a search for new meanings and roles of hip hop as expressions of transition and new realities. Edited by a sociologist and an ethnomusicologist, this volume brings together scholars who are specialists in their respective fields, including political science, literary theory, philosophy, media theory, and ethnomusicology. Scholars analyze hip hop using theoretical approaches from schools of thought in the United States, the United Kingdom, the European Union, the former Soviet Union, and former Yugoslavia. This richness of dialogue augments the extensive literature on hip hop that exists today. More importantly, it sheds light on the processes through which and the reasons why hip hop has been appropriated and become such a significant musical genre worldwide.

PART I

HIP HOP, POST-SOCIALISM, AND DEMOCRACY

CHAPTER 1

RAPPING INTO POWER

The Use of Hip Hop in Albanian Politics

Gentian Elezi and Elona Toska

SINCE ITS BEGINNINGS in the 1970s among African Americans in the South Bronx, New York, hip hop has been a vehicle for promoting messages of dissent for culturally, sociopolitically, and economically alienated communities. Given its role in giving voice to the marginalized, it is no surprise that it became one of the most popular art forms of its kind, alongside jazz, blues, and be-bop. Though it has a short history, hip hop in one of its three forms—rap, break dancing, and graffiti—has been a strong influence in many political movements, using linguistic and stylistic tools to push forward politically charged messages.

One of the unique features of hip hop, and particularly rap, the musical genre of hip hop, is its local specificity. Despite being embraced in many marginalized communities in the United States and abroad, rap lyrics are full of lyrics of *home*, whatever that might be to the rapper or hip hop artist (Perry 2004). This artistic and creative flexibility enabled "hip hop [to be] a cultural form that attempts to negotiate the experiences of marginalization, brutally truncated opportunity, and oppression" (Rose 1994). Most importantly, through choices of vernacular, messages, and beat, hip hop was able to go global, an artistic and social movement with a global reach through local expressions (Mitchell 2001). Inspired by the US hip hop movement, Brithop emerged in the United Kingdom among urban communities. Hip hop was embraced as a tool for mobilization by Islamic movements in the United States, United Kingdom, and France (Das 2005); disenfranchised Middle Eastern and sub-Saharan African youth in France (Cutler 2007); national identity in the Basque country (Urla 2001); redefining a concept of place and identity in Istanbul (Solomon 2005); and gender discourse in the Czech Republic (Oravcová 2012), among other such expressions.

Perhaps exactly because it was born among marginalized youth in the multiethnic melting pot of New York City, hip hop was attractive to many other groups in other parts of the United States and the world. In many hip hop scenes around the world, New York included, artists and their performances are recognized as having "mainstream" and "underground" components, each carrying out different functions in the rebellion of the marginalized against race, gender, economic, or sociopolitical injustice. Some of the new scenes noted above have been more mainstream, while others have had more of a purist, underground nature. Tools such as language (vernacular lexicon, English vs. mother tongue), style (clothing, adornment, gesture, and hairstyles), ethnic markers (dialectisms, national symbols such as flags), gender norms, and self-identified authenticity are inextricably linked to how hip hop artists and particularly rappers build their identities (Cutler 2007). Their application is a fluid process that enables artists both to appeal to members of the community they are aligning themselves with and to distance themselves from others.

Hip hop's overt engagement in dissenting against power structures defined by racial, social, economic, and political inequities has been played out outside the formal political structures of the communities whose concerns it voices. Though significant, compared to its sociocultural and economic influence, hip hop's political power remains weak compared to its social and cultural impact (Butler 2004). Despite this overall trend, in recent years, perhaps due to the increased popularity of many hip hop singers among African Americans, but also in the white middle class, there has been a greater overlap of hip hop as a social movement and political campaigns or elections. The United States is a particular example of this intersection of hip hop and formal political structures. Though hip hop's potential contribution to politics was dismissed following the 1984 elections, hip hop artists across the United States have been vital and active participants in the most recent elections. In 2003–2004, Russell Simmons's Hip Hop Summit Action Network, P. Diddy's "Vote or Die," and Jay Z's "Voice Your Choice" campaigns were significant bipartisan social movements aimed at political engagement. In the last eight years, the engagement of hip hop with mainstream politics in the United States has taken the form of bipartisan promotion of voter registration from bodies such as the League of Young Voters, the Hip Hop Caucus, the Hip Hop Summit Action Network (NBC 2004), or formal endorsements of political candidates, such as the grassroots mobilization by Questlove of The Roots and Jay Z and Beyoncé's $40,000-a-seat fund-raising dinner for the Obama campaign (Grant 2012). Leaders of the League of Young Voters propose that as a result of the increased participation of hip hop artists in getting out the young vote, the highest number of previously marginalized 18- to 24-year-old African Americans registered and voted in the 2008 and 2010 elections. Despite disagreements over the effectiveness of the electoral system among hip hop artists in the

United States,[1] many analysts agree that the engagement of hip hop with mainstream politics has been useful for both politics and hip hop. Particularly in the case of the Obama campaign over the last two elections (2008 and 2012), but also during local elections in 2010, many believe that it was through the involvement of the hip hop movement that greater political engagement of marginalized youth was reached. However, there are those who argue that this political engagement was reached because, in many ways, President Obama's path, like that of many hip hop artists and the movement itself, was paved with struggle and dissent.

POETRY AND BEAT IN ALBANIA

The hip hop movement came to the Balkans and Albania in the early 1990s, alongside many other new musical forms previously forbidden by the communist regime. In a vacuum of postindustrialization, amid racial and religious majorities and minorities, hip hop succeeded in taking root and becoming one of the most popular musical forms, easily accessible through the media. Dozens of new Albanian artists chose rhythm-and-blues (R&B) and hip hop as their genre, often shifting between the two forms while exploring newfound freedoms of artistic expression.

This chapter explores the role of Albanian hip hop in Albanian politics during the last decade. Through the case study of the involvement of a hip hop band in political campaigns in 2003 and 2009, it will explore the utilization of hip hop as a vehicle for creating an alternative identity for a political candidate and the Albanian electorate. It will focus on the case study of Edi Rama (artist-turned-politician and main opposition party leader) and West Side Family, one of Albania's best-known hip hop bands, during Edi Rama's political campaign for mayor of the capital, Tirana, in 2003 and the general elections in 2009. During these two campaigns, West Side Family's Edi Rama created two songs: "Tirona" (local dialect for the name of the capital) during the 2003 local elections for mayor of the capital, and "Çohu!" (Rise Up!), the soundtrack of the Socialist Party's campaign for the national general elections in 2009. Our analysis will explore themes of hip hop as a tool of political and radical dissent as well as increased political engagement and will assess to what degree this case study represents an example of a social movement co-opted into a partisan political fight under the guise of dissent and rebellion.

The global hip hop movement, in its full span of local forms, has been studied through a variety of academic lenses: ethnomusicology, anthropology (Solomon 2005), sociolinguistics (Morgan 1993, 2001; Cutler 2007), cultural studies (Mitchell 2001), postmodernist social theory (Potter 1995; Caldwell 2007), and many other social sciences and humanities. However, research on the development of the hip hop scene in Albania and Albanian communities is scarce. The aim of this chapter is to present a case study through an interdisciplinary lens. The chapter draws on themes of cultural studies and the globalization of hip hop, social theory and hip hop as a force of resistance challenging the dominant forces, and sociolinguistic analysis of dialects, lexicon, and identity creation.

UNDERSTANDING THE ALBANIAN CONTEXT

In Albania, music has been used as a tool for ideological control and political promotion, especially during the highly repressive communist regime. Prior to 1944, there was a rapid development, referred to as the National Renaissance of Albanian art and culture, whose study and performance was banned during the communist regime for ideological reasons (Koco 2005). During World War II, fighters for the National Liberation Army of Albania wrote and performed military songs used to inspire and galvanize the troops to continue in their path of guerrilla-style fighting against the foreign invaders. Following the war, art and culture succumbed to a "socialist realism" ideology whose main aim was to create the "New Socialist Man" (Capaliku and Cipi 2011). During the 40-year dictatorship, songs were written to praise leaders, inculcate ideology, and promote specific sociocultural and political norms and lifestyles, glorifying the *new man* of the Communist Party—known in Albania as the Party of Labor of Albania. While these musical creations belonged to several musical genres—classical, folk, or light rock—the range of exploration and innovation remained strictly controlled by the socialist regime. The censorship process established clear demarcations of what counted as Western influence—bourgeois tendencies considered to be threatening to the peace and well-being of the socialist Albanian society (Koco 2005).

Cultural events were mostly organized in Tirana, which was home to the Opera and Ballet Theatre, Theatre of the People, the Hall of State Variety Show, the Concert Hall of the Palace of Culture, the Hall of the High Institute of Arts. Performances at these venues, and many others in smaller cities and rural centers, were focused on keeping morale high through positive lyrics, mainstreamed use of formal Albanian language (the Tosk dialect), and specific beat patterns. To attain this purpose, the content and form of songs were controlled and strictly censored to fit with the dictatorship's specific agenda, particularly with regard to "Albanian" as a uniform ethnic, linguistic, socioeconomic, and political identity. The main musical genre was defined as "light music," which is folk in style.

Nonetheless, American (i.e., Western) influences were felt in Albanian arts and culture. Voice of America and various other programming sources were available to the public, though in many cases only after being filtered through the Soviet system. This does not mean that Albanians were encouraged to access these art and media forms. People were persecuted and jailed for "agitation and propaganda" for listening to the Voice of America or other stations such as Rai Uno (an Italian TV station) and, after 1961, Yugoslav TV stations such as JTR-1 and JTR2 (Kadija 1994).

Despite this rigorous control, most art forms, including music, developed in two streams: the visible and the hidden. Unlike literature, which could be smuggled and published abroad, the hidden struggle of music could hardly remain silent. Though many Albanians continued to listen to forbidden music and read forbidden books, a large number of artists were not able to experiment, create, or perform their chosen genres freely. Whenever they battled the socialist regime, any nonapproved music genre or performance was met with harsh censorship. Perhaps one of the most notable examples is the case of the more "jazzy" creations of the second and eleventh National Festivals of Albanian Music, which were met with censorship and repression in 1972 (Satka Mata 2011). Following performances at the festivals in 1963 and 1972, the party and its leader, Enver Hoxha, discharged and actively prosecuted the organizers of the festival by declaring them "enemies of the people" for introducing "immoral values" in the songs and performances (Këlliçi 2002). However, even then, access to foreign media was increasing, setting up the scene for many musical genres to flourish after the end of the communist regime in 1992. Nonetheless, the relationship between music and politics in Albania history up to 1992 is fraught with suppression, censorship, and one-sided imposition of norms that had to be followed.

Hip Hop in Albania: Rapping in the Era of Post-Communist Freedoms

Before introducing our case study, it is important to acknowledge that Albanian music was not limited to the Republic of Albania prior, during, and after communism. Albanian hip hop is a rich musical and social movement that encompasses artists from Kosovo, Macedonia, Montenegro, and other culturally and ethnically Albanian communities. Most of these communities were part of former Yugoslavia, and as such experienced varying levels of freedom to engage with the global hip hop movement. However, for the purposes of this chapter, we are focusing on the hip hop scene in Albania, particularly West Side Family.

Starting in the early 1990s, Albanian singers and songwriters have explored a wide range of music types: rock, country, jazz, classical music, turbo-folk, and hip hop. Given the dearth of experimental and innovative Albanian music prior to the end of communism, these creations have been strongly influenced by Western musicians. Albanian hip hop artists emulated in particular the nature of performances of American rappers and singers. Freedom of expression also extended to the use of art, including music, in politics. Albania's social fabric, a primarily artificial construction during the communist regime that disintegrated in the era of transition to democracy, was enriched by the experimentation in music and the arts.

However, the hip hop scene in Albania is clearly distinct from that in the United States and elsewhere. First, the Albanian hip hop and R&B scenes are not as uniquely segregated as those in the United States or elsewhere. The distinction is not necessarily clear even in the United States, where hip hop originated, so it will be not discussed at length in this chapter. While many academics distinguish between hip hop and R&B in terms of lyrics, rhythms, and political engagement, rap and R&B are considered two subcategories of hip hop music in the Grammy Awards—the most prestigious awards given annually to performers in the United States. For the purposes of this chapter, we recognize hip hop as a social movement, with rap as its musical genre, while R&B as another specific musical genre, characterized by softer, mellower rhythms and romantic lyrics, and as a predecessor to rap and hip hop. The hip hop scene in Albania has been inspired in appearance and performance style primarily through rap and hip hop artists, while R&B has had stronger influence on content, resulting in a mixed Albanian version of hip hop.

Since the 1990s, the Albanian hip hop scene has seen a prolific growth, with dozens of artists within Albania and an even livelier hip hop scene among Albanian speakers in Kosovo, Macedonia, Montenegro, and the United States. A unifying theme among these hip hop artists is the use of the Albanian language in their songs, interspersed with English words, not unlike the patterns observed in Italian and German hip hop by Androutsopoulos and Scholz (2002, 2003). West Side Family is one of the oldest bands in the hip hop scene in Albania. One of the pioneers of hip hop as a style, they paved the way for many other hip hop artists.

The intersection of music and politics in Albania was not uncommon during the communist regime, with songs used to promote political messages and idealized visions of society in the vein of socialist realism. Perhaps as a result of socialist realism co-opting artists to sing the communist regime's political tunes, or because engagement in politics has been considered a "serious" matter, after 1992 the involvement of artists and musicians was scarce. The choice by Edi Rama and West Side Family to cooperate in two election campaigns did not go unnoticed by other politicians. Soon, other singers joined campaigns, such as Ermal Mamaqi, a pop singer, who joined Sokol Olldashi, former minister of transportation, in the campaign for mayor of Tirana in 2007. As explored in more detail in the discussion section, including music in the marketing component of the electoral campaign was quickly embraced by the Democratic Party in the 2009 national elections. They were joined on the campaign trail by Youth Democrat leader and sex-symbol-turned-singer-turned-politician Çiljeta, who campaigned for the Democratic Party in 2009 and 2011.

Edi Rama: Rebelling into Conformity?

Edi Rama has been one of the most dominant public and political actors in the Albanian scene since 1992. With a controversial and dynamic personality, he was part of the group of intellectuals who started to oppose the Albanian communist regime after the fall of the Berlin Wall. Back then, working as a professor in the Academy of Arts of Tirana, he organized one of the first dissident public events, called *Refleksione* (Reflections). A book with the same title followed, written by Rama and his friend Ardian Klosi, another intellectual (Rama and Klosi 1992). He became popular at the time, although later he refused to be part of the first opposition political party in 1992.

A painter, writer, lecturer, and former basketball player, in the early 1990s Rama started to wander through different European countries, detaching himself from the early transitional developments in his country. However, after his return, his continual clashes with the policies and party line of the new president of Albania, Sali Berisha, brought troublesome experiences to his life. In 1996, he was beaten badly and left for dead in one of the Albanian capital's streets. Photos of him covered in blood went around the world and represented somehow a signal for what was going to happen one year later, during the violent year of 1997. He left Albania again to recover in Paris.

After the civil unrest and the political changes of 1997, Rama returned to Albania and was appointed minister for culture in the government of Prime Minister Fatos Nano, then leader of the Socialist Party. He started a process of transforming the capital of Albania, Tirana, which he continued later in 2000 in his capacity as mayor of the city. As some of the major Albanian newspapers pointed out at the time, "Rama is the first minister of culture who speaks to artists as an artist" (*Koha Jone* 1998; *Shekulli* 1998). The public and media perception of him was that of a modern reformer and innovator, an artist willing to rebel against existing norms and structures around what being a "politician" meant in Albania. The major newspapers followed this approach, and he used this relation in a brilliant manner (Budini 2008). This visibility and media attention helped Rama create and establish his image as a man on a mission who came to change the city.

In this new position, he became one of the most popular politicians in Albania, implementing important changes and bringing some quality and color to the capital city. His performance guaranteed him not only reelection in 2003, but also the title of Mayor of the World 2004, an internet-based voting competition. Riding the wings of this success, he ran and won the leadership of the Socialist Party in 2005, after the electoral defeat of the socialists and the resignation of the party's long-standing leader, Fatos Nano. In this new and important role, he ran for the third time as mayor of Tirana in 2007 and won by a sound margin. Holding the two positions, mayor of Tirana and leader of the opposition party, he prepared for the big step: the political elections and his ambition to become prime minister of the country during the 2009 elections. Although he did not win, he remained in his position as leader of the Socialist Party and, after four years of harsh opposition and after losing the municipality of Tirana in 2011, he prepared for and won the general elections of June 2013 (which political analysts considered to be his last chance in politics). Despite losing national and local elections in 2009 and 2011, Rama is still remembered in Albania and globally as the mayor who saved Tirana from dreary memories of communist pre-fab construction and the illegal construction that boomed post-1992, as documented by his May 2012 appearance in TEDxThessaloniki (Rama 2013).

An introvert by nature, Rama is nevertheless extremely passionate about the changes he believes await Tirana and Albania. His approach has been deemed ruthless but effective by many who appreciate his results, if not his methods. Ready for battle at all times, Rama has portrayed an image of "him against the world [of Albanian suffering and evil]," independent of the level of political involvement, a rebel ready to bring about change by whatever means are available. He transformed Tirana's shabby buildings and drug-ridden central park both as minister of culture and as mayor of Tirana.

WEST SIDE FAMILY, THE ALBANIAN HIP HOP PIONEERS

West Side Family, an Albanian hip hop group, was established by three young men—Roland, Miri, and Flori (*nom d'art,* Dr. Flori)—who met while attending the same high school in Tirana. The name of the band refers to the West Coast rappers in the United States who inspired them, such as Tupac Shakur, Snoop Dogg, and Dr. Dre (Shahini interview, 2013). Initially, their style was raw rap, with no chorus or melodic features in the songs. Their lyrics focused on socioeconomic problems of everyday life in Albania. Civil unrest in 1997 shocked them and influenced the spirit of their themes (Shahini interview). They became popular in 2000 with their debut song "Deluzion" (Delusion), and, later, in 2002 with the more popular "Mesazh" (Message), which they performed at the national song competition "Kenga Magjike 2002" (Magical Song 2002). Rama, then mayor of Tirana, was a member of the jury.

Though popular with the audience, they did not win any prizes, but the trio was asked to write a song for the city and then invited to perform with Rama for Mother Teresa Day in October 2003. Their first album, titled *Jeta Shkon* (Life Passes By), was produced in 2003 by Super Sonic Albania, including the song "Tirona." Their second album, *West Side Family,* which includes several songs performed in festivals in Albania, was finished in 2007. While *Jeta Shkon* was a much more hip hop–focused album, their second album experimented with multiple styles, including pop, folk, and classical music. In addition, while their first album was more carefree in content, their second album attempted to bring social issues to the forefront through Dr. Flori's poignant and tasteful lyrics. Their musical career has slowed since 2010, though Dr. Flori was the author of the lyrics of the winning song of the National Festival 2012. The song "Identitet" (Identity) represented Albania at the Eurovision contest that was held in Sweden in May 2013.

Rama asked West Side Family to write "Tirona" in early 2003, a local elections year. Initially, the song was not related to the campaign, but rather a sought to promote the city through music, branding the new era under Rama's administration. The band accepted Rama's proposal without any hesitation, since they were inspired by his personality, vision, and performance as an artist-turned-mayor. Alongside many others, the hip hop artists saw Rama as different from other politicians; they believed he was a good manager and that he could change Tirana and Albania (Shahini interview).

Following Rama's request, the band brainstormed with him to write the lyrics and the music. The song was followed by a video entirely conceptualized by Rama. He appeared in the video as well, rapping a few lines as a solo. His image of being young, out of the ordinary, and innovative was further developed by this new experiment. The performance put a good spin on his campaign for mayor of Tirana later that year. Rama ran for his second term with "Tirona" as the official campaign song. In the meantime, it had become one of the most popular songs in the country. This made it very easy for him in terms of sending a message to the electorate. Due also to his personality and his commitment to changing Tirana in the first term, he won the elections of 2003 and became even more popular, and not just in the capital.

The band did not participate in his campaign, although they supported Rama. This was only one of the differences between this campaign and the one in 2009. The most important is probably that "Tirona" was not composed specifically for the campaign, but, strategically, it was created and launched several months ahead. In this way, it created its own appeal and popularity in the people, and afterward it was used for the campaign, carrying its own weight as a winning card rather than as one of the many campaign messages (Shahini interview).

After nine years of local management as mayor and four years as leader of the opposition party, in 2009, Rama finally ran for the prime minister's office for the first time. By then he had become a central and leading political figure, who dominated the public sphere in terms of presence, image, and influence. This "natural" rise built on his multiple political roles since 1998, first as minister of culture and mayor of Tirana in 2000, and then as leader of the Socialist Party in 2005. He was no longer the controversial mayor/artist who painted the city's façades; he had changed and adapted himself to the new role of political leader (Budini 2008), playing the game in a highly partisan political arena with the

Democratic Party and Socialist Party dominating the discourse. Since 2005 he had gradually changed his look (no more colorful suits), his style (no more agendaless engagements and improvisation), his tone of voice (calmer, slower, and more reflective), and, last but not least, the content of his public discourse. He was aware of the fact that now he was communicating to a larger and different kind of electorate.

However, following the successful experience with West Side Family in 2003 and the positive impact that his participation in the song had in further improving his image and likability (reflected in voting patterns as well), he decided to go for another collaboration with the band. Considering the fact that the band was very popular among young people, this strategy was also based on the need to engage first-time voters (Fuga interview, 2013). Thus Rama asked the band to write a new song for him and to be fully involved in the national campaign this time. This would mean playing their music and songs at each of his campaign events (around 50) and being with him on the stage to sing the new song at the end of political speeches. The band agreed to endorse his campaign and write the campaign song.

Since Rama wanted to repeat the success of "Tirona," he expected to be in the video of the new song and sing with the group. However, following the band's suggestions, he agreed not to sing in the video, but to give a speech within it. This short speech was an intermezzo, in which he made statements taken directly from his political speeches. This adaptation to the new style of Rama and the decision not to sing in the song were explained mainly by his new ambition and the scope of its mission: becoming prime minister.

An Authentic Albanian Blend

West Side Family's members recognized that their style has been influenced by US hip hop and other global trends. However, in both of the campaign songs they chose to embed Albanian rhythms in the percussionist beat required of a hip hop song. The rhythm in the song "Çohu!" (Rise Up!) is much more active, while "Tirona" has the beat of a popular football club fans' song, a beat known to many in the capital and beyond. In addition, despite the fact that they claim to be influenced directly by US West Coast rappers, their style has softened and become more melodic over time. In a few songs they have also included Albanian folk music melodies, following the trend of the music market in Albania.

The combination of socially and politically aware hip hop artists and artistically aware politician is unique to the Albanian case. It is precisely because the two combined forces that their songs were so successful. In 2003, "Tirona" and West Side Family were popular in the musical scene in and of themselves, but it was Rama's direct involvement that gave them an extra edge in widespread popularity. The band reflected in an interview after the first performance of the song at a charity concert that while "the public welcomed us very well, when Edi Rama came on to the stage there was a huge rupture from the audience, as if we were at the Champions League," a very popular European soccer tournament (Panorama Plus 2009.)

"Tirona" was probably one of the first cases of actual endorsement by celebrities (US-style) in Albania. Edi Rama and his staff were captivated by the Obama campaign of 2008 and its effectiveness in garnering the youth vote. Under this influence, they tried to adopt several of its elements in their campaign. Although they had a previous successful experience with the band, West Side Family's direct involvement in the 2009 campaign was a new element, appealing more to the expected effects of celebrity endorsements in an Obama-style campaign involving stars such as Beyoncé, Jay Z, and others.

Most importantly, the motivation for making the two songs was strong on both sides—both Rama and his team, and the West Side Family artists strongly believed that joining the campaigns was the politically, socially, and artistically right thing to do. The three hip hop artists, representing disenfranchised youth disillusioned with the last two decades of limited progress in Albania (Shahini interview), wanted to voice their discontent, and nothing does that better than rhythmic rapping. The artist-turned-politician wanted to repeat the success of 2003, where people could see him as an artist even though he had put down the paintbrush and taken up the busy agenda of the capital's mayor. The relationship was a win-win situation, though it did not result in Rama's election in 2009, a result that was due to other factors.

An analysis of the lyrics of the two songs reveals a couple of important points: first, the Albanian vernacular used, and second, the content of the two songs. Whether intentional or not, the choice of both was intrinsically linked to the purpose of each song.

"Tirona" offers a rather popular, sketchy, and funny description of the city, its life, its people, activities, and so on, adopting a descriptive approach by trying to gather paradoxes and all the positive and negative perceptions of life in Tirana. Using the local dialect of the Tirana region, the song had no partisan political references, but aimed at strengthening the common ground of the citizens of Tirana and awakening their pride while their city was being radically reconstructed and improved. By celebrating the Albanian capital for the complex, paradoxical, and constantly improving city that it was, "Tirona" was fit for a reelection campaign, as it aimed to unite people, not to highlight divisions and inequality. Though corruption, gender and income inequality, and other social issues are portrayed in it, there is hope in the future that it depicts.

While "Tirona" was celebratory, "Çohu!" was a militant call to action. In many ways, it embodied hip hop's raison d'être, protesting profound social injustices observed in Albania. In other ways, it is different, as neither Edi Rama nor the Socialist Party are marginalized in the Albanian society. In many respects, Rama's engagement with the Socialist Party makes him part of the system and the political game that resulted in some of Albania's social issues. While he was not prime minister of Albania, he was mayor of Tirana, where nearly a third of all Albania's residents live, and the Socialist Party controlled some of the biggest municipalities in the country, such as Durres, Korca, Vlora, Fier, and Gjirokastra.

In his book *Decoded*, Jay Z describes hip hop as the perfect combination of poetry and boxing. When asked about their participation in the 2009 campaign, West Side Family noted their revulsion at the lack of change and improvement in the 17 years since democracy had arrived (Panorama 2007). West Side Family has embodied Jay Z's description through many of their other creations, including the song "Mjaft" (Enough), sung with opera singer Edit Mihali. "Çohu!," sung in the official Albanian language (rather than the local one in "Tirona") with a call to action in the lyrics, built a parallel to the speeches and poetry of Albanian Renaissance writers of the 1920s, who paved the way for the overthrow of feudalism and the monarchy in Albania.

"Çohu!" had a clear political content and message. It called for a general awakening of the citizens, to take their fate in their own hands and bring about change. This revolutionary attitude of the lyrics and message was inspired to a certain degree by Fan Noli, one of the Albanian intellectuals and political activists of the Albanian Renaissance during the first half of the twentieth century. In one of his famous poems,[2] Noli calls on all the groups in Albania, from south to north, to stand together against what he considered to be the authoritarian rule of the feudal system and the Albanian monarchy of the period. These references were present throughout Rama's political campaign. Many of his speeches contained direct quotations from Noli's work. Once again it was a clear strategy of attaching his own image to that of a widely appreciated historical personality in Albania. This connection to Noli's work was the main suggestion that Rama had for the band when writing the lyrics of the song (Shahini interview). As for the video, once again, all the ideas and concepts of that work came from Rama himself. In the video he was shown in many different scenarios, close to the main social and interest groups in Albania (miners, workers, fishermen, farmers, etc.), working with them, as one of them. Of course, particular attention was paid to the younger generation, and thus the video has many scenes with children singing the chorus of the song (the video starts with a little girl singing the chorus with no background music).

As discussed in the introduction, hip hop music has been considered as rebellion, containing messages of protest and revolution. It has been associated with marginalized groups in society, fighting for their rights against injustice, prejudice, inequality, and so on. From this point of view, our case study seems to reveal a paradox: The leader of a mainstream party has used hip hop music for his electoral campaigns, performing in the respective videos and on stage with the band.

However, when analyzing the case in depth, especially using the primary data gathered during the interviews, we could elucidate a different and more coherent perspective. Although Edi Rama is the leader of a mainstream party, he has been perceived as an outsider in mainstream politics—as a revolutionary and an independent actor. The path of his political career has been characterized by unconventional patterns and behaviors. The public image that he created over the years was that of a controversial leader who played by his own (new) rules. The members of the band claimed that Rama's image reflected a rebellion against the "old politics." They considered him as beyond political parties (Shahini interview). As a result, attaching his style to hip hop was not particularly difficult. Not only was Rama perceived as being beyond mainstream politics, but he defined himself as a "nonpolitician," or antipolitical (Rama 2008; Zaloshnja 2008). He considered himself a man with the mission of changing his country, but not interested in politics as we know it.

In addition, the ideological line he embraced for his campaign was based on the concept of inclusiveness and unification of the population against the political elite of the time. He claimed to pursue a polity "beyond the left and the right," beyond flags, encouraging the rise of Albanians to face and confront the old politicians (Tare 2008). These concepts are also reflected in the lyrics of "Çohu!"[3]

These analyses and considerations give us a better picture of the relation between Edi Rama and hip hop music in his electoral campaigns. Although he was leading a mainstream party, he was not perceived as a mainstream leader. Thus, the verve and the revolutionary spirit that hip hop music brought to his campaign were consistent in tone with his personality, his political activity, and his mission.

Conclusions

Like all other hip hop movements, Albanian hip hop is embedded in the sociopolitical realities of its source, in this case, postdemocratic Albania. It has a strong connection with everyday realities, challenges, and perspectives. However, perhaps due to the communist regime and its use and abuse of music, Albanian hip hop is apolitical compared to the movement in its initial shape as a dissenting voice of marginalized groups.

Despite its popularity, rap in the United States has always had a very politically charged relationship with the wider society, as a result of which it has often been vilified for its violent, sexual, racist, and criminal depictions (Perry 2004).

Interestingly, Albanian hip hop music does not have the same connotations. The themes it deals with are some that Albanian society grapples with on a daily basis: reinventing new identities for the communities in the postcommunist vacuum, and reimagining the past, present, and future. Within this context, hip hop has developed as a communication instrument used mainly by young persons, targeting other young people.

By focusing on and analyzing the case study of the collaboration between Edi Rama and West Side Family, we have tried to explore the patterns of the use of hip hop in Albanian political campaigns and to shed light on what this collaboration highlighted about the nature of the hip hop movement in Albania. The analysis of the development and utilization of the two hip hop songs explored whether and how Albanian hip hop was co-opted into representing a mainstream political party and its messages. We tried to elucidate the tensions between the nature of hip hop as a tool for rebellion and alternative expression on the one hand, and the rebranding of a well-established political apparatus on the other hand.

These mutually beneficial experiences, for both the politician and the hip hop band, were developed thanks to the particular context of our case study. The public image of the controversial leader and the characteristics of Albanian hip hop created the bases for interesting synergies and for a successful impact in the political campaigns. Although in the second case Rama did not win the elections, the use of a hip hop song appeared to be strategically valuable, especially in terms of further branding his image and better communicating his political message. His direct involvement in singing and acting in the video of the song could be considered an innovative approach to political marketing and its evolution in Albania. This last consideration might be an interesting starting point for further in-depth research.

NOTES

1. "You might get killed if you don't listen enough / Well I guess I'm dead / 'Cause I ain't listen to Puff / Best believe our system it sucks / And a person like me don't believe in assisting in such / Nah I be rippin' 'em up / But for every pond there's different ducks / I believe if you participate at a lower level / You can get a lot more things done / Like working with the alderman / But I ain't alterin' this song to be a political statement / Let's take it back to the basement." Lupe Fiasco, "Outty 5,000," as cited in Butler 2004.

2. In the poem "Anes lumenjve," Noli expresses his anger and rebellion against the regime and calls for everyone (*katundare e punetore*: villagers and workers), everywhere in Albania (*qe nga Shkodra gjer ne Vlore*: from Shkodra to Vlore) to stand up, confront the regime, and bring change.

3. *Pertej gjithe flamujve ka vetem nje Shqiperi* (Despite all flags there's only one Albania). *Pertej cdo partie ka vetem nje Shqiperi* (Despite any political party, there's only one Albania).

References

Androutsopoulos, Jannis, and Arno Scholz. 2002. "On the Recontextualization of Hip Hop in European Speech Communities: A Contrastive Analysis of Rap Lyrics." *Philologie im Netz* 19:1–42. http://web.fu-berlin.de/phin/phin19/p19i.htm (accessed March 26, 2013).

Androutsopoulos, Jannis, and Arno Scholz. 2003. "Spaghetti Funk: Appropriations of Hip Hop Culture and Rap Music in Europe." *Popular Music and Society* 26:463–480.

Arie, Sophie. 2003. "Regeneration Man: Tirana's Pop-Star Mayor Has Cheered Up Albanians by Giving Their Capital a Facelift." *The Guardian.* http://www.guardian.co.uk/world /2003/oct/22/worlddispatch.sophiearie (accessed March 22, 2013).

Budini, Belina. 2007. "WEST SIDE FAMILY Do krijojmë parti politike [West Side Family We Will set up a political party]." *Panorama.* http://www.merbraha.com/index.php /kulture/muzike/85.html (accessed March 23, 2013).

Budini, Belina. 2008. "Edi Rama. Politikani pop(ulist)-star" [Edi Rama—popul(ist) star politician]. *Polis* 8(Winter):3–19.

Butler, Paul. 2004. "Much Respect: Toward a Hip Hop Theory of Punishment." *Stanford Law Review* 56:983–1016.

Caldwell, David. 2007. "The Rhetoric of Rap: A Challenge to Dominant Forces? Bridging Discourses." *ASFLA Online Proceedings.* http://www.asfla.org.au/wp-content/uploads /2008/07/the-rhetoric-of-rap.pdf.

Capaliku, Stefan, and Kastriot Cipi. 2011. "Country Profile: Albania." *Compendium of Cultural Policies and Trends in Europe*, 13th ed. Council of Europe/ERICarts. http://www.culturalpolicies.net/down/albania_012011.pdf (accessed March 26, 2013).

Cutler, Cecelia. 2007. "Hip-Hop Language in Sociolinguistics and Beyond." *Language and Linguistics Compass* 1(5):519–538.

Das, N. Deepa. 2005. "Listen Conniving Haramzada." Junior thesis, Department of Politics, Princeton University, Princeton, NJ.

Decker, Jeffrey Louis. 1993. "The State of Rap: Time and Place in Hip Hop Nationalism." *Social Text* 34:53–84.

Eastman, Carol. M., and Roberta F. Stein. 1993. "Language Display: Authenticating Claims to Social Identity." *Journal of Multilingual and Multicultural Development* 143:187–202.

"Edi Rama do të këndojë së bashku me West Side Family këngën e fushatës së PS-së [Edi Rama will sing the SP campaign song together with West Side Family]" *Panorama Plus.* http://www.merbraha.com/index.php/revista-vip/1547.html (accessed March 23, 2013).

Grant, Ronald. 2012. "We the People: Hip Hop's Role in the 2012 Election." *HipHopDX.* http://www.hiphopdx.com/index/editorials/id.1963/title.we-the-people-hip hops-role-in-the-2012-election (accessed March 26, 2013).

Kadija, Refik. 1994. *American Studies in Albania in the Past and the Future.* Berlin: John F. Kennedy-Institut für Nordamerikastudien.

Këlliçi, Skifter. 2002. *Festivali i njëmbëdhjetë* [The 11th festival]. Tirana: Botimet Toena.

Koco, Eno. 2005. "Shostakovich, Kadaré and the Nature of Dissidence: An Albanian View." *Musical Times* 146(1890):58–74.

Koha Jone. 1998. "Rama, i pari minister kulture qe flet me artistet si artist" [Rama, the first minister of culture to speak to artists as an artist]. *Koha Jone* 9:26.

Mitchell, Tony. 2001. *Global Noise: Rap and Hip Hop Outside the U.S.A.* Middletown, CT: Wesleyan University Press.

Morgan, Marcyliena. 1993. "Hip Hop Hooray! The Linguistic Production of Identity." Paper presented at Annual Meeting of the American Anthropological Association, Washington, DC.

Morgan, Marcyliena. 2001. "Nuthin' but a G Thang: Grammar and Language Ideology in Hip Hop Identity." In *Sociocultural and Historical Contexts of African American English,* ed. Sonja L. Lanehart (pp. 187–210). Athens: University of Georgia Press.

NBC. 2004. "Hip Hop Artists Unite to Get Young Citizens to Vote: Russell Simmons Created the Hip Hop Summit to Give Young Adults the Chance to Learn More Voting." *Hardball with Chris Matthews,* NBC News. http://www.nbcnews.com/id/5529282 /#.UVFioBxvDW8 (accessed March 26, 2013).

Oravcová, Anna. 2012. "The Real Czech Emcees Please Stand Up! Construction of Authenticity in Czech Rap Music." In *New Cultural Capitals: Urban Pop Cultures in Focus,* ed. Leonard R. Koos. Oxford: Inter-Disciplinary Press.

Perry, Imani. 2004. *Prophets of the Hood: Politics and Poetics in Hip Hop.* Durham, NC: Duke University Press.

Potter, Russell. A. 1995. *Spectacular Vernaculars: Hip Hop and the Politics of Postmodernism.* Albany: SUNY Press.

Rama, Edi. 2008. "Pse nuk jam politikan" [Why I am not a politician]. *Gazeta Panorama.*

Rama, Edi. 2013. *Take Back Your City with Paint.* TEDxThessaloniki. http://www.ted.com /talks/edi_rama_take_back_your_city_with_paint.html (accessed January 21, 2013).

Rama, Edi, and Ardian Klosi. 1992. *Refleksione* [Reflections]. Tirana: Botime Albania.

Rose, Tricia. 1994. *Black Noise: Rap Music and Black Culture in Contemporary America.* Middletown, CT: Wesleyan University Press.

Satka Mata, Fjoralba. 2011. "Albanian Alternative Artists vs. Official Art under Communism." *History of Communism in Europe* 2:73–84.

Shekulli. 1998. "Rama leviz ujerat e ndenjura ku vegjetonin institucionet kulturore" [Rama moves the stagnant waters where cultural institutions were languishing]. *Shekulli.*

Solomon, Thomas. 2005. " 'Living Underground Is Tough': Authenticity and Locality in the Hip Hop Community in Istanbul, Turkey." *Popular Music* 24(1):1–20.

Tare, Ilva. 2008. "Cfare jeni ju Edi Rama?" [What are you, Edi Rama?]. http://www.panorama .com.al.

Urla, Jacqueline. 2001. " 'We Are All Malcolm X!': Negu Gorriak, Hip Hop and the Basque Political Imaginary." In *Global Noise: Rap and Hip Hop Outside the U.S.A.,* ed. Tony Mitchell (pp. 171–193). Middletown, CT: Wesleyan University Press.

West, Chelsi Amelia. 2008. " 'Mic Check, One Two, One Two': Globalization, Cultural Transfer and the Production of Hip Hop Identities in Tanzania and Albania." Unpublished honors thesis, Millsaps College.

Zaloshnja, Eduart. 2008. "Politikan Edi Rama?" [Edi Rama, politician?]. *Panorama.* http://arkivalajmeve.com/lajme/artikull/iden/9073/titulli/Politikan-Edi-Rama.

INTERVIEWS

Interview with Endri Fuga, political campaign manager and advisor to Edi Rama, March 14, 2013.

Interview with Miri Shahini, member of the hip hop band West Side Family, March 22, 2013.

DISCOGRAPHY

West Side Family. 2003. *Jeta Shkon.* Super Sonic. Particularly songs: "Deluzion," "Mesazh," "Tirona (feat. Edi Rama)." Official video for "Tirona": http://www.youtube.com/watch ?v=QPktvccn1so.

West Side Family. 2007. *West Side Family*. Super Sonic. Particularly song: "Mjaft (feat. Edit Mihali)."

West Side Family. 2009. "Çohu! (feat. Edi Rama)." Official Video for "Çohu!": http://www.youtube.com/watch?v=FVCXWMZ_q8A.

CHAPTER 2

NOTHING LEFT TO LOSE

Hip Hop in Bosnia-Herzegovina

Jasmin Mujanović

THE CENTRAL ARGUMENT of this chapter concerns the function of hip hop in postwar Bosnia-Herzegovina (BiH).[1] I observe that thematically, BiH hip hop is still working through the horrors and absurdism of the dissolution of the Socialist Federal Republic of Yugoslavia (SFRJ) and the kleptocratic postwar "democratic" transition, focusing in particular on the results of the Dayton constitutional order. In a country where peace has meant depoliticization and disenfranchisement, hip hop represents one of the few youthful, militant, politicized voices of critique, protest, and resistance. This voice, then, is both a rejection of the nominal "Europeanization" project of the European Union (EU) and the United States in BiH, as well as of the dominant (though internally fractured) ethno-chauvinist paradigm.

As such, this chapter is divided into two primary sections, the first explaining the present political arrangement of the state of BiH and the second detailing the thematic concerns and perspectives of Bosnian hip hop, in direct response to the political and social conditions within the country. It is necessary, however, to contextualize the emergence of the present political situation in BiH, as well as the emergence of BiH hip hop in a broader historical narrative.

THE DISSOLUTION OF YUGOSLAVIA & DAYTON BiH

The dissolution of the SFRJ had its origins not in Robert Kaplan's famed "ancient ethnic hatreds" thesis (Kaplan 1993), but rather in a narrow, conservative, antidemocratic reaction against the move toward decentralization and democratization that had begun with the 1974 constitutional reforms. The 1974 reforms seismically decentralized the Yugoslav state, the new order itself being a result of lasting liberal–conservative tensions within the federation (Gagnon 2004). Conservative elements within Yugoslavia's ruling establishment resented these reforms as an "anarcho-liberal" turn (Rusinow 1978:156). Liberals, on the other hand, were frustrated by the strictly institutional nature of the reforms. Ever the strategist, Tito managed a precarious balancing act between the two sides, with lasting consequences: "While Tito ended the reforms, he retained the decentralization of power to the republics (and two autonomous provinces of Serbia). The result was eight unreformed republic-level economic and political systems with institutional interests in the maintenance of their institutional bases of power (Gagnon 2004:59–60).

The emergence of Slobodan Milošević in 1987 was a coup for the forces of reaction in Yugoslavia. Fundamentally, Milošević accomplished his meteoric rise to power by marrying the visions of authoritarian Yugoslav communists and Serb nationalists. While the authoritarians merely resented the reformers for fracturing Belgrade's central authority, the nationalists insisted on the presence of a vast anti-Serb conspiracy. To the nationalists, the 1974 constitution was an attempt to divide the Serb nation across republican borders, thus reducing the Serbs to a systematically marginalized and discriminated-against minority. The 1986 publication of the so-called *Memorandum of the Serbian Academy of Sciences and Arts* (SANU) (Mihailović and Krestić 1995) proved to be the ideological manifesto—invoking the specter of an impending "genocide" of the Serb nation—on which Milošević relied in his initial confrontations with Serbian reformists in 1987, and then later across the federation (Glaurdić 2011:65–66).

The subsequent war in BiH was almost entirely the product of the wider dissolution of the SFRJ and had its origins in Belgrade (and Zagreb) rather than in Sarajevo. As Milošević's attempt to recentralize the federation was rejected by republican cliques in Slovenia, Croatia, and BiH (and he was unable to topple them in turn as in Serbia, Kosovo, Montenegro, and Vojvodina), his strategy shifted. Having become a patron of the post-Tito Yugoslav National Army (JNA), Milošević turned to carving out of Yugoslavia at least a "Greater Serbia" (Udovički and Ridgeway 2000:180–181).

The ensuing maelstrom of violence Milošević unleashed was ideologically chauvinist, yet practically characterized by abject criminality and profiteering. Peter Andreas refers to the emergence of a "patriotic mafia" across the region—smugglers, hit men, thugs, and gangsters—whose objectives masqueraded as "national liberation" and the "defense of our people," while in reality pursuing simple plunder (Andreas 2008:28). Understanding the use of ethnic cleansing and genocide in this process became critical to understanding the postwar BiH space, in particular (Toal and Dhalman 2011).

The postwar BiH state that emerges was an exercise in what David Campbell has called "apartheid cartography" (Campbell 1999). Through the internationally brokered/imposed 1995 General Framework Agreement for Peace in Bosnia and Herzegovina, generally known as the Dayton Accords, peace in BiH came through institutionalizing the effects of Serb (and Croat) nationalist ethnic cleansing and genocide. Contemporary BiH is an administrative quagmire—characterized by isolated ethnic enclaves that have replaced once-thriving multicultural cities, towns, and villages.

In short, present-day BiH comprises two highly autonomous entities: the Bosniak-Croat Federation of BiH (FBiH), itself further divided into ten cantons, and the Serb-dominated Republika Srpska (RS), as well as a jointly administered Brčko District. There is then a nominal central government in Sarajevo, headed by a three-member presidency, though final authority resides in the internationally appointed Office of the High Representative (OHR). The BiH state is officially composed of "three constitutive peoples" (Bosniaks, Serbs, and Croats), while the "Others" (persons identifying simply as Bosnian, Roma, Jews, and/or other minorities) are constitutionally barred from many public offices (Claridge 2010). Asim Mujkić astutely refers to this as an "Ethnopolis," a system whereby "[u]nder cover of the legitimacy conferred by free and fair elections, citizens as individuals are stripped of any political power" (Mujkić 2007:113). The official political discourse is thus dominated by a cartel of "competing" (or rather, *electioneering*) ethno-nationalist oligarchs and a facile, disinterested supervisory echelon of international observers and representatives.

It is in this context that BiH hip hop emerges as a voice of critique, protest, and resistance against both the ethno-chauvinists who insist on preserving this state of affairs and their partners in the international community who have institutionalized these relations in the first place.

Contextualizing the Yugoslav Roots of BiH Hip Hop

To understand the perspective(s) of contemporary BiH hip hop artists and MCs, it is necessary to situate their emergence in the vibrant Yugoslav rock and punk music scene of the 1980s. I understand the profound sense of loss and displacement felt by these artists and many ordinary citizens in the wake of Yugoslavia's dissolution in structural, political terms. As Gagnon notes, to a significant extent, while nominally authoritarian, Yugoslavia enjoyed a far more vibrant "civil society" than virtually any of its successor states (Krasniqi and Stiks 2011). This fact is most readily evidenced in cultural terms.

Iva Pauker notes that the lasting popularity of Yugoslav pop culture in the region (and the diaspora) is proof of a once genuine character of "organic coexistence" in the SFRJ; she traces how the emergence of ethno-nationalist movements was marked by a direct attack on the rock and punk ethos of the period (Pauker 2006:73–76). This fact is unsurprising when taken in conjunction with recent archival work, salvaging not merely the technically progressive elements of Yugoslav pop music, as in the case of the then-nascent electronica scene (Bulc 2012a) but also its politics. As one author argues, by 1974, Yugoslavia had seen the release, arguably, of its first transparently queer hit—Muharem Serbezovski's "Ramo, Ramo"—the subject becoming a reasonably frequent theme thereafter, across genres (Bulc 2012b).

The most significant contributions of this period were not merely proof of the viability and organic qualities of a genuine young "Yugoslav" perspective, in contrast to the supposed explosion of "ancient, ethnic hatreds," but a pronounced social critique that informed much of these performances. The so-called "New Partisans" and "New Primitives" represented two faces of this musical turn (Mišina 2010:266). Commenting on a collection of bands whose biggest hits continue to enjoy regular airplay across the Balkans, and whose concerts attract massive audiences in the Yugoslav diaspora, Dalibor Mišina writes that

> the socio-cultural praxis of New Partisans was animated by militant Yugoslavism as a counter-logic to the nationalist dissolution of a distinctly Yugoslav fabric of the socialist community in crisis. Thus, the movement's revolutionary "spirit of reconstruction" permeating its poetics of the patriotic was a mechanism of socio-cultural resistance to political, cultural and moral-ethical de-Yugoslavization of Yugoslav society. (Mišina 2010:266)

By fusing both the themes and melodies of Partisan revolutionary songs, rock 'n' roll ballads, and traditional Yugoslav folk music, these bands attempted a "conscious and deliberate integration of the folkloric and revolutionary stylistic and musical idioms into the rock music template as a strategy for evoking and mobilizing the broadly appealing patriotic sentiments among their audiences" (Mišina 2010:268). It was a youthful reworking of the marriage between working-class militancy and the traditions of peasant insurrections that had guided the original Partisans during the 1940s guerrilla years.

Mišina notes that emergence of the New Partisans in Sarajevo was a reflection of the important historic and cultural position the city enjoyed within Yugoslavia as a whole. This is not coincidental, he writes,

> and has to do with Sarajevo's reputation at the time as the most Yugoslav city of Yugoslavia. Just as [BiH] was, for a variety of cultural and ideological reasons, considered the most Yugoslav republic in the sense that it was perceived as the most harmoniously multicultural and, in that, a model of what the whole country was supposed to be like, Sarajevo, as the most Bosnian city of all (meaning the most multicultural, open, and unsuspecting of the "others"),

enjoyed the reputation of being the epicentre of a specifically Yugoslav brand of socio-cultural arrangement. (Mišina 2010:266)

"In other words," he concludes, "Sarajevo was in many respects thought of as Yugoslavia condensed into one city."

In contrast to the New Partisans' "militant Yugoslavism," Sarajevo also gave birth to the so-called New Primitives, an "authentic Yugoslav answer to punk" (Telibečirović 2011). The Primitives were a loose association of young comedians, musicians, and entertainers who, beginning in 1981, introduced into Yugoslav popular culture, arguably for the first time, a genuine Bosnian, specifically Sarajevan, voice (Spaskovska 2011:360).[2] Almost invariably, their skits and songs dealt with the misadventures of local hoodlums and hustlers, petty crooks, corrupt politicians, bamboozled workers, and uneducated peasants, among others. The absurdist character of their work, however, was guided by serious political messages. The now infamous "Top Lista Nadrealista" (Top List of Surrealists)[3] program gained popularity and notoriety for the scathing nature of its comedy: a typical skit featured a visit to a "factory for the production of nothing"; another portrayed the hiring of new university graduates as statues in local government offices as a measure to deal with chronic unemployment. Today, the program is perhaps best remembered for the almost (appropriately) surreal prognostic qualities of many of the troupe's sketches: One classic skit featured a news report on "rising ethnic tensions in northern Sweden between Eskimos and penguins," fueled by the desire of the region to secede and join with its "motherland, the Arctic" (Telibečirović 2011).

However, the critical reengagement within Yugoslav popular culture that had begun in the 1980s was cut short by the violence unleashed by the forces of reaction beginning in 1991. The cataclysmic experience of the war in BiH, however, was unable to destroy entirely the cultural terrain established by that point, and its essential antichauvinistic and antiauthoritarian character became the basis for a new musical revival: hip hop.

Hip Hop in BiH

Hip hop in BiH began in 1999, centered on the FM Jam production house based in the old steel city of Tuzla. The geography is relevant: Tuzla, like Sarajevo, is an urban center and, more importantly, had during the war largely resisted fracturing along ethnic lines (Hoare 2004:108–110). After the war, this process continued, with authorities (uniquely in the region) spending funds to rebuild and keep up Yugoslav-era Partisan statues and sites of commemoration, and in other cases refusing to ethnically segregate the burial sites of youth killed during the war by Serb nationalist shelling (Armakolas 2011).[4] Nor was the form, hip hop, without significance. As Daniel White Hodge notes, hip hop and rap have "offered definition, value, understanding and a shared language and linguistic form to ghetto communities, which are often otherwise characterized by social isolation, economic hardship, political demoralization and cultural exploitation. . . . Not limited to merely Black or Brown people, rap esteems the ghetto poor experience as valid and real" (Hodge 2010:41).

Initially stripped down and raw, the genre is largely "imported" into BiH through the return of exiles and refugees, as in the case of Edo Maajka and Frenkie, who spent much of the war in Croatia and Germany, respectively.[5] The parallels between racialized urban youth in the United States and the general social malaise in BiH, as well as the broader ghettoized experience of Yugoslav refugees in Europe and North America, are evidenced not merely in the adoption of the genre by local artists, but also in their repeated citing of (and references to) acts like KRS-One, Redman, and N.W.A. as influences and predecessors.[6] This recognition of the "borrowed" nature of hip hop and its history in the culture of black youth in the United States, in particular, accounts in part for the politically progressive and radical perspectives expressed by local MCs. The genesis of BiH hip hop is deeply political, and BiH hip hop artists, in turn, view the genre as itself inherently political. As Frenkie suggests, "*hip hop je religija, ja sam vjernik, ne volim lažne repere kao partizani četnike*" (Frenkie 2007b).[7] Frenkie, in particular, has made these overt political commitments even clearer in his media interviews (Karabeg 2012), though others have expressed similar sentiments (Boračić 2013).

A number of acts emerged from the FM Jam fold, the most noteworthy being Edo Maajka, Frenkie, and, to a lesser extent, HZA. Significant also are Dubioza Kolektiv (Dubious Collective), currently signed to the Gramofon label, whose 2011 album *Wild, Wild East* was a crossover hit (as it is almost entirely in English) (McManus 2011), while their 2013 LP *Apsurdistan* once again had the band dissecting regional politics. Maajka's debut album, the 2002 *Slušaj mater* (Listen to Mother), was an immediate hit. From the outset, songs like "Šverc Komerc" (Smuggling as Commerce) and "Pare, Pare" (Money, Money) established the central themes for BiH hip hop: the criminality that defined the war years and the subsequent transition, corruption, xenophobia, and nationalism. While the album also featured light-hearted tracks, it was the political commentary that gained Maajka and his peers their reputation and their following. It is in his 2004 follow-up album, however, *No sikiriki* (No Worries), that Maajka makes his clearest, most succinct comment on the whole of the BiH situation, describing BiH in the song "Mater Vam Jebem" (Motherfuckers) as a place where "*nije bitna ideologija, bitna je biologija, bitna je genetika* balije, ustaše *i* četnika" (Maajka 2004).[8]

Maajka's implication is clear, and it is one shared by Asim Mujkić. Because of both the war experience and, in particular, the subsequent institutionalized ethnic chauvinism of the Dayton constitutional order, political discourse and democratic aspirations in BiH are reduced to a cynical, fatalistic logic. Essentially: *we, the Bosniaks/Serbs/Croats, need our state/entity/canton to consolidate its authority and secure territories in order that they, our historic ethno-national enemies, will not exterminate us as individuals and as a group.* This "antipolitics" in effect eliminates the possibility of any sort of progressive, change-oriented, collective social project, and instead reduces politics to a contest of permanent, zero-sum hostility and suspicion.

Unsurprisingly, a central concern of BiH hip hop artists becomes the dismantling of this reactionary ideological edifice through both a salvaging of a collective Yugoslav past and social memory, invoking the need for a popular insurrection against ruling oligarchs, and a defense of the diversity of contemporary identities.

To this end, Dubioza Kolektiv, in their hit "Valter" (Walter),[9] invoke both Yugoslav pop culture and the Partisan guerrilla aesthetic as part of their call to arms:

> It's a new time, with new people,
> with a new occupying force,
> but their motives are the same.
> Call them by their right name,
> go out in into the streets,
> and fight for yourself.
> The air flickers
> as though the sky is burning![10]

> No one else will fight for your rights,
> there's no room for fear,
> when the masses speak.
> We're ready for action,
> call out for Valter
> and he will appear!

> Valter will be back, you motherfuckers! (Dubioza Kolektiv 2010)

HZA, meanwhile, laments the lack of precisely such a people's movement, blaming it for the dissolution of Yugoslavia itself, the collective betrayal of Tito's ideological insistence on "brotherhood and unity," and the miseries of postwar BiH life:

> Dear Tito, there's no more *Juga*,[11]
> we're being fucked by imams, priests and hatred,

we've got thieves in charge now.
They've taken your name off of the streets,
nothing is the way it was before,
the whole of Europe is laughing at us.
The economy and the standard of living is totally fucked,
and the hillbillies have come down from the mountains and into the cities.
There's no jobs, no money, no brotherhood and unity,
these kids today will have shit for childhoods.

Where are we now?
Where we deserve to be, because we didn't rise up! (HZA 2007)

Frenkie, however, provides a more critical assessment of the Yugoslav legacy, even as he, like Dubioza Kolektiv, evokes the Partisan liberation struggle: "I won't bullshit you how things were ideal as though things were better in the time of Tito. Bro, it wasn't ideal. Behind the stares, hatred was hiding" (Frenkie 2012a).

Indeed, the young Bijeljina native has established himself with each new album as the most sophisticated of political commentators among these artists, on a range of topics, and increasingly has been recognized as such by the (alternative) media (Imamović 2012). His 2012 album *Troyanac* (Trojan) likely represents his most nuanced rhymes to date. Nevertheless, like Edo Maajka, Frenkie established himself as a political provocateur from his earliest work. Picking up earlier suggestive queer[12] threads, Frenkie penned an unequivocal commentary on his second album, *Povratak Cigana* (Return of the Gypsies):

Hey, *Hodža*,[13] tell me if it's okay
if my buddies Mirza and Samir are gay?
Hey, *Hodža*, tell me if it'd be okay
if tomorrow you found out your son was actually gay?
Hey, *Hodža*, let me know what that would mean,
if you would still love him or you'd throw him away?
If my *Hodža* explains it, I'll understand,
would you allow your son to marry a Croat tomorrow?
Hodža, please tell me the truth,
would you allow your son to bring home a Serb? (Frenkie 2007a)

The song is easily the most overtly pro-queer song ever to have come out of the region. Yet the analysis Frenkie provides is not merely about homophobia or heteronormativity, but a generally chauvinist and reactionary bent to postwar BiH society and, in particular, the use of perceived difference as a means of control and dispossession by local elites.[14] This theme is echoed in Edo Maajka's latest album *Štrajk Mozga* (Brain on Strike), specifically the song "Drukčiji" (Different), which also features rhymes (appropriately) by the Serbian and Croatian rappers Marchello and Kandžija, respectively:[15]

> Don't be afraid, buddy, I'm only different,
> I have nothing against you, though it may seem like that to you.
> I know that they've taught you that being different is to be alien,
> that all those that are different are guilty and ugly.
> They're guilty in an environment that loves to place blame,
> an environment that you can never satisfy or make peace with.
> They've always judged the different,
> and it's all they know how to do.
> . . .
> Actually, it's all in our heads,
> otherwise, how would we know:
> who is beautiful, who is hungry,
> who is attacking, who is defending,
> which ones are fake, which ones are real,
> who is in charge, who is pathetic,
> who is first, who is last,
> who on this track is a Serb, who is Croat, who is a Bosnian,
> Stop! (Maajka 2012)

Yet it is still the junior, Frenkie, who has taken on the political and cultural sacred cows of BiH society most head-on; two cuts, in particular, deserve mention. His 2009 album *Protuotrov* (Anti-Venom) features the song "Nerko," an extended monologue by an eponymous veteran and friend of the artist:

> Nerko, my old chum, is a Golden Lily,[16]
> I've got one of his old crumpled war photos.
> He was wounded twice, and when he recovered,
> he was back on the frontline and he didn't hide.
> Three long winters he spent in the trench,
> he didn't fight for Alija [Izetbegović],[17] but for his family.
> "There's no state on this Earth, which I love more than my little girl,
> you could add a million more to this country
> and it still wouldn't be worth as much as her pinky.
> Fuck this new flag and this new anthem,
> I was defending her," he tells me over a beer.
> . . .
> They used us and in the end threw us away,

we were manipulated, some didn't understand this.
It doesn't matter what side you're on, my friend,
if you believe them today still, then you're a fool. (Frenkie 2009)

After recounting his growing destitution, his children's hunger, the song concludes with Nerko asking his compatriot, "So, tell me, what am I to do with this
Golden Lily?" For Bosnians (and Bosniaks, in particular) sympathetic to the cause
of an independent BiH during the war years and thereafter, the Golden Lily (*Lil-
ium bosniacum*) is a powerful symbol. As the country had at no point in its modern history been allowed a substantive or collective iconography, the "flag with
the lilies" was seen as evoking an ancient, medieval, proudly *Bosnian* (rather than
Yugoslav or, especially, Serbian or Croatian) history—though it was meant to include both Bosnian Catholics and Orthodox Christians. When the OHR unilat-
erally changed the design of the flag to a nondescript yellow triangle on a blue
field in 1998 (Tanner 1998), at the behest of Serb and Croat nationalists, many
Bosnians, and Bosniaks especially, saw the move as a stark visualization of an
unjust peace: first genocide, then apartheid, now revisionism. Frenkie's use of the
emblem, however, is anything but devotional, and the song strongly suggests that
the entire "patriot" narrative is a false one: "We're not important, we're pawns,"
he has Nerko explain.

The betrayal of one's own tribe, as the MC comes to conceptualize it, is center
stage on the album *Troyanac*. Here, however, the narrative is entirely Frenkie's—a
"letter" to Milan. While it is unclear whether Milan is an actual person, he is
clearly also meant as a stand-in for a Bosnian Serb everyman.[18] The song is worth
quoting nearly at length:

A three-winged scale, a symbol of Bosnia and the Balkans,
it's always mine, yours or their side,
it's constantly in use.
They tell me to keep my eyes on my own gate and my own yard.
We committed atrocities and then there is a big "but,"
you burnt and stole as well.
So, for years like that among our own people,
never turning to one another.
And that's why I'm writing you this letter, Milan,
so you can see that we're not all the same.
Mine will fault me but that's my choice,
my intentions are honest and that's why I'm at peace.
I wouldn't agree to their rules today,
time will tell whether I fought or I was a traitor.
There's been enough taking it, it's boiling over in me,

I've decided to offer my hand first.
. . .
Let's stop lying and cheating each other.
I know you're afraid walking through Sarajevo,
you see the Arabic script, your hear the call of the *azan,*
I'm afraid too when I see the *Wahhabis.*
And I'm afraid now as I write these lines,
They'll tell me I've spat on my fallen and my grandfathers.
And I believe you're waiting for a signal from the other side,
I know this well because I'm waiting for it too.
We have so much in common this moment,
when we visit, we lie about our names,
you feel like a swine in Teheran,[19]
much like when I visit Trebinje.[20]
It's easier if we don't pretend anymore,
what matters now is who's a majority in each town,
strength in numbers and we like it.
Nothing good will come of this, you know this, I know this too.
. . .
I won't bullshit you how Dodik is lying to you all,[21]
taking the cash while he blinds you with nationalism.
We're not brothers and fuck the old days
when we went to each other's *Eids* and *slavas,*[22]
all that fell apart quickly and passed,
as brothers butchered each other overnight.
I don't want to compare victims and count the dead,
burnt mosques and destroyed churches.
I'll leave that to those who want to
but I won't manipulate another's pain.
I want to listen and for us to talk,
because we're not going anywhere like this.
I know it's hard when they blame you constantly
and when you hear that line from our end: "a genocidal nation."[23]
You're not like that and it can't be easy, I figure,
but you should know, I don't think that of you.

It's not easy offering others your condolences,
yours will give you the boot and the others will spit on you,
abuse you and shove you into a new conflict,
and that's how the flames will explode again.
It's not easy offering others your condolences,
yours will give you the boot and the others will spit on you.

We can extend our condolences to others,
or keep going in circles for another twenty years. (Frenkie 2012b)

It is difficult to overstate the importance of Frenkie's intellectual contribution, with *Milan* in particular. Contemporary BiH, after all, is a space where one of the country's largest dailies, *Voice of Srpska*, in the twenty-first century can publish an op-ed (utterly confusingly) condemning the practice of mixed marriages as a "Nazi program" that brings families into "bloodshed and . . . throws individuals into chaos, into a small, personal hell" (Pejaković 2012). It is a place where in the twentieth century, just as apartheid was ending in South Africa, it was here being (re)constructed (Campbell 1999:404). Only by understanding the utterly depraved, reactionary, fascistic nature of contemporary BiH politics and discourse can we begin to appreciate the significance of Frenkie's commentary, along with the work of his peers.

It is, thus, a tragedy that speaking out against institutionalized racism and chauvinism and celebrating shared histories, anywhere in the world, would be considered a revolutionary act or make one worthy of the title of "hero," as local alternative media have referred to Frenkie—as it is unfathomable that such a system could continue to persist. Yet such a system persists, indeed, in BiH and it is internationally sanctioned and administered. It is this cruel, persistent reality, even more than the war years, that informs and motivates BiH hip hop as a means of likewise persistent dissent—so much so that when Frenkie describes the crumbling of global systems of domination and dispossession ("Wall Street is burning, the IMF is burning . . . Brussels is burning, Washington is burning. Burn, burn, burn, Babylon!") he cannot but draw particular attention to the BiH context, an acute manifestation of said systems: "Dayton is burning . . . you're burning and I'm burning" (Frenkie 2011). Yet, he insists: "We are the ones we have been waiting for."[24]

Conclusions

"There has never been a consensus within [hip hop] about its purpose, identity, or destiny," argues S. Craig Watkins (2005:5). While this is certainly true of American hip hop, as the genre has become truly global, the claim warrants reassessment. In the case of BiH, hip hop has been consistently and unapologetically political. Edo Maajka notes this himself: "Fancy rims, fancy pussy, fancy houses, who's got more? I'm really glad it's not like that with us. Some tried to pull it off, but it wouldn't go" (Maajka 2008).

The reasons for this are structural. American hip hop emerges from a place of marginality and now struggles to make sense of mainstream acceptance and commercialization. Hip hop in BiH, on the other hand, has a "memory" of a moment in time where now-marginal voices were, in fact, leading a cultural movement toward emancipation. Yugoslavia in the 1980s, though undergoing economic crisis, was for ordinary citizens a popular polity with genuine potential. Its purposeful, violent dismemberment was and continues to be a source of immense social trauma and confusion, especially in BiH, where the actual institutions of state perpetuate a kind of structural violence, suspicion, and absurdism.

Insofar as BiH hip hop artists are attempting to salvage the past, they are doing so with their eyes firmly fixed on the future. They are confronted with the reality that there is no escape from their ghetto because, as Frenkie argues, "the whole of Bosnia is a ghetto" (Frenkie 2006). They are prevented from even entertaining the idea of "bling"[25] and commercialization due to wholesale social collapse, and so are only left with the option to fight: "*nemam više šta izgubit.*"

Notes

1. This paper would not have been possible without the ongoing commentary and editorial assistance of E. Wang of Princeton University. Any errors or faults to be found in this discussion, however, are entirely my own. All translations, and thus any errors in translation, are likewise my own.

2. The troupe was composed of several musical wings, all of them very much embracing a light-hearted, antiestablishment punk-rock aesthetic: Zabranjeno Pušenje, Elvis J. Kurtović and His Meteors, and Bombaj Štampa. During the war, Pušenje would fracture in two: a Sarajevo-based ensemble, composed of most of the original Primitives crew, would largely continue with the same antiestablishment, antichauvinist message, releasing their most recent (appropriately titled) albums *Muzej Revolucije* (Museum of the Revolution) in 2009 and *Radovi na cesti* (Road Work) in 2013. A Belgrade-based ensemble composed of former front man Nele Karajlić and director Emir Kusturica, now redubbed the No Smoking Orchestra, almost completely abandoned the ethos of the old group, instead embracing ethno-nationalist garb, rhythms, and themes.

3. To the best of my knowledge, no complete "official" compendium of the series exists. Thus, while the show is a regular staple of local entertainment programming, and can be viewed in its entirety online, it is difficult to provide "proper" citations of relevant excerpts. Accordingly, I have attempted to fill out my argument using available texts.

4. Importantly, in February 2014, Tuzla also became the ignition point for a series of violent protests across the country that featured masses of citizens torching government offices in response to decades of political corruption, unemployment, and poverty, all with an explicitly antinationalist message (Mujanović and Domi 2014).

5. Maajka, Frenkie, HZA, Moonja, and DJ Soul have occasionally performed together as Disciplinska Komisija (The Disciplinary Commission), though all are better known for their solo work.

6. In a personal correspondence, however, E. Wang notes that "hip hop itself is fundamentally referential and citational—all hip hop artists cite their predecessors and quote and sample other rappers' beats . . . the conversational aspect is inherent in the medium."

7. "Hip hop is a religion; I am a follower. I don't like false rappers like the Partisans don't like Chetniks." The *četnici* were World War II–era Serbian quislings. Though the *četnici* initially opposed the fascist occupation, ideologically they were Serbian nationalists and monarchists. As such, they soon found themselves in league with both the Nazis and the Croatian *ustaše*, likewise quislings, in combating the communist Partisan liberation movement.

8. "Ideology isn't what matters, biology matters, genetics matters: *balije, ustaše,* and *četnika.*" As the above context might suggest, the terms *ustaša* and *četnik* are today pejorative labels for Croats and Serbs, respectively, while the term *balija* similarly applies to Bosniaks— though its meaning and etymology are difficult to translate. Maajka's intent here is not to promote chauvinist rhetoric but precisely the opposite: to note the structural impossibility, under the Dayton system, of being a Bosnian citizen rather than a nationalized, ethnic subject.

9. Vladimir "Valter" Perić was a Yugoslav Partisan from Serbia, who had died in the closing hours of the liberation of Sarajevo on April 6, 1945, and subsequently became a martyr of the Partisan cause (Donia 2006). Valter became an icon of the city, commemorated most famously in a 1972 Yugoslav film titled *Valter brani Sarajevo* (Valter Defends Sarajevo).

10. These two lines are from an exchange between two characters from the above-mentioned film, who use the code to recognize each other as undercover Partisan operatives and begin preparations for the liberation of the city. Like latter-day Partisans, Dubioza Kolektiv invokes this reference as a code to like-minded, contemporary, would-be revolutionaries.

11. A common nickname for Yugoslavia.

12. E. Wang is likely right in suggesting that these texts are better referred to as antihomophobic rather than queer. However, I view Frenkie's work, in particular, as still being *in medias res*, where each new album has displayed a greater tendency toward challenging boundaries and social norms. As such, my use of the term queer is rooted in hope of an *emerging* queerness in BiH hip hop.

13. Imam.

14. Frenkie is perhaps following in the footprints of Edo Maajka's 2008 song "Sve prolazi" (Everything Passes), where the latter observes that "everything changes, nothing is a secret. It used to be shameful to be gay, now they openly declare it" (Maajka 2008). However, while Frenkie repeatedly cites Maajka as the elder statesman of BiH hip hop, Maajka's passing reference here pales in comparison to Frenkie's anthem. Nor, it must be said, is Maajka's interpretation of the "coming out" process entirely clear.

15. However, as my colleague Anita Tavra notes, the attitude toward female-gendered persons remains ambiguous, at best. In many songs, women's bodies remain as territory to be "captured" or "conquered."

16. The Golden Lily was the highest civilian and military order awarded by the Republic of Bosnia-Herzegovina (1992–1996). Named for the fleur-de-lis motif found on its flag, and taken from the thirteenth-century coat of arms of the House of Kotromanić, the one-time rulers of the medieval Bosnian Kingdom crushed by the Ottoman conquest, the "lilies" were offered as proof of a historic antecedent for the newly independent Bosnian state.

17. The first president of independent Bosnia-Herzegovina.

18. And, correspondingly, that Frenkie would be perceived as a "Bosniak," regardless of his actual politics.

19. A local expression meaning "to not fit in," like a pig in a presumably Islamic city.

20. A town in Herzegovina, presently in the RS entity, from which, as elsewhere in eastern BiH, the vast majority of the non-Serb population was expelled or murdered during the war.

21. Milorad Dodik, the longtime and hard-line nationalist president (former prime minister) of the RS, widely suspected of wartime profiteering and postwar racketeering and corruption.

22. Serbian Orthodox feasts, Saint's days or "name days."

23. A frequent Bosniak nationalist claim about Serbians as "inherently genocidal," citing anti-Bosniak/Muslim atrocities, during both the nineteenth and twentieth centuries.

24. A line originally from June Jordan's "Poem for South African Women."

25. E. Wang, however, also argues, "bling is such a central concept in American hip hop *because* it is absent in the social collapse of the American city. It is an obsession born out of a lack. One could make an analogy to Frenkie's topics—he writes about dialogue and criticism because it is lacking."

References

Andreas, Peter. 2008. *Blue Helmets, Black Markets: The Business of Survival in the Siege of Sarajevo.* Ithaca, NY: Cornell University Press.

Armakolas, Ioannis. 2011. "Reconstructing Cultural Heritage in Bosnia: The Case of the Slana Banja Memorial Complex in Tuzla." *Transconflict.* http://www.transconflict .com/resources/perspectives-on-conflict/perspectives-on-the-balkans/reconstructing -cultural-heritage-in-bosnia-the-case-of-the-slana-banja-memorial-complex-in-tuzla/ (accessed May 4, 2012).

Boračić, Selma. 2013. "Muzičari iz regiona ujedinjeni u akciji 'Zašto sam antifašista.'" Radio Slobodna Evropa. http://www.slobodnaevropa.org/content/muzicari-iz-regiona -ujedinjeni-u-akciji-zasto-sam-antifasista/24909049.html (accessed March 23, 2013).

Bulc, Gregor. 2012a. "Dancing under Socialism: Rare Electronic Music from Yugoslavia." *B-Turn.* http://bturn.com/9479/dancing-under-socialism-electronic-music-yugoslavia (accessed March 23, 2013).

Bulc, Gregor. 2012b. "Hard Bosom: Top Pro-Gay Tracks from ex-Yugoslavia." *B-Turn.* http://bturn.com/8384/hard-bosom-top-pro-gay-tracks-from-ex-yugoslavia-part-one (accessed March 23, 2013).

Campbell, David. 1999. "Apartheid Cartography: The Political Anthropology and Spatial Effects of International Diplomacy in Bosnia." *Political Geography* 18(4):395–435.

Cerkez-Robinson, Aida. 2009. "Bosnian President Angry over Plavsic Release." *The Guardian.* http://www.guardian.co.uk/world/feedarticle/8778300 (accessed March 23, 2013).

Claridge, Lucy. 2010. *Discrimination and Political Participation in Bosnia and Herzegovina: Sejdic and Finci vs. Bosnia and Herzegovina.* Minority Rights Group International. http://www.minorityrights.org/9773/briefing-papers/discrimination-and-political -participation-in-bosnia-and-herzegovina.html (accessed November 14, 2011).

Donia, Robert J. 2006. *Sarajevo: A Biography.* Ann Arbor: University of Michigan Press.

FM Jam. n.d. "FM Jam." http://www.fmjam.com/crew/fm-jam (accessed May 4, 2012).

Gagnon, V. P. 2004. *The Myth of Ethnic War: Serbia and Croatia in the 1990s.* Ithaca, NY: Cornell University Press.

Glaurdić, Josip. 2011. *The Hour of Europe: Western Powers and the Breakup of Yugoslavia.* New Haven, CT: Yale University Press.

Hoare, Marko Attila. 2004. *How Bosnia Armed.* London: Saqi Books.

Hodge, Daniel White. 2010. *The Soul of Hip Hop: Rims, Timbs and a Cultural Theology.* Downers Grove, IL: InterVarsity Press.

Imamović, Emir. 2012. "Heroj generacije: Adnan Hamidović Frenkie." Radio Sarajevo. http://www.radiosarajevo.ba/novost/95167/heroj-generacije-adnan-hamidovic-frenkie (accessed March 23, 2013).

Kaplan, Robert. 1993. *Balkan Ghosts: A Journey through History.* New York: St. Martin's Press.

Karabeg, Omer. 2012. "Mladi muzičari za BiH bez podjela i mržnj." Radio Slobodna Evropa. http://www.slobodnaevropa.org/content/most-mladi-muzicari-za-bih-bez-podjela-i -mrznje/24811828.html (accessed March 23, 2013).

Krasniqi, Gezim, and Igor Stiks. 2011. "How to (De)mobilise Citizens: An Interview with Chip Gagnon." *Citizenship in Southeast Europe.* http://www.citsee.eu/interview/how -demobilise-citizens-interview-chip-gagnon (accessed May 3, 2012).

McManus, Liam. 2011. "Dubioza Kolektiv: Wild Wild East." *PopMatters.* http://www .popmatters.com/pm/review/146651-dubioza-kolektiv-wild-wild-east/ (accessed May 4, 2012).

Mihailović, Kosta, and Vasilije Krestić. 1995. *Memorandum of the Serbian Academy of Arts and Sciences: Answer to Criticisms.* Belgrade: Serbian Academy of Arts and Sciences.

Mišina, Dalibor. 2010. "'Spit and Sing, My Yugoslavia': New Partisans, Social Critique and Bosnian Poetics of the Patriotic." *Nationalities Papers* 38(2):265–289.

Mujanović, Jasmin, and Tanya L. Domi. 2014. "Bosnian Spring Signals New Possibilities for Bosnia-Herzegovina." *Harriman Magazine* (Summer):22–25.

Mujkić, Asim. 2007. "We, the Citizens of Ethnopolis." *Constellations* 14(1):112–128.

Pauker, Iva. 2006. "Reconciliation and Popular Culture: a Promising Development in Former Yugoslavia?" *Local-Global: Identity, Security, Community* 2:72–81.

Pejaković, Nikola. 2012. "Miješani brakovi su naci-program komunista." Radio Sarajevo. http://www.radiosarajevo.ba/novost/95010/mijesani-brakovi-su-naci-program -komunista (accessed December 23, 2012).

Rusinow, Dennison. 1978. *The Yugoslav Experiment: 1948–1974.* Berkeley: University of California Press.

Spaskovska, Ljubica. 2011. "Stairway to Hell: The Yugoslav Rock Scene and Youth during the Crisis Decade of 1981–1991." *East Central Europe* 38(2–3):355–372.

Tanner, Marcus. 1998. "Outside World Chooses New Flag for Bosnia."*The Independent.* http://www.independent.co.uk/news/outside-world-chooses-new-flag-for-bosnia -1142950.html (accessed March 23, 2013).

Telibečirović, Amir. 2011. "Sarajevska verzija Montija Pajtona." *Protest.* http://protest.ba/v2 /sarajevska-verzija-montija-pajtona/ (accessed April 29, 2012).

Toal, Gerard, and Carl Dhalman. 2011. *Bosnia Remade: Ethnic Cleansing and its Reversal.* New York: Oxford University Press.

Udovički, Jasminka, and James Ridgeway. 2000. *Burn This House: The Making and Unmaking of Yugoslavia.* Durham, NC: Duke University Press.

Watkins, S. Craig. 2005. *Hip Hop Matters: Politics, Pop Culture and the Struggle for the Soul of a Movement.* Boston: Beacon Press.

DISCOGRAPHY

Dubioza Kolektiv. 2010. "Valter." *5 do 12.* Sarajevo: Gramofon and Menart.

Frenkie. 2005. "Hajmo Rušit." *Odličan.* Tuzla: FM Jam.

Frenkie. 2006. "Mr. Policeman." *Dosta!* Tuzla: FM Jam.

Frenkie. 2007a. "Ej, Hodža." *Povratak Cigana.* Tuzla: FM Jam and Menart.

Frenkie. 2007b. "Yes, Yes." *Povratak Cigana*. Tuzla: FM Jam.

Frenkie. 2009. "Nerko." *Protuotrov*. Tuzla: FM Jam and Menart.

Frenkie. 2011. "Gori." Tuzla: FM Jam.

Frenkie. 2012a. "Francuz." *Troyanac*. Tuzla: FM Jam.

Frenkie. 2012b. "Milan." *Troyanac*. Tuzla: FM Jam.

HZA. 2007. "Dragi Tito." *Opušten Ko Lexaurin*. Tuzla: FM Jam.

Maajka, Edo. 2004. "Mater Vam Jebem." *No sikiriki*. Tuzla: FM Jam.

Maajka, Edo. 2008. "Sve prolazi." *Balkansko a naše*. Tuzla: FM Jam.

Maajka, Edo. 2012. "Drukčiji." *Štrajk Mozga*. Tuzla: FM Jam and Menart.

CHAPTER 3

RUSSIAN RAP IN THE ERA
OF VLADIMIR PUTIN

Philip Ewell

THE SPOKEN WORD has always held a special place in the hearts of Russians.[1] From the poetry recitations by Evgeny Evtushenko in the 1960s that filled stadiums to the inspired lyrics of Russian bards like Vladimir Vysotsky, Russians have sought not only beauty but also repose in artistic literary forms. This is not surprising given Russia's troubled political history over the centuries, which reached its height in the twentieth century with the repressive Soviet era. Countless volumes have been written over the years on censorship in the USSR and on the ensuing balancing act that Soviet artists endured at the hands of the authorities.

That Soviet and post-Soviet Russian rappers felt that same repression is not in doubt. What sets rap, as a genre, apart from other literary forms in Russia is its place in time: It really took hold only in the early 1990s, immediately after the fall of the Soviet Union, so one cannot speak of rap, as a genre, influencing political events in the USSR. Though one could argue that the first rap in Russia was "Rap" from 1984 by the group Chas Pik, an unabashed rip-off of The Sugarhill Gang's "Rapper's Delight" from 1979—widely recognized as the first commercial rap hit ever—it was not until the 1990s that Russian rappers and rap groups such as Bogdan Titomir, Liki MC, Bad Balance, and Mal'chishnik became widely known in the former Soviet Union and, with them, the rap genre itself. The fit was perfect for Russia, with its rich literary tradition and its strong history of performance art.

There are currently two rather well-defined camps in Russian rap: a party/house camp, which features light-hearted lyrics on themes such as love, having fun, and hanging out, while the second might be called a socially active political/artistic camp, which features poignant lyrics of a topical nature. There are, of course, other types of rap in Russia, but most artists, or at least most songs, could fit into one of these two groups.[2] This is important for one simple reason: Your choice of camp will likely determine your chances of making it in Russian rap.

In this article, I wish to place recent developments in Russian rap into a political and cultural context. I will show how rap, in the face of the current political situation within Russia, in which freedom of speech has come under attack, has been able to provide a consistent avenue for artists to promote dissent and question power. The era of Vladimir Putin began on August 9, 1999, when President Boris Yeltsin appointed him prime minister of Russia. On New Year's Eve of that year, Yeltsin resigned and Putin became acting president until his election to the presidency a few months later. For 14 years he has been the undisputed ruler of Russia, and during this period Russia has seen tremendous growth and relative stability. In the past few years, however, it has also seen enormous tension between Putin and the Russian populace. This tension is manifested in the work of several Russian rappers. More generally, one could also say that rap, as a genre, finally found its footing in Russia during Putin's 14-year reign and broke away from its blanket imitation of the American artists who defined it in the 1990s. It is my intention to analyze the interaction of the political context with the cultural production of rap and hip hop music in the era of Putin. Further, insofar as most political tension in Russia has been concentrated in the last few years— since then-Prime Minister Putin announced in September 2011 that he and then-President Dmitri Medvedev would switch places when the president's term expired at the beginning of 2012—I will focus my analysis mostly on the past few years, and on a few key figures in particular.

Perhaps the best-known social activist rapper in Russia is Ivan Alekseev, better known as Noize MC (b. 1985). Noize began his music studies in classical guitar at the age of 10. He was soon performing with various hip hop artists, and by the time he was 20, he had already gained notoriety as a rapper. He is generally considered the best freestyle rapper in Russia, and comparisons with Eminem are frequent. His budding acting career began with the film *Rozygryshch* (2008). Though he had many recording successes prior to his solo career as a rapper, his first album, *The Greatest Hits, Vol. 1,* was only released in 2008. It was named album of the year by the popular Russian lifestyle magazine *Afisha*. Noize acknowledged the irony of the title for his first album, since in fact he already had performed more than 200 tunes by the time the album came out, so in this sense it was his "greatest hits" (Noizemc.ru).

In the past few years, he has increasingly made his political views known. In August 2010, he was placed under administrative arrest and incarcerated for 10 days in Volgograd (formerly Stalingrad) for "offending the authorities" at a concert there three days earlier. His group had performed a skit that highlighted the extreme corruption of the Russian police. Noize was forced to tape a video confession in order to gain his release. The confession was ironic and insincere, though it was not perceived as such by the authorities. Later, Noize used this video confession as the chorus for his song and video "10 sutok v raiu (Stalingrad)" (10 Days in Paradise [Stalingrad]). So, as in the United States, Russian rappers have problems with law-enforcement authorities, though in Russia it has only been going on for the past several years, and only under Putin. Further, unlike in the States, there is far greater latitude in Russia with respect to what the authorities can do to someone when held in custody. Noize points out that "they didn't let me communicate with my lawyer, my producer, or anyone else" at the time of his arrest (Alekseev 2010).

Perhaps more than any other hip hop artist, Noize MC voices his dissent from official views of the Russian government. As is well known, there has been a strong surge in nationalism during Putin's tenure in office, and often this national-ism manifests itself in racist activity. One of the most horrific incidents happened in August 2007 when a Russian neo-Nazi group beheaded two men of color, one from Tajikistan and the other from Dagestan, and uploaded the video of the event to the internet (Chivers 2007). Though the leaders of this particular neo-Nazi group were calling for Putin's resignation, many believe that such nationalist fringe groups generally support Putin; it is therefore not surprising that Putin does not seem to be doing too much to crack down on such groups (Barry 2011).

Another arena for racism in post-Soviet Russia is the football (i.e., soccer) stadium. In that regard, St. Petersburg's Zenit football team is often considered the worst in Russia. In March 2011, in response to the first nonwhite player to play for the team, Roberto Carlos, a fan brandished a banana, which is a common rac-ist meme used against players of color playing in European football leagues. Zenit is notorious for such behavior (Longman 2012). Noize MC's answer to this overt racism was "Pushkinskii Rap" (Pushkin Rap). Generally considered to be the greatest Russian writer of all time, Alexander Pushkin had a great-grandfather who was African, and by all accounts, Pushkin himself had non-Russian physi-cal traits and slightly darker skin. Noize uses this fact to answer the racist fans of Zenit. The animated video for this song begins in the stadium with football fans chanting "Peter," another name for Zenit (Alekseev 2011b). Noize uses Pushkin as the narrator for the song and questions the intentions of the simpleton racist fan. Here is a translation of the lyrics:

Verse 1:
My name is Aleksander Sergeevich Pushkin
My skin doesn't look like a cheese Danish filling
Dark-skinned face and black curly curls
Thanks to my great-grandfather for all of these features

Those with small minds
Think it necessary to call me an ape

And even in school those bullies frequently joked
That my ancestors were swinging from branches not long ago

Like, my great-grandfather was the moor Hannibal
Peter the Great bought him for a bottle of rum from a dealer
Who accused me of everything
But you yourselves know how it all ended up

I didn't create a memorial to myself by hand
Both scholars and students consider me great
If you study Russian language and don't read my books
That's straight down a dead-end road

Chorus:
Where do these smarty-pants come from
Who think that "Racism" and "Russia"
Come from the same root word
You know, Pushkin's against people like you, yo

You look askance at people who don't look like you
You're blabbering something about Russian culture?
From that culture here's an answer for you:
"What, like, Pushkin's not a Russian poet?"

Verse 2:
You see, someone is lengthening the queue to paradise for you
Everyone is pushing through on the highway and you're on the shoulder
Who's bothering you, foreign workers?
Foreign students and everyone like them?

Without them your life would be lighthearted movie
With an awesome beginning, middle, and end
And you yourself would be the best dancer to everyone
If your balls didn't rub up against each other

Also, in short, about national dances:
Russians have always been a friendly nation
We only beat those who throw the first punch
Xenophobia is a thing of Neanderthals

Let's leave racism for the apes and the Australopithecus
Tell everyone "hi" from the nineteenth century
Great, your progress is impressive
There's only one thing that A. S. Pushkin can't understand. . . .

Repeat chorus

The clear mocking tone of the rap is evident from the start. Using Pushkin, who is revered by all Russians, is appropriate, insofar as racism in Russia is usually directed at persons of color and, even though many Russians don't realize it, their favorite author Pushkin was, himself, such a person. Noize is famous for his social-activist songs, and it is worth mentioning that he has a massive following in Russia. This points to the fact that, in the face of a repressive vertical power structure in which freedom of speech is under attack and racist acts often go unpunished, there is a need for legitimate sources of information that deviate from the official versions of events—hip hop songs often bridge the gap between reality and the Russian government's retelling of an event.

Noize's latest album, *Novyi al'bom* (New Album), has several songs that protest the rise of racism and fascism in Russia. When asked about these "antifascist" songs, such as "Edem 14/88" (Eden 14/88), and why he felt the need to address this issue, Noize answered:

> It upsets me that these views are gaining popularity. I get the chance to hang out with many different people. Currently, it's not shameful to be a xenophobe or a racist. As if it's OK to think that way. It's difficult to say why this is so. First, people simply forget what is inherent in this way of thinking. Too much time has passed already; the generation that remembers World War II is gradually fading away. Also, there are concrete political figures who, through their actions—consciously or unconsciously—exacerbate the situation. (Alekseev interview, 2012)

Clearly, Noize considers Vladimir Putin to be one such figure. Noize is becoming more and more political in the face of the crackdown on political dissent in Putin's Russia. The fact that he has a massive following is comforting as Russians face the difficult situation regarding nationalism and racism in their country.

Noize's most famous protest song has to do with a well-known car accident in Moscow that happened on February 25, 2010. In order to understand the song "Mersedes S666" (Mercedes S666), it is important to understand a few things about driving in contemporary Russia. They have a special, powerful, and nationwide law-enforcement agency dedicated to traffic safety, called the Gosudarstvennaia inspektsiia bezopasnosti dorozhnogo dvizheniia (State Inspectorate of Automotive Traffic Safety), or GIBDD for short, which is actually part of the Russian Ministry of Internal Affairs. It is widely known as a nefarious organization whose primary goal, it would seem, is to extort money from drivers. (I myself have been pulled over on various occasions while driving in Russia, and the methods they use to get bribes are highly sophisticated.) The traffic accident was between a large black Mercedes S500, which carried Vice President Anatoly Barkov of Russian oil giant Lukoil, along with his driver and bodyguard, and a much smaller Citroën C3, which carried Olga Aleksandrina and Vera Mikhailovna. By most accounts, the head-on collision on Leninskii Prospekt occurred when the Mercedes, in an effort to thwart Moscow's insufferable rush-hour traffic, crossed the double lines to travel in the oncoming traffic lane. Surprisingly, this is common in Moscow, especially for official cars that carry a blue flashing light on top. That Barkov's Mercedes was traveling toward the city center during the morning rush hour while the Citroën was traveling away was sufficient proof for most Russians that Barkov's car was in the wrong. There is no need for a car traveling freely with little traffic to swerve into the oncoming rush-hour's slow-moving traffic. Aleksandrina and Mikhailovna died in the crash, while the three occupants of the Mercedes suffered only minor injuries. Quickly, the official account of the accident reported that the driver of the Citroën, Aleksandrina, was to blame and, since the driver of the at-fault car died in the crash, the case was closed.

Almost immediately, Noize MC composed "Mercedes S666"—he is a friend of Aleksandrina's sister, Anastasia Aleksandrina, and felt he needed to act. Almost immediately after the accident, Anastasia Aleksandrina herself, who is also known as the hip hop singer Staisha, published an open letter to the authorities about the accident on the rap portal rap.ru. About the necessity to shine a light on the injustice of the accident, Noize said:

> In this situation, I am not blindly worshiping the principle of the presumption of innocence. If you don't attract attention to the situation dramatically then everything gets hushed up. . . . [The police] acted quickly and with one specific aim, saying the driver of the Citroën was the guilty party. If I hadn't drawn attention quickly, then it would have been easier to cover this up. I understand that I will have a mess to clean up later, but I could not stand on the sidelines. (Werman 2010)

"Mercedes S666" is a take on the Rolling Stones' "Sympathy for the Devil" (Werman 2010), and the video depicts Anatoly Barkov as Satan. The video is extremely scathing in its indictment of Barkov, specifically, and of the current power structure in general. What follows is a translation of the entire song:

> Verse 1:
> Allow me to introduce myself, I'm Anatoly Barkov
> I don't have leathery wings, no vampire fangs.
> In my position I'm not interested at all
> In such low-class things.
> Vice president of Lukoil is something to be reckoned with.
> You need to look respectable, without excessive glitz.
> All of these satanic spoofs you are doing are complete childishness,

Any resemblance I have to the actual devil is totally lacking
Because a real demon has nothing to do with a clown.
Let's leave the masquerades for the heavy-metal stars.
I'm a different kind of person, of the higher sort.
I don't see problems that can't be solved with bribes.
I don't know people whose lives are more important than my interests.
I'm not concerned what the press writes about me.
So if you are in the way of my Mercedes
In any account you'll be guilty of the traffic accident.

Chorus:
Mercedes S666
Out of the way pleb, don't get hit,
Pitiable mob, tremble, there's a king on the road,
We're late to hell, make way for the chariot.

Mercedes S666
Out of the way pleb, don't get hit.
Pitiable mob, tremble, there's a king on the road.
We're late to hell, make way for the chariot.

Verse 2:
In the underworld I'll be stewing in the next pot alongside Evsiukov
But now I'm alive, healthy, and fully stocked
100 percent insured from any problems
And, moreover, I've known Putin for a long time.
I possess the skill to change space and time.
All surveillance cameras stop working at once.
But if there is any evidence of my crime recorded on them
Then you can stuff your popular opinion up your ass.
People will yackity yak, and then calm down
The dog barks and the elephant keeps a clean reputation.
I have to be honest, I don't even really remember
Who Vera Sidel'nikova and Olga Aleksandrina were.

Repeat chorus

When Noize raps, "I'm a different kind of person, of the higher sort / I don't see problems that can't be solved with bribes / I don't know people whose lives are more important than my interests / I'm not concerned what the press writes about me," he is tapping into an angst and a sense of helplessness that lie in the hearts of all Russians. He skillfully creates a picture of Barkov as Satan, changing the number of the car to 666 and making many artful allusions to the underworld.

The chorus of the rap accurately depicts how many of those in power feel with respect to their fellow citizens on the road. Finally, the fact that Barkov has "known Putin for a long time" speaks to the fact that if, indeed, someone knows Putin personally in Russia, there is the general feeling that that person is above the law—such incidents as this traffic accident prove the fact.

Largely because of this rap and a few other journalistic interventions, an investigation was launched into the true cause of the accident, making it all the way up to then-President Dmitri Medvedev. In this fashion, Noize and other activist rappers are able to alter the course of events in Russia. Ultimately, in September 2010, it was determined that Barkov was not at fault in the accident. However, the seeds of revolt had been planted by late 2010; a solid case could be made that incidents such as this famous traffic accident caused the intense unrest and political protests after the contested Russian parliamentary elections in December 2011. An even stronger case could be made that Noize's incarceration in August 2010 in Volgograd, mentioned above, was a result of "Mercedes S666."

Vasya Oblomov is a Russian rapper whose lyrics are, arguably, even more controversial than Noize's. Vasya Oblomov is the pseudonym of Vasily Goncharov (b. 1984), who currently lives in Moscow. His first megahit as Oblomov, "Magadan," was released in 2010 and won several awards. The song displays his keen sense of satire and humor, as he ridicules many current memes of contemporary Russia. The song also represents his first foray into rap. Oblomov—a musician, rapper, writer, activist, and intellectual—often draws the ire of the authorities, which can be risky in present-day Russia. Though his style can certainly be described as rap, he prefers the term "songs of a conversational style," and he often mixes these songs with interesting and introspective musical soundtracks. He started his career not as the rapper Oblomov, but as the frontman of Cheboza, a Britpop-inspired rock group from Rostov-on-Don, in 1999.

Oblomov's songs deal with the many injustices in the Russian political system and the various peculiarities of Russian culture: the endemic corruption in the Russian police force in "Kto khochet stat' militsionerom?" (Who Wants to Become a Police Officer?), the shady side of Russian politics and the Russian judicial system in "Zhal'" (Too Bad), the hopelessness of the cultural elite in "Magadan," or the disputed elections of December 2011 in "Paganen'kii u nas narod" (Our Rotten Little Nation). Three particularly contentious songs are those written by Oblomov and performed along with two famous political activists and television personalities, Ksenia Sobchak and Leonid Parfenov: "Poka Medved" (So Long, Medvedev), "VVP" (for Vladimir Vladimirovich Putin), and "Rap Moleben" (Rap Prayer). The first is an open letter to then-President Medvedev. Its openly mocking tone chides Medvedev about his decisions surrounding the return to power of Putin. The second is about Putin himself and is not praiseful of the leader, which is to say quite enough about the song. The third, "Rap Prayer," is about the craziness surrounding the now-famous Pussy Riot episode.

About the crackdown on dissent currently going on in Russia, and about censorship, Oblomov says:

> I write about that which I think is important. I act according to the principle "I can't be quiet." Lev Tolstoy wrote his books according to the same principle. As far as freedom of speech is concerned, of course, in a different world it would be possible for my songs to be heard on radio stations or state television and so on. One state television station wanted to invite me on to its program and sing a song in connection with an album launch, but since they could not find one song that they could play, they said: "We can't invite you, since we can't find one appropriate song." They invite me to a radio broadcast to have a conversation and give an interview, but at the same time they're afraid to put my songs in their rotation for whatever reason. It's a fact, but it doesn't mean that I shouldn't write about it. First I write a song, and then something happens with it, or doesn't happen. . . .
>
> About censorship, because of the internet you can upload anything you like. Thus there's no censorship at all. I write that which I think is necessary and act as I see fit. After all, the internet essentially helped musicians open a path to the public. Since, if earlier there was an editor-in-chief of a radio or television station who needed to approve your clip before an audience saw it, then now all those barriers are gone. You film a clip as you like and make a song as you like, upload it to the internet and, if anyone at all likes what you did, then that person will find it. And thus, of course, in the event you write a song, there is not even any question of censorship. There's no one to demand it. (Oblomov 2013)

Oblomov's "Zhal'" is a good example of his incisive poetry. The song is a laundry list of complaints about contemporary Russian society and of things in which Oblomov does not believe. What follows is an excerpted version of the song:

> I don't believe the deputies, they're in the system, and it doesn't matter whether they're with them or not.
> I don't believe what they write in Russian newspapers, or in the answers during the Q&A.
> I don't believe in documentary TV programs, since they're all made for us at someone's urging.
> I don't believe in honest billionaires, and I don't believe Gazmanov when he sings about officers.
> I don't believe in an honest president, nor do I believe in doctors or their patients.
> I don't believe in jurisprudence or justice—tell me, why would I?!
> I don't believe the beggars or the bums in the subway, nor do I believe in those who voted for United Russia.

I don't believe in the future of Russian soccer, and I don't believe that we've got the same Coca-Cola.

But time will put everything in its place and, chances are, we are already right there.

We'll walk around and smile at each other, and at difficult times we'll hold out a hand.

Morality will become more important than any letter of the law and no icon will be necessary to do good deeds.

Civil society in a law-abiding state, and the person whom they just yesterday reproached for nonconformity

Will not be able to find a reason for dissatisfaction, mistrust, or banal anxiety.

The thought is that all of this will be true, a classic author once wrote us in a letter.

But it's too bad that neither you nor I will get a chance to live in that beautiful time.

And I'm sad that neither you nor I will get a chance to live in that beautiful time. (Oblomov 2011)

At first Oblomov raps about what it is that he doesn't believe in, but toward the end of the song, he talks about a beautiful future. However, in the penultimate line—in which he quotes directly from the famous Russian poet Nikolai Nekrasov's collection of poetry "Railways"—Oblomov comes back to a common overriding feeling among intellectuals in Russia, the notion that things will certainly get better in Russia in the future, but that Russians currently alive will simply not live to see it. One gets a sense of Oblomov's political underpinnings when he writes about several of the things in which he does not believe: Russian newspapers and TV, an honest president or honest billionaires, or the judicial system.

As is well known, on February 21, 2012, five members of the punk-rock collective Pussy Riot staged a mock concert in Moscow's Cathedral of Christ the Savior, demanding, among other things, the removal of then-Prime Minister Vladimir Putin from power. The ensuing court battle and incarceration of three of the five, and Putin's personal involvement in the case, garnered worldwide media attention. This event put all Russian artists on notice—you could either play by the rules or go against them and face the consequences. Like Noize MC, Oblomov is firmly part of the latter group. About the Pussy Riot episode, Oblomov said:

It seems to me that everything that happened was simply the result of a huge universal stupidity. At first, certain people with church titles had the great idea to campaign for political power and participate in political life. And after that stupidity, different people had the great idea to dance in a church and sing a song. And then a third group of people had the great idea to begin a judicial process for this. One stupidity resulted in another. And nothing would have happened if that Russian court had had enough brains to not incarcerate those women and punish them in some other way. But no, the court decided to incarcerate them. It was yet another stupidity. This ball of stupidity multiplied and became this global absurdity, leaving the confines of Russia and getting discussed in the world media. Most shameful, it's simply a result of universal stupidity. And then, when it became clear that different people had made many idiotic decisions, the propagandists were left no choice but to accuse some secret enemies of Russia and say that they want to ruin us. After all, one must vindicate oneself. In my view it was simply stupidity after stupidity and a huge ball of craziness. This is what "Rap Prayer" was about. I didn't make anything up; I simply outlined all of the absurdity that has taken place in the country for the past year. In Russia, we had a great actor, Yuri Nikulin, who often said: "I don't create anything funny—it's enough to look at life, notice some things, list them, and this will seem funny and absurd." But, just the same, it's from life. The song "Rap Prayer" is about the same thing. Moreover, I didn't lie with one word, didn't make anything up, I simply connected the whole chain together, and it already looks like nonsense. This was the point. Generally, I feel sorry for all people in that situation, because it's really a situation of global idiocy. I was dismayed with how it all went down. I don't like Pussy Riot, the music or the women. It was just a classic Russian stupidity—one person said something, another one did something, a third went somewhere, the court decided something, unrightfully or rightfully, the media wrote something, and as a result, millions were wasted by Russian authorities on the image of Russia abroad, money was simply thrown into the trash can, and in the eyes of the world Russia turned into a place where Putin is fighting with Pussy Riot. To be completely honest, I was ashamed by this. That this happened. I experienced a feeling of shame when this all happened, precisely the process of the prison sentence. I had a feeling of shame. It seemed to me that this was all wrong. I signed a letter that other artists were signing calling for the release of those women. I really believe that what they did does not call for a prison sentence. (Oblomov 2013)

This long quotation encapsulates the frustration that many Russian artists now face under the current political situation. More than anything, the fact that one must choose sides in the debate is becoming more and more obvious; either you back Putin and the present power structure, or you do not. The fact that he became involved in the Pussy Riot case means that he is part of the popular culture, and Putin wants contemporary artists to know that.

Oblomov's response was a brilliant trio, again with Sobchak and Parfenov, entitled "Rap Prayer." The video begins with Russian Eastern Orthodox music and all three "rappers" dressed in black religious garb. What Oblomov does with his lyrics is exactly what Yuri Nikulin did, as evidenced from the quote above, "I don't create anything funny—it's enough to look at life, notice some things, list them, and this will seem funny and absurd." The rap is addressed to the Holy Mother, and simply goes through all of the events surrounding Pussy Riot. What follows is my English translation of "Rap Moleben":

This is a rap prayer in support of religion
Preserving stability and a sense of moderation
Oblomov, Parfenov, and Ksenia Sobchak
Are sending a sign to the Holy Mother

Dear Mother, pay attention
To what kind of sufferings we're enduring
All winter our country fought with a foreign enemy
There were several protest meetings and then

A group of particularly dangerous girls in a church
Shouted something and stomped their feet
Demanding immediately to drive someone out
Do we all really need this, Holy Mother?

How did the people gang up on the patriarch?
Because of the watch? Because of some gift?
His holiness doesn't look at clocks
He doesn't even really know whether they're there or not

Evil bloggers are urging us to sink the boat
Along with the patriarch, with his tobacco and vodka
Along with the nano-dust in his apartment
Along with that girl living there, either Lena or Ira

With the drivers of the Gelandewagen and BMW
With the clergy and the perpetrators of traffic accidents
With the president and prime minister
They are shaking the boat slowly so that it sank quickly

Along with the envoy from the Ural wagon factory
Not waiting for 2018
Dear Holy Mother, please guide us
And at the same time wipe out the accounts of the protests' sponsors

The religious gatekeepers' feelings are offended
Bikers with flags are cruising around memorials
The patriarch wisely kept silent for a long time
But the sinners won't repent

After all, doesn't it enter their minds that Russian justice
Tries us for our sins, even if we are stupid

And will certainly put us on the right path
By means of an Orthodox Christian prison sentence

Orthodox Christianity is the only unity for us
Chekism, nationalism, and self-preservation
Echo-Moskva engages in sacrilege
And sows discord in the minds of our citizens

But the sacred support for our Orthodox faith
Strengthened the people's spirit and our judicial system
And blessed the criminal case of May 6
And the driving away of the students from "Occupy Abai"

And didn't allow the investigation to return those millions to Ksenia
So that the devil didn't confuse her for sponsoring the violence
And god-servant Ksenia was rejected from the saintly Mus TV, from ORT
   and TNT
And all kinds of evil TV.

And the Moscow OMON were given apartments
Bastrykin apologized and was forgiven
We thank You for Your angelic patience
Don't pay any attention to public opinion

You definitely know what is necessary for our country
Who should be in the Duma and who in the Kremlin
Holy Mother Russia lives justly
The courts will decide the fate of Pussy Riot impartially

Thank you for your support, all Russians are with us
Holy Mother, don't kick anyone out. Stay -with us!

As with any rap song, there are numerous allusions to current events. For instance, the "foreign enemy" is the United States (immediately after the December 2011 protests, Putin went on record as saying that US Secretary of State Hillary Clinton and the US government were to blame), while the "someone" in "demanding immediately to drive someone out" is Putin, since Pussy Riot was demanding his departure from government in their song. But, as Oblomov points out, he is simply commenting on what has happened recently, and is not making anything up. One of the main issues that the Pussy Riot episode highlighted was the increasing involvement and interdependency of the national government and the Russian Eastern Orthodox Church, led by Patriarch Kirill I. There was a famous episode of an expensive Breguet watch, worth roughly $30,000, which Kirill I wore to a meeting with a government official. Realizing that this did not give the right impression of the church, editors airbrushed the watch off his wrist for publication of the photo, but they forgot to airbrush the reflection of the watch on the table (Schwirtz and Mackey 2012). This famous episode is part of "Rap Moleben," in the fourth stanza.

In a larger sense, though, what happened with Pussy Riot highlights greater problems with the Russian government. It also has soured people's relationship to the church. About this, legendary rapper Vladi, from the group Kasta, says:

> In Russia there exists a loyal relationship to Christianity, to Eastern Orthodox Christianity, but this situation with Pussy Riot somewhat worsened this relationship with Christianity and, more specifically, with the church.
>
> Because the church should, in theory, simply ignore what happened and somehow forgive. That's how the church should conduct itself. However, it all ended with prison sentences and loud trials. And people, looking at all that, began to understand that the church was not at all doing what Jesus urges us to do. (Vladi 2013)

What all of this underscores, then, is a top-heavy Russian governing system in which freedom of speech is under attack, and artists are forced underground. It is a system in which one must take sides: there is little opportunity to simply ignore the situation.

Without question, the most famous rapper who supports the Putin government in Russia today is Timati (b. 1983 as Timur Yunusov). He is an artist in the party camp of hip hop, and his lyrics are for the most part uncontroversial. He has become more of an entrepreneur in the past few years, launching several ventures in clothing and producing, and he has appeared with such American artists as Snoop Dogg (at Timati's great expense), Busta Rhymes, Timbaland, and P. Diddy. Judging by a concert by Timati and one of his many protégés, L'One, that I attended, his fans are numerous and faithful.

Before the Russian presidential elections of March 2012, Timati famously filmed an election commercial in support of Putin's candidacy (Timati, 2012a).[3] Even more famously, Timati's support for Putin resulted in an invitation for a postelection party commemorating Putin's victory, to which only 40 guests were invited. One of the more famous photos of Timati features him, in full hip hop garb, with Putin, both waving a victory sign.

Timati's involvement in politics does not endear him to Russia's cultural elite, but it needs to be said that he, more than others, is a true hip hop artist. By this I mean that he uses all available channels at his disposal to further his career and achieve his goals. To be sure, there are those who would call this opportunism as well as those who might call him a sell-out, and that might be a fair judgment for Timati. But no one can deny that, in the face of "keeping it real," the most successful hip hop artists in the United States are, to one extent or another, opportunistic. That Timati has branched out to start his own line of clothing (Black

Star by TIMATI) and his own production company (Star Factory 4) is in line with many of the biggest names in American hip hop, such as P. Diddy or Jay Z. Timati is concerned with promoting Russian artists beyond Russia's borders. He says:

> I want to bring new big names to the market and make them big stars. So that they can shine not only in our country but also beyond its borders. . . . My goal is to take a Russian self-made product and raise it to an international level and make it the equivalent of anything from America, Asia, or Europe. My goal is to break stereotypes and promote so that Russia could be proud of its heroes in the West. (Timati, 2012b)

In following Timati, one gets the sense that there is an obsession on his part to prove himself in the West as a great hip hop artist. This obsession, which is part of Russia's larger obsession with the West and, more specifically, with the United States, is unique to Russian hip hop. Those who are invested in hip hop in Russia are aware of its American roots and, for these hip hop fans, making it in America would be a coup.

Beyond the obsession with American hip hop that this camp of rap represents in Russia, Timati's alliance with the current Russian power structure has proven quite beneficial for him. All channels are open, and he is free to pursue any project that he desires. Notably, there is a strong audience for this brand of hip hop in Russia, and many interesting new artists have aligned themselves with Timati, an artist who represents an antipode, in many ways, to Noize and Oblomov.

The fact that both Noize and Oblomov were classically trained brings up another interesting point about Russian rap—people who engage in the genre often come to it later, and from backgrounds as instrumentalists and performing musicians. Further, unlike in the States, Russian rap did not emerge as part of a cultural movement, and it is not therefore perceived as a dissident art form by itself. Russians hip hop fans are generally aware of the history of the genre in the States, and many of these fans listen to great American rappers. However, they usually don't understand the lyrics, and they are listening either as an act of protest or an act of American solidarity. The following quotation, from a history of Russian rap, summarizes:

> The main problem with Russian rap today is that there is very little "home-grown" talent in rap and too many prejudices around this theme, which places rap in Russia into an unfavorable situation. It's extremely interesting that, if hip hop arose as a music and subculture of the "African American ghetto," with its strongly aggressive attitude toward the white population (which is fair to say not only of the USA but, for instance, of France as well), then in Russia hip hop appeared as an international culture predominantly perceived by the

"white" segment of the population, and therefore one cannot speak of a "ghetto subculture" in Russia. ("History of Russian Rap" 2009)

The typical Russian hip hop fan generally comes to the genre out of interest in American culture, listening to American artists, and then migrates over to local Russian artists once it becomes clear that such artists are around. This is an important point in order to understand how rap is perceived in Russia, and how it began. It is getting to the point where fewer people have a good understanding of the American roots of rap and hip hop. At a recent concert in Moscow, by Timati and L'One, I was impressed by how younger audience members knew almost nothing of American rap (only Wu Tang Clan was mentioned), while knowing quite a lot about Russian hip hop artists. Not surprisingly, as Russian rap matures and its following grows, the link to rap's American roots becomes more distant.

It is also worth pointing out that, with respect to "representing" regions of the country (a time-honored element of rap in the United States), all roads ultimately lead to Moscow, even in 2013. Sure, there are famous rappers outside of Moscow, but if you've made it in the rap game, you are likely in Moscow, like the following big-name rappers and rap groups who now reside there: AK 47 (originally from Beriozovskii), Kasta (Rostov), Noize MC (Iartsevo), Vasya Oblomov (Rostov), Basta (Rostov), and Dzhigan (Odessa). Occasionally, a big-name artist who lives in Moscow is actually from Moscow, like Timati or Guf, but more often than not, people still come to Moscow to make their career in rap.

That nationalism is prominent in Putin's Russia is not in question. Hardly a day goes by when there is not news of some new patriotic or nationalistic trend. This nationalistic environment, and the backlash against it, affects hip hop in Russia in various ways. Because rap is a poetic art form, it is scrutinized to a far greater extent than other art forms. Also, the authorities realize that it is wildly popular, and they can see its influence on its citizens. It would seem that the sadness of being a rap artist, or any artist, in Putin's Russia lies in the fact that one *must* choose sides—either to be with Putin or to be against him. To do neither is to wither away in obscurity. Of course, there are many talented hip hop artists who practice their craft without getting involved in politics, but the fact that everyone must take a stance on Russia's present power structure is unique. In the States, we saw this to some degree during the Bush administration, for example, when the Dixie Chicks were excoriated for taking a political stance against the president. However, the type of political pervasiveness that is present in Putin's Russia could never be part of the artistic environment in post–Cold War America.

Perhaps it could be said that Russian rap represents the best and the worst of present-day Russia: its dissident voice crying out for freedom, and its opportunistic underside playing the patriotic card for self-advancement. Rap, wherever it is made, has always been controversial, and this is quite evident in Putin's Russia.

I think Oblomov says it best when speaking about what can be done and what needs to be done in order to improve Russia's lot:

> I think that if you don't do anything, then nothing will ever happen. I think that one needs to request, to demand from one's country that it become better. One needs to be able to recognize one's problems in order to be able to fix them. Nor must one sit and say, "We're the best, the most beautiful," with no good reason to do so. In that case there's nothing to strive for. If you think that you're the best then you have nothing to strive for, and that's not really the case. One needs to acknowledge one's mistakes in order to fix them. (Oblomov 2013)

NOTES

1. I would like to thank Vasily Goncharov, Andrei Konovalov, Vladislav Leshchkevich, Charles Maynes, Marina Sarest, Ruslan Volkov, and Marina Vytovtova, all of whom helped in one way or another with this paper. All translations from Russian to English are my own. I have used the transliteration system of the US Library of Congress throughout this work.

2. The party camp would include artists such as Dzhigan, KReeD, L'One, Mot, and Timati, and the political and artistic camp would include artists and groups such as AK 47, Assai, Basta (aka Noganno), Guf, Kasta, Krovostok, Noize MC, and Vasya Oblomov.

3. Notably, the YouTube version of this video has only 477 likes versus 2,769 dislikes as of April 8, 2013, which shows, to an extent, what people think of Timati's support for Putin.

REFERENCES

Baranovskii, Artem. 2010. "Vse o DTP na Leninskom prospekte. Kto vinovat i chto teper' delat'?" [Everything about the traffic accident on Leninsky Prospect. Who is to blame and what can now be done?]. http://www.autonews.ru/autobusiness/news/1585794/ (accessed April 3, 2013).

Barry, Ellen. 2011. "Russian Nationalist Urges Support for Putin." *New York Times,* September 21. http://www.nytimes.com/2011/09/22/world/europe/russian-nationalist -supports-a-putin-presidential-bid.html?_r=0.

BBC. 2006. "Russian Racism Out of Control." http://news.bbc.co.uk/2/hi/europe/4969296 .stm (accessed March 20, 2013).

BBC. 2011. "Zenit St. Petersburg fined for Roberto Carlos Race Abuse." http://www.bbc.co.uk /sport/0/football/12998953 (accessed March 31, 2013).

Boiarinov, Denis. 2012. "Detskaia komnata" [The nursery]. http://os.colta.ru/music_modern /events/details/35492/?expand=yes#expand (accessed February 16, 2013).

Chivers, C. J. 2007. "Beheading and Shooting by Russian Neo-Nazis on Video." *New York Times,* August 15. http://www.nytimes.com/2007/08/15/world/europe/15russia.html.

"History of Russian Rap." 2009. http://www.jump-street.ru/history_rus_rap.html (accessed February 10, 2013).

Longman, Jeré. 2012. "Russian Soccer Fans Marching Backward to Intolerance." *New York Times,* December 18. http://www.nytimes.com/2012/12/19/sports/soccer/russian-soccer -fans-marching-backward-to-intolerance.html?_r=0.

Noizemc.ru. Accessed February 20, 2013.

Radio Free Europe, Radio Free Liberty. 2010. "Scandal Erupts over Fatal Car Crash Involving Russian Oil Executive." http://www.rferl.org/content/Scandal_Erupts_Over_Fatal _Car_Crash_Involving_Russian_Oil_Executive/1973679.html (accessed March 22, 2013).

Schwirtz, Michael. 2010. "Tale of Botched Traffic Operation Increases Russians' Mistrust of Moscow Police." *New York Times,* March 11. http://www.nytimes.com/2010/03/12/world /europe/12russia.html?_r=0.

Schwirtz, Michael, and Robert Mackey. 2012. "Russian Church Admits Photo Was Altered to Hide Patriarch's Watch." *New York Times,* April 5. http://thelede.blogs.nytimes.com /2012/04/05/russian-church-admits-photo-was-altered-to-hide-patriarchs-watch/.

Werman, Marco. 2010. "Noize MC and the Mercedes Song." BBC. http://www.pri.org/stories /2010-03-16/noize-mc-and-mercedes-song (accessed August 25, 2014).

INTERVIEWS

Alekseev, Ivan (aka Noize MC). 2010. Interview with Aleksandr Shchadov. http://www .rusnovosti.ru/programms/prog/61884/103927 (accessed March 27, 2013).

Alekseev, Ivan. 2012. Interview with Aleksandr Gorbachev, March 26. http://www.afisha.ru /article/noize_newalbum (accessed April 8, 2013).

Oblomov, Vasya. 2013. Live interview with the author.

Vladi (from the group Kasta). 2013. Phone interview with the author.

FILMOGRAPHY

Alekseev, Ivan. 2011a. "10 sutok v raiu (Stalingrad)" [10 Days in Paradise (Stalingrad)] [video]. https://www.youtube.com/watch?v=zymCyPDWcu8 (Accessed March 18, 2013).

Alekseev, Ivan. 2011b. "Pushkinskii Rap" [Pushkin Rap] [video]. https://www.youtube.com /watch?v=rnm3aieV1wg (Accessed August 25, 2014).

Alekseev, Ivan. 2012. "Mersedes S666" [Mercedes S666] [video]. https://www.youtube.com /watch?v=XX5NPcg_FxE (accessed March 15, 2013).

Oblomov, Vasya. 2010. "Magadan" [video]. https://www.youtube.com/watch?v=sIRTrsabL_M (accessed February 19, 2013).

Oblomov, Vasya. 2011. "Zhal'" [Too Bad] [video]. https://www.youtube.com/watch?v =KPZbHl-yxok (accessed August 25, 2014).

Oblomov, Vasya. 2012. "Rap Moleben" [Rap Prayer] [video]. https://www.youtube.com/watch ?v=bqTbNvC9XjA (accessed April 3, 2013).

Timati. 2012a. "Ia golosuiu za Putina" [I'm voting for Putin] [video]. Pre-election commercial. https://www.youtube.com/watch?v=1PGxy57RBqU (accessed April 8, 2013).

Timati. 2012b. "Timati Documentary" [video]. http://www.youtube.com/watch?v =msknzf9zdW8&feature=youtu.be (accessed February 15, 2013).

CHAPTER 4

RAP MUSIC AS A CULTURAL MEDIATOR IN POSTCONFLICT YUGOSLAVIA

Alexandra Balandina

IN THE WAR-TORN Balkans, music has often been used to generate, foment, or support conflict. Popular music in former Yugoslavia has been inextricably linked with attempts to construct nationalistic ideologies and to provoke interethnic violence. Similarly, rap music has been used as a platform to express ethnic and cultural differences and interethnic dissent in the territories of former Yugoslavia. Nevertheless, as I will show in this article, rap may also be used as a cultural mediator to bridge ethnic divides and other expressions of conflict among different youth groups in the Balkans.

This study is situated in the city of Kumanovo in Macedonia (officially FYROM)—a former republic of the Socialist Federal Republic of Yugoslavia—which today experiences tensions between various ethnic communities and the ambivalences embedded within cultural pluralism and ethnic identity.

The Republic of Macedonia declared its independence from Yugoslavia after the violent break-up of the latter in September 1991. Although Macedonia did not take part in the Yugoslav civil war, it experienced an armed conflict in 2001 between the Albanian National Liberation Army and the Macedonian state army, which ended after six months of military crisis and negotiations.[1]

Kumanovo, the third-largest city in Macedonia, is located 40 km northeast of the capital Skopje. The conflict brought a general climate of interethnic tension and violence to the city, which exemplifies Macedonia's multilingual and culturally mixed society, containing, besides a large Macedonian population, Albanian, Roma, Serbian, and Turkish minorities. These diverse ethnic inhabitants experience linguistic, religious, cultural, and political dissonance, and in the last few decades, mutually antagonistic nationalisms, which are very prominent, especially between

Macedonians and Albanians. After the 2001 conflict, ethnic tensions between Macedonians and Albanians increased dramatically and became an integral part of daily life and local culture.

Young people in Kumanovo are significantly affected by this postconflict situation and by the war in Yugoslavia. There is very little interethnic collaboration among the various young ethnic groups. This lack of interaction is perpetuated by the ethnically separate schooling system, separate neighbourhoods, and distinct entertainment venues that keep apart especially Albanian and Macedonian youths. Thus, the Centre of Intercultural Dialogue (CID),[2] a nongovernmental organization in Macedonia, initiated the Youth Open Festival (YOF) in Kumanovo as an opportunity for the various ethnic communities to mix together, to foster interethnic cooperation, and to promote and strengthen peace in the region by using music as a peace-building tool.

My participation in the YOF project as anthropologist/ethnomusicologist gave me the opportunity to employ applied or action ethnomusicology/anthropology in order to intervene in community life. This type of applied research rests on the premise that music making offers influential means of collaboration within and across cultures, and that music making has the power to unite, to promote nonviolence and respect.[3]

The YOF project operates on the premise that music making constructs new possibilities for cross-cultural understanding and provides a paradigm for peaceful coexistence among various ethnic groups in a nation-state. Broadly, therefore, I want to point to the importance of popular music and particularly hip hop in intercultural youth musical collaborations as mediator of political and cultural conflicts.

The objective is to examine how anthropologists and ethnomusicologists can use hip hop for peaceful and effective conflict transformation[4] in a region where hip hop has often been employed as an avenue to disseminate sociocultural and political meaning in divergent ways.

THE MANY FACES OF RAP MUSIC IN FORMER YUGOSLAVIA IN SNAPSHOTS

In the territories of former Yugoslavia, popular music has been used not only to express opposition and critique against the war, the state, and its hegemonic forces, but also to provoke interethnic violence, to instigate and endorse conflict, and to promote particular nationalistic and political ideologies (Laušević 2000; Pettan 2009; Ramet 2002; Gordy 1999; Hudson 2003; Sugarman 2007). Rap music, like other popular music genres in the region, does not escape from its many conflicting usages. It is often commercially oriented, lacking any demonstration of social criticism. It is frequently protest oriented, following traditional hip hop themes of social criticism and signaling political awareness, although numerous examples testify that it is also used to enhance nationalistic ideas and ethnic violence in the region.

When first introduced in Yugoslavia during the 1980s, it was a fairly marginal music genre, lacking a local ethos and identity. It was imitating to a large degree its source: the American rap scene, and especially its ostentatious and erotic language. The spread of hip hop culture in the beginning of 1990 in former Yugoslavia coincided with the development of hip hop national scenes and markets in Europe (see Androutsopoulos and Scholz 2003). In Yugoslavia, as elsewhere in Europe, rap and hip hop are products of a popular music industry, culturally dominated by the United States and driven by both local artists and fans (see also Mitchell 2001:2).

A distinct hip hop temperament began to develop, especially since the mid 1990s, "a time of war, sanctions and isolation" (Mitic 2003:2). In most big cities in the former Yugoslavia, it became spread in its local dialects, commenting on burning political issues related to the war experience, the dissolution of Yugoslavia, and everyday socioeconomic problems. In a way, hip hop music undertook this role from rock music, which during this period failed to relate to the aftermath of the civil war and became gradually marginalized.[5] Croatian rap, for example, provided commentary on important social and political events, as well as issues related to morality, religion, future, and ecology (Bosanac 2004:118).

In post-Milošević Serbia and Montenegro, the single "Govedina" (literally "beef," meaning "pig," "swine," "bastard"), issued in 2002, aided the popularization of hip hop all over the country. In this protest song, the group Beogradski Sindikat used hard language to criticize the new political elite. In Serbia, as Mitic comments, hip hop found fertile ground in Belgrade, especially among youngsters who identified themselves as ghetto dwellers and could find connections between their lives in Belgrade's poverty-stricken, dodgy neighborhoods, stigmatized by years of conflict and underground economy and US gangsta rap (Mitic 2003).

In Macedonia, as in the other urban centers in Yugoslavia, hip hop was imported in the 1980s and developed by reflecting the dissolution of Yugoslavia and its aftereffects. By the end of the decade, it had become quite popular with the antiwar song "Rapovanje" by the rock/rap group Supernova. The lyrics of the song with the catchy and memorable phrase *"Bolje da se rapuje nego da se ratuje"* (Better to rap than to wage war), were sung in Serbo-Croat in order to appeal and to relate to the war experience all over Yugoslavia. Today, it is not uncommon for Macedonian rappers to use Serbian text or to listen to Serbian rap. While regional variations exist, new political boundaries have not erased common political and cultural histories or the constant flow of people, ideas, culture, and music among the territories of the former Yugoslavia. According to a Macedonian rap listener:

> Well, we also listen to Serbian rap. We are all in the same boat. We have similar political problems, maybe that's why we are similar people culturally. We have same problems: what is a trouble [*maka*] for them, it's also for us. I think that is why we listen here [to Serbian] rap.

Cross-regional flow of rap music beyond the cognitive maps of ethnicity and nation show that, despite the breakdown of the country and the demarcation of boundaries, people in the territories of former Yugoslavia today share common everyday struggles, burning problems of economic oppression, interethnic tension, and political instability and insecurity. Indeed, according to Soysal, rap music as an expressive genre crosses analytical boundaries with seeming effortlessness, including boundaries of culture, nationality, class, political orientation, identity, and manages to create moral, cultural, commercial, and political tremors of varying degrees (Soysal 2004:79).

YouTube is one of the most important outlets for dissemination of rap music in a way that facilitates cross-regional dialogue among rappers and the wider audience in the former Yugoslavia and abroad among its diaspora. Rap music videos on YouTube, like rap music itself, have been used in many different, often contradictory, ways. Many rap videos refer to sexist symbols, others provide sociocultural and political criticism, while still other express nationalistic fantasies and ideals. At the same time, war rhetoric is very prominent on numerous hip hop YouTube videos, which often combine in imaginative ways the musical and lyrical text to war snapshots. The Serbian band Beogradski Sindikat has released a number of music videos on YouTube ("Ovlovni vojnici," "Niko ne moze da zna," "Crvene beretke") that depict war images from older Yugoslav World War II films, but also powerful images from the recent war, such as soldiers holding weapons in front of the camera, crying mothers, burning houses, bombed churches, and wounded children. Other images offer visual narratives that fulfill national fantasies and shape historical and political consciousness, especially among young audiences. Such images include Orthodox representations (old women lighting a church candle, a policeman kissing an icon), Serbian national symbols (the Serbian flag, the coat of arms of Serbia with the double-headed white eagle—a common symbol in Serbian heraldry—and the Serbian cross), negative images of Albanians (such as an Albanian kissing a photo of former U.S. President George W. Bush), and Albanian nationalistic propaganda, expressed clearly in a map of Albania showing the competing claims to Macedonian territories in Macedonia, Serbia, and Greece.

Similarly, "Srceto na Lavot" (The Heart of the Lion), a rap music video by the group Bad Contract from Ohrid city in Macedonia, reconstructs Macedonian history by using nationalistic images to enhance the lyrics. The video begins with an image from Vergina's "Sun"[6] and the English words: "The truth is like the Sun, Macedonia forever." It depicts random, incoherent images from Macedonian history—wounded Macedonian soldiers from the Second World War, a massive exodus of small children, dirty and hungry children eating bread. Also, it interjects a well-known Macedonian folk song in the beginning and the middle of the music video with the lyric "*I nie sme deca na Makedonija i nie imame pravo da ziveeme*" (We are also children of Macedonia, and we have the right to live).[7] It follows with images from recent Macedonian history, depicting Macedonian politicians since 1991, the murder of Kiro Gligorov, a NATO summit, symbols of the EU, Alexander the Great (at this image the lyrics say, "Alexander is ours; I know history"), and a map illustrating the division of Macedonia among Greece, Albania, Kosovo, and Bulgaria.

The text in "Srceto na Lavot" also expresses in a highly emotional manner Macedonian hard-line nationalism and the contested issues related to Macedonian national identity and the Macedonian name:

We are not Serbian Bulgarian or Greek
Keep your heads up, up, brothers Macedonians
our neighbors have divided our land
stole a lot and changed our name
till when FYROM?[8] I will fuck your mother—[it's] Macedonia!
The sun[9] always shines here
the heart of the lion[10] will always beat[11]

Some Serbian rap music videos on YouTube have over 5 million views, while some Macedonian videos have over 180,000 views.[12] These numbers clearly indicate that rap music has become a powerful avenue for dissemination of social and political meanings.

Overall, after the break-up of Yugoslavia, rap music progressively acquired its own distinctive style, especially when it began to relate to the interethnic Yugoslav wars and their repercussions. The decisive turn was the adoption of a local language and dialect, thus becoming the voice of disenfranchised youth by reflecting the social, economic, and political realities of their lives. Rap's diversity and contradictory articulations—its war rhetoric and nationalistic usages and its antiwar messages and ideals—offer contrasting cultural, social, and political interpretations. They are signs of a polyvocal society, deeply wounded by its history.

However, as will be shown in this paper, anthropologists, ethnomusicologists, and other practitioners working in postconflict environments may benefit from rap aesthetics and use rap music processes and symbols as a peace-building tool among youth groups.

Unity within Musical Diversity

The Youth Open Festival (YOF) was based on an ideological motivation that I shared: It was conceived, initiated, developed, and implemented by local youth from Kumanovo to address issues of conflict caused by perceptions of ethnic differences among Kumanovo youth.[13] This bottom-up ownership of the festival ensures local orientation in cultural development projects, as it is the local youth who are in tune with the needs and interests of the young people in the region.

My participation in the project was voluntary, and my initiatives were both personal and professional. As I was raised in Macedonia, in Skopje (before the break-up of Yugoslavia), I sympathized with these young people and their cause, because as a teenager I had experienced the same difficulties that these young people experience today in terms of facing daily interethnic tension. As an ethnomusicologist with a strong interest in performance theory, I could function as a facilitator to empower the peace-building goals that festival organizers had set.

In effect, I had a double identity. On the one hand, I was an insider with personal experience of life in former Yugoslavia. This "native self" assisted me in comprehending the importance of the historical dimension of the current political situation of ethnic tension. On the other hand, I was also an outsider, a scholar of Greek origins, who had a life and a career abroad. In the eyes of the participants, my second identity ensured impartiality in communicating musical and cultural advocacy, which was fundamental to developing relationships based on trust. These two identities, the native on the one hand, and the scholar on the other, are complementary in ethnographic research as they may offer a greater depth of reflection and contextualization on how young people live in postconflict communities, and how hip hop music may contribute to conflict transformation.

As a child growing up in socialist Yugoslavia, I did not question the ideals (or strategy) of "brotherhood and unity"[14] as they were implemented in Yugoslavia. However, in everyday life I experienced quite the opposite: sociocultural and religious distance among the Albanian, Macedonian, and Roma population. The area where I lived in Skopje, Topansko Pole, was divided into ethnic geographical pieces. There was the Roma district and the Roma fraction in a nearby building; there was the Albanian zone, where I rarely trespassed; and there was the Macedonian area where I lived and hung out with my Macedonian friends. In school, the situation was similar: the distance between the Albanian and Macedonian populations was pervasive, as we attended separate classrooms in both primary and secondary school. Today, reflecting on these experiences, I can see that these cultural and geographical divisions overemphasized the unknown, maintained existing cultural barriers, and incited feelings of antipathy in both Albanian and Macedonian populations.

I suggest that tensions between the Macedonian and Albanian ethnic communities in the Republic of Macedonia are not simply the result of the armed conflict in 2001 or a simple memory of the ethnic divisions and inequalities of the Yugoslav era. Ethnic divisions have deep historical roots apparent in politics and everyday life practices that continue to nourish negative stereotypes and prejudices about the "others."

In present-day Kumanovo, it was interesting to observe that, while I did not have personal experience of living in Macedonia after the break-up of Yugoslavia, the local youth (organizers and participants) did not have my experience of Yugoslavia before the war. Although 20 years have passed since the day I left Yugoslavia (in 1988), hearing young people talk about their problems with their relationships with other ethnic groups was nothing new to me. However, some things have changed in the last two decades, and these changes indicate a different texture in the relationship between Macedonian and Albanian communities.

For instance, positive predispositions toward cultural communication were apparent in the music sphere. As one of the volunteers remarked, "Today, Albanians are not that different from us. They listen and dance to Macedonian traditional music and hire Macedonian traditional bands for their weddings."

There are also indications that many Macedonians today are also positively inclined toward ethnic Albanians. Many times I have heard Macedonians in Kumanovo making a distinction between "our Albanians" (*nashite Albanci*) and "other Albanians" (*ne se nashi*), a distinction that helps them to have a more positive attitude toward local Albanians. The "our Albanians" to which Macedonians in Kumanovo refer are the local Albanians with whom they have lived for many years "under the same sky" (*pod istoto nebo*). Macedonians in Kumanovo would often say, "It is not our Albanians who provoke conflicts and fights," or "It is the other Albanians responsible for the fights"—those "who have entered illegally in Macedonia from Kosovo and Albania," "whom we don't know," "who are unknown to us." This "demonization" of the "other Albanians" and the construction of external opponents indicate that Macedonians are also inclined to improve their relationships with their Albanian cohabitants.

Arriving in Kumanovo, the idea of brotherhood and unity was floating in my head as I was thinking how I could help to forge unity and bridge the distance among the Kumanovo youth in a bottom-up manner, rather than in the top-down manner exercised under the concept of Yugoslav supranationality.

A bottom-up approach in this project was ensured by the voluntary involvement of all participants. To preserve this bottom-up approach, I decided to emphasize "unity within musical diversity." I realized that diversity—in the sense of cultural plurality—is the key concept that they (and I) should try to defend and empower and that unity can be achieved only if music diversity becomes accepted and respected.

Rapping in the Balkans: The Volunteer-Based Music Ensemble

Twelve teenagers (ages 17–22) of Macedonian, Albanian, Roma, and Serbian origin, and of different religious and socioeconomic levels, participated as volunteers in this music project that I coordinated. Half of the group had some musical background, either as active amateur musicians (two, one Albanian and one Roma, introduced themselves as rappers) or as music students (one at the graduate level and one in private music school).

With regard to repertoire, we decided to incorporate traditional and contemporary music and dance representing Macedonian, Albanian, and Roma heritage, and popular music from the English-speaking world.[15] Musically speaking, young people are familiar with their own traditional repertoire but less so with those of the other ethnic groups. My aim was to bring cultures together musically, that is, to encourage young participants to connect with the ethnically diverse musical cultures of their region. I hoped that intercultural music making would promote acceptance of and respect for diversity and cultural differences, and that it would reduce negative stereotypes (which by and large are sustained by the lack of contact among these various ethnic groups), and thus assist the reconciliation process.

The main teaching and learning strategy focused on peer learning through rote imitation, which often leads to the exploration of improvisatory techniques. Both peer learning and rote imitation are very successful informal strategies for group bonding as they promote active participation, face-to-face interaction, and dialogue (see Cowie and Wallace 2000).

The repertoire included five languages—Kumanovski (Macedonian with Kumanovo dialect), Macedonian (formal), Albanian, Roma, and Serbian—in order to represent all ethnic groups that participated in the concert and to appeal to the multiethnic Kumanovo youth audience. For the public, the use of diverse ethnic languages displays inclusiveness and cultural equity. On a personal level it induces positive emotions that enact the values of interethnic respect and cooperation. As one Albanian participant remarked:

> It is so fulfilling to see Macedonians and Roma singing "Rrokka Mandolinën" [Albanian traditional song]. It's amazing how fast they [Macedonians] have memorized the lyrics. I am happy to see everyone enjoying themselves when singing this song.

The highlight of the repertoire was the final rap song "Ajde Site," composed entirely by the young participants. The creative processes for producing this song—such as exploration with musical ideas, intuitive music making, blending, and experimenting with lyrics—gave everyone the opportunity to work creatively together, unfolding their music skills and assisting group bonding.

The solo sections were composed and sung in the Albanian and Roma languages by the two rappers belonging to those ethnic groups, which added an important degree of rap originality to the song. Both solo sections stressed peace messages. According to the Albanian rapper, "I sing mainly political messages. I sing about respect, acceptance, and equality." While the Roma rapper underlined the aspect of love that can be found in his peace messages, ":

> Peace is life, with conflict we destroy life, peace is love and music is also love.
> Without love, without peace and without music there is no life.

The lyrics and the melody of the refrain of "Ajde Site" were composed entirely by the participants themselves. The refrain of the song, sung in Macedonian and Serbian by all the participants, calls for harmonic interethnic cooperation:

> C'mon, all together, let's sing in one voice. C'mon, all sing with us.
> C'mon, all together, let's sing in one voice. C'mon, you too sing with us.[16]

This rap song, a property of the entire group, is the song the volunteers mostly identified with and felt a sense of ownership for that derives from the process of creating their own music through group composition and improvisation. One of the volunteers expressed affectionately this feeling of commonality and fraternity: "This is a small project, but it's ours. It will stay locally, and it will be talked about and remembered locally. We should give our best." Interethnic group bonding was thus strongly empowered by bottom-up dynamics of musical ownership and creativity that rap music entails.

The Power of Rap Music Making in Reconciliation Processes

Many NGO's in the territories of former Yugoslavia have used community based art activities and music performances to help facilitate reconciliation between ethnic groups or give youth the tools to make their voice heard (see Zelizer 2003 for Bosnia and Herzegovina).[17] A good example of an intentional strategy to use hip hop as activist music has been undertaken by the NGO R-Point in Srbia and the Association of Roma Students, financed by the British NGO Our Point in Vojvodina. These NGOs have supported the dissemination of Roma hip hop in order to give to marginalized Roma youth a voice to express their cultural identity and confront Roma stereotypes (see Banić-Grubišić 2010 and Kaufaman 2007).

It is not by chance that NGOs choose rap music performances to facilitate intercultural interaction and connectedness and to give youth the power to express themselves.[18] Hip hop has become the representative voice of youth globally, a vehicle for global and local youth affiliations, and "a tool for reworking local identity" (Mitchell 2001:1–2).

In Kumanovo, hip hoppers represent all ethnic groups. They are mainly young male amateur musicians in their early twenties, few of whom have acquired a professional musician's status. They rarely have the opportunity to transgress ethnic boundaries, and this project gave them the opportunity to communicate beyond ethnic affiliations. As one of the rap singers remarked, "This is something completely new. We never had the opportunity to sing together. But, we both use hip hop to sing against violence in the Balkans. This makes easier for us to rap together."

"Ajde Site" empowered the participants themselves; it gave them the sense of musical ownership that stems from common creative improvisatory processes. Performing this rap song, volunteers experienced what Sawyer calls "group flow," where "everything seems to come naturally; the performers are in interactional synchrony" (Sawyer 2006:158). Group flow is a property of the entire group as collective unit, where emotional empathy is strong and the cohesiveness of the ensemble is powerful (Sawyer 2006). One group member exemplified this well:

> I liked the rehearsals very much because all ethnic groups were together and there was no difference among us. I never experienced this [collaboration] before. It feels even better when the song sounds good. Perhaps it's the feel of enjoyment that makes the music.

Such experiences of group flow can provide us with a better understanding of the essence of group communication, not only in musical ensembles but also in everyday life. As Sawyer (2006:164) states, "Musical collaboration can help us to understand all collaboration." In effect, I argue that interethnic musical interaction, good communication, and group creativity in rap music making have powerful transformative effect and may foster group flow in daily life as well. In other words, rap music provides new aesthetic and artistic experiences that point toward new social experiences.

The aesthetic and artistic experience of rap music, although imported, can be imbued with local aesthetic overtones, providing the opportunity to express local issues by endorsing the freedom to improvise melody, and perhaps more importantly by allowing the freedom to improvise in local languages and dialects.

With regard to language, hip hop provides the opportunity to use language as a symbol of meaning beyond its lyrical content (Bennett 1999:82). The use of four local dialects in our rap song was as powerful as the lyrics appealing for peace and unity. After the disintegration of Yugoslavia, the national imagining of one language was strongly promoted as the core element of ethnic identification (Petrović 2000:174–175). The incorporation of languages representing all ethnic groups in "Ajde Site" alludes to peaceful coexistence, mutual respect, and fraternity, as it represents a novel paradigm against language as an ethnic marker that stresses national difference and cultural distance.

And while hip hop has been often used as a nationalized discourse in many parts of former Yugoslavia, especially during and after the war, as discussed in the beginning of this article, it is still largely considered "part of the 'alternative' and valued resistance toward dominant discourses and nationalism" (Baker 2009:41).

In Macedonia, although hip hop has been used with nationalistic overtones by a few bands, it is not identified as the cultural or ethnic property of a particular ethnic group. On the contrary, young musicians draw their sound aesthetic from global hip hop. This, in turn, makes the genre more appealing to young audiences in Macedonia, as it strengthens their relationship to Europe and the West. From the data discussed so far, it becomes evident that hip hop can act as a cultural mediator. It mediates between the global and the local, facilitating better interaction among ethnic groups. The basis for cultural mediation is the inclusion in hip hop music making processes of elements from local cultures and traditions, including lyrics, musical idioms, aesthetics, and cultural experiences. For instance, although the making and performing of "Ajde Site" was based on common local identity, it opened up the opportunity for new spaces of identification. It induced a shared sense of cultural identity, giving youth the opportunity to relate to the global postmodern dimension of hip hop. It is the global identity of rap music that helps to transgress political, ethnic, and national identity on the local level.

It is important to emphasize that music-making processes in rap music—and not simply the miraculous meaning of music—have a significant role in reconciliation processes. According to Small, "The act of musicking establishes in the place where it is happening a set of relationships, and it is in those relationships that the meaning of the act lies" (Small 1998:13). Thus, the act of rap music making in its totality and all that it represents—performing, improvising, learning and teaching music, dancing, talking about music, listening to music—has polymorphous powers. In this project, rap music making enabled processes of creative music making and performing that could only be completed by a group effort. It gave young people the opportunity to accept ethnic and cultural differences and to diminish existing prejudices. In addition, the effectiveness of rap music making in repairing conflictual relationships lies in its emotional sensibility, as it enhances young people's experience of positive forms of interethnic communication. The intense emotional experience and the enjoyment that arise from collective effort and rap musical creativity strengthen intercultural cohesiveness and interconnectedness. For instance, group bonding and feelings of enjoyment, befriending, and good interethnic acceptance and communication became obvious, especially on the day of the concert, when volunteers would express their joy by singing "Ajde Site" together, embracing each other, and laughing both off and on stage.

The aim of any such short-term project or individual mission should not be overly ambitious. According to Jakobsson Hatay, "In the aftermath of violent conflict, a long-term perspective on reconciliation, spanning decades or even generations is required." Improving interethnic relations and promoting reconciliation necessitates multidimensional peace operations (Jakobsson Hatay 2005:41) and both bottom-up and top-down contributions.[19]

Adopting a more open-ended evaluation—instead of imposing dichotomous value judgments in terms of "success" and "failure"—we may observe that even musical projects limited to specific periods that use rap music effectively may inspire young people to collaborate and assume a more critical approach within the context of their social and political reality (Jakobsson Hatay 2005). Intercultural music making, and in particular rap music making, in the context described in this article, empowers individuals and groups to assume control and mastery over their lives, and as such it may be seen as an agent for social change in people's everyday lives. By performing on stage, young people become active agents in fostering interethnic acceptance and increasing public awareness of the need to promote interethnic understanding, peace, and equality.

My role as an applied researcher and facilitator of the music group was to reflect unbiased and ethical ways of cultural interaction by granting equal status and rights to all participants. I could activate the power of rap music to achieve group bonding and connectedness by acknowledging the importance of history, language, and culture in the formation of all ethnic groups. Rap music making provided a neutral ground where participants would enjoy positive experiences. As an ethnomusicologist, I tried to enhance a common youth identity by emphasizing the freedom of creativity in rap music making processes. Toward the end of the project, dichotomies such as "us" and "them" weakened and were broadened by the collective "we": "We care about the concert"; "We will give our best, hoping that the concert will be great." Multimusical, collective music making, in turn, stimulates new forms of cultural dialogue that may be relocated in everyday life.

CONFLICTING IDENTITIES AMONG KUMANOVO YOUTH: LANGUAGE, RELIGION, AND HIP HOP

Although rap music making has the potential to help bridge the ethnic divide, different languages, religious practices, and cultural characteristics often remind us of existing ethnic divisions and fuel negative stereotyping. In this section, I will consider obstacles and challenges in realizing project goals and discuss in particular how language issues, hip hop, and religion may comprise areas of ethnic tension among the young volunteers during the YOF. I will also consider my role as facilitator and applied ethnomusicologist in transforming tension and enhancing connectedness.

Throughout the project, language matters often hampered interpersonal communication among the young participants and encouraged ethnic divisions. On my first meeting with the volunteers, ethnic and cultural considerations prompted me to speak in both Macedonian (the dominant language of the republic) and English. This was a conscious choice. First, I did not speak Albanian, and English was a neutral language. I did not want to show a prejudice in favor of Macedonians. Second, English is a distinctive mark of global hip hop and an alternative paradigm of communication.

Language in the Republic of Macedonia and its Kumanovo particularities is a sensitive issue for interethnic relationships, as it constitutes a site of power, a symbol of cultural identity, and a potential social stigma. Issues related to linguistic—and consequently ethnic—differences would often arise in daily encounters among the Kumanovo youth, expressing their multiple identities and alliances. Consider the following example: K. (a Macedonian volunteer) asks everyone during the rehearsal in a polite manner, "Do you understand me when I speak Kumanovski?" which is the Macedonian dialect of Kumanovo. J. (an Albanian volunteer) replies somewhat offended. "Of course I understand; I am from Kumanovo." J's inability to speak fluent Kumanovski is the result of segregation (social and in the educational setting), an indication of poor interethnic interaction, and it can lead to potential negative experience in social communication across ethnic borders. In this sense, poor language abilities may constitute a potent social stigma and generate friction among youth. At the same time, Albanian youth is caught up in a process of cultural conflict: "poor Kumanovski" creates tension between their "ethnic self" and their identity based on locality. For the Macedonian youth, the Kumanovo dialect is an integral part of their Kumanovo identity. I believe, though, that conflating Kumanovo identity with Kumanovo language suggests cultural hegemony over the Kumanovo identity on behalf of Macedonians, as Kumanovski is basically a Macedonian dialect.[20]

Thus, although the Kumanovo identity may appear to be a common foundation for the youth, in practice it represents potential divisions as it reveals difference and diversity, which are expressed as stigma rather than value.

The experience of the Roma youth with regard to language was quite different. The ability of S. (a Roma child) to speak Kumanovski with the proper accent and grammar was much better than S.'s official Macedonian language skills, which were limited because of S.'s poor school record. S.'s Kumanovski dialect was fluent, as S. feels much more comfortable socializing with Macedonians than with Albanians, although with the latter they share a Muslim identity. This was generally emphasized to me by the parents of several Roma from Kumanovo. As one of them said, "I prefer my children to be fluent in official Macedonian;

this is the language of the country we live in, and they ought to master it. That is why they attend Macedonian schools."

On the other hand, since the break-up of Yugoslavia, many Macedonians have realized the importance of learning Albanian for future employability. But the use of the Albanian language by Macedonians still remains primarily in the business field and is very rare in daily associations. This situation is reflected in Macedonian youths' unease in conversing with Albanians in Albanian. For example, while 16-year-old M. (Macedonian) is taking lessons in Albanian language, because, as she says, "Today you must know Albanian if you want to get a job," she feels unhappy about practicing Albanian with the Albanian members of the ensemble, even if this would advance her language abilities. It was, thus, a great success for the project to see Macedonians enjoying themselves while memorizing and singing the Albanian songs.

And while tensions among the Macedonians and Albanians are rooted in ethnic and cultural rather than religious biases (Neofotistos 2002:93–109), religion is a potential bone of contention among the Albanian and Roma youth. In one incident a pious Roma boy criticized an Albanian boy, saying, "You are not a good Muslim, because you drink alcohol." In another incident, again related to religious identity, one of the Roma boys mocking an Albanian girl about her ignorance of dervishes was asking her, "Are you a Muslim? Then how come you don't know what dervishes are?" These types of tensions would normally arise between the opposite poles of the same religion, conservatives and modernists. These incidents capture how even common religious identities may become barriers to communication among the youth in Kumanovo, as they reveal divisive identities and beliefs that may provoke friction. However, cultural encounters do not necessarily involve clashes and conflict. It should be stated that Islam is also a cohesive force among the Albanian and Roma youth. The same boy who one day accused the Albanian volunteer of excessive drinking would say on another day in friendly manner, "We are Muslims, just like you."

Negative attitudes among the volunteers were also expressed in rap music making. Common hip hop identities were another field where ethnic differences were accentuated. While S. (Roma rapper) and J. (Albanian rapper) had good rapport as hip hop performers, whenever S. addressed J. as a "brother" (a hip hop slang call), J. would reply, "How can you tell my mother?," implying that they do not have a mother of the same color and that they belong to different ethnic groups.

CONCLUSIONS

Among the Kumanovo youth, language, religion, and hip hop are areas where young people may share common identities and interests. On the other hand, they constitute fields where ethnic, religious, and cultural difference can arise and bring about contestations.

Complex layers of youth identities—different classes of physical characteristics, national affiliations, age traits, affiliations to particular religions and cultures, political and philosophical ideas, and style of life—coexist, overlap, and interact with one another, thus highlighting multiplicity. According to Ramnarine, multiplicity of identities reminds the "multi" of the "multicultural," and thus it "is subject to unceasing divisions" (Ramnarine 2007:10). In other words, with so many complexities of multiple identities and forms of group identification and differentiation, cultural misunderstandings, intergroup tensions, stereotypes, and disputes inevitably arise.

In conclusion, while ethnomusicologists like Ramnarine have argued that "interculturalism does not provide ready solutions to the problem of otherness" (Ramnarine 2007:8), in my view, the opportunities in interethnic communication outweigh the challenges, however daunting they may appear. Thus, while cultural encounters may provoke various levels of dissatisfaction among participants, shared aims and targets and the final success of the projects, in this case the music concert during YOF and rap music making, can unite the participants and empower conflict transformation processes.

NOTES

1. Various reasons are cited to explain this conflict, such as the resurgence of ethnic nationalism and demands for more rights on behalf of the Albanian ethnic minority, including cultural freedom, human rights, and political and territorial autonomy (see Babuna 2000).

2. The Centre for Intercultural Dialogue (CID) is a nongovernmental, nonprofit youth organization that works on the regional level in Macedonia; it was formed in May 2006 by active youth leaders and youth workers. See CID's website: http://cid.mk/ (accessed May 4, 2013).

3. Music not only has positive powers; it may also increase conflict by articulating differences within society. For the nonpeaceful uses of music, see Kent 2008 and Stokes 1994.

4. The field of music and conflict transformation is very new and relatively small. See Cohen Evron 2007, Urbain 2008, and the journal *Music and Arts in Action*'s special issue on "Music and Arts in Conflict Transformation and Peace Building," Winter 2009–2010. On music and reconciliation processes in former Yugoslavia, see Pauker 2006.

5. Yugoslav rock music was a distinct and important sociocultural force in socialist Yugoslavia in the period from the mid 1970s to the late 1980s. (See Mišina 2013.)

6. The Vergina Sun, also known as the Star of Vergina, a symbol of the heroic accomplishments of Alexander the Great, excavated in 1977 in Vergina, in the Greek region of Macedonia, has become an object of political conflict between Greece and the Republic of Macedonia. While Greece has exclusive rights to the official use of this national symbol, for Macedonians Vergina's Sun is a symbol of continuity with ancient Macedonians (Danforth 1997:163–173).

7. Often rap musicians fuse rap music with folk music instruments or songs that symbolize ethnic or national identity, particularly when rap is used to promote nationalistic ideas and goals (see also Baker 2009; Pettan 2009; Sugarman 2007).

8. The acronym FYROM (Former Yugoslav Republic of Macedonia) has been enforced, especially by Greek international politics over the single name Macedonia that Macedonians prefer. For the official stance of the Greek government, see the following article on the website

of the Greek Ministry of Foreign Affairs: http://www.mfa.gr/en/fyrom-name-issue/ (accessed May 1, 2013).

9. Referring here to Vergina's Sun.

10. Referring here to the Golden Lion, a symbol that was proposed and rejected as a coat of arms after the independence of Macedonia, and which is today used especially by the nationalist party VMRO-DPMNE.

11. Nie ne sme Srbi, Bugari ni Grci
glavata gore gore braka Makedonci
sosedite nashi zemjata ja podelija
ukradoa mnogu ama ime ni promenija
do koge be FYROM?, mater da vi ebam—Makedonija!
ovde vecno sonce gree
srceto na lavot vechno ke cuka.

12. The difference in numbers points to differences in local productivity and market size but also population numbers in each country. Several rappers have founded small independent record companies in Serbia with professional record studios in order to produce and promote their work. Automatik Records, Prohibicija, One Records, Magmedic, Bassivity Music, Multimedia Records, Ltdfm Music, and Take It or Leave It Records are among the most popular companies producing Serbian rap music. However, at the same time, the black market music industry is an ever-growing market for dissemination of rap music.

13. The festival was a noncommercial venture, organized in the summer of 2008 by the Kumanovo nongovernmental organization Centre for Intercultural Dialogue (CID) with financial support by the Youth in Action program of the European Union.

14. An ideological slogan that became an omnipresent symbol for reconciliation in the Socialist Federal Republic of Yugoslavia soon after World War II. This unique concept, promoted under the watchful eye of the authoritarian communist/socialist regime, often played an important ideological role in repressing expressions of ethnic rivalry and religious identity.

15. The initial idea for an interethnic music program was mine, but the actual choice of songs and dances belongs to the participants.

16. Ajde Site da peeme na glas. Ajde Site zapejte so nas.
Hajmo Svi sad da pevamo na glas. Hajde i Ti zapevaj uz nas.

17. However, not many have theorized about such endeavors.

18. For other projects, see Soysal 2004.

19. Peace-building and conflict transformation projects are flourishing in former Yugoslavia. See, for example, Rosandic 2000; Petroska-Beska and Najcevska 2004; Jakobsson Hatay 2005; McGlynn et al. 2009; Ackerman 2003; Siani-Davis 2003; Sampson 2003.

20. The Albanians in Kumanovo whom I met who spoke fluent Macedonian were not as fluent in the Kumanovo dialect. This emphasizes their higher education rather than their willingness to share the "Kumanovo-Macedonian" identity. Also, there is no distinct Kumanovo dialect in the Albanian language.

References

Ackermann, Alice. 2003. "International Intervention in Macedonia: From Preventive Engagement to Peace Implementation." In *International Intervention in the Balkans since 1995*, ed. Peter Siani-Davis (pp. 105–119). London: Routledge.

Androutsopoulos, Jannis, and Arno Scholz. 2003. "Spaghetti Funk: Appropriations of Hip-Hop Culture and Rap Music in Europe." *Popular Music and Society* 26(4):463–479.

Babuna, Aydin. 2000. "The Albanians of Kosovo and Macedonia: Ethnic Identity Superseding Religion." *Nationalities Papers* 28(1):67–92.

Baily, John. 2008. "Ethnomusicology, Intermusability and Performance Practice." In *The New (Ethno)Musicologies*, ed. Henry Stobart (pp. 121–138). Chicago: Scarecrow.

Baker, Catherine. 2009. "War Memory and Musical Tradition: Commemorating Croatia's Homeland War through Popular Music and Rap in Eastern Slavonia." *Journal of Contemporary European Studies* 17(1):35–45.

Banić-Grubišić, Ana. 2010. "Romski hip hop kao multikulturalistički saundtrek R-point: Pedagogija jedne politike." *Etnoantropološki problem* 5(2):85–108.

Barker, Chris. 2008. *Cultural Studies: Theory and Practice*, London: Sage.

Bennett, A. 1999. "Hip hop am Main: The Localisation of Rap Music and Hip Hop Culture." *Media, Culture and Society* 21:77–91.

Bennett, W. John. 1996. "Applied and Action Anthropology: Ideological and Conceptual Aspects." *Current Anthropology* 37(1):23–53.

Blacking, John. 1987. *"A Commonsense View of All Music": Reflections of Percy Grainger's Contribution to Ethnomusicology and Music Education*. Cambridge: Cambridge University Press.

Bosanac, J. 2004. "Transkulturacija u glazbi: Primjer hrvatskog hip hopa." *Narodna umjetnost* 41(2):105–122.

Cohen Evron, Nurit. 2007. "Conflict and Peace: Challenges for Arts Educations." In *International Handbook of Research in Arts Education*, vol. 16, ed. by Liora Bresler (pp. 1031–1058). Dordrecht: Springer.

Cowie, Helen, and Patti Wallace. 2000. *Peer Support in Action: From Bystanding to Standing By*. London: Sage.

Danforth, Loring. 1997. *The Macedonian Conflict: Ethnic Nationalism in a Transnational World*. Princeton, NJ: Princeton University Press.

Franovic, Ivana. 2008. *Dealing with the Past in the Context of Ethnonationalism: The Case of Bosnia-Herzegovina, Croatia and Serbia*, Berlin: Berghof Research Center for Constructive Conflict Management.

Gordy, E. D. 1999. *The Culture of Power in Serbia*. University Park: Pennsylvania State University Press.

Hudson, Robert. 2003. "Songs of Seduction: Popular Music and Serbian Nationalism." *Patterns of Prejudice* 37(2):157–176.

Jakobsson Hatay, Ann-Sofi. 2005. *Peacebuilding and Reconciliation in Bosnia and Herzegovina, Kosovo and Macedonia 1995–2004*. Uppsala: Department of Peace and Conflict Research, Uppsala University.

Johnson, Henry. 2007. " 'Happy Diwali': Performance, Multicultural Soundscapes and Intervention in Aotearoa/New Zealand." In *Musical Performance in the Diaspora*, ed. Tina K. Ramnarine (pp. 71–94). London: Routledge.

Kaufman, Jane. 2007. "Roma in Vojvodina: Expressions of Cultural Identity through Performance." Paper submitted in partial fulfillment of The Balkans: Gender, Transformations and Civil Society, SIT Study Abroad, spring semester.

Kent, George. 2008. "Unpeaceful Music." In *Music and Conflict Transformation: Harmonies and Dissonances in Geopolitics*, ed. Olivier Urbain (pp. 104–114). London: I. B. Tauris.

Laušević, Mirjana. 2000. "Some Aspects of Music and Politics in Bosnia." In *Neighbors at War: Anthropological Perspectives on Yugoslav Ethnicity*, eds. Joel M. Halpern and David A. Kideckel (pp. 289–301). University Park: Pennsylvania State University Press.

McGlynn, Claire, Michalinos Zembylas, Zvi Bekerman, and Tony Gallagher, eds. 2009. *Peace Education in Conflict and Post-Conflict Societies: Comparative Perspectives*. New York: Palgrave Macmillan.

Mišina, Dalibor. 2013. *Shake Rattle and Roll: Yugoslav Rock Music and the Poetics of Social Critique*. Farnham: Ashgate.

Mitchell, Tony. 2001. "Introduction." In *Global Noise: Rap and Hip-Hop Outside the USA*, ed. Tony Mitchell (pp. 1–38). Middletown, CT: Wesleyan University Press.

Mitic, Aleksandar. 2003. "Rap against the Machine: A 21st-Century Style Protest Song Has Belgrade Marching to a New Beat." *Transitions Online*. http://www.tol.org/client/article /8653-rap-against-the-machine.html.

Neofotistos, Vasiliki Panagioti. 2002. *Resisting Violence: Hegemonic Negotiations of Ethnicity in the Republic of Macedonia*. Unpublished PhD thesis, Harvard University, Cambridge, MA.

Pauker, Iva. 2006. "Reconciliation and Popular Culture: A Promising Development in Former Yugoslavia?" *Local-Global: Identity, Security, Community* 2:72–83.

Petroska-Beska, Violeta, and Najcevska, Mirjana. 2004. "Macedonia: Understanding History, Preventing Future Conflict." Special Report No. 15. Washington, DC: US Institute of Peace.

Petrović, Edit. 2000. "Ethnonationalism and the Dissolution of Yugoslavia." In *Neighbors at War: Anthropological Perspectives on Yugoslav Ethnicity, Culture and History*, eds. Joel M. Halpern and David A. Kideckel (pp. 164–176). University Park: Pennsylvania State University Press.

Pettan, Svanibor. 2009. "War, Music and Ethnomusicology at the Break-Up of Yugoslavia: Notes on Croatia." In *Militärmusik im Diskurs: Eine Schriftenreihe des Militärmusikdienstes der Bundeswehr* (pp. 107–124).

Ramet, Sabrina. 2002. *Balkan Babel: The Disintegration of Yugoslavia from the Death of Tito to the Fall of Milošević*, 4th ed. Boulder, CO: West View Press.

Ramnarine, Tina K. 2007. "Musical Performance in the Diaspora: Introduction." In *Musical Performance in the Diaspora*, ed. Tina Ramnarine (pp. 1–18). London: Routledge.

Rosandic, Ruzica. 2000. "Peace Education in Serbia." *Peaceworks* 33. Washington, DC: US Institute of Peace.

Sampson, Steven. 2003. "From Forms to Norms: Global Projects and Local Practices in the Balkan NGO Scene." *Journal of Human Rights* 2(3):329–337.

Sawyer, Keith R. 2006. "Group Creativity: Musical Performance and Collaboration." *Psychology of Music* 34(148):148–165.

Siani-Davis, Peter, ed. 2003. *International Intervention in the Balkans since 1995*. London: Routledge.

Small, Christopher.1998. *Musicking: The Meaning of Performing and Listening*. Middletown, CT: Wesleyan University Press.

Solís, Ted, ed. 2004. *Performing Ethnomusicology: Teaching and Representation in World Music Ensembles*. Berkeley: University of California Press.

Soysal, Levent. 2004. "Rap, Hiphop, Kreuzberg: Scripts of/for Migrant Youth Culture in the WorldCity Berlin." *New German Critique* 92:62–81.

Stokes, Martin, ed. 1994. *Ethnicity, Identity and Music: The Musical Construction of Place*. Oxford: Berg.

Sugarman, Jane. 2007. "'The Criminals of Albanian Music': Albanian Commercial Folk Music and Issues of Identity since 1990." In *Balkan Popular Culture and the Ottoman Ecumene: Music, Image and Regional Political Discourse*, ed. Donna A. Buchanan (pp. 269–308). Lanham, MD: Scarecrow.

Urbain, Olivier, ed. 2008. *Music and Conflict Transformation: Harmonies and Dissonances in Geopolitics.* London: I. B. Tauris.

Zelizer, Craig. 2003. "The Role of Artistic Processes in Peace-Building in Bosnia-Herzegovina." *Peace and Conflict Studies* 10(2):62–75.

INTERVIEW

Agovski, Vladimir. 2010. Interview with Vladimir Agovski—Ago (DNS Ekipa). http://hiphop .mk/intervjua/427-2010-03-19-18-42-47.

PART II

HIP HOP AND EMERGING MARKET ECONOMIES

CHAPTER 5

DIESEL POWER

Serbian Hip Hop from the Pleasure of the Privileged to Mass Youth Culture

Goran Musić and Predrag Vukčević

IN ORDER TO analyze local manifestations of hip hop as a global phenomenon, it is useful to start from a simple recognition that the culture was born and defined in the ghettos of the United States by the lower-class youth of racial minorities. Like many earlier musical styles and products of American pop culture, hip hop arrived in other countries as a cultural transfer. It is habitually assumed that the social place and cultural meanings that hip hop acquired in the United States are automatically replicated on the receiving end. Hip hop is seen as a universal language of the oppressed (Osumare 2001:172). However, in peripheral societies, it is often youth from privileged social backgrounds, and not marginalized groups, who are best positioned to adopt the latest Western cultural exports. Inside the receiving societies, hip hop culture can attain new values and social interpretations, very different than those it embodied in its country of origin.

This chapter looks at the change and spread of hip hop expression over the course of three decades in Serbia, a society undergoing transformation from state socialism to capitalism, where hip hop developed from a subculture, claimed and jealously guarded by a socially privileged, closed circle of rap adherents, to one of the most popular cultures among Serbian youth. This expansion was in part made possible by the fusion of hip hop with other, more authentic, local youth subcultures. The major milestones along this path were: (1) hip hop's initial spread among the already existing disco/funk scene and its cohabitation with local subcultural traditions in the 1980s; (2) the proliferation of hip hop as a distinct subculture oriented to street-level themes, with appropriation of the g-funk subgenre sound and fashion in the 1990s; and, finally, (3) its full emancipation as the preferred language of expression for the local proletarian youth, through open exchange with the youth subculture traditionally associated with turbo-folk, eurodance music, and street crime known as *dizelaši*[1] at the turn of the century.

In the scholarly treatment of contemporary popular culture in Serbia, the emergence of *dizelaši* and turbo-folk in the early 1990s is often seen as a state-sponsored project, introduced to weaken existing urban cultures. Turbo-folk is also regularly seen in connection with nationalism and authoritarian politics (Gordy 1999:19). This reasoning is to a large extent a reflection of the dominant popular discourse inside Serbia, which tends to place the blame for rising inequality, crime, corruption, and other social problems accompanying the transition to capitalism on the shoulders of lower-class youth aspiring to change their social position by any means at hand. Throughout the 1990s, the hip hop community in Serbia was composed mostly of middle-class youth, adopting moralistic views similar to lower-class youngsters and their culture. The opening up of the local hip hop scene to other youth subcultures, and *dizelaši* in particular, was therefore a protracted process full of tension and controversy.

This chapter rejects the notions of turbo-folk and *dizel* culture as a top-down, engineered social phenomenon with fixed social and political outlooks (Dimitrijević 2002; Đurković 2002, 2004). Instead, it treats *dizelaši* as a grassroots urban youth movement shaped by the social realities of Serbian mafia capitalism. It argues that, of all the phases in the development of Serbian hip hop mentioned above, it was open communication with the *dizel* ethos that decisively contributed to transforming it into a widely accepted culture among youth. The carefree attitudes and plebeian musical choices of the *dizel* movement helped Serbian hip hop reconnect to its forgotten party roots and socially mixed crowds from the early days of disco.

Among other things, this new, more inclusive orientation of the Serbian hip hop community is reflected in partial recognition and acceptance of urban Roma youth as essential to the shaping of local street culture, and thus hip hop (Matić 2005).

DANCE, DANCE, DANCE . . .

As a result of the policy of open cultural exchange with the West, the early artifacts of hip hop culture reached the Socialist Federative Republic of Yugoslavia (SFRY) in the first half of the 1980s, parallel to their arrival to Western Europe. In the capital city of Belgrade, hip hop found its very first followers among the disco/funk dancers, DJs, and aficionados. In 1981, Boban Petrović—one of the most popular, if not the most popular disco DJ and promoter in Belgrade, Serbia, and Yugoslavia—published a quintessential disco funk LP titled *Žur* (House Party). Petrović himself was an intriguing figure, managing to fill the club with partygoers from all walks of life: celebrities, sons and daughters of the communist party bureaucracy, sportsmen, but also criminals, disco dance enthusiasts, and working-class youth looking for a good time (Musić and Vukčević 2009).

On a symbolic level, one could argue that the track "Đuskaj" (Get Down) from the *Žur* LP serves as a manifesto for the incipient hip hop generation in socialist Yugoslavia (Petrović 1981). Although Petrović sings on it, his rhymes suggest the start of something new, clearly distinguishable from rock 'n' roll—the music by then already appropriated by the Yugoslav communist authorities and promoted as a desirable urban youth culture.[2] Petrović takes a stand in defense of party music and funky spirit against all the rock critics who had been diminishing their value, stating to the listener that the music doesn't have to convey "a message and an advice," because people can figure things out using their own mental capacities, and inviting the listener to simply dance. He wraps up the track in a genuine hip hop "represent" style, stating that personal image and lyrics are the main thing and suggesting to all musicians to *recite* their lyrics because "that is the real gift" (Petrović 1981).

Following Boban Petrović's "Đuskaj," many new and aspiring artists attuned to the funk music tradition started to incorporate elements of hip hop in their work. Belgrade's new wave band Du Du A put out the track "Hop Ap Du Ap" on their debut LP, *Primitivni ples* (Primitive Dance) from 1983—arguably the first track featuring rapping verse in any of the Yugoslav languages (Du Du A 1983). Data, a team of electropop producers from Belgrade, published a b-boy electro funk EP *Degout* in 1984, under the moniker the Master Scratch Band, with "Break War" as the A1 track (Master Scratch Band 1984). In the song, the female announcer states that "the streets are filled with turntables and cassette players" and "our reporter is in the hospital, but he has managed to send in a report that says, 'Break war started!'"[3] (Master Scratch Band 1984). That same year, Curtis Marlow's book *Break Dancing* was translated to Serbo-Croatian and published in Belgrade (Marlow 1984). Around this time, state-owned record labels started publishing numerous hip hop, electrofunk, and disco rap compilations and singles, licensed from US and UK labels such as Sugar Hill Records, CBS, Charisma, and so on. Thus, by the mid-1980s, break dancing reached the level of a "craze" among Yugoslav school youth, with kids in the streets imitating dance moves and fashion styles seen in the media.

Diverse aspects of this new urban subculture tended to diffuse unevenly and in specific ways among the youth from different social and ethnic backgrounds. Early hip hop–influenced records had been created and consumed mostly by youth from the upper and middle classes who were already in touch with the latest musical trends.[4] After the great impact of the punk movement, an artistically diverse and avant-garde new wave and post-punk scene blossomed in Yugoslav urban environments throughout the 1980s. The artists most open to new influences started incorporating hip hop and rapping into their sound (e.g., Disciplina Kičme 1987;

Rambo Amadeus 1989). Despite a wave of negative reaction from fellow artists and conservative music journalists who grew up on rock guitar, various individuals from the new wave/post-punk scene started developing a keen interest in the newest trends in "black music."[5] One of the most charismatic musicians coming out of this milieu—Dušan Kojić-Koja, the leader of the cult band Disciplina Kičme—started promoting the emerging rap groups of the late 1980s, such as Public Enemy, through his interviews, radio guest slots, and by working as a disc jockey in alternative clubs.[6]

The alternative rock crowd adopted rap music with a punk ethos. It was seen as a rebellious music of hard drums, guitar samples, and a clear social message. On the other hand, the party/dance tradition of hip hop culture continued to live among kids from the lower social strata. Many of these youth had no previous contact with rock music and adopted the new styles from their peers in the United States, often mixing them in a carefree fashion with other Western pop culture influences and local traditions. Break dance became the element of hip hop most present on the streets and in working-class neighborhoods. Roma kids, being socially marginalized, discriminated against by the educational system, and often speaking Serbo-Croatian as their second language, were especially attracted to the possibility of proving themselves through the display of physical fitness and virtuosity (Matić 2005:117–122). As with kung fu movies, this cultural import in which the main characters were nonwhites had great appeal for the Roma youth (Musić and Vukčević 2009).[7] By the end of the 1980s, hip hop had also entered the broader music market, with some underground artists who experimented with rap music gaining mainstream success, and well-established pop musicians borrowing rap snippets, hip hop clothing, or street dance routines to refresh their image (Balašević 1989). In the early 1990s, even folk singers started to incorporate elements of hip hop into their media appearances (e.g., Babić 1991; Dabetić 1992). This trend only increased the visibility of hip hop culture for the broader public and working-class youth.

RAP 'N' ROLL

As the 1980s drew to a close, the early spirit of "peace, unity, and love through having fun," promoted by disco/funk DJs such as Boban Petrović was all but lost. Hip hop had spread its influence far beyond the clubs playing dance music, but there was still no coherent youth movement able to embody the culture as a whole. On one hand, hip hop was nurtured by avant-garde artists of the post-punk generation who borrowed particular components of rap music for their sound. On the other, there was a broader layer of youth receiving only glimpses of hip hop culture and fashion filtered through the lens of popular media. It was only in the early 1990s, with the spread of satellite television, music videos, bootleg cassettes, and, most importantly, the appearance of a number of local artists fully immersed into the culture, that hip hop started to exist as an independent, integral youth subculture.

The second half of the 1980s, however, had seen Public Enemy's records being welcomed and promoted by a select number of rock music critics, and Yugoslav record labels were putting out some of the biggest titles from the Def Jam music label catalogue—Beastie Boys, Run DMC, LL Cool J, and so on—which attracted the layer of youth more prone to electric guitars and raw drum machine sounds.[8] Toward the start of the 1990s, Serbia had witnessed the birth of something that could be called the first Belgrade/Serbian demo rap scene. Bands such as Budweiser, Geto Blaster, Bez kaucije, Green Kool Posse, Robin Hood, and Who Is the Best? had all been making rap music in a classic Def Jam/Rick Rubin manner, while putting more emphasis on lyrics containing hardcore crew/local represent, vivid descriptions of everyday life in the city, and sociopolitical commentary.

This shift toward a "whiter" sound and "harder" lyrics alienated the part of the hip hop crowd that was more into party/dance side of the culture. As Matić vividly depicts in his essay on the famous dancer Đogani as a Yugoslav urban myth:

> Our fellow citizens, those from the margins—laborers, proletarians—and especially those from the "ethnic" margin—Roma, Albanians, our "Gypsies and Shqiperie," as we used to call them paternalistically—couldn't relate to rock 'n' roll, to problems that it posed, to such stylistics. They simple couldn't feel it—too "white" and middle-class. They needed their own sound, and when they've finally got it, they've got it with a vengeance. With the expansion of disco clubs, this scene also got its own values and heroes. (Matić 2005:120)

At the turn of the 1980s and into the 1990s, these party/dance hip hop kids had switched to the sound of party hip hop and eurodance groups (e.g., Technotronic, Snap! Mantronix, Bomb the Bass) or more mainstream US rap artists (e.g., MC Hammer). They started emulating the dance and music styles of the aforementioned acts and laid the foundation for their own local scene. Despite the internal differences—primarily between kids who were into dancing to party tracks and rap 'n' roll kids who were more into rapping hard rhymes over rap crossover beats—and although being relatively small, this generation that came to age in the late 1980s, taken as a whole, is the first generation whose members started perceiving hip hop as a rounded, multifaceted urban culture and lifestyle.

The track "24 sata" (24 Hours) by the most popular rap 'n' roll band from this period—Budweiser—recorded in 1988, contains perhaps the first documented lyrical (self) references to a "rapper" as a subcultural identity in Belgrade and Serbia:

> Chain around the neck, ring on the finger
> Rappers always dress the best
> Put on your jeans and Adidas on your feet
> No one is dressed better than us[9]

These lyrics showcase a clear recognition of hip hop's subcultural fashion/style identity displayed through battle/represent rhymes. In the same song, which tries to represent an ordinary day in the life of young Belgrade rappers, Budweiser—which had dubbed its own style of music "rap 'n' roll"—are showing an appreciation for rock music, saying that they are playing it at their rehearsals, but it's clear that rap is their first musical and subcultural choice. Their MC raps the following rhymes:

> I arrived to a rehearsal right on time
> My people have already started rehearsing without me
> They have played rock noisy and loud
> I said: "Enough! Do I make myself clear?!"
> Then we've started playing rap with a strong beat
> and we've played it for a while, 'til nightfall[10]

A recurring motif in these early declarations of independence for rap music is that rap should be recognized as a distinct local urban youth subculture—different, in the first place, from rock 'n' roll in general and, more specifically, from punk rock. Probably the most accurate and balanced representation of the first demo rap scene's view of the relation between the developing hip hop subculture and rock 'n' roll as the most visible local urban youth culture was given by MC Best, a member of the band Who Is the Best? in its song from 1990 titled "Rap Is My Life":

> They just say "Hit the road, rap!"
> And look upon it as a musical disgrace
> I'm a rocker but I love rap
> To me, it's imaginative and beautiful[11] (Who Is the Best? 1990)

Despite their strong sense of belonging to hip hop culture, the effort these artists invested in distinguishing themselves from the rock milieu reveals just how close they still were to their guitar music roots, in every aspect. By the mid-1990s, however, the Serbian rap scene managed to spread to a wider circle of urban youth and establish itself as a clearly separate stream among the urban subcultures. This development was enhanced by the rising influence of American West Coast gangsta rap, a subgenre that even the most generous rock critics were not ready to embrace. The new gangsta sound, which relied more on a funk heritage than on heavy beats and guitar samples, as well as street-oriented subject matter, definitely cut the ties between the local rap scene and the alternative music circles stemming from the rock heritage.

THE *GETO* MESSAGE CARRIERS

The weekly radio show called *Geto* (The Ghetto) , which became the main source for the dissemination of new rap acts from the United States, played a crucial role in this turn. With authoritative hosts, lists of foreign singles supported by up-to-date reports of a member of the *Geto* crew who was studying in the United States at the time, a local demo chart, and regular live phone interactions with listeners on a wide range of issues concerning the music and life in a big city, the show quickly established itself as the cornerstone of the Belgrade rap scene, and even went on to win the title of most popular specialized radio show in the country.

Geto was not simply mirroring the main trends taking place in the United States, but shaped specific local tastes. Over time, the show developed a tendency to promote gloomier gangsta rappers nurturing sinister sounds, such as MC Eiht, Spice 1, and Scarface. *Thug Life: Volume 1*—an album made by Tupac Shakur and his crew—gained a cult-like status among local rap fans. Shakur's straightforward language and raw, emotional delivery brought foreign rap closer to many young-sters who had limited knowledge of English. Cassette tapes with songs recorded from radio, VCR tapes carrying rap videos from MTV, hip hop movies, and, oc-casionally, copies of *The Source, Hip Hop Connection,* or similar magazines cir-culated from hand to hand. By 1995, the g-funk sound became the norm in the local scene, and groups such as Rhythm Attack, Gru, CYA, Plan B, 187, and others brought the subject matter of Serbian rap much closer to the actual streets, trying hard to find local parallels to the gangster themes of American rap.

Nevertheless, hip hop expression was still unable to catch the raw feel of lo-cal neighborhoods. MCs often used indirect speech, narrated in the third person, avoided bragging, and rarely mentioned their names and specific local markers in rhymes, and the songs contained moral distancing from the more controver-sial topics. In spite of being obsessed with the raw reports from city streets, lyrics and the whole "MC represent" of the g-funk generation, Serbian rap was, in a strict hardcore rap MCing sense, a step back compared to the rap 'n' roll genera-tion's rap. More often than not, Serbian rap songs sounded generic, almost as direct translations of American songs. They often managed to offer informative reports about the street culture, but rarely offered genuine insight into the local proletarian milieu and its understandings of social reality.

An illustrative example of the lack of locality in the songs of the "g-funk gen-eration" is the first single from the famous group 187, called "Tamna strana" (The

Dark Side) (187 1995). From a conversation with Predrag Radisavljević, a former member of the group, we learned that in the first version of the song, the start of his verse "We are driving down the street wasted on cocaine . . ." (*Vozimo niz ulicu mrtvi od koke . . .*)." contained a specific local reference to Požeška (name of a street in Belgrade). Radisavljević and his group members took out the street name from the song because they thought more people would relate to the rhyme if it weren't so openly local (Vukčević 2013).

Throughout the g-funk years, the idea that rap music had a duty to be politically engaged remained present. The rap 'n' roll generation of artists, recording during the late 1980s and early 1990s, was the first to set the trend of profound social commentary delivered from the perspectives of youth from lower-middle-class and working-class backgrounds. Budweiser set it straight, saying:

> We are not a pop group that got money to burn
> We came from the street and climbed to the top[12] (Budweiser 1989)

The song went on to draw the line between its members and kids from wealthy families living in Belgrade's prestige residential area of Dedinje:

> Cafés are expensive, you ought to have money
> Boys from Dedinje run the city now[13] (Budweiser 1989)

Probably the most poignant sociopolitical commentary in Serbian rap from the start of the 1990s would be "Drama"—a track from the first officially published Serbian rap LP, *Milenijum posle—Misterija I* (A Millennium After—Mystery I), made by Belgrade rap group Tapiri. "Drama" encapsulates the experience of the year 1993—the most traumatic year in recent Serbian history, when rampant inflation, war in the former Yugoslavia, and the criminalization of society caused unprecedented rapid social decay. Tapiri recorded the whole album during 1993, and it was published same year by the state-owned record label PGP RTS.[14] On this track, leader of the group and lyricist-in-charge Milan Bojanić starts by rhyming that the friends of the band are suggesting to band members to start making music for girls. The band leaves open the possibility of taking that advice, but "in a year or two,"[15] because the situation in 1993 is too urgent and band members have to rhyme about it. Throughout the song, the band calls out ruling party bureaucrats from Serbia—especially from Dedinje, a high-class Belgrade residential neighborhood—and Croatia, as warlords and those most responsible for the crisis in the former Yugoslavia,[16] but they still manage to portray the situation from the standpoint of the average city kid, rhyming that prices are shockingly high and that it's virtually impossible for them to attain sneakers and perfumes, while "jackets and pants are from the stone age." The rest of the album also contains a few rhymes that depict the social realities of Belgrade and Serbia in 1993, but the vast majority of lyrics point to the parallel party tradition, dealing with funny storytelling and strictly "MC represent" rhymes.[17]

A transition to gangsta themes and a West Coast sound, therefore, did not introduce a complete break from the commitment to social commentary or spread the "real niggaz don't give a fuck" attitude with a lot of lyrical boasting made popular by the new g-funk stars in the United States.[18] For the second generation of rap groups in Serbia, political activism remained a necessary, if not crucial, element of hip hop culture. However, social and political positioning was not so easy and straightforward for local g-funk artists. The spread of rap music inside Serbia overlapped with the breakup of the country, civil wars, international economic sanctions, increasing poverty, criminalization, and the beginning of the transition from the Yugoslav variety of self-management socialism toward capitalism. The entire last decade of the twentieth century was marked by intense political struggle between the authoritarian regime, personified by Slobodan Milošević, and oppositional forces, which often spilled out into the streets in the form of rallies, protests, and clashes with police.

Under these circumstances, it was pretty much inevitable for local rappers to start identifying their social position with that of African American youth. The rapping voice in the opening jingle of the *Geto* radio show declared:

You can't put no veto on us
All types of schemes do us no harm
The rise and fall, hunger and crime
'cause I'm a warrior and this is a ghetto[19]

The intent to draw a parallel between the poverty-stricken and isolated Serbia of the 1990s and US inner cities was clear, but the question of where one drew lines of class and ethnic distinction, which seemed so clear-cut in the United States, remained open. Who was the local equivalent of the "young black male" that Chuck D or Ice Cube rapped about? What should the rap community stand for, and against whom should it fight?

As late as 1992, the Romani leader of the famous Serbian rap, later eurodance, group Beat Street, Husa, rapped in a carefree manner on a national TV show, on the group's demo rap track "Beat Street"—"with a street beat, everyone is a nigger" (*uz ulični bit nigeri su svi*) (Stanojević 1992). Yet the rise of g-funk was accompanied by a struggle to conceptualize a place in hip hop culture and MC represent for Serbian, that is, non–African American, rappers. A common view inside the rap scene organized around *Geto* was that rap groups should fight against Milošević's regime alongside rock 'n' roll bands, support political forces opposing Milošević, and defend the "urban" spirit from all cultural and political attacks, including the party-oriented rappers seeking commercial success by mixing hip hop with eurodance or turbo-folk.

In Defense of the "Urban"

The early years of transition to a free market economy brought a drastic lowering of the living standards for the vast majority of the population, and enrichment for a tiny number of the elite. Unable to maintain the old industrial facilities or open new workplaces, the regime opened the doors to an informal economy as a security valve at the bottom of the social ladder. Working-class families in the urban areas started engaging in black markets of goods in shortage, such as gasoline, oil, and cigarettes, smuggled under the wall of economic sanctions. This widespread street entrepreneurialism "from below" injected a new dynamism into society and spread hopes of fast enrichment. Also, despite international isolation, Western cultural influences and consumer culture started penetrating the country at a pace never before witnessed under state socialism. The market was soon flooded with genuine and bootleg consumer goods, which symbolized the good life and luxury: sport shoes, brand-name sweat suits, foreign liquor, electronic items, and so on.

With no other paths to climb the social ladder, working-class youth were especially prone to absorb this new ethos of instant consumerism and the fast life. The soundtrack to this socioeconomic transformation became "turbo-folk." Under socialism, folk music came to the cities with migrant workers, but its lyrics and sounds remained loyal to traditional themes of harmonious rural life. By the early 1990s, folk music started opening up to influences from American pop music and eurodance, but also Greek and Turkish pop folk traditions. The lyrics switched as well from longing for the idealized rural past to a hedonistic embrace of new opportunities arising under mafia capitalism. One of the most popular folk artists of the time was Džej Ramadanovski, a Belgrade Roma who built his image as a streetwise entertainer and spoke openly about his experiences with petty crime. Džej introduced James Brown–like shouts in between his tongue-in-cheek lyrics, did not abstain from using slang words, and incorporated street dance moves in his stage performances.

Various individuals from the street dance scene played crucial roles in this development. One of the most notable was Hamit Đogaj, a youth of Albanian Roma descent from Mirijevo and Zemun, Belgrade's working-class neighborhoods. Đogaj, a.k.a. Đogani, started appearing in Belgrade disco funk gatherings as early as the late 1970s, gathering professional experience as a studio dancer for the Italian national television Rai Uno show *Fantastico* during the 1980s, only to return to Serbia in the early 1990s, where he opened a school for street dance and performed with his group Đogani Fantastiko as a back-up dancing act for many turbo-folk stars (Musić and Vukčević 2009; Matić 2005). Later, during the 1990s, Đogani Fantastiko started putting out its albums and scored a few major hits—mainly eurodance, but also some new jack swing tracks with an oriental/turbo-folk touch. In addition, Đogani's younger brothers and cousins—Funky G, Baki B3, and Sani Trik FX—built their own careers in the Serbian eurodance and pop music scene, becoming the first stars of Roma descent—alongside Džej Ramadan-ovski and Husa from Beat Street—to appear regularly on Serbian mainstream TV shows in the 1990s.

The first half of the 1990s was marked by the informal economy and orga-nized crime. The neighborhoods of bigger cities came under the control of local crime figures, presenting themselves as fighters against the powers that be and defenders of the poor.[20] The young people associated with this new breed of ur-ban music, social street hustling, gyms and body building, tough attitudes, fast cars, and expensive sporting gear,[21] looking up to young gangbangers who were coming up in the Serbian urban neighborhoods as local "Robin Hoods," were soon dubbed *dizelaši* by the local media.[22] *Dizel* subculture was a local social phe-nomenon whose aesthetic and values stood close to the gangsta attitude of the American inner city youth. As Quinn points out while trying to provide an account of African American g-funk generation, "Gangsta's governing ethic of aggressive economic self-determination is clearly legible when seen as a tactical response to the steady depletion of resources, rights, and modes of resistance" (Quinn 2005:169). *Dizelaši* were developing this gangsta attitude to life in the same vein as their African American peers were doing on the West Coast, across the American South, and elsewhere at the time. The limited opportunities to advance in society were pushing them into idolization of "conspicuous consumption and self-determined business practice," leading them to the conclusion that "living well is the best revenge" (Quinn 2005:170).

The g-funk generation of rappers in Serbia was wary of coming closer to *dizelaši*. Ding Dong, a rap group from Niš, the third-largest Serbian city, rapped in its 1999 hit single "Ćelav sam pa šta" (I'm Bald, So What?), that members didn't want to be compared to *dizelaši* even though they sported a similar hairstyle—"And if you tell me that I'm a dizel, I will do you like Sean Penn did Madonna" (*A ako mi kažeš da sam dizel, ja ću tebe kao Madonu Šon Pen*) (Ding Dong 1999). The main target of criticism in rap rhymes remained the corrupt politicians and the upper classes, but rappers also started directing their anger toward those below them. The rap scene took an active part in the popular wave of moral indignation against the *dizel* culture and other members of marginalized social groups try-ing to come up during hard times.

The main problems with *dizel* counterculture, from the rappers' point of view, were: (1) generic and oversimplified romantic and feel-good party anthems, without any social or political commentary, which they saw as an effort to dumb down and to turn the attention of the audience away from the real problems, thus helping the regime; (2) the fact that these songs were not censored by TV and radio stations, while political rap and rock songs were; and (3) the fact that *dizels* were very aggressive, often initiating physical clashes with other sub- or countercultural groups.

The rap band Magic People from Novi Sad—the second-largest Serbian city—openly represented tough *dizel* atittudes in their demo track "Diesel People" from the late 1990s, rhyming about the regular night out in the city and beating up other non-*dizel* crews (Magic People 1998). One edition of *Geto* also reflected this mood very well. Listeners were invited to voice their opinions about the social group they had the most problems with and declare it unworthy of a place in Belgrade. Rap fans usually listed turbo-folk music, *dizelaši*, war refugees, and Roma as the main problems in their immediate surroundings.

All of these social groups were usually lumped together under the label "peasants" (*seljaci*)—the term used to put down newly arrived migrants from the countryside, but also the lower social strata in general, who allegedly were resistant to integration and attaining the "civic" manners of the middle and upper classes. In 1994, MC Best, the founder of *Geto* and the leader of Who Is the Best? (one of the rare groups from the rap 'n' roll generation that managed to accommodate to the new g-funk sound), wrote the following lyrics:

> For stupid peasants it remains inscrutable . . .
> Because this is my city, you scum
> Out with all you scoundrels and bastards
> over Drina river, go back where the hell you came from![23] (Who Is the Best?
> 1994)

Hip hop was therefore jealously guarded, being seen by many as an exclusive right reserved for urban dwellers sophisticated enough to fully understand and appreciate the art. This antagonism toward working-class youngsters practicing hip hop culture on their own terms and other more authentic street subcultures in the city was rationalized on two levels. The first was the "true heads versus phonies" argument so often utilized in the hip hop community. Those who danced,[24] listened to more commercial rap acts, or mixed hip hop with turbo-folk were rejected as "wannabes" contributing to negative stereotypes of rappers in the eyes of general public and other more appreciated youth subcultures (grunge, alternative rock fans).

Yet there were also deeper cultural and political notions involved under the surface. In Serbia, hip hop was understood primarily as an "urban" culture. In the original American context, the term "urban" clearly pointed to postindustrial inner cities and their deprived citizens, in contrast to the middle-class suburbs. In a country such as Serbia, where the process of urbanization and migration from the countryside is still taking place, traits of "urbanity" represent cultural capital associated with the more privileged layers of society. In the midst of political and economic crisis, the urban middle classes formed under socialism felt threatened by the social stirrings of the time, taking a defensive stance against the newly forming property-owning class, but also the lower social layers trying to survive through the informal economy.

The oppositional political movement, which had its base in big urban centers and was supported by most rap groups, used the discourse of orientalism and capitalist modernization to criticize the ruling clique gathered around Slobodan Milošević (Đurković 2004:271). They alleged that the regime consisted of the remaining communists relying on the support of the working class, peasants, pensioners, and criminals to stay in power. In the view of the oppositional activists, this alliance was destroying the urban population and its culture based on Western cultural imports of the previous decades. The system kept pushing the society eastward, away from modern Western democracy and the prosperity of the market economy. For instance, turbo-folk was mostly criticized for adopting Oriental melodies and preventing the development of Western-style mainstream pop music. *Dizelaši* were thus not perceived as victims, but beneficiaries of Milošević's regime. Most rappers preferred to play the conservative role of keepers of the old values and hope for better days, instead of embracing the new urban realities of peripheral capitalism.

And You Thought We Had Settled Down?!

After the NATO bombing in 1999 and Milošević's overthrow in 2000, Serbian society entered the new millennium with high hopes. The economic and social development strategy of the new, openly pro-Western and neoliberal government was based on financial credits and investments arriving from global financial organizations and multinational corporations, which were supposed to raise the general standard of living and bring Serbia closer to "normality" as imagined in the societies of Western Europe. Very soon, however, the realization that the 1990s had never left, as well as fear that they never would, started to spread among the population. The economic hardships continued and the politics remained highly contentious, with open feuds between the main political parties, state security agencies, and organized criminal groups. Scandals over shady privatizations of public enterprises by domestic and foreign buyers were flooding the media.

With the well-established culture of electronic dance music gatherings and the wide selection of cheap drugs on the black market, youth turned to radical hedonism and the booming nightlife for comfort. There were no more regrets, reminiscences of better days, or illusions that everything would be better with the future changes in the government. Paradoxically, this new spirit of demoralization and powerlessness opened the possibility for the hip hop community to reconsider its surroundings and finally recognize the potential of real-life Serbian streets to inspire rap language. By the early 2000s, along with techno, hip hop became the most widespread youth culture in Serbia. Apart from the rap scene, new b-boy and graffiti scenes also started taking shape and became stronger on a national level. Hip hop/R&B DJ parties became big in Belgrade clubbing after 2002, allowing for more a relaxed and inclusive space that had rarely existed in the puritan and self-righteous atmosphere of the 1990s rap scene.

The emergence of a new hip hop aesthetic was announced with the release of a track titled "Ko će to da plati?" (Who Will Pay for It?). The song was recorded by the group VIP, consisting of Juice, a rapper already active during the 1990s,[25] and two up-and-coming Belgrade MCs, Ikac and Rexxxona. While they managed to record only one track before they parted ways, that track became the blueprint for hardcore street rap in Serbia. The intense rhymes crystallized in the chorus arguably represent the strongest generational scream in local rap, which captured the state of mind of the majority of urban Serbian youngsters at the start of the twenty-first century:

> Ten years in poverty, bro—who's gonna pay for it?!
> Ten years of patience, bro—who's gonna pay for it?!
> Expensive cars, black leather, air conditioning—who's gonna pay for it?!
> Livin' large every day—who's gonna pay for it?!
> Our respect costs some money, bro—who's gonna pay for it?!
> To take the crew off the street corners—who's gonna pay for it?!
> Pretty chicks, new things—who's gonna pay for it?!
> Travels, restaurants—who's gonna pay for it?![26] (VIP 2001a)

Such a passionate display of city kids' hunger for material wealth and their need to attain social status, vividly depicted using local symbols, was unheard of in Serbian rap. There were no cries about lost urban identity, self-victimization, or scapegoating of others. Juice rapped in a systematic *dizel* attitude, identifying the accumulation of luxury goods as the only way to win social recognition, with no reservations:

> Thousand Deutsch marks, I need a new pair of shoes and sneakers
> Without cash I feel like a farmworker
> I want BMW 3 TDI, two or three VW Golfs, CRX Honda
> and Mondo's total night income[27] (VIP 2001a)

In 2001, Ikac recorded a similar anthem titled "Atlantida (Malo para—puno stida)" (Atlantis, Small Cash—Big Shame), in which, for the first time, *dizel* subculture is explicitly connected with rap music:

In these four walls I'm not used to lose
Rapper and a dizel, bro—a true Serb!
I'm used to kissing, I love to fuck
to make money, to cheat a bit[28] (VIP 2001b)

In the years to come, Ikac continued to deliver strong rhymes that proclaimed the street kids/*dizel* worldview. In the song "Moj život" (My Life), for instance, Ikac delivers the true *dizel* state of mind:

I started working out, my spirit is restless
It's all about mine—I often don't choose the means
I get nervous, I get into fights
I decided to win in this life all by myself (VIP 2002).

Still, the full localization of rap, through its evolving relation with the *dizel* counterculture, had to wait for Juice's solo take on the subject matter. Juice put out his solo debut LP *Hiphopium* in 2002. Already an accomplished graffiti artist and MC, and viewed as the preserver of a "true hip hop" spirit—something that most of the Serbian hip hop heads wouldn't even put in the same sentence with *dizel* counterculture—Juice managed to achieve a great success with his first single off the album, a song called "Keš kolica" (Cash and Ride) (Juice 2002a). The song became an instant classic among rap fans, as well as across the genre's borders, despite—or due to—the fact that it was heavily embedded in a *dizel* setting. Rap fans who suspected there was something "awkward" going on in the song chose to perceive it as a sarcastic take on young wannabe hustlers, usually coming out of *dizel* subculture and/or sharing *dizel* manners and worldviews. Apart from this song, the album featured a skit with a portion of a song by Roma folk music legend Muharem Serbezovski (Juice 2002c). The general hype surrounding this album as one of the first pronouncements of the new generation of Serbian rap, as well as Juice's stature as a "true hip hop head," kept it safe from accusations of selling out to the *dizel* audience and cemented its classic status.[29]

Another important historical moment that occurred on Juice's debut album was his cover version of Boban Petrović's "Đuskaj" (Juice 2002b). The extraordinary value of this remake is comprehensible only if we contextualize it against the majority of the Serbian rap tracks at the start of the twenty-first century, which were trying to emulate New York rap styles of the 1990s, as well as the popular belief that party-rap tracks were, at least, subpar to raw represent or politically engaged ones. Besides drawing a direct connection between the roots of Serbian rap music at the start of the 1980s and its newest developments some 20 years later, Juice's cover of "Đuskaj" announced an important new development that would become clear on his second album.

Juice returned to the scene in 2006, with his sophomore album, *Brate minli*. The first single, the title track, hit the rap scene hard, immediately creating a controversy. Juice and his 93 FU crew appeared in the video for "Brate minli" with the haircuts, tracksuits, and Nike Air Max sneakers popular among the members of *dizel* subculture in the 1990s. Accompanied by two half-naked female go-go dancers, Juice rapped the following rhymes:

And you thought that we have settled down?!
But, in fact, we just got disturbed
You were flauntin' with chicks a bit, you were showin' off a bit
You were stealing someone else's thunder
While we are in the hood and live the reality
You are askin' gratitude for your petty songs[30] (Juice 2006a)

It was clear from the get-go that Juice was battling the whole rap scene, accusing it of being less "real" than *dizelaši*, if real at all. However, the *dizel* identity he and his crew had chosen to represent was not used just for its shock or battle value. Throughout the album it was clearly shown that the concept relies on a premise that rap should represent the urban life through local symbols, a victorious tone, and from the street level—or, more precisely, from the perspective of working- and lower-middle-class kids—and that *dizel* subculture and its worldview are the most appropriate local equivalent of the street culture of American inner cities.[31]

In "Uvertira lektira" (Overture Lecture), the opening track of the album, Juice conveys advice to his generation to cease the shootings and drug abuse, to start working out, and so on—mainly advice that a grown-up *dizel* would give to another *dizel* (Juice 2006b). This track sets the tone for the entire album; Juice is serious when telling the story of Serbia "since '91, '92, '93," when the *"story starts moving in the wrong direction"* (Juice 2006b). But, on the other hand, he also represents harsh reality through bittersweet humoristic insights, ironically delivered anecdotes, and often surreal-sounding life episodes. Most of the time there is also a party going on.[32] Just a quick glance at the list of the album guests and artists sampled—Tapiri, Husa from Beat Street, Ivan Gavrilović, that is, the crème de la crème of the 1990s Serbian eurodance and party rap scene—makes it self-evident that, as Juice later explained in an interview, his intention was to refresh the whole Serbian rap scene of the mid-2000s, to shock and to put an end to the proliferation of dull and too-serious rap songs (Vukčević 2008).[33]

Intense and complex lyrical developments on the *Brate minli* album, addressing the real life of Serbian street kids on every level imaginable, flooded with local references and supported by Salier Del Flores's raw digital beats, which combined influences of g-funk and emerging Dirty South styles, with a few eurodance and folk touches here and there, made this album hard to follow or to swallow for the regular rap audience. The party and hedonistic aspect of the album is not limited to 1990s and *dizel* counterculture references. The very title of the album and the first single—"Brate minli" (My Mellow, My Ace, or literally "dear brother")—is actually a greeting of Belgrade partygoers, disco dancers, players, and hustlers from the 1970s—the people of the same funky milieu from which Boban Petrović went on to create his proto–hip hop/disco funk sound of Belgrade. This insight points toward a completely new symbolic level of Juice's rap, opening the space for an interpretation that presents "Brate minli" as an effort to establish a kind of virtual funky tradition of Belgrade street culture through the generations.

The price Juice paid for resurrecting his lyrical persona in such close exchange with the real-life proletarian cultures was the scorn of the more conservative core of the Serbian rap community. On the other hand, his daring work helped bring about a watershed in the local rap expression, with *dizel* subculture becoming an integral part of the local rap scene's discourse. Moreover, the new generation of youngsters who had never experienced the turbulent 1990s embraced the *dizel*-flavored style without reservations. The fact that Serbian hip hop had finally caught up with the streets was confirmed by Belgrade street riots in the winter of 2008. The 1990s were marked by mass street rallies organized in support of official policies by the regime of Slobodan Milošević, as well as opposition demonstrations. In 2008, the conservative Serbian government decided to mobilize the citizens one more time against the secession of Kosovo, Serbia's southern province inhabited by an Albanian majority. The government declared a day off for public schools, hoping to attract the youth to the nationalist-colored protests. The youth indeed came out into the streets, but many of them split from the main column of the demonstrations, breaking into the sport boutiques and stealing brand-name goods. A Nike shop was one of the main targets, with youngsters grabbing the retro Air Max models, the shoe that had become a symbol of the *dizel* generation of the early 1990s.

In 2009, one of the most popular Serbian rap groups of the latest generation, THC La Familija, put out a hit track called "Trenerka stil" (Tracksuit Style), in which the rappers openly recognize the influence and street credibility of the *dizel* subculture:

Tracksuit style—everyone's wearing it
The streets echo the spirit of the '90s (THCF 2009)[34]

A young Serbian rap star named Marlon Brutal, representing ruthless football hooligan crews from his block in New Belgrade, took this point further, stating:

I haven't been growin' up with pussies but with football hooligans
and I haven't been growin' up with rappers but with *dizel* crew (Marlon Brutal
2009)[35]

Finally, one of the biggest national hits of 2010, called "Dizel Power"—a track by
Juice's protégé and hardcore rapper, the self-proclaimed "Dance Don" Shwarz,
virtually an adaptation of eurodance sound for 2009, made in collaboration with
Slađa Delibašić, ex-wife of Hamit Đogaj and former lead female vocalist of Đogani
Fantastiko—sums it up for the generations to come:

Player is on the mic, old dogs in Nike
Comin' to your speakers like I started a hunt
Digits are counted, let the big men stand
Everyone get out the way when we're takin' ours
Just business, no leasing
Just big money, no small amounts
We are overbearing in everything—when are you gon' get that?
We are *dizel* power—can you follow in our steps?[36] (Shwarz 2010)

CONCLUSIONS

Throughout the past three decades, peer groups and individuals immersed in hip
hop culture in Serbia felt constant pressure to look for new subcultures, identities, and practices that were more "real," meaning local social phenomena cor-
responding to those described in US rap music. Hip hop was therefore able to
evolve and gain a mass following by constantly negotiating imported sounds and
images with the actual styles, languages, and fashions present on the streets of
Serbian cities. The capacity to filter imported styles and apply them to homegrown
contexts depended largely on the social position of the transmitters. Due to better purchasing power and knowledge of foreign languages, individuals from the
upper classes were in a better position to acquire and translate hip hop as a scarce
imported cultural good. These were usually "rap heads," with a keen ear for de-
tails and an understanding of hip hop as an integral cultural form. On the other
hand, individuals from lower social backgrounds were more likely to receive only
certain elements of hip hop, usually transmitted by the mainstream culture.

In the 1980s, hip hop was picked up and propagated by sections of the new
wave/post-punk scene attracted to the hard beats and guitar samples of early Def
Jam recordings, and to rap's subversive image. Simultaneously, the culture entered the more plebeian disco crowds and spread among working-class youth in
the form of break dancing. In the 1990s, this dichotomy continued with the development of a close-knit community of rap fans insisting on street topics and

social messages on the one hand, and the party/dance-oriented groups in closer contact with proletarian youth subcultures, such as *dizelaši* and local tastes (e.g., turbo-folk) on the other. By the end of the 1990s, rap music became much more accessible to wider audience, and the core rap scene managed to translate and disseminate the style among broader layers of youth. The time was ripe for a synthesis. It was in the early years of the new century that cultural transfer from the United States found affinities to more authentic local trends and proletarian youth subcultures, such as the hedonistic traditions of the local clubbing scene, turbo-folk, or football hooligan culture.

The relationship between *dizel* and hip hop subcultures proved to play a crucial role in this process. The appropriation of *dizel* attitudes, symbols, and language granted Serbian rap cultural and class credibility and added much-needed local flavor. In return, rap lyrics gave the marginalized *dizel* subculture a public voice. For the first time since the early 1990s, lower-class youth striving to attain social status in Eastern European transitional capitalism, through legal or illegal schemes, were being represented by matter-of-fact descriptions, without moralizing undertones. The future development of the rap expression in Serbia depends precisely on this ability of the artists to pick up local urban styles and sentiments, which are close to rap sensibility, and interpret them by relying on the hip hop worldview, free from the pressures of dominant political and media discourses in their home society.

Notes

1. "Diesel crew" or, more precisely, "*dizel* crew."

2. In the mid-1960s, the LCY officially adopted rock 'n' roll as a legitimate youth culture capable of reflecting socialist values. After that, rock music was widely played on the radio stations and became an integral part of state-sponsored youth manifestations. Those performers willing to integrate official state symbols and revolutionary messages into their songs were particularly favored by the authorities (Vučetić 2012; Đurković 2004:276–278).

3. Meaning "our reporter is in the hospital, but he has managed to send in a report that says, 'Break war started!'"

4. The Yugoslav version of "market socialism" encouraged social inequality on a larger scale than was the case in other societies inside the Eastern Bloc. The urban middle classes consisted of white-collar employees in more successful companies or state administration. The most privileged youth came from the families of high-level party bureaucrats or managers of social enterprises. On the other end of the social ladder, in urban surroundings, stood the blue-collar working class, which often maintained ties to the countryside, migrant workers, and Roma population. For a closer understanding of social differentiation in SFRY, see Archer et al. 2016.

5. The most common critique against rap music was that it is not music, since there were no live instruments. Rapping, or "reciting," as rock critics called it, was also looked down upon as too simplistic and inferior to singing.

6. Those rock musicians who were not rejecting hip hop a priori acknowledged only its more or less "harder," r'n'r or funk-sounding elements. Dušan Kojić Koja's interview for *Ritam*

magazine reveals these attitudes. In it, Koja openly despises sounds of Grand Master Flash and Afrika Bambaataa for being "too disco" and acknowledges only Public Enemy's sound, while still remarking that there is nothing new about their music, that "it's all Wattstax" (soundtrack) (Čikara 1989:20).

7. There is also a significant historical episode from the late 1960s, when the band Elipse played soul and funk music for the first time in Belgrade, and the majority of the audience were people of Roma descent. According to Zoran Simjanović—leader of Elipse and the most famous Serbian film music author—the vibe that Roma people created to soul and funk music that Elipse played at their gigs was as in Harlem, New York (Vukčević 2010).

8. The Def Jam sound was preconceived as the ultimate integrationist crossover between "white" and "black" music (Chang 2005:244–246).

9. Lanac oko vrata, prsten na ruku
    Reperi se uvek najbolje obuku
    Navuci farmerke, obuci Adidas
    Niko se ne oblači bolje od nas

10. Na probu sam stigao tačno na vreme
    Moji su svirku počeli bez mene
    Svirali su rok, bučno i glasno
    Rekao sam: "Dosta! Je li jasno?!"
    Počeli smo rep uz ritam jak
    i svirali smo dugo dok nije pao mrak

11. "Hit the road, rap!" samo kažu
    i vide ga kao muzičku blamažu
    Ja sam roker, ali volim rep
    Za mene je on maštovit i lep

12. Mi nismo pop grupa koja se u parama kupa
    Sa ulice smo stigli i na vrh se digli

13. Kafići su skupi, potrebni su novci
    Gradom sada vladaju sa Dedinja momci

14. The fact that the state-owned record label put out Tapiri's LP with a track such as "Drama"— the track that included harsh criticism of Milošević's regime—serves as a strong argument for theorists who deny the thesis that there was a significant state-governed cultural policy in Serbia during 1990s, and that, consequently, turbo-folk was a governmental project. It serves as an argument for the opposing thesis that the cultural policy was dealt with in a laissez-faire manner, left to be governed by the dynamics of the free market.

15. These rhymes turned out to be prophetic, because Tapiri really got into mainstream eurodance music in 1995, when it changed its name to Tap 011 and started working with two of the most notable Serbian female vocals of the 1990s, Ivana Pavlović-Peters and Gordana Goca Tržan. Later, they became the most successful Serbian band of the decade.

16. Milan Bojanić represents a similar standpoint in the demo song "Time's Up," which he ghostwrote for the young rap band Belgrade Posse in 1994.

17. We have to point out a g-funk posse cut from the year 1994, "Sutra je novi dan" (Tomorrow Is a New Day), a track from the debut album *Samo u snu* (Only in a Dream) of Funky G, younger brother of Đogani. The song was written by Milan Bojanić from Tapiri and recorded by the crème de la crème artists of Serbian eurodance scene from 1990s—Funky G, Tapiri, and Duck. On this track, artists who would later create a vast number of eurodance hits adored by the *dizel* audience represent their carefree and party loving attitude while claiming their urban

identity. Funky G acknowledges and complies with his listeners' musical choice, allegedly including rap 'n' roll, rap, funk, and pop music, while Duck denies folk music and asks listeners to spit on folk music and despise it because folk musicians are bringing the "countryside to the city" (*selo u grad*).

18. For an understanding of the change in overall hip hop philosophy brought by g-funk artists in the United States, see Quinn 2005.

19. Na nas ne možeš da staviš
Razne igre—ne pomaže sve to
Uspon i pad, kriminal i glad
jer ja sam ratnik a ovo je geto

20. For the traditions of social banditry in the Balkans, see Eric Hobsbawm 2000, pp. 77–91.

21. Some of the favorite sport shoes brands of *dizels* were Nike Air Max, Puma Disc, and Reebok Pump, which were sold at a price of approximately 20–30 times the typical monthly wage at the time they were released in mid-1990s. It was common for teens to be robbed for their sneakers on the streets, in broad daylight, often with the use of physical violence.

22. The name derived from Diesel—the popular jeans brand of the time. The movie *Rane* (The Wounds) and the documentary *Vidimo se u čitulji* (See You in the Obituary) shed more light on the microcontext in which *dizel* counterculture came to being.

23. Za glupe seljačine to je nešto peto . . .
Jer ovo je moj grad smradovi
Napolje ološ i gadovi
s one strane Drine u tri materine!

24. For rap fans in Serbia who missed the break dance era or early rap's Golden Age back-up dancers and entered the culture through hardcore rap acts of the first half of the 1990s, such as Wu Tang Clan, or the stoned sounds of West Coast gangsta rap, dancing was never seen as a part of the hip hop experience. There were very few girls present at rap shows, and crowd behavior often resembled that of hardcore punk concerts, with mosh pits and a generally tense atmosphere.

25. In the 1990s, Juice was part of Full Moon—a band which released their debut LP in 1998, filled with teenage introspective rhymes and boom bap beats.

26. Deset godina u bedi, brate—ko će to da plati?!
Deset godina strpljenja, brate—ko će to da plati?!
Skupa kola, crna koža. klima—ko će to da plati?!
Svaki dan da se ima—ko će to da plati?!
Naše poštovanje košta, brate—ko će to da plati?!
Da se ekipa skine s ćoška, brate—ko će to da plati?!
Lepe ribe, nove stvari—ko će to da plati?!
Putovanja, restorani—ko će to da plati?!

27. Mondo was the most famous Belgrade electronic dance music club at the start of the 2000s.
Hiljade maraka, treba mi nov par cipela i patika
Bez keša osećam se poput zemljoradnika
Ja hoću BMW 3 TDI, 2–3 Golfa, CRX Honda
i pun noćni pazar Monda

28. U ova četiri zida nisam navik'o da gubim
Reper i dizelaš, brate—pravi Srbin!
Navik'o da ljubim, volim da karam
Pare da stvaram, malo da varam

29. It is important to note that appropriation of *dizel* attitudes was not the only way that hip hop was localized at the time. Apart from Juice's dialogue with *dizel* youth culture, another equally significant development came from 43-23 cipher, started by Ajs Nigrutin and Timbe (a.k.a. Bdat Džutim), founders of the famous rap group Bad Copy. Established at the end of the 1990s, 43-23 cipher grew in the first half of 2000s to include the legendary hardcore rap band Prti Bee Gee; the first Serbian female hardcore rap act, Bičarke na travi; multitalented instrumentalist, freestylist, and party MC Wikluhsky; and a number of established hardcore rap MCs with distinctive styles—Bvana, Seven, Luća H8R. Their represent and style ever since has been somewhat more laidback and nonconfrontational than 93 FU's, with more emphasis on various hedonistic aspects of everyday life in the hood. Despising everything that was not underground and downright dirty occasionally led members of 43-23 cipher to revive open mockery of the *dizel* materialistic aspirations of their peers. However, their amusing and ingenious hood reports, and the authentic slang words they created and popularized helped them become a mainstay of hardcore hip hop in Serbia.

30. *Vi ste mislili da smo se smirili?!*
   U stvari smo se uznemirili
   Malo ste ribe furali, malo se širili
   Malo se tuđim perjem kitili
   Dok mi smo u kraju i živimo realnost
   za vaše pesmice vi tražite zahvalnost

31. There is also an important intertextual reference to Tapiri's "Drama" in "Brate minli," when Juice raps about looking for fresh new sneakers in a city where none are to be found, especially not the famous Nike Air Max models from 1990s that were a status symbol for *dizel* crew.

32. The same kind of duality is deeply rooted in the concept of 93 FU—the name of Juice's crew. The number 93 refers to the year 1993—the year of the total system breakdown in Serbia and Yugoslavia, with high inflation, a crime wave, food shortages, and so on—while FU can be interpreted as a slang word used to express excitement created by something so wicked/mad fresh/crazy tight, but also as an abbreviation of "fuck you," which also holds two possible interpretations when taken together with "93." One interpretation would be something like, "We are '93, fuck you!"; the second one would be "Fuck the year 1993." All in all, the concept is trying to capture the rage toward everyone who created the collapse of society symbolically attached to the year 1993 and, at the same time, the triumphant life philosophy of Juice's crew (and *dizel*), based on the success in surviving the worst possible social circumstances (Vukčević 2012).

33. This whole turn in Juice's sound was announced by his notorious guest rap appearance on Funky G's hit song from 2005, "U tvojim kolima" (In Your Car), when he enraged rap audiences for the first time in his career by laying some playalistic rhymes over an Oriental hip hop beat that Funky G took from the French rap hit "Just Married" by Relic & Amine.

34. Trenerka stil—nose je svi
   Ulice prati duh devedesetih

35. Nisam rast'o s pičkicama nego s navijačima
   i nisam rast'o s reperima nego s dizelašima

36. Plejer je na majku, stari dogovi u Nikeu
   U zvučnike ti stižem ko da podig'o sam hajku
   Cifre nek' se broje, velikani neka stoje
   Sada sklonite se svi kada uzimamo svoje
   Samo biznis, ništa lizing
   Samo krupno, ništa sitniš

Mi smo bahati u svemu, brate, kad ćeš to da shvatiš?
Mi smo dizel power—da li možeš da nas pratiš?

References

Archer, R., et al., eds. 2016. *Social Inequalities and Discontent in Yugoslav Socialism*. Farnham: Ashgate.

Chang, J. 2005. *Can't Stop Won't Stop: A History of Hip-Hop Generation*. New York: St. Martin's.

Dimitrijević, B. 2002. "Globalni turbo-folk." http://www.nin.co.rs/2002-06/20/23770.html (accessed January 27, 2016).

Đurković, M. 2002. "Kulturna industrija i problem nacionalnog identiteta: Slučaj popularne muzike u Srbiji." *Diktatura, nacija, globalizacija* 77–190.

Đurković, M. 2004. "Ideološki i politički sukobi oko popularne muzike u Srbiji." *Filozofija i društvo* 25:271–284.

Gordy, E. 1999. *The Culture of Power in Serbia: Nationalism and the Destruction of Alternatives*. University Park: Pennsylvania State University Press.

Hobsbawm, E. 2000. *Bandits*. London: Weidenfeld & Nicolson.

Marlow, C. 1984. *Brejkdensing*. Belgrade: Branko Gavrić.

Matić, Đ. 2005. "Đogani Hamed." In *Leksikon YU mitologije*, eds. Andrić Iris et al. (pp. 117–122). Belgrade: Rende.

Osumare, H. 2001. "Beat Streets in the Global Hood: Connective Marginalities of the Hip Hop Globe." *Journal of American and Comparative Cultures* 24(1–2):171–181.

Quinn, E. 2005. *Nuthin' but a G Thang: The Culture and Commerce of Gangsta Rap*. New York: Columbia University Press.

Vučetić, R. 2012. *Koka-kola socijalizam: Amerikanizacija popularne kulture šezdesetih godina XX veka*. Belgrade: Službeni glasnik.

Vukčević, P. 2012. Personal communication with Juice, December 20.

Vukčević, P. 2013. Personal communication with P. Radisavljević, February 25.

Interviews

Čikara, A., et al. 1989. "Interview with Dušan Kojić Koja", *Ritam* 1(5):18–21.

Musić, G., and P. Vukčević. 2009. "Đogani šampion (istorija BEEGEE FONKa): An Audio Interview with Hamit Đogaj Đogani." https://soundcloud.com/djapee/djole-shampion (accessed January 27, 2016).

Vukčević, P. 2008. *Rispekt za iskrene ortake* [Interview video file] (interview with Juice). http://www.popboks.com/article/6980 (accessed January 27, 2016), and http://www.popboks.com/article/646.

Vukčević, P. 2010. "Sa ove strane soula: Intervju sa Zoranom Simjanovićem." http://www.popboks.com/article/8105 (accessed January 27, 2016).

Filmography

Bjelogrlić, D., et al., producers, and Dragojević, S., director. 1998. *Rane* [motion picture]. FR Yugoslavia/Germany: Cobra Film Department/Pandora Filmproduktion.

Baljak, J., director. 1995. *Vidimo se u čitulji* [motion picture]. FR Yugoslavia: RTV B92.

Stanojević, M., director. 1992. *Talenti 2000* [TV show]. First aired December 2, 1992. FR Yugoslavia: RTS.

DISCOGRAPHY

187. 1995. "Tamna strana." *Tamna strana* [CD]. Belgrade: CentroScena/PGP RTS.

Babić, S. 1991. "Sneki Rep." *Hopa-Cupa* [LP]. Belgrade: PGP RTB.

Balašević, Đ. 1989. "Sugar Rap" [Proces diferencijacije u Kombinatu za proizvodnju i preradu šećerne repe]. *Tri posleratna druga* [LP]. Zagreb: Jugoton.

Belgrade Posse. 1994. "Time's Up" [demo]. www.youtube.com/watch?v=B7SSOfe5Pvw (accessed January 27, 2016).

Budweiser. 1988a. "24 sata" [demo]. www.youtube.com/watch?v=woQUHOg_myA (accessed January 27, 2016).

Budweiser. 1988b. "God Save the Rap" [demo]. www.youtube.com/watch?v=oiSYOAVR61Q (accessed January 27, 2016).

Budweiser. 1989. "Čuješ li buku" [demo]. *Omladina '90* [LP]. Novi Sad: "M" Produkcija Radio Novog Sada.

Dabetić, A. 1992. "Noć ludila." *Anđeo za umornu dušu* [LP]. Belgrade: PGP RTB.

Ding Dong. 1999. "Ćelav sam pa šta?" *South Side* [CD]. Belgrade: CentroScena.

Disciplina Kičme. 1987. *Dečija pesma* [LP]. Belgrade: PGP RTB.

Du Du A. 1983. "Hop Ap Du Ap." *Primitivni ples* [LP]. Belgrade: PGP RTB.

Funky G. 1994. "Sutra je novi dan." *Samo u snu* [cassette]. Belgrade: MAT/Zmex.

Funky G. 2005. "U tvojim kolima." *Nedodirljiva* [CD]. Belgrade: City Records.

Juice. 2002a. "Keš kolica." *Hiphopium* [CD]. Belgrade: BK Sound.

Juice. 2002b. "Đuskaj." *Hiphopium* [CD]. Belgrade: BK Sound.

Juice. 2002c. "Zovi me" [skit]. *Hiphopium* [CD]. Belgrade: BK Sound.

Juice. 2006a. "Brate minli." *Brate minli* [CD]. Belgrade: City Records.

Juice. 2006b. "Uvertira lektira." *Brate minli* [CD]. Belgrade: City Records.

Magic People. 1998. "Diesel People" [demo]. www.youtube.com/watch?v=RgamOKCb5po (accessed January 27, 2016).

Marlon Brutal. 2009. "HCZ KCZ" [demo]. www.youtube.com/watch?v=WNIZ3Jhp_wQ (accessed January 27, 2016).

Master Scratch Band. 1984. "Break War." *Degout* [LP]. Zagreb: Jugoton.

Petrović, B. 1981. "Đuskaj." *Žur* [LP]. Ljubljana: ZKP RTVL.

Rambo Amadeus. 1989. *Hoćemo gusle!* [LP]. Belgrade: PGP RTB.

Shwarz. 2010. "Dizel Power" [demo]. www.youtube.com/watch?v=gwG98baHZ88 (accessed January 27, 2016).

Tapiri. 1993. "Drama." *Milenijum posle—Misterija I* [LP]. Belgrade: PGP RTS.

THCF. 2009. "Trenerka stil." *Majmun idzuo* [CD]. Belgrade: Tilt.

VIP. 2001a. "Ko će to da plati?" [demo]. www.youtube.com/watch?v=oXYZIBdJaH8 (accessed January 27, 2016).

VIP. 2001b. "Atlantida (Malo para—puno stida)." *TILT Volume 1*. Belgrade: Tilt.

VIP. 2002. "Moj život." *Bassivity Mixtape—Prvi put* [CD]. Belgrade: Bassivity Music.

Who Is the Best? 1990. "Rap Is My Life" [demo]. *Soul Food Music* [CD]. Belgrade: City Records. 2005.

Who Is the Best? 1994. "WITB Strikes Again" [demo]. *Welcome to Belgrade* [CD]. Belgrade: ITMM. 1995.

CHAPTER 6

"THE UNDERGROUND IS FOR BEGGARS"

Slovak Rap at the Center of National Popular Culture

Peter Barrer

ONCE A PERIPHERAL form of popular music, indigenous rap production is now at the very center of Slovakia's popular music culture. The intention of this chapter is to discuss the key properties of Slovak rap as a dominant popular music idiom through an analysis of media texts as well as some of the most widely circulated tracks and videos. Slovak rap in the mainstream is characterized by a masculine narrative of capitalism which champions upward social mobility through financial enrichment and celebrates practices of conspicuous consumption. This narrative, which now dominates Slovak rap's lyrical and visual content, was present (but not so prevalent) when this music idiom first shifted to the mainstream in the mid-2000s; at that time there were other narratives in popular rap tracks, including descriptions of home locality, commentaries on social and political issues, and a general sense of disdain toward social and cultural hierarchies (Barrer 2009:64–72). In general, the lyrics of Slovakia's most popular rap artists no longer genuinely engage in public debate concerning pressing social issues such as corruption, interethnic relations, or social inequality. Instead, these artists endear themselves to advertisers by avoiding political controversy. Slovak rap remains closely bound to the "white" majority population, who listen to rap as a consumer activity and are not confronted with any critical assessment of sensitive subjects (such as, for instance, the discrimination and social exclusion experienced by Slovakia's Romani community). The commercial motives behind Slovak rap are present even when the videos and lyrical content appear to have a noncommercial focus; at first sight, they seem unlikely candidates for commercial success due to their "objectionable" content. Rytmus is Slovakia's most prolific rap artist and the most influential figure on the local scene: he embodies the music idiom's commercial direction, and his work (and reactions to it) will be discussed in detail throughout this chapter. Another defining feature of Slovak rap which will be briefly discussed is the emergence of a "nationalist" narrative in the work of artists who are on the fringes of the mainstream in terms of circulation but who constitute a central theme of media attention given to rap in Slovakia in recent years.

Most of the Slovak population certainly know of Slovak rap, whether they follow popular music or not. For the most part, public perceptions of rap have been formed from the Slovak mass media, which circulate condensed images of Slovak hip hop informed by a mixture of facts, symbols, and stereotypes. Since the success of Kontrafakt's 2003 rap video "Dáva mi" (What Rap Gives Me) and the first wave of commercial album releases in 2004 and 2005, which signaled Slovak rap's move into the mainstream, this music idiom has moved to the center of the national popular music industry. Slovak rap videos posted on video-sharing websites such as YouTube attract millions of views, and while some of the most popular Slovak rap tracks have had their airplay on music radio and television restricted because broadcasters are legally obliged to avoid the use of foul language or objectionable imagery during primetime hours, rap artists regularly win national music awards and have best-selling albums on the national charts (Danko 2011; Kizek 2013; Krekovič 2013; "Vyhrá Hit roka reper Ego?" 2012). In addition to being used for a range of commercial purposes in popular culture outlets, particularly television programming and commercials, Slovak rap reached beyond these realms with the 2008 hip hop musical theater production *Príbeh ulice* (The Story of the Street), which proved so popular in both Slovakia and the Czech Republic that it spawned a sequel (Janda 2011). Slovakia's foremost rap artists (all of whom are male) are media celebrities who regularly appear on television and in celebrity newspapers and magazines; their concert performances, album sales, and rap videos have made rap a dominant force in the Slovak popular music industry. This is particularly the case in terms of Slovak rap's internet presence, where videos by prominent rap practitioners such as Rytmus, Ego, and Majk Spirit have millions more views than those of other Slovak popular music artists. This is an important consideration because the internet is a primary form of popular music consumption. Slovakia has a higher level of internet penetration than the European average: up to three-quarters of the national population go online for information and entertainment (Johnson 2013:160–161; Salovaara-Moring 2013:103). In addition, the number of album sales in Slovakia is low. A domestic album need only sell 5,000 units to receive gold certification—a figure considerably lower than other European countries (e.g., Denmark, Finland, Ireland, or Norway) with similarly sized populations—and there are high levels of music piracy (Bernstein, Sekine, and Weissman 2007:137, 153). Therefore, rap artists' revenue from their music production (over which they maintain ownership) is primarily generated through increasing their internet presence, appearing on television, performing at concerts and corporate functions, and ultimately attracting sponsorship from advertisers. Given the importance of the internet as a primary site of popular music consumption in Slovakia, this chapter will refer whenever possible to those rap videos and tracks that are freely available online and endorsed by the artists who made them.

In addition to their mutual linguistic intelligibility, there is a strong dynamic of reciprocity, openness, and seamlessness between the popular music industries of Slovakia and the Czech Republic. Like other forms of domestic popular music, Slovak rap is not limited to Slovakia but functions on a Czecho-Slovak basis. Major music publishers now control their Slovak operations from head offices in Prague, and the tendency to broadcast transnational versions of popular music talent shows such as Česko Slovensko má talent (Czecho-Slovakia's Got Talent), Česko slovenská superstar (Czecho-Slovak Superstar), and Hlas Česko Slovenska (The Czech/Slovak Voice), on which Slovak rappers have participated as performers, judges, and coaches, is further evidence of an integrated Czech and Slovak popular music industry. Czech rap compilation albums routinely feature Slovak artists, and it is common practice in the music retail outlets of both countries to group Slovak and Czech popular music together within "domestic" displays. Czech and Slovak rap artists also have a strong presence on regional music television stations such as MTV, Óčko, and Musicbox. Slovak rappers are very popular in the Czech Republic; they regularly perform there and appear alongside their Czech counterparts in collaborative videos. Indeed, the most prolific Slovak rap artists are truly "Czecho-Slovak" in popularity.

There is some exposure of Slovak rap in other European countries, most notably Poland. The Slovak rappers Ego and Rytmus both performed in the video clip "I tak to osiągnę" by the Polish group WWO, which also featured the Czech rapper Orion and the French group Soundkail (WWO et al. 2008). In 2009 Rytmus appeared in another Polish rap video, "Stoprocent 2," with the Polish rappers Sobota, Gural, and Wall-E; the German rapper Kool Savas; and the British rapper Bigz (Sobota et al. 2009). A key characteristic of these videos is their multilingualism, with rappers delivering their lyrical pronouncements strictly in their native tongue. However, even though Rytmus has stated that the "Czech and Slovak market is too small" for his ambitions (Kušnierik 2012), there does not appear to be any significant movement of Slovak rap beyond Slovakia, the Czech Republic, and Poland. Slovak rap therefore remains limited to those countries where the Slovak language is either fully or partially understood.

Men Making Money

One fact that stems from the popularity of Slovak rap is that its authenticity is now negotiated along commercial lines. In sharp contrast to Dennison Bertram's comment regarding Czech rap in the early 2000s, that "if someone picks up a mike . . . , they never do it for the hope of getting rich" (Bertram 2003:43), the lyrical centerpiece of Slovak rap in the 2010s is financial enrichment. Though the spatial imagery of Slovak rap videos remains characterized by the rappers' "home" localities—urban environments of aging panel-style apartment buildings and desolate-looking industrial spaces—which is a deliberate acknowledgment of mainstream rappers' modest "street" origins and a symbolic engagement with local experiences of economic deprivation, this is often juxtaposed with attractive female dancers, designer clothing, and other images of a "champagne lifestyle." The cultural capital of Slovak rap today is centered on upward social mobility: on possessing the necessary technical abilities and physical appearance to "shift units," make money, and move from one's street origins to wealthier environs and the very center of the popular culture industry (Hess 2005). It is hardly surprising that "talk of the economic" (Rehn and Sköld 2005:26) now makes up a lot of mainstream Slovak rap lyrics. As Alf Rehn and David Sköld (2005:22–23) state, "assuming that most rap artists come from modest means, or at least exist in a culture where economic hardship is seen as characteristic for lived experience ('keeping it real'), having achieved financial success is not necessarily something one would keep quiet about."

While Slovak rap's foremost practitioners—such as Rytmus and Ego (both from Kontrafakt), Majk Spirit (H16), and Bacil (Drvivá Menšina, Názov Stavby)— have all emerged from long-standing formations in the hip hop subculture, their most widely circulated lyrics and videos no longer offer any social critique or highlight locally specific realities. For sure, Slovak rap has remained countercultural relative to other forms of mainstream popular culture in terms of its linguistic rebellion against standard Slovak (particularly its popularization of regional dialects, teenage slang, and foul language) and its championing of the aesthetics of the wider hip hop arts movement. However, the lyrical fixations and visual features of mainstream rap songs primarily seem to emphasize the acquisition of commodities (e.g., jewelry, designer clothing, and cars) and the practice of bravado and self-aggrandizement. Slovak rap stars can be seen in concerts, videos, and advertisements promoting commodities aimed at young people: for instance, Majk Spirit is sponsored by Nike; Rytmus has undertaken campaigns for Adidas, Tatra banka (a commercial bank), and Slovak Telekom; and, in addition to promoting Slovak Telekom, Ego is the Czech and Slovak "ambassador" for the backpack manufacturer Eastpak and the local face of Monster Energy Drink (Bartošová 2013; Krekovič 2013; Monster Energy Drink 2014). By local standards,

Rytmus is a prodigious pitchman for merchandise and has gone one step further than other rappers in fusing celebrity and commodity; he even promotes an energy drink bearing his own name and image (Rytmus Energy Drink 2014). As Rytmus himself has acknowledged, "My name is a brand and I try to get as many deals as I can" ("Rytmus a politická pieseň" 2012). More than anything else, Slovak rap serves a multitude of commercial purposes and is a regular feature of television commercials and even children's programming. According to the rapper Lyrik H:

> [Slovak] rap is becoming a space to promote products. Rappers are making songs for [brands of] beer, whisky, and videogames, or in their recordings they mention certain clothing and footwear labels or political parties. That's OK; such are the times. Otherwise there would be no way to make decent money. (Lyrik H, cited in Jaslovský 2010)[1]

The level of commercialism in Slovak rap has been criticized by cultural observers for a number of years. Vladislav Gális (2009), for instance, has claimed that Slovak rap has been bled of political or social criticism, becoming something only listened to by children and teenagers, who, of course, constitute a highly lucrative market for the commodities rappers sell. According to journalist and self-confessed hip hop head Marek Vagovič, meaning in rap lyrics and rap's countercultural ethos have been sacrificed for market share:

> Rytmus likes to show off his luxury lifestyle and brand clothing, and he makes fun of the underground from which he once came. . . . This one-time orthodox rapper started the second wave of the hip hop boom, which, however, has little to do with the fundamental aspects of this music style. And it seems that Rytmus has his successors—the rapper Ego, his buddy from Kontrafakt, sings about the blue sky with an ice cream in his hand. Majk Spirit raps about a sexy woman who is the "Beyoncé" to his "Jay Z." And that poor devil Bacil is shaking it up in some cheap [Balkan-style] clip with some chicks. (Vagovič 2012)

The commercialization of Slovak rap has been more gradual than instant: rap's focus on capitalist values was already apparent in 2006, when H16 released the track "Zarabaj keš" (Make Cash), whose message is self-evident in the title and in lines such as "I need cash. I can't eat from love alone," "They say money is not everything, but I see it differently," "I do not want to live like a beggar," and "I am addicted to cash like an addict to drugs . . . I want to be fucking rich" (H16 2006:track 5). Such ambitions have turned into reality for Slovakia's top rap artists, who, instead of feeling any obligation to continue representing their urban audience, actually illustrate their distance from them through visual displays of ostentatious wealth and lyrical content championing their ambition and their journey to financial self-enrichment. In doing so, they are showing their fans an alternative path of upward social mobility as opposed to that found, say, in the curricula of business schools. In "Som aký som" (I Am What I Am), Majk Spirit (2011) celebrates the fact that he has wealth and now enjoys fame "from Prague to the Tatras," that is, on a Czecho-Slovak scale. In the 2014 video "Keď jazdíme my" (When We Ride), Ego and Rytmus (as Kontrafakt) demonstrate their journey from ordinary circumstances to considerable wealth by riding BMX bicycles in the obligatory rap video settings of urban decay before "upgrading" to a Hummer luxury SUV and Bratislava's Eurovea waterfront—a high-end residential area and a favorite site of consumption and relaxation activities for the well-heeled. This visual emphasis on wealth acquisition is accompanied by references to the expensive commodities the rappers can now afford (e.g., a Maserati Quattroporte car with leather seats, Philipp Plein designer clothing, and Ray-Ban sunglasses), with a brief acknowledgment of their modest upbringing in lines such as "my mother did not know what comfort was" (Kontrafakt 2014a). Another Kontrafakt video, entitled "V Mojom Svete" (In My World), features guest appearances by the Bratislavan rapper Separ and the Czech rapper Ektor, and places all of the rappers back in their home localities (Kontrafakt 2014b). It presents visual and lyrical references to the apparent edginess of these spaces and carries suggestions of a thug lifestyle through images of drug dealing, acquisitive and violent crime, and a cash economy. This is accompanied by repeated assertions of competitiveness, toughness, gruffness, and pride in one's origins. However, the actual detachment of the video's protagonists from their home localities is evident in their conspicuous display of high-end commodities. Rytmus actually flies into his dilapidated neighborhood on the south side of the town of Piešťany in a private helicopter before energetically rapping on the pavement and then departing; it is clear that he only came "home" for a visit. The video then concludes with a scene showing all the rappers in a spacious dining hall where they enjoy a medieval-style feast replete with goblets and the consumption of fine meats, which are eagerly bitten into and masticated. Rytmus employs the same idea of moving from rags to (explicit) riches in "Started from the Bottom"—a rap video that uses the same riff as the Canadian rapper Drake's 2013 rap track of the same name—in which he and his muscular posse drive into an impoverished urban settlement populated mostly by Roma (Rytmus is himself of Romani descent) in luxury vehicles before moving to more affluent environs, where they enjoy dressed salads and espressos at a terrace cafe (Rytmus 2013). His lyrical pronouncements throughout the track emphasize the centrality of financial enrichment in everyone's lives and the insincerity of any claims to the contrary.

Despite his commercialization, Rytmus possesses significant subcultural capital in hip hop circles. His rap career stretches back to the early 1990s, when he gained a reputation as a highly competent b-boy and rapper. Rytmus gained nationwide attention when, as a member of Kontrafakt, he released the previously mentioned breakthrough video "What Rap Gives Me" and Kontrafakt's debut album *ERA*, released in 2004, which became the first Slovak rap album to receive platinum certification. Since that time, Rytmus has progressively become the epitome of Slovak rap's popularity and has embarked on a successful solo career, which has been characterized by a seemingly unlimited self-belief, as the titles of his solo albums *Kral* (King) and *Fenomen* (Phenomenon) illustrate. In addition to his success in selling albums, Rytmus has a massive following on the internet by Czech and Slovak standards, with his posted videos on YouTube having attracted well over one hundred million views ("Rytmus je fenomén" 2012). Rytmus's much-publicized relationship with Dara Rolins, a prominent Slovak pop singer, has been used in advertising campaigns and television appearances, which has helped make Rytmus a familiar figure to all who come into contact with Slovak media culture. The couple's love of luxury items, which apparently extends to the use of bodyguards, is well documented (Kühnelová 2012; "Rytmusa stráži ochranka" 2013).

While for the general public he is a divisive figure due to his very public use of foul language, Rytmus has garnered much criticism among the hip hop community for his apparent *volte-face* regarding the commercialization of his music (Andrejčáková 2008; Marek 2009; Nedorostová 2011). Rytmus's onetime vitriol for those who had gone "mainstream" and "sold out," which was apparent throughout *ERA*, has been replaced by an embrace of the commercial, to the extent that he now openly makes fun of those from the hip hop "underground," literally waving in their faces a big wad of banknotes and informing the audience that "the underground is for beggars" (Rytmus 2010a; Rytmus 2011a). This turnaround in perspective was clearly illustrated in the 2010 rap video "Rytmus A.K.A Best Rapper in Europe," where Rytmus (2010a) fires a tirade of vulgar invective at *Czecho-Slovak Superstar* (a talent show based on the *Pop Idol* format) only to appear a year later on that show, as well as on the Czecho-Slovak version of *The Voice* as a judge/coach. Rytmus justified this choice by stating that "they are paying me well. We are all there for the money, that's the way it is. I won't say anything false" (Kovačevič 2011), demonstrating a fundamental embrace of the established order of advanced capitalist society.

Slovak rap's propulsion into the mainstream, and the apparent contradiction between its commercial success and its "street" origins, have been noticed and parodied in Slovak popular culture. Rytmus is often the target of such satire: in the web-based animated series *LokalTV,* he is disparagingly referred to as "Rytmaus" (in reference to a campaign for Slovak Telekom in which he wore a Mickey Mouse hat) (*LokalTV* 2014), and on various internet fora he is referred to as "Riťmus" (the Slovak word *riť* means "ass") and Riťhnus (*hnus* refers to something disgusting or vile). In 2007 the punk rock band Horkýže Slíže released a video called "R'n'B Soul," which flagged Slovak rap in general, and Rytmus in particular, as targets for comedic entertainment. The video shows lead singer Peter "Kuko" Hrivňák performing as a rap star (recognizable as Rytmus) and having sex with a luxury automobile, complaining about catching lice from a male neighbor and pulling a stuffed deer on a leash (Horkýže Slíže 2011). After its release, this video became the most viewed Slovak music clip on YouTube, surpassing anything released by an authentic Slovak rap star up to that time and spawning a number of fan versions ("Horkýže Slíže lámu rekordy na youtube" 2007). While briefly the most popular "rap" track, this parody of rap was not perceived as a dissin' track by Rytmus or others in the rap community, who did not react to the video. If anything, "R'n'B Soul" represented an acknowledgment of rap's centrality to Slovak popular music, as Horkýže Slíže's parodies only target performers who are well known in Slovakia or on a worldwide scale.

Sometimes Rytmus has appeared to tackle topics outside the dominant commercial narrative. The moderately successful 2012 rap video "Už toho bolo dosť!" (There Has Been Enough of This!) deals with that year's nationwide "Gorilla" protests against political corruption. The Gorilla scandal refers to a file leaked online in 2011 containing summaries of transcripts from secret service wiretaps, which suggested there was a massive amount of corruption across the whole spectrum and at the highest levels of Slovak politics; the file claimed that politicians had received bribes from business executives in return for lucrative contracts involving privatization and the provision of services. The publication of the Gorilla file triggered widespread public anger, resulting in the largest demonstrations seen in Slovakia since the end of communist party rule (Bagin 2012). In the aforementioned video, Rytmus combines his condemnation of Slovak politics with a sense of patriotism in statements such as "Slovakia, I love you with pride, [but] hoodlums in suits run this state. How long will such people represent us?" (Rytmus 2012b). On the surface, the video appears to be an earnest attempt to return to a critical and confrontational view of the established social order, which characterized some Slovak rap tracks in earlier times (Barrer 2009:70–71), but such an analysis would be highly speculative. Rytmus is nowhere to be seen in the video, which only shows footage of the protests and demonstrators clashing with police, and Rytmus did not take any noticeable part in the protests themselves. Furthermore, in contrast to the invective in his dissin' tracks, which are often aimed at other Slovak popular music artists, Rytmus's condemnation of politicians and big business is rather vague: he does not name names, even though the Gorilla scandal implicated specific politicians, political parties, and financial groups. In sum, this track appears to have been an undeclared part of a marketing campaign for a new political party called Právo a spravodlivosť (Law and Justice), for which Rytmus performed on a number of occasions in the 2012 election campaign ("Rytmus Trencin 7.3.2012" 2012; "Rytmus a politická pieseň" 2012). The words *právo* (law) and *spravodlivosť* (justice) pepper the text in statements such as "Kde je moje právo?" (translatable as "Where are my rights?") and "Kde je naša spravodlivosť?" (Where is our justice?). It is clear that the purpose of the video is actually to sell a political commodity. Indeed, Rytmus is no alienated observer; he has happily associated himself with politicians at both the local and national levels in the hope of securing more media exposure for himself, as Slovak rap has now evolved to providing government-sponsored messages (Kováčová 2011; Marec 2012; Valček and Rehák 2012; "Rytmus sa dal na politiku" 2009). In addition to rapping about public safety, fellow rapper Ego even secured a place on the board of directors of the central hospital in his home locality of Piešťany (Krempaský 2012). It appears, then, that there is nothing genuinely subversive in the meanings presented in mainstream Slovak rap production.

To hip hop heads, the mainstreaming of Slovak rap may be a disappointment; after all, it no longer reflects the everyday struggles and realities of the ordinary population, preaches dissent, or genuinely promotes social change. However, this does not make mainstream Slovak rap necessarily "inauthentic": its practitioners are simply presenting their experiences and ambitions as they move up the social ladder. Furthermore, it could be argued that Slovakia's most popular rappers offer a relatively positive model of financial enrichment in a country where the political and corporate spheres are characterized by corruption, clientelism, cronyism, and nepotism (Deegan-Krause and Haughton 2009; Malová and Účeň 2011; Školkay and Ondruchová-Hong 2012). Their discussion of wealth in the plebeian language of the street offers a new expression of financial well-being which is in meritocratic contrast to the seedy world of Slovakia's politicians, lobbyists, and favored corporations (Vagovič 2012). Indeed, the success of Slovak rap actually "deterritorializes the ways in which business is being spoken and thought of" (Rehn and Sköld 2005:26). While Slovakia's most successful rappers have acquired their wealth quite transparently through individual ability and effort, this has come about at the expense of any lyrical engagement with localized social discourses, particularly those concerning structural inequality. This apparent sacrifice has led Marek Vagovič to ask important questions concerning the legitimacy of the art form:

> Let there be no mistake: rappers are not politicians. They do not have to answer to anyone as to why they have changed their minds, their style [of music], and way of life. They do not have to explain to anyone where they got the money for their new car or house because in contrast to many politicians they have earned their money in an honest fashion. However, are the compromises they make in order to sell more albums worth it? Really is hip hop, which once based itself around strong texts, just a money factory? Where is the boundary which Slovak rappers would never cross? (Vagovič 2012)

While Vagovič expresses concern at the lack of lyrical protest and subversion in mainstream Slovak rap, there is no reason for rap not to be commercial. After all, its fans are predominately "ordinary" youth and consumers of mainstream popular music who are not subject to any entrenched social disadvantage or disenfranchisement. Slovak rappers come from suburban neighborhoods that, despite appearances, have always been integrated into municipal infrastructures; they did not grow up in "ghetto" hardship and have more or less escaped the entrenched isolation from public services, generational un(der)employment, poverty, and gang criminality that characterize marginalized communities. The only Slovak equivalents of ghetto communities are the informally segregated settlements of Slovak Roma in rural areas and the notoriously troubled Košice housing estate of Luník IX, a Romani urban slum (Jurásková, Kriglerová, and Rybová 2005). With the notable exception of Rytmus, Slovak rappers all come from the "white" Slovak-speaking majority, and they do not undertake anything more than a minor engagement with the peripheral position of ethnic minorities. Because of their ordinary upbringings, no Slovak rappers in or near the mainstream can rap about "life in the ghetto" from any personal experience. This is particularly true of rap's mainstream texts, which, as described, simply reaffirm the core messages of capitalism, albeit using a new vocabulary.

Rytmus's success, given his Romani origin, is certainly important considering the overwhelmingly negative image of Roma in Slovakia. Rytmus publicly presents himself as a "Gypsy" and even has the word *Gitano* (the Spanish word for a male Gypsy) tattooed on one forearm. Coming from the modest means of a single-parent family, but by no means a ghetto background, Rytmus's performance of affluence "in extremis" (Rehn and Sköld 2005:23) is important in the Slovak context, for it offers proof of "a notion of success that isn't tethered by the aesthetic notions of the white plutocracy and through this a culturally specific 'economy'" (Rehn and Sköld 2005:24). However, aside from emphasizing the fact that he has "made it" in Slovakia in spite of his ethnic background, Rytmus has done nothing significant to challenge the difficult situations Roma face in everyday life. This lack of engagement is evident in the video to his rap track "AKM," where the Romani participants, all exhibiting accentuated markers of poverty and social degradation, are shown dancing, getting drunk, and fighting in a raucous celebration upon Rytmus's visit to an isolated Romani settlement (Rytmus 2012a). If anything, this representation only affirms mediated images and other ascribed stereotypes of Roma as being barely literate, unreliable, innately asocial, and possessing insurmountable cultural differences from the rest of Slovakia's population (Guy 1998; Vermeersch 2002). Videos like "AKM" validate long-standing myths and prejudices concerning Roma and do not alienate the white audience. A rap video decrying the racialized inequality and discrimination Roma face in gaining access to quality education, housing, and meaningful employment, for instance, would hardly be as popular among Rytmus's fans, even if that is what Roma themselves might prefer to see. Roma are not Rytmus's target market: they constitute less than 10 percent of the total Slovak citizenry, and, in any case, many of them suffer from chronic poverty (Vašečka and Vašečka 2003). In "AKM," Rytmus avoids any discussion of racial inequality in favor of a personal narrative presenting his own path to riches. This in turn comforts white consumers of Rytmus's videos because racism and racial tensions are easier to ignore when the audience is presented with images of Roma who seem happy enough with their lot in life and where the figure of Rytmus as a Romani rapper-hero supports the myth that racism is not really a problem in Slovakia. Rytmus certainly knows his mainstream (white) audience, and he has tailored his image to meet market needs.

Bereft of any genuine political and social criticism, rap videos by mainstream Slovak artists employ a lot of foul language and sexually explicit content. While music television and radio stations are loath to broadcast Slovak rap songs in their uncensored versions during daytime and early evening for fear of attracting fines for objectionable content, the sheer mediated presence of Slovak rap has led to a popular desensitization of the shock value of foul language; after all, uncensored rap songs and videos are widely available on the internet, which, over and above music radio and television, is the key domain of Slovak rap in the present day.

In addition to being at the center of Slovak rap's commercialization, Rytmus has been instrumental in the desensitization of foul language. He has firmly maintained his constant usage of swear words and offensive expressions as he has moved into the position of Czech/Slovak rap icon. The lyrics of his most popular rap videos make generous use of words such as *kokot* (dick), *piča* (cunt), and various expressions derived from *jebať*, the Slovak verb for "fuck" in its coarsest form. Indeed, sometimes his tracks contain very little else in terms of lyrical content. In 2011, Rytmus released a video simply entitled "Jebe" (translatable here as "Fucked in the Head"), in which he disses a number of Czech and Slovak celebrities, repeatedly stating that "they are fucked in the head" (*im jebe*), while reminding viewers that he is a "phenomenon" and the "King of Pop" (Rytmus 2011b). This video gained further public attention when, during the 2011 season of Czecho-Slovak Superstar, when Rytmus was a judge, the show's Czech host Leoš Mareš commented in a live primetime broadcast to both republics that perhaps Rytmus was "a little fucked in the head" (Rytmusovi trochu jebe) for giving a harsh judgment on a contestant's performance (Kováč 2011). While this expression in Czech does not carry quite the same weight of offense as it does in Slovak, Mareš's statement, which contained an explicit reference to Rytmus's aforementioned video, illustrates the desensitizing of foul language in the mass media, in which Slovak rap has played a significant role.

Female rappers have yet to make a noticeable mark on the Slovak scene, and there is no feminist rap in the mainstream or even near it. Most Slovak rap videos and lyrics project a strong heterosexual masculinity and present the rap artist as an "alpha male" and urban warrior. Women have a minor presence and are often sexually objectified: either they appear somewhere in the background nodding their heads to a rapper's pronouncements, or they dance in various provocative states of (un)dress. Women function as eye candy for the male gaze and as indicators of the rappers' success. Some videos venture into pornography, which is now a well-established part of television, film, music, and advertising in Western liberal societies. Indeed, "the line that once divided pop culture from porn culture continues to be blurred" (Watkins 2005:208–209). Relevant literature suggests that such representations of women in mainstream rap are problematic because they legitimize adverse sexual beliefs and play down the importance of misogynistic messages (Aubrey, Hopper, and Mbure 2011; Conrad, Dixon, and Zhang 2009; Rose 2008). Perhaps the most explicit example of pornography in Slovak rap is a 2010 music video released by Hajtkovič and Rytmus entitled "Do sce jebat" (Who Wants to Fuck?), in which naked women engage in explicit sexual activity with each other under the rappers' approving gaze (Hajtkovič and Rytmus 2010). It is worth noting that in the same year as this "hip hop porn" was released, Rytmus (adorned in a Mickey Mouse hat) was selling mobile phone services in a nationwide advertising campaign targeted at preadolescent children: something which speaks volumes about the rapper's commercial versatility (Rytmus 2010b). While perhaps shocking some in the Slovak audience (although media reaction to the video appears to have been nonexistent: most versions of the video available online are censored), "Who Wants to Fuck?" is not that surprising in an international context. After all, hip hop porn has been around since at least 2001, when the "Snoop Dogg's Doggystyle" video was released by *Hustler* magazine, and this is just a Slovak appropriation of an earlier trend present in US hip hop culture.

As noted above, the sexual objectification of women in Slovak rap videos and lyrics is commonplace, and, alongside the use of foul language, this seems to be something which is expected of the music idiom. Much of the lyrical sexism in Slovak rap seems to go unnoticed. A case in point is Bacil and Rakby's video "Ukáž mi" (Show Me), in which bikini-clad women gyrate to the rapidly spoken yet sexually fueled pronouncements of the two rappers, who, among other things, warn the women that "if you resist me, then I will put [my penis] in your ass" (Bacil and Rakby 2011). This track gained nationwide attention after it was reported that Slovakia's national men's ice hockey team had played it nonstop in the locker room during the 2012 International Ice Hockey Federation World Championships, even dancing to it upon their celebratory return to Bratislava as silver medalists ("Hit roka" 2013; Zelinka and Benčat 2012). The broad acceptance of this song as the year's summer hit and the lack of any notable controversy concerning its lyrics could be because it was primarily accepted by the audience as a sonic experience. The most sexually explicit statements, including "she will soon jump on my dick without hesitation" and as a result "will not be able to shit for a day," are camouflaged in an array of dance beats, which makes it difficult to initially ascertain what is being said. "Show Me" was widely played on music radio and only attracted a €100 fine for objectionable content (Poláš 2014). Another possible reason for the lack of protest at the obvious sexual objectification of women in Slovak rap videos such as "Show Me" may be the continued acceptance of sexist attitudes; Slovakia has a considerably lower level of gender equality than, say, the United States or Western Europe, and there is an absence of a vocal feminist lobby or indeed any widespread respect for such a movement in the country (Groch 2007; Napier, Torrisdottir, and Jost 2010:411).

NATIONALIST RAP?

An important aspect of Slovak rap's ownership by the majority "white" population is that it reflects concerns and prejudices common in this group. A self-perception of being "victims of history," with "enemies" both external and internal, has played a role in making latent racism a socially acceptable part of public life among Slovaks. These sentiments have found fertile ground in Slovak rap, which may seem surprising considering hip hop's initial role as a means of engagement for nonwhite communities in localized social discourses, especially those concerning the lack of economic and political influence (Forman 2004; Keyes 2002). Admittedly, such tracks are not really "mainstream," because they are not as widely circulated as the tracks and videos mentioned above. However, nationalism in Slovak rap has caught the public eye due to recent media attention on the emergence of a nationalist hip hop movement, and therefore it deserves a brief discussion. "Trápi ma" (It Bothers Me) is a track by the rapper Vladis that decries Slovakia's apparent fate of having had its own history decided by other nations. It projects Slovak patriotism alongside a defiant attitude to those with whom ethnic Slovaks have shared their history:

> I love our country, a country of which I am proud. I love our people, people who are similar to me. My heart beats for the Slovak nation, but I am bothered by the fact that we are always second and never first. . . . Others have always told us how to live: in poverty, with a bare ass and working for the benefit of others. . . . Those rats executed Tiso, the first president. A Frenchman is proud, an Italian is stupid; a Czech's [mouth] stinks and a Russian is a hard case. Arabs lie and Gypsies cheat; Jews rule with their money, and we have our heads down. Don't feel desperate. Slovak! It is up to you whether you assert yourself. (Vladis 2010:CD 1, track 12)

In the above track, Vladis not only supports the previously mentioned Romani stereotypes but also taps into Slovak nationalist grievances against other ethnic groups. Of particular interest here is the defense of Jozef Tiso, leader of the wartime Slovak state (allied with Nazi Germany), who was executed in 1947, and the stereotyping of Jews as scheming money hoarders. Anti-Semitism, an official policy of wartime Slovakia, still exists there today and is "based on a very strong tradition, greatly influenced by Christianity. . . . There is also jealousy, both intellectual and material, and in the case of Slovaks it is also a matter of ignorance" (Jaroslav Franek, cited in Fila 2003). Put into a wider context, Vladis's track is one of a number of public attempts in recent years to rehabilitate the wartime Slovak state and its political leaders, and indicates the understated yet continued presence of anti-Semitism in Slovak society, which, despite the minuscule size of Slovakia's Jewish community, is at more prevalent than in many countries of Western Europe (compare Bergmann 2008; Fila 2003; Lesná 2007; Nicholson, 2007).

A more explicitly aggressive nationalist tone is noticeable in the video "Náš svet" (Our World) by the rappers Kali and Mates, who perform together under the name 85101 (the postal code for Bratislava's Petržalka, Slovakia's largest urban dormitory community and the strongest textual backdrop to contemporary Slovak rap lyrics and videos). The video shows known neo-Nazis and football hooligans dressed as if for battle and standing behind an unfurled Slovak flag; their faces are masked, they are clad in clothing labels connected to the far-right subculture (e.g., Thor Steinar, Pretorian, and others), and they are carrying baseball bats and other street weapons ("Kali, Mates, neonacisti a hip hop" 2011; Vagovič 2011). Despite the assertions of the rappers that the video was not intended to promote a neo-Nazi worldview, but simply football, martial arts, and an anti-drugs messages (Vagovič 2011), "Our World" is undeniably militant and nationalist. This is evident in the video imagery and in lines such as "Whoever throws a stone at you, throw 200 back," "The law is written by the street," and "We are not trying to be American; we have our own rules and we shall stick together to lift up our own culture" (85101 2011). The baseball bats and other handheld items in the video are clearly weapons and cannot have any sporting purpose. Baseball is, after all, an undeveloped sport in Slovakia.

CONCLUSIONS

The semantic values of Slovak rap now seem a long way from presenting urban malaise or meaningful political protest. While rap lyrics remain staunchly in the Slovak language, the concerns of the rappers themselves have moved away from localized discourses to more universal fixations concerning upward social mobility through financial enrichment. The textual absence of provocative subjects of discourse has made Slovak rap in the mainstream similar to other forms of popular music; there is a noticeable reduction of references in rap lyrics to personal experiences, opinions, and desires, and an avoidance of critical reflections on modern urbanism. Slovak rappers ultimately sidestep the hard questions concerning social inequality and the lack of economic and political influence. Despite this, Slovakia's most successful rap artists are still authentic hip hop performers. After all, one of their most notable lyrical characteristics is their outspokenness and a fixation on their own concerns and lived experiences. The fact that Slovak rappers' lyrics focus on their financial success is simply an indication of Slovak rap's widespread popularity. To present a complex rap narrative on the social inequality and injustice faced by Slovak Roma or the sexual objectification of Slovak women is beyond the brief of the most popular Slovak rap artists. After all, they can only represent themselves and their own experiences. For consumers of Slovak rap, who are mostly young and middle class, simple messages concerning financial enrichment and "having fun" are far more easily understood, and are more appealing than something they would be unfamiliar with. While local political discourses are outside the rap mainstream, they do sometimes attract media attention. However, as shown above, these messages express views, concerns, and prejudices held by the "white" majority population. Despite hip-hop's original intentions, messages in Slovak rap from the social and ethnic periphery are simply not heard by most of its listeners.

NOTE

1. All of the translations from the Slovak are my own.

REFERENCES

Aubrey, Jennifer Stevens, K. Megan, Hopper, and Wanjiru G. Mbure. 2011. "Check That Body! The Effects of Sexually Objectifying Music Videos on College Men's Sexual Beliefs." *Journal of Broadcasting and Electronic Media* 55(3):360–379. doi: 10.1080/08838151.2011.597469.

Bagin, Peter. 2012. "Thousands Join Gorilla Protests." *Slovak Spectator,* February 2. http://spectator.sme.sk/articles/view/45248/2/thousands_join_gorilla_protests.html.

Barrer, Peter. 2009. "'My White, Blue, and Red Heart': Constructing a Slovak Identity in Rap Music." *Popular Music and Society* 32(1):59–75. doi: 10.1080/03007760802207825.

Bartošová, Veronika. 2013. "Rytmus: Som 'fejsbukár.'" *Mediálne.trend.sk*, December 4. http://medialne.etrend.sk/marketing/rytmus-som-fejsbukar.html.

Bergmann, Werner. 2008. "Anti-Semitic Attitudes in Europe: A Comparative Perspective." *Journal of Social Issues* 64(2):343–362. doi: 10.1111/j.1540-4560.2008.00565.x.

Bernstein, Arthur, Naomi Sekine, and Dick Weissman. 2007. *The Global Music Industry: Three Perspectives.* New York: Routledge.

Bertram, Dennison. 2003. "Czech Hip Republic Hop." *New Presence: The Prague Journal of Central European Affairs* 5(1):42–43.

Conrad, Kate, Travis L. Dixon, and Yuanyuan Zhang. 2009. "Controversial Rap Themes, Gender Portrayals and Skin Tone Distortion: A Content Analysis of Rap Music Videos." *Journal of Broadcasting and Electronic Media* 53(1):134–156. doi: 10.1080/08838150802643795.

Danko, Marek. 2011. "Rytmus: Z ľudí hovorí závisť." *SME.sk*, August 20. http://korzar.sme.sk/c/6022359/rytmus-z-ludi-hovori-zavist.html.

Deegan-Krause, Kevin, and Tim Haughton. 2009. "Toward a More Useful Conceptualization of Populism: Types and Degrees of Populist Appeals in the Case of Slovakia." *Politics and Policy* 37(4):821–841.

Fila, Lukáš. 2003. "Anti-Semitism a Hidden Part of Slovak Life." *Slovak Spectator*, February 10. http://spectator.sme.sk/articles/view/11789/1/.

Forman, Murray. 2004. "'Represent': Race, Space, and Place in Rap Music." In *That's the Joint! The Hip-Hop Studies Reader*, eds. Murray Forman and Mark Anthony Neal (pp. 201–222). New York: Routledge.

Gális, Vladislav. 2009. "Koniec hip-hopu na Slovensku." *Týždeň*, May 27. http://www.tyzden.sk/kultura/koniec-hip-hopu-na-slovensku.html.

Groch, Michal. 2007. "Feminism in Slovakia: Finally Escaping the Clichés?" *Český rozhlas*, December 12. http://www.radio.cz/en/section/ice_special/feminism-in-slovakia-finally-escaping-the-cliches.

Guy, Will. 1998. "Ways of Looking at Roma: The Case of Czechoslovakia". In *Gypsies: An Interdisciplinary Reader*, ed. Diane Tong (pp. 13–68). New York: Garland.

Hess, Mickey. 2005. "Metal Faces, Rap Masks: Identity and Resistance in Hip Hop's Persona Artist." *Popular Music and Society* 28(3):297–311. doi: 10.1080/03007760500105149.

"Hit roka: Ukáž mi lásku, pospevovali si ich pesničku strieborní hokejisti." 2013. *Čas.sk*, January 6. http://www.cas.sk/clanok/240251/hit-roka-ukaz-mi-lasku-pospevovali-si-ich-pesnicku-strieborni-hokejisti.html.

"Horkýže Slíže lámu rekordy na youtube." 2007. *Pravda.sk*, July 30. http://kultura.pravda.sk/hudba/clanok/35836-horkyze-slize-lamu-rekordy-na-youtube/.

Janda, Radek. 2011. "Hip-hopový muzikál 'Príbeh ulice' se dočkal druhého dílu." *Musical.cz*, March 7. http://www.musical.cz/zahranici/hip-hopovy-muzikal-pribeh-ulice-se-dockal-druheho-dilu/.

Jaslovský, Marian. 2010. "Je slovenský hip hop mŕtvy?" *SME.sk*, September 2. http://kultura.sme.sk/c/5530791/je-slovensky-hip-hop-mrtvy.html.

Johnson, Owen V. 2013. "Entertaining the People, Serving the Elites: Slovak Mass Media since 1989." In *Media Transformations in the Post-Communist World: Eastern Europe's Tortured Path to Change*, eds. Peter Gross and Karol Jakubowicz (pp. 149–166). Plymouth: Lexington Books.

Jurásková, Martina, Elena Kriglerová, and Jana Rybová. 2005. "Roma." In *Slovakia 2004: A Global Report on the State of Society*, eds. Grigorij Mesežnikov and Miroslav Kollár (pp. 187–206). Bratislava: Institute for Public Affairs.

"Kali, Mates, neonacisti a hip hop." 2011. *Antifa.cz*, August 9. http://www.antifa.cz/content/kali-mates-neonacisti-hip-hop.

Keyes, Cheryl L. 2002. *Rap Music and Street Consciousness*. Urbana: University of Illinois Press.

Kizek, Marián. 2013. "Rytmus: Nemôžem chodiť ako vandrák." *SME.sk*, May 10. http://korzar.sme.sk/c/6795072/rytmus-nemozem-chodit-ako-vandrak.html.

Kováč, Patrik. 2011. "Rytmusovi trochu j.e, povedal v priamom prenose Leoš Mareš." *Aktuality.sk*, April 2. http://www.aktuality.sk/clanok/184944/rytmusovi-trochu-j-e-povedal-priamom-prenose-leos-mares/.

Kovačevič, Vedran. 2011. "Rytmus o účasti v SuperStar: Mám čas a dobře mi zaplatí." *iDNES.cz*, February 2. http://revue.idnes.cz/rytmus-o-ucasti-v-superstar-mam-cas-a-dobre-mi-zaplati-pdv-/lidicky.aspx?c=A110201_212115_lidicky_ved.

Kováčová, Nikoleta. 2011. "Video: Fico vzdal "poklonu" Tine—V televízii pôsobí ako veľká obluda." *Aktuality.sk*, December 13. http://m.aktuality.sk/clanok/198530/video-fico-vzdal-poklonu-tine-v-televizii-posobi-ako-velka-obluda/.

Krempaský, Ján. 2012. "Na zdravie v Piešťanoch dozrú raper Ego a Smer." *SME.sk*, November 29. http://trnava.sme.sk/c/6621577/na-zdravie-v-piestanoch-dozru-raper-ego-a-smer.html.

Kühnelová, Tereza. 2012. "Dara a Rytmus se topí v luxusu: Prsteny za 2 miliony!" *Blesk.cz*, October 15. http://www.blesk.cz/clanek/celebrity-ceske-celebrity/183416/dara-a-rytmus-se-topi-v-luxusu-prsteny-za-2-miliony.html.

Lesná, Ľuba. 2007. "Matica Journal Doubts Holocaust." *Slovak Spectator*, February 12. http://spectator.sme.sk/articles/view/26631/2/.

LokalTV. 2014. "Zapál Rytmausa." http://www.lokaltv.sk/zapal-rytmausa (accessed September 2).

Malová, Darina, and Peter Učeň. 2011. "Slovakia." *European Journal of Political Research* 50(7–8):118–129. doi: 10.1111/j.1475-6765.2011.02040.x.

Marec, Samo. 2012. "Rytmus, Biela Revolúcia a kampaň Práva a Spravodlivosti." *SME.sk*, February 16. http://samuelmarec.blog.sme.sk/c/289951/Rytmus-Biela-Revolucia-a-kampan-Prava-a-Spravodlivosti.html.

Monster Energy Drink. 2014. "Ego." https://www.monsterenergy.com/sk/sk/athletes/ego/ (accessed September 10).

Napier, Jaime L., Hulda Thorisdottir, and John T. Jost. 2010. "The Joy of Sexism? A Multinational Investigation of Hostile and Benevolent Justifications for Gender Inequality and Their Relations to Subjective Well-Being." *Sex Roles* 62(7–8):405–419. doi: 10.1007/s11199-009-9712-7.

Nedorostová, Lucia. 2011. "Rytmus: Na toto si už zabudol?" *Pluska.sk*, March 24. http://www.pluska.sk/soubiznis/spravy-klebety/nase-celebrity/rytmus-toto-si-zabudol.html.

Nicholson, Tom. 2007. "Church Continues to Distort Truth of WWII." *Slovak Spectator*, January 8. http://spectator.sme.sk/articles/view/26223/11/.

Poláš, Martin. 2014. "F*ck, sh*t a r*ť v pesničkách: Čo môžu a nemôžu púšťať rádiá do éteru." *Mediálne.trend.sk*, April 4. http://medialne.etrend.sk/radia/f-ck-sh-t-a-r-t-v-pesnickach-co-mozu-a-nemozu-pustat-radia-do-eteru.html.

Rehn, Alf, and David Sköld. 2005. "'I Love the Dough': Rap Lyrics as a Minor Economic Literature. *Culture and Organization* 11(1):17–31. doi: 10.1080/14759550500062268.

Rose, Tricia. 2008. *Hip-Hop Wars: What We Talk about When We Talk about Hip-Hop—And Why It Matters*. New York: Basic Civitas.

Rytmus Energy Drink. 2014. http://www.rytmusenergy.com/#/home (accessed September 10).

"Rytmus je fenomén. Prekonal hranicu 100 miliónov na Youtube!" 2012. *Aktuality.sk*, October 30. http://www.aktuality.sk/clanok/216824/rytmus-je-fenomen-prekonal-hranicu-100-milionov-na-youtube/.

"Rytmusa stráži ochranka, bodyguarda má aj jeho Dara! Čoho sa bojí?" 2013. *Čas.sk*, February 2. http://www.cas.sk/clanok/241948/rytmusa-strazi-ochranka-bodygarda-ma-aj-jeho-dara-coho-sa-boji.html.

Salovaara-Moring, Inka. 2013. "Digital (R)evolutions? Internet, New Media and Informed Citizenship in Central and Eastern Europe." In *Media Transformations in the Post-Communist World: Eastern Europe's Tortured Path to Change*, eds. Peter Gross and Karol Jakubowicz (pp. 99–114). Plymouth: Lexington Books.

Školkay, Andrej, and Mária Ondruchová-Hong. 2012. "Slovakia: Reinventing Media Policy without a Practical Perspective. In *Understanding Media Policies: A European Perspective*, ed. Evangelia Psychogiopoulou (pp. 182–197). New York: Palgrave Macmillan.

Vagovič, Marek. 2011. "Nazi hip-hop?" *Týždeň*, October 23. http://www.tyzden.sk/casopis/2011/43/nazi-hip-hop.html.

Vagovič, Marek. 2012. "Je slovenský hip-hop mŕtvy?" *Týždeň*, September 9. http://www.tyzden.sk/nazivo-doma/je-slovensky-hip-hop-mrtvy.html.

Valček, Adam, and Oliver Rehák. 2012. "Štát zaplatil za klip s raperom Egom desaťtisíc eur." *SME.sk*, December 6. http://ekonomika.sme.sk/c/6629703/stat-zaplatil-za-klip-s-raperom-egom-desattisic-eur.html.

Vašečka, Imrich, and Michal Vašečka. 2003. "Recent Romani Migration from Slovakia to EU Member States: Romani Reaction to Discrimination or Romani Ethno-Tourism?" *Nationalities Papers* 31(1):27–45. doi: 10.1080/0090599032000058893.

Vermeersch, Peter. 2002. "Ethnic Mobilisation and the Political Conditionality of European Union Accession: The Case of the Roma in Slovakia." *Journal of Ethnic and Migration Studies* 28(1):83–101. doi: 10.1080/13691830120103949.

"Vyhrá Hit roka reper Ego? Jeho klip videlo 20 miliónov ľudí!" 2012. Čas.sk, December 19. http://www.cas.sk/clanok/239031/vyhra-hit-roka-reper-ego-jeho-klip-videlo-20-milionov-ludi.html.

Watkins, S. Craig. 2005. *Hip Hop Matters: Politics, Pop Culture, and the Struggle for the Soul of a Movement*. Boston: Beacon Press.

Zelinka, Adam, and Benčat, Stanislav. 2012. "Pilot Šatan aj lietajúci Vůjtek. Hokejisti pobláznili Slovensko!" *Pravda.sk*, May 21. http://hokej.pravda.sk/ms-2012/clanok/125534-pilot-satan-aj-lietajuci-vujtek-hokejisti-poblaznili-slovensko/.

INTERVIEWS

Andrejčáková, Jarmila. 2008. "Rytmus: Som chalan z ulice. Len bohatší" (interview with Rytmus). *Život.sk*, January 23. http://zivot.azet.sk/clanok/2870/rytmus-som-chalan-z-ulice-len-bohatsi.html.

Krekovič, Miloš. 2013. "Majk Spirit: Atlantída? Viem, že existovala" (interview with Majk Spirit). *SME.sk*, January 31. http://kultura.sme.sk/c/6682349/majk-spirit-atlantida-viem-ze-existovala.html.

Kušnierik, Juraj. 2012. "Český a slovenský trh je pre mňa primalý" (interview with Rytmus). *Týždeň*, September 9. http://www.tyzden.sk/casopis/2012/37/cesky-a-slovensky-trh-je-pre-mna-primaly.html.

Marek. 2009. "Rytmus: Hip hopové publikum je pre mňa tak malé, že mám pocit, že hip hop tu ani neexistuje (rozhovor)" (interview with Rytmus). *90bpm*, December 14. http://www.90bpm.sk/news/7567/78/Rytmus-Hip-hopove-publikum-je-pre-mna-tak-male-ze-mam-pocit-ze-hip-hop-tu-ani-neexistuje-rozhovor/.

FILMOGRAPHY

85101. 2011. "Náš svet" [video]. http://www.youtube.com/watch?v=BkA9Ob_C3jc.

Bacil and Rakby. 2011. "Ukáž mi" [video]. http://www.youtube.com/watch?v=ihAqhcucwGQ.

Hajtkovič and Rytmus. 2010. "Do Sce Jebat" [video]. http://www.youtube.com/watch?v=EoolN1FYb4I.

Horkýže Slíže. 2011. "RNB Soul" [video]. https://www.youtube.com/watch?v=I9SFvEsoghI.

Kontrafakt. 2014a. "Keď jazdíme my" [video]. https://www.youtube.com/watch?v=odp6sdJNUtg.

Kontrafakt. 2014b. "V mojom svete feat. Separ, Ektor" [video]. https://www.youtube.com/watch?v=RsDZ-lm2zxo.

Rytmus. 2010a. "Rytmus A.K.A Best Rapper in Europe" [video]. http://www.youtube.com/watch?v=JAjuCjdQ1Aw.

Rytmus. 2010b. "Keď si šťastný" [video]. http://www.youtube.com/watch?v=vJZM8pGKB6c.

Rytmus. 2011a. "Hateri sú v Pičí" [video]. http://www.youtube.com/watch?v=w6LYgErMxjk.

Rytmus. 2011b. "Jebe" [video]. http://www.youtube.com/watch?v=runQo_hRRrs.

Rytmus. 2012a. "AKM" [video]. http://www.youtube.com/watch?v=R9foO1ohXtM.

Rytmus. 2012b. "Už bolo toho dosť!" [video]. https://www.youtube.com/watch?v =XrWzHAeGlq4.

Rytmus. 2013. "Started from the Bottom (Gypsyking Freestyle)." [video]. https://www .youtube.com/watch?v=j5TukJ2zovE.

"Rytmus a politická pieseň." 2012. [video] February 20. http://www.aktuality.sk/clanok /201802/video-rytmus-a-politicka-piesen/.

"Rytmus sa dal na politiku: Spieva pre stranu Braňa Zahradníka!" 2009. [video] Čas.sk, October 27. http://www.cas.sk/clanok/136274/video-rytmus-sa-dal-na-politiku-spieva -pre-stranu-brana-zahradnika.html.

"Rytmus Trencin 7.3.2012." 2012. [video]. https://www.youtube.com/watch?v=7JsOIItmG4k.

Sobota, Kool Savas, Gural, Wall-E, Rytmus, and Bigz. 2009. "Stoprocent 2" [video]. http:// www.youtube.com/watch?v=rnidyiFT14Y.

WWO, Orion, Kontrafakt, Wlodi, and Soundkail. 2008. "I tak to osiagne" [video]. http:// www.youtube.com/watch?v=ge5M2387L5U.

DISCOGRAPHY

H16. 2006. *Kvalitný materiál*. HIP-HOP.sk and EMI Czech Republic.

Majk Spirit. 2011. *Nový človek*. BeatBan Records.

Vladis. 2010. *Generácia*. EMI Czech Republic.

CHAPTER 7

MUSIC, TECHNOLOGY, AND SHIFTS IN POPULAR CULTURE

Making Hip Hop in e-Estonia

Triin Vallaste

IT IS NOW widely accepted that hip hop, and rap as one of its elements, serves as an expressive resource in contexts far afield from its historical origins in African American, Caribbean, and Latino youth cultures. As Tony Mitchell states, "[Rap] has become a vehicle for global youth affiliations and a tool for reworking local identity all over the world" (Mitchell 2001:1–2). Strong local currents of hip hop indigenization have taken root across the world, including in Europe (see Bennett 2000, Krims 2000, Mitchell 2001, Brown 2006, Helenon 2006, Barrer 2009, Helbig 2014). As proposed by James Lull, the indigenization, or reterritorialization of a musical genre from a globally available popular culture, is a helpful framework for examining the emergence of rap in Europe and the creation of a new cultural territory. As Androutsopoulos and Scholz interpret Lull's concept, "an indigenized cultural pattern is integrated into the artistic repertoire of the host society, and, as a consequence . . . the pattern is now appropriated as a native form of expression" (Androutsopoulos and Scholz 2003:468). Therefore, since there is now enormous musical and cultural diversity in hip hop, one can talk in Bakhtinian terms of a multivocality in hip hop discourse: Instead of one hegemonic voice, global hip hop discourse consists of multiple unique voices (Bakhtin 1981). In other words, each local tradition has its own sonic and cultural voice.

The reasons behind the broad and rapid indigenization of the rap genre might lie in its musical components and available "fantasies of masculine power" (Keeler 2009:9). As Simon Warner notes, "perhaps the very fact that [rap's] musical components were, technically, relatively simple to replicate and that its core was a lyric-based message made it an adaptable, user-friendly structure onto which far-flung performers could graft their own local subjects, their own narratives, their own concerns" (Warner 2004:164). Combining models and idioms from hip hop in the United States with local musical and linguistic idioms, rap in local languages has become "an innovative form of musical and linguistic expression" across Europe (Larkey 2003:140). At the same time, the use of local language is not the only relevant feature of indigenized rap in Europe. Hip hop's sampling aesthetic leads rappers and producers to draw on local popular music, films and other media, traditional music, and even classical poetry to express their viewpoints on local issues, not only in a local language but also through sonic citations often comprehensible and relevant exclusively to cultural insiders.

Hip hop's indigenization in Estonia coincides with the collapse of the Soviet Union in 1991 and the regained independence that followed. After the dissolution of the USSR, dominant Estonian social discourse eagerly celebrated reentering the Euro-American world and embracing its values (Plakans 2011:402–404). The uncensored global media outlets that opened up after 1991 and the rapid developments in information technology shortly thereafter were crucial to the story of Estonian-language rap. Hip hop artists' extensive involvement with new media and technologies requires an examination of the ways in which an extremely swift transition from ill-equipped to fluent manipulation of technology affects cultural production and structures participation in various sociocultural communities. The early 1990s also represented a pivotal moment in U.S. hip hop, with the rise of West Coast gangsta artists, mainstreaming of the genre on local, national, and global levels via commercial radio and music videos, and increasingly accessible technology for digital sampling and track production. All these developments contributed to Estonian perceptions of hip hop as a musical genre accessible to virtually anyone who had something to say and owned a computer.

Since 1991, Estonia has undergone and is still undergoing a double transformation: resuming the modernization that was interrupted by Soviet occupation in 1940, in tandem with postmodernization as it becomes a part of a globalized world (Vetik 2012). The contradictory nature of these two processes—trying to negotiate conflicting ideas of a homogenous society and the prevalence of difference and multiculturalism within a single state—is at the heart of numerous political, economic, and artistic projects in Estonia, including hip hop. Since the dialectic of the local and the global is an intrinsic aspect of globalization, the local transformations of certain commodities or cultural practices are clearly part of the broader processes of globalization (Guibernau 1996:132; Tsing 2005). In the Estonian case, however, strong currents of ethnolinguistic nationalism, which have increased since the early 1990s, confirm that nationalism will not "necessarily go away in an era of globalization" as well as the fact that "nationalism will only persist to the extent that individuals, movements, and groups choose to be nationalists" (Kaldor 2004:162). In the current context of societal transformation, both de-Sovietizing and proglobalization in nature, it is challenging for the Estonian state and cultural elites to reconcile narratives of victimhood and repression under Soviet occupation with multicultural ideologies of the European Union, of which Estonia has been a full member since 2004.

While the first Estonian national awakening of the 1860s was enabled by the spread of print capitalism (Anderson 1983), rapid developments in Estonian society during the 1990s and 2000s and the rise of nationalist state ideologies were partially achieved via "new media"—television, the internet, CDs, DVDs, and so on (Kaldor-Robinson 2002; Kaldor 2004). The use of radio as an "old medium" in the early 1990s and the rapid impact of the internet in the mid-1990s were crucial to the emergence and development of hip hop in Estonia. Radio, user-friendly and accessible to a variety of populations, has "regularly allowed new or silenced voices to enter the public sphere, especially in times of social or technological change" (Tucker 2013:150; Taylor 2005). Certain radio hosts, promoting Estonian hip hop artists' works, may be regarded as cultural gatekeepers who "foster the feeling of belonging to a community" (Simonett 2001:45). Meanwhile, rapidly increasing access to cheap, high-quality sound recording equipment facilitated the democratization of music production and distribution, which also helped mature the hip hop scene in Estonia (Théberge 1997; Peterson and Bennett 2004:6).

In an attempt to sum up Estonian-language rap, which emerged in the mid-1990s, it is difficult to come up with any unifying themes in terms of the content of rhymes or the aesthetics of beat-making: There are stories about competitive binge drinking as well as making pancakes with grandmother, and beats range from reggae to heavy-metal and drum and bass. Also, there is an immense variety in rappers' rhyme schemes as well as in beatmakers' (*biidimeistrid*[1]) and producers' use of production software and know-how. Additionally, there is no homogeneity in terms of the hip hop artists' public image or style of dress: One can encounter bohemian rappers in self-knitted sweaters, plaid shirts, and corduroy pants, or intentionally swaggering producers with baggy pants, way-too-big hoodies, baseball hats, and flashy jewelry—and everything in between. This diversity among hip hop practitioners emerges from a group consisting exclusively of male middle-class ethnic Estonians with, in most cases, good education and well-respected public personas.

One of the main reasons for the abundance of hip hop lies in the local music industry, or, more precisely, the lack thereof. Due to the minuscule size of the market, major record labels have not taken any interest in Estonian-language popular music. Some Estonian-language rap circulates on compilation albums put out by local independent labels, usually owned by an active member of the hip hop scene, while the majority finds its public outlet through social network channels such as Facebook, YouTube, SoundCloud, MySpace, and various Estonian hip hop community websites. Therefore, since there is no industry-driven pressure and no conventions around producing rap in certain ways, local artists have the freedom and urge to experiment with and modify their styles from one track to another. I would like to offer two examples from the late 1990s—two tracks by the Estonian hip hop group A-Rühm (A-Team)—to illustrate this kind of experimentation.

Hip Hop, Technology Literacy, and e-Estonia

In 1998, just three years after the release of the very first Estonian-language hip hop album (*O'Culo* by Cool D), A-Rühm became hugely popular across various audiences with its single "Popmuusik" (Pop Musician). The first hip hop act to achieve national attention stirred up discussions about hip hop as a vulgar genre and, more specifically, issues connected with freedom of speech in post-Soviet Estonian society. "Pop Musician's" explicit rhymes were seen as playing on the border of virtuosic wittiness and outright inappropriateness, and were at the center of public discourse for a while. In January 1999, on the annual Estonian national radio program *Aastahitt* (Hit of the Year), A-Rühm won second place with "Pop Musician." Although some foreign hip hop songs had appeared in the top five in earlier years, such as Coolio's "Gangsta's Paradise" in 1995, A-Rühm's "Pop Musician" was the first Estonian-language hip hop song to make it to the most prominent chart, which catalogues the 40 most popular local and foreign songs from the previous year, based on listeners' votes. The huge popularity of "Pop Musician," which was beaten on the chart only by a rock ballad, demonstrated how the musicians of A-Rühm had savvily carved out and filled the until-then uninhabited resistance niche in Estonian mainstream pop while, at the same time, securing themselves a central position in the very same field to which the band seemingly set itself in opposition. As Kozy, one of the band members, put it in an interview from this time, "We don't claim that pop music is bad in and of itself and that we are not part of it. The issue [that made the band release the song] here is about the quality of this fucking Estonian pop music. It is made by brainless guys, and there is even no hope in sight that they will start to come up with anything original that would express their own opinions and ideas" (Jänese 1999). Genka, another MC from the band, continues Kozy's criticism and declares in the same interview: "Listen, it can't be a good band that has a guy somewhere dictating what can or can't be done" (Jänese 1999).

Besides shifting Estonian-language hip hop from the underground into the mainstream, A-Rühm introduced new (digital) ways of thinking and talking about the creation of popular music in the Estonian context. These new ways, made possible by "truly amazing technological developments [that were] coupled with a major price drop in digital recording and signal-processing equipment" (Moorefield 2005:xvii), rejected the traditional separation between performer, engineer, and producer, making the artist(s) the embodiment of all three.

Paul Théberge reminds us how "an understanding of the various issues relating music and technical innovation cannot be separated from a broader analysis of contemporary social and economic relations" (Théberge 1997:5). Thus, what is additionally significant about "Pop Musician," as well as Kozy's and Genka's statements in the media, is how well they exemplify two simultaneously evolving processes in Estonian popular culture and socioeconomic realms at the end of the 1990s. First, "Pop Musician" displayed the localization of globally circulating modes of musical resistance, which A-Rühm based on the genre of Estonian-language hip hop, antiauthoritarian rhymes, and independent, artistically "all-in-one" public personas. It must be added, however, that "Pop Musician" was by no means the first popular song exhibiting resistance,[2] but it was certainly the first that gained national attention as such after 1991 when Estonia become independent from the Soviet Union. The catchy sing-along-style chorus, which asked a mainstream pop musician not only to not "yell into my ear" and to "piss into your own pocket," but reveals a plan to "murder you, pop musician," became quickly an integral part of youth vernacular in 1998.

The rapid economic growth of the late 1990s, which brought with it a higher standard of living and the "e-Estonia" project, granted a wide part of the population easy access to computers and high-speed internet connections. The e-Estonia project,[3] launched in the mid-1990s, was a large-scale, state-funded initiative that supplied every educational institution with computers and a high-speed internet connection. The Estonian national information technology (IT) program was launched in February 1996 by President Lennart Meri, with the goals of modernizing the Estonian educational system, creating conditions for the formation of an open learning environment, and adapting the nation to the demands of an information society (Miljan 2004:471). The immediate objective was to put a computer in every classroom in every school in Estonia, and to rapidly introduce information and communications technology (ICT) in the public and private sectors. By 2000, four years later, ICT access had moved Estonia into the front ranks of internet use in Europe.

The Tiger Leap Foundation, founded to develop and expand the reach of computer and network infrastructure, was created in February 1997 as a nonprofit body consisting of the Ministry of Education and 37 computer companies and private individuals to organize the execution and financing of the program. Initially, to the general public, Tiger Leap became associated with the slogan "one computer for every twenty pupils." The foundation rapidly evolved a three-level strategy, with the national level developing the target program; the national level coordinating the supply of computers and skills; and, at the local level, each school implementing the ICT program of learning and utilization of IT resources (Miljan 2004:471).

The educational part of the program provided training for teachers, computers, and software; assisted in setting up Estonian-language educational databases for schools; and encouraged pupils to set up chat rooms and online newspapers. The Tiger Leap program caught the imagination of the Estonian population and became the motor of virtualization of the Estonian economy and the public sectors. To encourage Estonians to use IT outside work and education, the foundation provided a large number of public-access internet labs around the country. As early as 1999, almost all government forms were accessible to the public on the internet, and the administrative reform of 2000 began by making all internal documents available online to eliminate paper jams. All ministries, including the prime minister's office, sent Christmas cards in 1999 online only (Miljan 2004:471). By 2000, cabinet meetings used only documentation read on computer screens, and traveling ministers participated in cabinet meetings by laptop internet connection. In 2002, the Tallinn City Council inaugurated its own advanced Tiger Leap to increase the number of computers in the schools from the one per 42 pupils to one for every 10 by 2005; and that June, a program funded by banks and telecom firms was inaugurated to teach computer and internet access skills to 100,000 computer-illiterate adults in Estonia (Miljan 2004:472).

Additionally, government funds subsidized Estonian families investing in these technologies. It has been possible ever since to manage the virtual paperwork related to banking, schooling, and even national-level voting without leaving one's house. One producer told me about his grandmother living in the countryside with an outhouse and no running water but enjoying the perks of high-speed internet thanks to "e-Estonianization."[4] Similarly, access to global TV channels via satellite providers, which proliferated after the collapse of the Soviet Union, was welcomed with open arms by Estonian viewers.

As a result of e-Estonia, Estonians acquired computer fluency and wider media literacy very quickly. This enabled previously ill-equipped hip hop musicians to acquire computer fluency and wider media literacy in addition to being able to purchase media and manipulate the technologies necessary for independent music production. In other words, as noted by Peter Manuel in his work on "cassette culture," "the spread of various forms of inexpensive, grassroots-based micro-media . . . provide[s] [previously] dominated social groups with an unprecedented degree of access to, representation in, and control of mass media" (Manuel 1993:3). DJ Paul Oja, Toe Tag's beatmaker and producer and a close friend and collaborator with all of the A-Rühm members, described his decision to start making beats in the mid-1990s (DJ Paul Oja interview, 2011):

I got very encouraged by the whole new digital direction in early 1990s music which proved that one didn't have to have [traditional] musical instruments, band members [to play them], and a separate room for band rehearsals. One could make music in one's own bedroom and not have to worry about what other guys might think about this music.

Oja's description hints at new kinds of artistic, communal, and masculine subjectivities (see Biehl, Good, and Kleinman 2007) that became available due to the political and cultural transitions under way in Estonian society after the end of the Soviet regime. His decision to make digital music using "technologies of wired sound" became part of the process that announced "new logics of music creation and [empowered] local cultural and expressive values" (Greene 2005:3).

At the same time, while MCs took advantage of democratized ways to make, record, and distribute (electronic) music and embraced "all-in-one" artistry, the need for effective beats, which meant the need for a masterful producer, claimed a central place. Kozy and Genka, the two MCs who denigrated "a guy somewhere [who is] dictating what can or can't be done" and who were promoting their autonomy and a "we make our own rules" attitude, would most certainly not have been able to enjoy the popularity of "Pop Musician" without their beatmaker—the DJ and producer DJ Critikal. It is a fact that "Pop Musician" is not a newspaper article or a poem but a piece of music that gained A-Rühm "access to channels of mass distribution and underpins their power and credibility" (Walser 1995:194).

Hip Hop and Transforming Popular Culture in the 1990s

DJ Critikal's[5] beats for "Pop Musician," produced in 1998, illustrate the technological processes transforming Estonian popular culture and the public sphere in general. When DJ Critikal started to be interested in digital music making around 1994,[6] he did not own a computer. In 1999, the first A-Rühm album, which included "Pop Musician," was released. The five years between making his first beats and completing a full album that he himself produced, recorded, and mastered, while holding a day job during all of these years, demonstrates both the rapid increase in the availability of technological and financial tools and the committed, hard-working nature of the producer. In an interview, DJ Critikal has described the conditions and equipment at the beginning of his career as a producer:

> First I didn't even own a computer—I visited homies at night to learn stuff on their computer; it was a great time. I think it was around 1994 and 1995. I actually tried to produce some sort of primitive drum and bass stuff first. It was very difficult to make hip hop stuff at that time: We couldn't afford any decent sound cards, not to mention any mics or studio time. Somehow, I did make lots of beats, but they remained without vocals for the most part. The program I was using was SoundClub, very old-school shit. We didn't have a sound card, we just connected a 286 computer directly into the amp with the Covox plug. A few years with SoundClub, I learned how to use a tracker called FT2

[FastTracker 2]. This is what I worked with to make beats for A-Rühm's [album] *Unsung Songs*.[7]

Working with FastTracker 2, DJ Critikal opens "Pop Musician" with a signature riff that reappears in the chorus as well as in the bridge, sampling (or imitating) a synthesized guitar riff from the 1979 international megahit "Pop Muzik" by the British artist M. Considering that "Pop Musician" aimed at drawing attention to the low level of Estonian pop music, it was a conscious choice to use a riff from "Pop Muzik," which critiques the mindless consumption of pop music. Here, by sampling from "Pop Muzik," DJ Critikal bolsters the local meaning of resistance by drawing on a global artifact, acquiring prestige and credibility among Estonian youth who valued everything Western and North American. At the same time, it is noteworthy that DJ Critikal's engagement with "Pop Muzik" *preceded* a boom in sampling from and covering this song by many internationally prominent artists.[8] This shows how, by taking advantage of technological resources becoming available in Estonia in the mid-1990s, DJ Critikal employs his deep knowledge of previous popular music styles as well as a refined sense for a catchy hook, to which his broad listening experience definitely contributes. He is also extremely up to date with global trends in production techniques in terms of putting together beats and mastering them within a short period of time:

> You know, I am used to going through different stages during the production process as a whole—beat making and post-production are very connected. Of course, I do listen to the finished product later on and sometimes do a new mixdown but usually I like to work from the start to the end within a single breath, as they say.[9]

This kind of working style became more and more common among (electronic) musicians during the 1990s. As Virgil Moorefield has observed: "[A] standard procedure is to . . . disappear into the studio for two weeks or so, 'work twenty-hour days, sleep four or five hours, then get back to work.' . . . This method of working is reminiscent of how Giorgio Moroder and other disco producers went about making music in the late seventies; at the time it was unusual, but now it's the way most pop music is created" (Moorefield 2005:96).

The four-beat-long riff appearing in "Pop Muzik" at 0:07 pops up in "Pop Musician" unaltered—DJ Critikal uses the riff, consisting of an ascending minor seventh and a descending major third (G#-F#-D#; two beats, one beat, one beat, respectively), in the same key and timbre of electric guitar blended with synthesized sounds. It is another conscious move to keep the riff as close to the original sound as possible, since it is possible in FastTracker to lower or raise a pitch. However, DJ Critikal has slowed down the tempo in comparison with the "Pop Muzik" from 120 bpm to 100 bpm. Possibly, the change in tempo was necessary to give MCs a more relaxed framework to rap comprehensibly as well as to allow Estonian audiences to perceive the layers of kick drum, snare, sleigh bells, and the bass line closer to 90 bpm, which, as one Estonian producer explained, is believed to be most typical and "authentic" for a hip hop track among Estonian hip hop practitioners and followers (DJ Melkker interview, 2011).

DJ Critikal, one of the two main hip hop producers—alongside DJ Paul Oja— in Estonia in the mid- and late 1990s, was certainly a role model for every aspiring beatmaker and producer. As he expressed it in an interview that appeared on the Estonian hip hop community website ehh.ee, "To create and record a hip hop track, you don't need to be some sort of rocket scientist at all. A computer and a mic will do very well! It is even feasible to use your cell phone to make beats."[10] In another online interview for the ehh.ee website, he encouraged young musicians to search for their original sound:

> In terms of inventing the ways to make the technology work for you and your ideas for sound, it is important to dig real deep in the internet to find all the necessary instructions since almost every trick for any kind of sound has been invented already, let's face it. All you need to do is find the instructions, which can sometimes take forever. And during this quest for instructions and playing around with your software, you might end up finding your "own" sound and wouldn't need these instructions anymore after all.[11]

DJ Critikal's statements about the accessibility of making beats, stressing the need to be methodical and creative, inspired a whole generation of young men who started to play around with various types of music sequencer software to make music. Although the Estonian-language hip hop pioneer Cool D had already released three albums,[12] and the first hip hop group Toe Tag with their producer DJ Paul Oja had made one album[13] available by 1999 when the DJ Critikal–produced *Unsung Songs* by A-Rühm came out, *Unsung Songs* can be regarded as the watershed in Estonian-language hip hop that paved the way for MCs and producers such as Chalice and Tommyboy in the early 2000s. The latter "all-in-one" hip hop musicians were the leading figures in the "nationalization" of and social activism through hip hop in Estonia, providing the sounds of Estonian-language hip hop with new and diverse qualities.

Estonian Hip Hop and the Accession to the European Union

Another example by DJ Critikal was released on the same album as "Popmuusik." The track "Rahvused on surnud" (Nations Are Dead) starts with an ominous synthesizer moving slowly in half-steps with some scratchiness mixed in, which persists throughout the sound fabric of the track. An extra-aggressive delivery of the rhymes matches the threatening and dark character of the beats. The rhymes summarize vividly, if controversially and with an exceptionally heavy dose of profanity, the heated debates in late-1990s Estonian society about the state-initiated goal of joining the European Union.

Estonia's accession to the European Union stirred up intense, long-standing public debate from 1998 to 2004. The state's negotiations with the EU started in March 1998 and officially concluded in December 2002, after which Estonia's entry into the EU was decided by a nationwide referendum in September 2003. The accession was supported by 66.83 percent of voters, with a turnout of 64.02 percent, and Estonia became a European Union member state on May 1, 2004.[14] At the time of this writing (2014), when the Estonian state is celebrating the tenth anniversary of joining the EU, earlier anti-EU movements and a failed referendum in 2001 have been largely eclipsed. Although rejoining Europe had been an inseparable part of independence for Estonians, most were not interested in joining the European Union, which they considered to be simply changing colonial rulers (Miljan 2004:230).

In the late 1990s, the most emotional argument against potential EU membership related to another union from Estonia's past—the Soviet Union. A-Rühm's MCs refer to "a new empire" that has come to Estonia's door.

Nations are dead
the circle is closed
a new empire has come
to our door[15]

In the popular imagination, especially for older generations and the financially insecure segments of the population, becoming an EU member state was associated with a significant rise in the cost of living; an opening up of the labor market, which would bring much-feared new immigrants into Estonia; and a slow-down in the Estonian economy ("Valitsuse saamatus . . ." 2001).

These were the three primary themes through which the conservative *euro-skeptikud/eurorealistid* (Euroskeptics/Eurorealists) managed to gain political momentum in 2001, when, during the first nationwide referendum on joining the EU, a slim majority of Estonian citizens voted in opposition (Rumm 2009). Political analyst Hannes Rumm summarized the results of the 2001 popular vote succinctly: "Emor's [a polling firm] sociologists were straightforward about wording the results: the majority of Estonian citizens looks at the world through the lens of money . . . [and] not in connection with an abstract maturation of our society" (Rumm 2009).

It is noteworthy that joining the EU was the issue that inspired Genka, Cool D, Kozy, Revo, and DJ Critikal to take an ultrapatriotic, conservative stance against an allegedly progressive step for the Estonian state and society. One commenter on YouTube categorized the track as *"tõupuhas eesti natsiräpp"* (pure-bred Estonian Nazi rap).[16] The xenophobic message in the track is indeed strik-ing, since during their first year of collaboration, A-Rühm, dubbed the "local rap super group" by a respected music critic (Nestor 2008), cultivated its image as progressive and cosmopolitan. A-Rühm's 180-degree turn in "Nations Are Dead" can be interpreted as the creation of a new persona through which to engage in wider public debates about the European Union. Mickey Hess argues that "rap artists obscure, confuse, or split their identities to subvert the often conflicting standards of authenticity and marketability" (Hess 2005:298), while Peter Bar-rer, looking at Slovak rap, similarly notes how in Slovakia rap is counted as au-thentic when rappers have the "ability to create personae . . . who display strong attachments to locality and present a social perspective from an alienated periph-ery" (Barrer 2009:62).

The controversial subject matter and profane rhymes of "Nations Are Dead" are delivered belligerently, with the half-steps from the synth part echoed in Gen-ka's flow. In the verses, insults built on stereotypes of different European nations test audiences' moral sensibilities and reveal a calculated effort to shock. Estonian media consumers have always been attuned to sensationalist approaches to cer-tain issues and have loved all sorts of local scandals. Also, the fact that the group's first single, "Viimane lumi" (Last Snow), which laid the foundation for forming a permanent rap act, was a commission[17] opens the possibility that A-Rühm set as a goal the voicing of multiple opinions despite their own viewpoints and appar-ent conflicts with their cosmopolitan profile. This kind of adoption of the *vox po-puli* becomes especially clear in the case of Genka, who is an avid promoter of progressive ideas such as green living (Kaur 2009) and social work with children (*Publik* 2008).

Protesting against the European Union in "Nations Are Dead," the lyrical whip turns to the old and new Europeans but, interestingly enough, not to the government officials behind the EU accession plan. The possibility of a subtle hid-den critique of the state remains open, although a more likely explanation connects to another role of popular music in post-Soviet contexts. In Soviet times, anti-government popular music exclusively targeted Moscow, and state government officials were viewed as innocent and resistant, as being forced to fulfill Moscow's orders. (See Helbig 2011 for an analysis of this dynamic in Soviet and post-Soviet Ukraine.) This image of oppressive centralized power carried over into indepen-dent Estonia, and might explain why A-Rühm never mentions the Estonian state. However, some politicians themselves drew this track into government discourse. For instance, Margus Õunapuu of the ultra-right Estonian Independence Party used the track in his most recent election campaign as "a song that contains a meaning and a message that should be thought about."[18]

The politician-endorsed message of "Nations Are Dead" consists of ruthless bashing of "black drug dicks," "Danish faggots," "Spanish *locos*," "Turks," and, last but not least, "Algerian, Nigerian, Rwandan felons" as the "main pieces of furniture in the large Euro room," after which the beat drops and Genka declares a cappella:

> I am not a racist, chauvinist but realist
> But in this new union I will be a pugilist
> Let a Kuuno live in Espoo and a spaghetti in Rome,
> And an HIV positive in a Berlin ghetto in a coma[19]

A-Rühm's aggressively xenophobic opposition to EU membership summarizes discussions taking place among young Estonians in the late 1990s (Elflein 1998:257) about German rap and renewed forms of nationalism after the fall of the Berlin Wall). The collapse of the Soviet Union in 1991 brought a significantly refreshed wave of nationalism as well as debates about the past that had not been permitted under the Soviet regime. Estonian anthropologist Aet Annist concludes in a recent study of two rural communities in southeastern Estonia that the "[the past] is a medium . . . to understand and interpret the current situation. [Estonians] have transferred images, changes in social values and goals from the past to the present. All they have experienced, heard, and learned about the past comes from previous generations" (Annist 2011:74). In this light, perceptions of Soviet-era ideologies of popular musics and their association with political and cultural resistance become all the more relevant in A-Rühm's case.

Estonian independence created space for a new, nationally coded youth culture. Especially with tracks like "Nations Are Dead," A-Rühm successfully entered the world of national(ist) popular music, showing how echoing local consumers' shifting tastes trumped the hip hop ethic of rhyming strictly about one's own perspectives and convictions. YouTube comments on A-Rühm's track include questions about its "truthfulness" to hip hop culture's principles. User Eestlaneonvisa (The Estonian Is Tough), for instance, criticizes the track, saying, "The point is good but there should have been more work on the rhymes." User Eesti85 (Estonia85) declares, "It is not at all determined in hip hop about what you can sing. This is merely a genre," to which user Nostalgia98 countered with, "What kind of f-ing track is this? The message of this track is against all sorts of principles in hip hop. This is a contamination of hip hop with racist and Nazi ramble." User EestiPuhtaks (Clean Up Estonia) tops the debate off with "Hip hop does not mean that we need to love blacks [*neeger*] or immigrants. Hip hop is like any other musical style for expressing one's opinion. These guys [A-Rühm] simply expressed their opinion. Period."[20] These conflicting opinions highlight the exceptional status of A-Rühm's track in terms of what some fans perceive as global hip hop's rules and how they should apply to local hip hop. Even when certain fans disapprove of catering to nationalist propaganda and demand that hip hop artists explicitly convey their own viewpoints, the general opinion is that a popular music genre is meant for expressing local sentiments and discussing local social developments such as EU accession.

To return to parallels with developments in German rap, Mark Penney claims that "the racial statements of U.S. rappers were felt to be sufficiently divorced from the German situation to be safely parroted" (Pennay 2001:116). He continues that "[rap artists] decided to concentrate on issues they saw around them, using their own language, rather than aping American styles" (Pennay 2001:121). Timothy S. Brown comments on the use of hip hop in German society as a site for voicing issues about various types of oppression (Brown 2006:146). He observes that "East German rap fans tended to see a real parallel between ghetto life and their oppression as citizens of a communist dictatorship" (Brown 2006:139). Jeffrey Baker, on the other hand, has argued that "[R]ap . . . tends to articulate protest against marginalization and inequality rather than against authority per se" (Baker 2005:372). With "Nations Are Dead," A-Rühm expressed sentiments loaded with the frustrations of post-Soviet reality and the fears of facing the future, while diligently avoiding a critique of the state and its wrongdoings. "Nations Are Dead" also exemplifies the Estonian style of lashing out against anyone or anything that is believed to receive more "undeserved" attention than their situation of historical and economic hardship.

CONCLUSIONS

With both "Pop Musician" and "Nations Are Dead," A-Rühm facilitated public discussion in late-1990s Estonian society about profanity and the right to self-expression in youth cultures. The group also challenged the indiscriminate consumption of pop music and marketed itself as a group of musicians who were composers, producers, and performers "all in one," making their own decisions about their music. At the same time, since A-Rühm chose to document the anti-EU sentiments prevalent in Estonian society during the late 1990s; in its production, the group revealed its eagerness to satisfy local consumers' shifting tastes, which contradicted their ethic of rhyming strictly about one's own perspectives and convictions.

A-Rühm's hip hop production in the late 1990s helped construct and present a new kind of pop music persona to Estonian audiences. Estonian youth, mostly attuned to and idealizing Euro-American forms of popular music, including U.S. hip hop, proved to be very receptive to the Estonian-language hip hop, with which they could identify as their own. DJ Critikal's beats certainly boosted positive reception since they sounded very similar to other hip hop artists' work from the UK or United States. The all-encompassing need prevalent in Estonian society, especially during the 1990s, to become an accepted part of "the West" expressed itself in the popular music scene through the conscious and diligent work of producing and consuming high-quality "Western-sounding" hip hop beats.

Rap artists in Estonia are aware of but not invested in the contexts and mythologies of U.S. hip hop, in which racial discourse and identity is a fundamental part of authenticity. Diverse hip hop practices, two Estonian examples of which I have analyzed, make bottom-up approaches and interpretations an entirely legitimate part of global hip hop studies. This means that there is an ever-evolving need to keep rethinking conventional positions and methods of analysis in global hip hop studies that constantly push beyond comparisons with hip hop culture and scholarship in the United States. In other words, hip hop artists in Estonia, as elsewhere around the world, aspire to connect with trends and ideas from global hip hop, but they do so using local materials: local language, lyrical themes, and culturally specific samples combine to create unique sounds and statements.

Notes

1. A local term explained to me as being used for individuals who come up with a catchy loop or a set of loops but have no knowledge or aspiration to develop them into a full-length track. This will be done by producers.

2. A stream of (implicitly) politically resistant pop songs were performed throughout the Soviet era. Additionally, the underground hip hop scene had existed in Estonia since the early 1990s.

3. Read more at http://e-estonia.com/.

4. Additionally, although founded by Scandinavian businessmen, Skype software was developed by a team of Estonian IT specialists in 2003.

5. Currently performing mostly under the stage name Bert on Beats and signed under this name with the Berlin-based label Man Recordings. More on Bert on Beats along with his remixes can be found at http://soundcloud.com/bert_on_beats.

6. DJ Critikal grew up studying piano at a community music school.

7. Interview available at http://www.ehh.ee/?main_id=13&text_id=123&highlight=DJ,Critikal. My translation.

8. Tricky, 3rd Party, Powerman 5000. Additionally, the song has been covered in the musical *Priscilla, Queen of the Desert* (2006).

9. See note 7 above.

10. Ibid.

11. Ibid.

12. *O'Culo* (1995), *Saaga läheb edasi* (The Saga Continues, 1998), *Pahade planeet* (Planet of the Bads, 1999).

13. *Real Kuhnja Homophobes* (1997).

14. See more at http://www.vm.ee/?q=en/node/8479.

15. Rahvused on surnud

ring on sulgund
uus suur riik on
ukse taha tulnud

16. User silmitsisinuga, at http://www.youtube.com/all_comments?v=oyGcPWVbkKU.

17. "Viimane lumi" was commissioned by the Estonian Red Cross to promote antidrug attitudes among Estonian youth. A-Rühm first performed it at the college fair for high school students in April of 1998.

18. Find the blog entry with props to A-Rühm by Tarmo Õunapuu from the Estonian Independence Party at http://ounapuu.ee/2011/02/rahvused-on-surnud/.

19. Ma pole rassist, sovinist, vaid realist,
kuid selles uues liidus saab minust pugilist.
Las Kuuno elab Espos ja spaghetti elab Roomas
ja HIV positiiv ju Berliini getos koomas

20. YouTube commentary thread on A-Rühm track available at http://www.youtube.com/all _comments?v=oyGcPWVbkKU.

References

Anderson, Benedict. 1983. *Imagined Communities: Reflections on the Origin and Spread of Nationalism.* London: Verso.

Androutsopoulos, Jannis, and Scholz, Arno. 2003. "Spaghetti Funk: Appropriations of Hip Hop Culture and Rap Music in Europe." *Popular Music and Society* 26(4):463–479.

Annist, Aet. 2011. *Otsides kogukonda sotsialismijärgses keskuskülas: Arenguantropoloogiline uurimus* [In search of community in a large post-socialist village: A study in the anthropology of development]. Tallinn: TLÜ Kirjastus.

Baker, Geoffrey. 2005. "¡Hip hop, Revolución! Nationalizing Rap in Cuba." *Ethnomusicology* 49(3):368–402.

Bakhtin, Mikhail. 1981. *The Dialogic Imagination: Four Essays,* ed. Michael Holquist, trans. Caryl Emerson and Michael Holquist. Austin: University of Texas Press.

Barrer, Peter. 2009. "'My White, Blue, and Red Heart': Constructing a Slovak Identiy in Rap Music." *Popular Music and Society* 32(1):59–75.

Bennett, Andy. 2000. "Hip Hop am Main, Rappin' on the Tyne: Hip Hop Culture as a Local Construct in Two European Cities." In *Popular Music and Youth Culture: Music, Identity, and Place* (pp. 133–165). Basingstoke: Palgrave Macmillan.

Biehl, João, Byron Good, and Arthur Kleinman, eds. 2007. *Subjectivity: Ethnographic Investigations.* Berkeley: University of California Press.

Brown, Timothy S. 2006. "'Keeping It Real' in a Different 'Hood: (African-)Americanization and Hip Hop in Germany." In *The Vinyl Ain't Final: Hip Hop and the Globalization of Black Popular Culture,* eds. Dipannita Basu and Sidney J. Lemelle (pp. 137–150). London: Pluto.

Elflein, Dietmar. 1998. "To Krauts with Attitudes to Turks with Attitudes: Some Aspects of Hip Hop History in Germany." *Popular Music* 17(3):255–265.

Greene, Paul D. 2005. "Introduction: Wired Sound and Sonic Cultures." In *Wired for Sound: Engineering and Technologies in Sonic Cultures,* eds. Paul D. Greene and Thomas Porcello (pp. 1–22). Middletown, CT: Wesleyan University Press.

Guibernau, Montserrat. 1996. *Nationalisms: The Nation-State and Nationalisms in the Twentieth Century.* Cambridge, UK: Polity Press.

Helbig, Adriana. 2014. "Hip Hop Ukraine: Music, Race, and African Migration." Bloomington: Indiana University Press.

Helenon, Veronique. 2006. "Africa on Their Mind: Rap, Blackness, and Citizenship in France." In *The Vinyl Ain't Final: Hip Hop and the Globalization of Black Popular Culture*, eds. Dipannita Basu and Sidney J. Lemelle (pp. 151–166). London: Pluto.

Hess, Mickey. 2005. "Metal Faces, Rap Masks: Identity and Resistance in Hip Hop's Persona Artist." *Popular Music and Society* 28(3):297–311.

Jänese, Kerttu. 1999. "A-Rühm: Ropendamine pole kuritegu!" [A-Rühm: Cursing is not a crime!]. *Õhtuleht*. http://www.ohtuleht.ee/34049.

Kaldor, Mary. 2004. "Nationalism and Globalisation." *Nations and Nationalism* 10:161–177.

Kaldor-Robinson, Joshua. 2002. "The Virtual and the Imaginary: The Role of Diasphoric New Media in the Construction of a National Identity during the Break-Up of Yugoslavia." *Oxford Development Studies* 30(2):177–187.

Kaur, Laura. 2009. "Genka: poes käies ma 95%-l kordadest kilekotti ei kasuta" [Genka: While shopping, I don't use plastic bags on 95% of the times]. *Publik*. http://publik .delfi.ee/news/muusika/genka-poes-kaies-ma-95-l-kordadest-kilekotti-ei-kasuta.d?id =27447155.

Keeler, Ward. 2009. "What's Burmese about Burmese Rap? Why Some Expressive Forms Go Global." *American Ethnologist* 36(1):2–19.

Krims, Adam. 2000. *Rap Music and the Poetics of Identity*. Cambridge: Cambridge University Press.

Larkey, Edward. 2003. "Just for Fun? Language Choice in German Popular Music." In *Global Pop, Local Language*, eds. Harris M. Berger and Michael Thomas Carroll (pp. 131–151). Jackson: University Press of Mississippi.

Lull, James. 2000. *Media, Communication, Culture: A Global Appoach*. New York: Columbia University Press.

Manuel, Peter. 1993. *Cassette Culture: Popular Music and Technology in North India*. Chicago: University of Chicago Press.

Miljan, Toivo. 2004. *Historical Dictionary of Estonia*. Lanham, MD: Scarecrow.

Mitchell, Tony. 2001. "Introduction: Another Root—Hip Hop outside the USA." In *Global Noise: Rap and Hip Hop outside the USA*, ed. Tony Mitchell (pp. 1–38). Middletown, CT: Wesleyan University Press.

Moorefield, Virgil. 2005. *The Producer as Composer: Shaping the Sounds of Popular Music*. Cambridge, MA: MIT Press.

Nestor, Siim. 2008. "Preili HU? Ja härrad HU?-d." [Miss HU? and misters HU?] *Ekspress*. http://www.ekspress.ee/news/paevauudised/elu/preili-hu-ja-harrad-hu-d.d?id =27677783.

Pennay, Mark. 2001. "Rap in Germany: The Birth of a Genre." In *Global Noise: Rap and Hip Hop outside the USA*, ed. Tony Mitchell (pp. 111–134). Middletown, CT: Wesleyan University Press.

Peterson, Richard A., and Andy Bennett. 2004. "Introducing Music Scenes." In *Music Scenes: Local, Translocal, and Virtual*, eds. Andy Bennett and Richard A. Peterson (pp. 1–15). Nashville: Vanderbilt University Press.

Plakans, Andrejs. 2011. *A Concise History of the Baltic States*. Cambridge: Cambridge University Press.

Publik. 2008. "G-Enka pani varjupaiga lapsed räppima" [G-Enka got orphanage kids to rap]. http://publik.delfi.ee/news/inimesed/g-enka-pani-varjupaiga-lapsed-rappima.d?id =18948709.

Rumm, Hannes. 2009. "Eesti esimesed viis aastat hiirelõksus" [Estonia's first five years in the mouse trap]. *Sirp*. http://www.sirp.ee/index.php?option=com_content&view=article

&id=8687:eesti-esimesed-viis-aastat-hiireloksus&catid=9:sotsiaalia&Itemid=13&issue=3250.

Simonett, Helena. 2001. *Banda: Mexican Musical Life across Borders*. Middletown, CT: Wesleyan University Press.

Taylor, Timothy D. 2005. "Music and the Rise of the Radio in Twenties America: Technological Imperialism, Socialization, and the Transformation of Intimacy." In *Wired for Sound: Engineering and Technologies in Sonic Cultures*, eds. Paul D. Greene and Thomas Porcello. Middletown, CT: Wesleyan University Press.

Théberge, Paul. 1997. *Any Sound You Can Imagine: Making Music/Consuming Technology*. Hanover, NH: Wesleyan University Press.

Tsing, Anna Lowenhaupt. 2005. *Friction: An Ethnography of Global Connection*. Princeton, NJ: Princeton University Press.

Tucker, Joshua. 2013. *Gentelman Troubadours and Andean Pop Stars: Huayno Music, Media Work, and Ethnic Imaginaries in Urban Peru*. Chicago: University of Chicago Press.

"Valitsuse saamatus ässitab euroliidu vastu" [Government's incompetence induces people to be against the European Union]. 2001. *Delfi*. http://www.delfi.ee/news/paevauudised/eesti/valitsuse-saamatus-assitab-euroliidu-vastu.d?id=1352732.

Vetik, Raivo. 2012. "Introduction: Estonian Nation-Building in the Double Context of Post-Communist Transformation and Globalization." In *Nation-Building in the Context of Post-Communist Transformation and Globalization: The Case of Estonia*, ed. Raivo Vetik. Frankfurt am Main: Peter Lang.

Walser, Robert. 1995. "Rhythm, Rhyme, and Rhetoric in the Music of Public Enemy." *Ethnomusicology* 39(2):193–217.

Warner, Simon. 2004. "Review: Global Noise: Rap and Hip Hop outside the USA." *Ethnomusicology Forum* 13(1):162–166.

INTERVIEWS

DJ Melkker, November 2011 in Rakvere, Estonia.

DJ Paul Oja, November 2011 in Tallinn, Estonia.

CHAPTER 8

WEARING NIKES FOR A REASON

A Critical Analysis of Brand Usage in Polish Rap

Milosz Miszczynski and Przemyslaw Tomaszewski

For more than thirty years of its existence, hip hop culture influenced and reflected changes in the culture, politics, and economy of different localities around the world. At its core, international hip hop emerged as an artistic movement that represented oppressed and marginalized groups whose difficulties were symbolically parallel to the hardships of the American ghetto. In most cases, hip hop developed as a bottom-up movement. International pioneers of rap, with a similar lack of equipment, discovered how to express themselves and convey their lived reality through poetics and the aesthetic seen in African American rap video clips from the United States (Androutsopoulos and Scholz 2003; Tervo 2013). Rap music allowed for artistic communication that connected local identity negotiations, historic narrations, or existential debates. Local artists have adopted the cultural pattern, configuring specific rules with local conditions and creating specific "global assemblages" (Ong and Collier 2005). In a similar way, everywhere that hip hop gained popularity the local hip hop culture was organized by a shared definition of authenticity, hypermasculinity, misogyny, criticism of the mainstream society, and references to hip hop's origins. Using categories of hip hop and reinterpreting its aesthetic, artists employed rap as a platform for sociopolitical dialogue that reflected the social attitudes of artists and their environments.

The mass popularity and commodification of American hip hop created a multibillion-dollar industry that has influenced global culture and economy. As Dan Charnas points out, in hip hop, an artist and a businessperson are often the same, and even the earliest hip hop parties were marketed and had a commercial dimension (Charnas 2010). With rap's impact on the economy, hip hop propels the rise and fall of brands, fashions, and trends that go beyond popular music.

Hip hop brand hype has generated new segments, trends, and collections, sometimes eroding the pristine luxurious image of products. Calling it a "tanning phenomenon," Steve Stoute and Mim Eichler Rivas argue that the development of those trends is based on the uniqueness of a shared point of view promoted by hip hop that is independent of the demographic or economic status of a consumer (Stoute and Eichler Rivas 2011).

On the artistic side, the symbiosis of hip hop and consumption is reflected in the way it is created and performed. This paper focuses on this relationship and studies the convention of using brands in constructing a rap message. In publications on hip hop, branded commodities recur in quoted lyrics, ethnographic descriptions, and interviews with rap fans (Dennis 2012; Rose 1994). Everywhere in the world, rappers use brands when describing their dreams and desires, but also when referring to everyday struggles or narrating social life. Brands prevail in lyrics, refrains, and song titles, and are explicitly filmed in video clips. Brands function as rhetorical figures, filled with culture-specific symbolic meaning, carrying emotional value, and making the message meaningful and realistic (Danesi 2006). With hip hop's global popularity, the convention of referring to brands, sometimes called "spitting brands,"[1] is practiced around the globe. Our study is an attempt to define and explain this phenomenon.

The goal of this study is to discover the functions and ways in which rappers employ rappers. To do so, we perform a textual analysis and, since merely naming the brands and categorizing the products is insufficient, we consider the ways in which the symbolic attributes of a branded product are culturally motivated in varying contexts or utterances. We focus on the case of Polish rap, which is among the most vibrant European hip hop scenes. Analyzing the connection between the cultural values of rap and brand identities reflects the way that rap and its ideology is processed and understood in different societies. We decode contexts and their origins by showing the ways in which rappers infuse symbolic meaning into brands, giving them a culture-specific meaning and function. By studying brand usage, we show how Polish rap nurtures the idea of classlessness and collective solidarity as well as constructs a new sense of self in reference to Polish neoliberal reality (Serazio and Szarek 2012).

Hip Hop and the Language of Consumer Society

Hip hop culture is deeply embedded in contemporary social life and employs the language of consumer society. As any form of consumption may be a foundation for economically powerful consumer segments (Katz-Gerro 2004), commodities and brands in rap act as an important element of identity construction. Since the pioneering study of the self by Ernst Prelinger (1959), the possession of various products has been identified as being among the fundamental elements of self.

Jean Baudrillard's *The Consumer Society* established a consensus that consumer motivation goes beyond the product's "use value" and is not solely based on properties of the product (Baudrillard 1998). Consumption patterns and shared meanings of brands work as a group-making mechanism. leading to the formation of consumption-related subcultures (Kozinets 2001). Participating in a consumer society requires sharing a map of meanings of the products and brands available on the market. Zygmunt Bauman (2007) identifies the "consumptionist syndrome" of modern society as a mental disposition. Consumption defines groups (Mazzocco et al. 2012), and expresses ethnic affiliation (Deshpande, Hoyer, and Donthu 1986) or value contestations (Halkier and Jensen 2011; Long and Villarreal 1998). Possession of goods serves as a tool for enacting particular social roles, and functions as a status marker.

Brian Goldman observes that rappers "drop at least one brand name reference and some cram in so many names that it can be difficult to hear much else" (Goldman 2007). Brands are referred to in rap in all sorts of contexts, serving as an important element of hip hop's vernacular (Potter 1995). Rap lyrics have been a platform for the communication of brand names since its beginnings. The first rap song with a brand name in the title was Run-D.M.C.'s "My Adidas," dating back to 1986. But even before this brand-praising song, the convention of referring to brands of commodities had become an important part of hip hop (Charnas 2010). For instance, the 1984 Swatch Watch NYC Fresh Festival Tour, a nationwide undertaking and a milestone in hip hop history, drew together an emergent cultural form with a then relatively unknown brand. Over the years, rappers influenced their fans, telling them what they consider to be in fashion, which products matter for performing the culture, and which products might be considered wrong or send an inappropriate message (Stoute and Eichler Rivas 2011). Thanks to the intense popularity of the music, rappers generate specific consumer trends, sometimes influencing sales of forgotten brands and classic products, or incorporating commodities seemingly unrelated to the urban lifestyle (Charnas 2010; Roberts 2002). During our study we identified competing claims, allowing us to hypothesize about why and how brands are repeatedly employed in hip hop expression.

The "bling era" of American hip hop correlated with Clinton-era prosperity and formed a stereotype that successful rappers are fond of displaying their wealth. At that time, shiny chains, furs, luxurious brands, and tuned cars became important requisites of rap. The compensatory consumption thesis assumes that high-end commodities serve as a means of self-affirmation. Conspicuous consumption, so visible in 1990s rap video clips, might be understood as compensation for social marginalization stemming from structural inequalities. As rappers and rap fans are often closely connected to the lower social strata, obtaining and demonstrating higher social status, in part through luxurious brands, might be read as a way of restoring power. Because self-affirmation through consumption correlates with low social status, referring to brands may be understood as "a desire to acquire" (Belk, Bahn, and Mayer 1982; Rucker and Galinsky 2008, 2009). The need to consume high-end products correlates with race (Charles, Hurst, and Roussanov 2007), social status, and vertical mobility (Mazzocco et al. 2012), and rappers often represent groups facing inequities based on those variables. Luxurious brands are the most important part of the hip hop model of conspicuous consumption (Mukherjee 2006), influenced and recreated in rap, and in the American context stereotypically referred to as "ghetto fabulous" (Mukherjee 2006). Continuing through today, this aesthetic, especially outside the American context, is often copied by international rappers; however, it is often influenced by local factors. For instance, in Eastern European hip hop, the traces of this fashion are manifested in *nouveau riche* claims and direct references to American hip hop's consumption patterns and product preferences.

But rap music also carries a set of brands that are far from being considered luxurious. The artists mention, for instance, how they "picked up their Nokia," "bought Durex condoms," "put Nikes on," or "drank a Red Bull." Rappers often communicate by referring to products that are popular locally and contain specific local or class-related meanings. In a manner similar to everyday communication, brands in this case replace nouns in order to make the message more realistic or understandable to the audience. Brand familiarity theory helps to understand this context of the usage of brands. An exposure to brand references in rap creates a specific structure of knowledge about the catalogue of commodities, which reflects first- and secondhand experience with the brand (Alba and Hutchinson 1987; Campbell and Keller 2003; Kent and Allen 1994). Rap guidelines concerning how to consume a product, under what conditions, and what meaning its possession carries might be understood as a way of delivering new information about the brand and generating a culture-specific familiarity. A lot of commodities mentioned in rap, especially nonluxurious ones, are known to the audience because they are part of the local consumption model. Putting a strong emphasis on a seemingly typical product is an important tool in constructing a rap message. Brands ranging from beer names to types of cough medicine become tools that facilitate more effective and detailed communication and reduce personal distance. Because of different significance outside and inside hip hop culture, those brands referring to mundane everyday consumption should be considered an important instrument in developing authenticity and coherence.

The symbolic potential of brands is a valuable means of communication between the artist and audience, and not only in hip hop. As historical studies prove, each decade, brands have become increasingly present in works of fiction (Friedman 1985). Also, hip hop uses brands as rhetorical figures; for instance, Polish rapper LJ Karwel raps: "Screw this soil, I shake the Durex down, in this same Durex I rap, so that I won't get any nasty stuff"[2] (*TenTypMes i Lepsze Żbiki* 2013). This passage illustrates how employing brands allows for certain emotions and reactions to be evoked. Brands on their own carry so much symbolic meaning that they can cause subconscious physical reactions (Walla, Brenner, and Koller 2011). In marketing practice, brands are intentionally stylized to cause emotional reactions; for example, Italian names are employed in naming pasta-related products to connect the consumer to a specific imaginary environment (Zilg 2011). Rap does this in a similar way by employing the symbolic value of language combined with the poetics of lyrics and the artistic ambiance of music. As brands correspond with memories and have multiple meanings for consumers (Suresh, Mohanan, and Naresh 2012), in hip hop brands are a tool that amplifies narrations and makes the process of communication more intimate.

Artists inspire not only audiences but also each other. Because of the global scale of hip hop's influence, rap's intercontextuality happens everywhere hip hop has developed (Charry 2012; Guibert and Parent 2005; Solomon 2009). This process occurs not only on one level of hip hop culture, but also on a transnational level. For instance, Polish rap extensively refers to and engages with the values, symbols, or quotes of U.S. rappers. This paper reflects this dialogue by considering the context and function of the usage of brands of commodities and their symbolic value. Considering the symbolic load of brands in Polish rap lyrics, we focus on their relation to local brand identities and contexts as well as to the global hip hop movement.

Polish Hip Hop in the Era of Neoliberalism

Polish rap music and hip hop culture emerged as a reaction to market freedom and capitalist reality after the political transformation of Eastern Europe (Serazio and Szarek, 2012). Similar to the other hip hop variations in the world (Condry 2006; Dennis 2012), for more than two decades, Polish hip hop underwent a long evolution: starting as a bottom-up movement, becoming a recognized commercial musical genre, creating its own artistic niche, and finally conquering mainstream popular culture and dominating record sales in Poland. Except for three years of a hip hop boom (1998–2001), hyped by major record companies, Polish rap music has received very little mainstream attention. In effect, since the early 2000s, it has been pushed into its own niche, which very strongly relied on the internet. With time, the Polish rap scene became as large and vibrant as the mainstream music industry.

In referring to Polish hip hop, we assume that it inherits both the form and content of the culture of its American predecessor. Tricia Rose writes that American hip hop forms alternative identities manifested in fashion, music, and language as a way of contradicting the dominant social frame that marginalizes black urban youth (Rose 1994). Although the American and Polish social contexts differ significantly, the less salient aspects of Polish society, such as racial discrimination, become transferred into different spheres, carrying a similar message based on inequality. Though not many rappers in Poland have a good command of English, their texts and attitudes are profoundly influenced by both the aesthetics and the conventions of American hip hop. The strongest influences come from the Golden Age of U.S. hip hop of the early 1990s, as the Polish scene was forming at that time. Through cultural transfer, Polish rappers adopted a similar form of hip hop culture, including rituals such as freestyle battles or online rap beefs (conflicts), themes and problems such as discussion of rap's authenticity, and fashion or on-stage gestures.

Currently, hip hop is the most competitive music scene in Poland, a country of 38 million people. Russell A. Potter describes how American hip hop culture counters commercial appeal and censorship. Potter claims that hip hop "is a counter-formation that takes up capitalism's gaps and contradictions and creates a whole new mode, a whole new economics" (Potter 1995). The case of Polish hip hop strongly supports that thesis. With highly independent promotion channels, since 2010, more than 100 albums have appeared, including 55 in 2012 (OLiS 2013). However, sales do not accurately reflect the size of the fan base, as most Polish hip hop fans download the music illegally. The records are most often purchased as collectibles and resold on internet auctions. On the internet, Polish hip hop is booming. Over 70 regularly updated video channels on YouTube.com count their views in the millions; they contain not only music video clips but also additional materials, such as video miniseries, concert reports, and interviews. Polish hip hop has its own daily tabloid (glamrap.pl); an uncounted number of official artist fan pages, 11 of which have more than 200,000 fans; over 30 clothing lines; and an online rap reality show. Concerts and hip hop events take place on a daily basis in all corners of Poland, drawing diverse audiences. Polish hip hop culture is geographically dispersed and represents various localities, targeting various age groups and all social strata.

The Polish rap scene connects different genres and styles. From street rappers with an authentic street message, through grime and avant-garde musical experiments, the scene accommodates a broad range of rap forms. Among the most popular are classical "boom-bap" beats produced in a way similar to the American East Coast beats of the 1990s. This era also strongly influences rap fashion and contributes to a stereotype of US-based rappers as conspicuous consumers. Because of the different context of their activity, the situation of Polish rappers is very different from the Americans. Despite the enormous popularity of hip hop in Poland, Polish artists often use a slogan, "This is Poland, not the US" (*to Polska, nie Stany*), and stress that rapping hardly allows them to support themselves. Being a rapper in Poland requires a do-it-yourself approach and attitude. The music is recorded in independent studios owned by the artists, as very few commercial studios provide equipment and conditions suitable for recording rap music. Besides artistic activities, rappers administer their businesses, book concerts, or package and sell their products, usually with very little help from hired staff. Most artists travel to their concerts in their own private cars or, if the concert happens outside of Poland, they fly low-cost airlines. Most rappers grew up in and, like millions of Poles, still inhabit big post-communist neighborhoods of concrete block flats. Those complexes, in Polish hip hop called the "projects" (*projekty*), are Polish hip hop's milieus and a symbol of urban Poland. All these factors foster a complex attitude toward consumption and wealth.

The ideas behind the message rap communicates, at their root, represent the Polish working class. This implicit identity of hip hop has its foundations in the concepts of Polish socialism, especially in regard to the project of flattening the social structure. The introduction of the free market economy, which happened before rap bloomed in Poland, has polarized Polish society. On the one hand, the free market stimulated dreams of Westernization and produced new consumers (Serazio and Szarek 2012), and on the other it marginalized low-skilled workers in industry and agriculture (Howard 2003). Rap very strongly reflects these attitudes toward the changes that have happened in the past 20 years. From describing the dreams and desires of the American middle-class idyll to pointing out the barriers to upward mobility and expressing disappointment with capitalist practices, Polish rappers influenced new identities based on combining the philosophy of hip hop with a strong critique of the new social order. As we show below, the mediated symbolic meaning of brands is a crucial instrument in that process.

TRACING BRANDS IN POLISH RAP

As we have not found any previous analyses of rap focused on brands, our research design was experimental in the way we applied our tools and collected data. On the preliminary level, the qualitative examination aimed at gathering the greatest possible number of lyrics and identifying all brands in the sample. The first step in the research process was to collect and review a sample that will, to the maximum extent possible, correspond with the state of art of Polish rap. The popularity of the internet in Poland and a solid base of hip hop fans participating in interactive web pages were helpful in acquiring the lyrics. Because the internet is the biggest channel for the distribution and consumption of hip hop, we were able to find four web pages providing hip hop lyrics. Their main function is to collect user-added content in a way similar to Wikipedia. They are usually moderated in order to avoid advertisements or irrelevant entries; however, the content is not verified in detail. In order to acquire the data from those pages, we designed a script that acquired all texts from the chosen pages. We then compared overlapping lyrics with each other, which allowed us to detect some of the mistakes of the transcribers. We concluded that the web page containing the greatest number of lyrics is www.tekstyhh.pl. On September 20, 2012, we acquired the database. The lyrics were verified, and we removed entries where the artist or a song could not be identified. In the end, we collected 8,603 song lyrics in Polish, starting from the first rap album in 1994.

Lyrics for each song were examined to determine references to brands and coded using qualitative data software. First, all content was coded for the presence of brands. We coded *in vivo* all of the brands in the texts, including slang and colloquial varieties, such as "*beema*," similar to the English "Beemer," for a BMW car. In this way, we identified 1,532 texts that mentioned at least one brand name, making up 17.8 percent of the 8,603 lyrics in our database. On the one hand, this result shows that brands are actually not "dropped in every text," as previous literature suggested. On the other hand, this number shows a tendency that, on the textual level, reveals an important trend and proves that brands are indeed instruments of rap lyricism, in some cases present also in repeated choruses. In the analysis, we coded 2,575 brand mentions, out of which we identified 266 unique brand names (codes). Some of the codes, such as brands of cars, had up to 14 different variations of designates, which were merged into one code, for instance "*S-Klasa*," "*E-Klasa*," and "*Merc*" were put into the Mercedes brand code. As Figure 8.1 indicates, the codes were categorized according to the function of the product that they refer to, as well as their origin. In the next stage, we built a nested hierarchy of categories according to the functional meaning of the products, such as brands of vehicles, fashion, or stimulants. To get a broader picture, during the final analysis, we went over our findings with rappers and hip hop fans.

Hip Hop as Disillusionment

The first theme that emerged from our analysis was that everyday and luxurious brands are referred to at an almost equal rate. On the one hand, we found brands referring to mundane everyday consumption (717 codes), which accounted for 27.84 per cent of the total number of brand references. These included the names of foods and drinks, stimulants, and pharmaceuticals. On the other hand, brands identified as luxurious in the Polish context made up 25.71 percent of the sample and were found in 662 fragments. The almost equal number of the two categories does not, however, imply that rappers support both types of consumption. The majority of texts avoided "bling" consumption and instead sought to emphasize the equality of rappers and the audience, and posed a critique of neoliberal reality.

> Sometimes I dream that I hardly leave my studio
> That I have a huge house and a private beach,

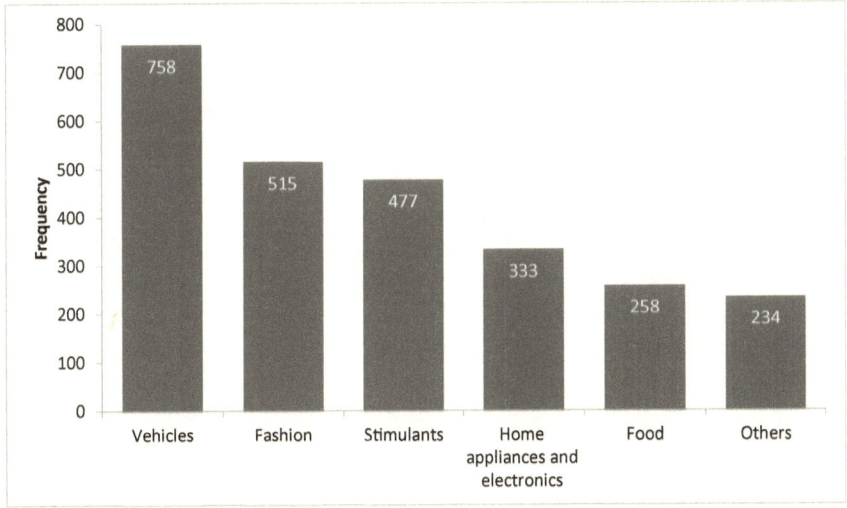

Figure 8.1. Top 20 most frequent brand references from Polish rap lyrics according to the category of product to which they refer. $N=8,603$.

In my garage a 4Runner and a Beemer
And I am just drowning in my money.
But this world is not real, it's all a dream
That will never happen here. (Tede 2001)

As the passage above indicates, many Polish rappers emphasize their aspirations using foreign brands. However, their conclusions are similar to Tede's: that their possession is impossible both for them and for most people in Poland. Our research reveals an extremely high presence of luxurious cars in the lyrics, with three luxurious German car brands—BMW, Mercedes, and Porsche—at the top of this category. However, very few rappers indicate possession of a car. Instead, the use of public transportation is often emphasized.

Because luxury goods are relatively rare on the Polish market, with very few shops offering them and prices that make their consumption almost impossible even for the most well-known Polish rappers, we assume that they were adopted from American hip hop and locally incorporated as part of the hip hop convention. However, the value of brand judgments differs. Polish lyrics pose a critique of the illusion of a liberal order full of brands. Rappers indicate that, like many Poles, they believed in a new order but found out that success was not achievable. Instead of showing success, high-end brands are elements of a critique of neoliberalism. The dominant position of Polish rap is completely opposed to the mainstream "high society," especially with regard to celebritism and Polish popular music. Most of the high-end goods mentioned in the lyrics might be seen as positive or gratifying in American rap and context, but in Poland they are presented in a negative way, as "Poland is not the States." This also includes seemingly usual products for Americans, perceived as exclusive in Poland. For instance, Starbucks, which has only three franchises in Poland and sells the most expensive coffee in the segment, is always used as a synonym for snobbism.

Moreover, the sample contained a group of brands from the luxury segment that did not match products available and known to the Polish consumer. We discovered that those brands were utilized to confirm an insider status in global hip hop. Brand references, especially to commodities absent on the Polish market, put a rapper in a situation where the lyrics introduce the audience to the new commodities. By showing new brands, rappers take the position of experts— not of consumer goods, but rather of the hip hop culture. Knowledge of brands such as Kenzo, Don Perignon, or Chivas Regal confirms rappers' cosmopolitism and especially their knowledge of foreign hip hop, which often employs those same products in its lyrics in a way that confirms the compensatory consumption thesis.

The category of commodities that we qualified as belonging to mundane consumption included 96 unique brand names. An overwhelming number of brands in this category represent brands that are the most recognizable in their market segments in Poland. Most of them refer to products that are leaders in their segments in Poland and are locally widely recognized, such as Coca-Cola or Marlboro cigarettes. Out of 717 brand references, only 254 referred to Polish product names—in particular, lower-end Polish alcohol brands, such as beer and vodka. Seemingly dull commodities belong to the language of Polish society, and rappers actively manipulate their brands, using them to reinforce their local identity and closeness to their audience. Following the hypothesis of brands as containers of emotions conveying meanings to consumers, our study confirms that claim. The context and high presence of brands belonging to the mundane consumption category are the strongest argument supporting this thesis. Similar to swearing, a natural part of hip hop lyricism, rappers consciously rely on the symbolic strength of everyday brands, trying to communicate with listeners using the words that are used in everyday communication, thus speaking using brands and employing their already generated symbolic potential as well as updating it.

GLOBAL SOLIDARITY OF HIP HOP

Similar to other cultures of consumption, sharing consumption activities, product categories, and brands in hip hop is an important source of social cohesion and a basis for interaction (Schouten and McAlexander 1995). In hip hop, some products might be identified as accessories necessary for performing the culture. Our data produced an extensive list of commodities essential to the hip hop culture, including ones that are culture-specific and unknown to outsiders. Often they took a culture-specific form of local interpretations of global brand identities. Our study proves that those brands are understood as an important, if not fundamental, element of the hip hop culture.

One American brand, Nike, emerged in our sample 160 times. Nike is a flagship brand of Polish and international hip hop culture. Even though for outsiders the brand is mostly known for its sports equipment, Nike is a staple product of urban fashion worldwide, synonymous with class identity and distinct from designer brands, such as Gucci, which symbolizes the upper class (Archer, Hollingworth, and Halsall 2007). Nike sneakers are praised and loved by hip hop fans all around the world, partially thanks to street-style advertising campaigns, often involving rappers and basketball players. For instance, one ad featured KRS-One rapping to footage from a basketball court and proclaiming revolution, using the Nike's swoosh logo as its symbol. A symbiosis between Nike and rap in Poland is not unprecedented on a global scale. Rap icons mentioning Nikes include rappers Rakim, KRS-One, and Mac Miller, as well as international artists such as the German Krudo, Brazilian MV Bill, Polish Sokół, and French rapper Kennedy. As the high number of references to Nike proves, Polish rappers inherited the preference for the cult sneakers. This preference is transmitted to the audience. Nike Dunk and Air Max One are the two most loved models among Polish rap fans, which is visible not only during rap events but also on the Polish streets. It is worth stressing that Poland does not have a strong basketball culture, and no rap references or parties have ever been sponsored by Nike in Poland.

The devotion to hip hop commodities is positioned against the anti-neoliberal message of Polish rap. The global hip hop consumption model is also negotiated within the local context. In effect, some of the brands or conventions get rejected—for instance, golden chains and other types of jewelry. The approved hip hop commodities work as the symbol of unity with global hip hop. Wearing Nike sneakers or New Era hats is a clear signal that allows for the internal coherence of hip hop and demonstrates a tight connection to its US predecessors, often treated as the founding fathers of the culture. Those brand identities are also a foundation of Polish hip hop's fashion and aesthetic. Despite the fact that in the American context, items such as baseball or basketball hats might seem usual, in Poland the possession of genuine accessories has an important meaning and proves the sophistication, hip hop unity, and cosmopolitism of artists and audiences. Similarly, in the early 2000s, Lacoste polo shirts and vintage tracksuits were incorporated into Polish hip hop. Though they are luxurious, they were considered a part of French hip hop fashion, partially thanks to the 1995 movie *La Haine,* depicting life in a multiethnic French housing project.

The tools for producing rap serve a similar function. The most important device of Polish rap is the MPC sampler (Music Production Center) by Akai, a piece of studio equipment used for combining musical samples. It was coded 43 times in the sample, and almost every Polish rap fan can identify its shape, as it is often represented in video clips. Its presence is also strongly connected to the preference for sampled, looped "boom bap" rap in Poland. Similar to referring to the turntable brands Vestax and Technics, mentioning MPC proves affinity with the culture and often reveals the fact that rappers produce their own beats, which is considered a merit. References to those brands reinforce rappers' authenticity, as music made or performed on this equipment has an important connection to the heritage of American hip hop. As our study proves, in a similar way, Polish rappers rap about graffiti accessories, such as spray paint brands Montana or Belton. Knowledge of these brands is verification of the rappers' insider status and serves as an important message for their audience.

Similarly, elements used to emphasize the street cred of American MCs were transplanted to Polish rap. For instance, the gun model Glock was coded 48 times. Hardly seen or possessed in Poland, Glock is an important requisite of American gangster rap and, as our study proves, an important point of reference for Polish rap. Though this brand had not belonged to the Polish social context, it became a prominent part of Polish hip hop. Even today, Glock has very little recognition outside of hip hop. In most lyrical descriptions, Glock symbolizes a powerful weapon that could be used in defense against outside forces, such as the pressures of commercial industry or internet haters. Many similar examples prove a deep interaction of local ideology, discourse, and meaning with outside brand identities.

Unity between Artist and Audience

Promoting brands remains a controversial issue in Polish hip hop. American rap music has a much longer tradition of cooperation with sponsors, and product placement and advertising by artists receives a higher degree of tolerance (Blair 1993; Charnas 2010). In Polish rap, very little is known about officially sponsored lyrics, and artists avoid direct involvement in mainstream media advertising. Recurring controversies and gossip about sponsored lines always heat up the audience. Though rappers provide a strong criticism of capitalism, reject the commodification of rap, and avoid conspicuous consumption, in two instances they are willing to promote brands. Moreover, they do it with the full acceptance of their fans and peers. The first is sponsored product placement. This is increasingly present, but never on the scale and extent of mainstream media and hardly ever touching the lyrical sphere. The second form involves promoting products sold by the rappers themselves. Buying these is considered a form of payment for musical activity.

Some Polish rappers have promoted an ethos that artists may advertise goods that are part of their own life. One of the best examples of advertising through Polish hip hop is the herbal vodka Wódka Gorzka Żołądkowa. Rappers associated with the micro-label Alkopoligamia have repeatedly referred it in their lyrics, put it on their album covers, and promoted it during mass events. In our sample, we were able to track it 29 times, of which 26 were in Alkopoligamia's lyrics. However, the alcohol brand was popular even before the campaign, and the meaning of the brand connects many important elements: It had been produced under communism since the 1950s; its layout, bottle, and recipe have not changed much since then; its flavor is distinctive from other products; and finally, it can be drunk without cooling, directly after purchasing at the store, unlike many other vodkas in Poland. For the hip hop audience, this classic drink is a symbol of an urban lifestyle and parties in the Polish "projects." Probably due to this fact, the campaign has not faced any strong criticism from other artists.

An alternative practice, which avoids intervening in the delicate sphere of lyrics, is based on financing the activity of rappers through corporate sponsors. For instance, mobile phone operator Orange sponsored an open rap video contest. The main prize was an opportunity to record an album with Koka Beats, a record label owned by rapper Pezet, who became the face of the contest. Except for Orange's logo in the videos covering the competition, nothing was said about mobile telephones. Another initiative, sponsored by Reebok, allowed for hip hop collaborations with promising young artists representing different musical styles. In a considerable number of countrywide tours, manufacturers acted as titular sponsors. In the most recent one, Red Bull allowed rap fans to vote for the 10 cities to which a rap tour bus would be sent. As our interviewees pointed out, in all these cases the understanding of collaboration goes beyond the simple form of product placement and takes the form of subtle and agreeable patronage. The prevailing interpretation is that these sponsorships support hip hop as a culture, and the artists stay independent and are not censored or influenced like those in the mainstream media and music industry.

Many rappers sell and promote their own products, usually clothing, and our data revealed the presence of independent Polish hip hop brands in lyrics. Similar to what Wu-Tang Clan started in the United States, Polish rappers have developed their own clothing brands or acted as brand ambassadors for a company with hip hop credit, usually owned by another artist. Because of music piracy, this activity is commonly recognized and accepted in Polish hip hop. Unlike selling music, producing clothes is considered profitable, and the audience sees buying branded clothes as a form of solidarity and support for the artists. Many fans are willing to buy a piece of clothing that for the Polish market is usually priced high (about $30 for a T-shirt, $100 for a hoodie). Strong emphasis is always put on the high quality of the product, and the fact that it is produced nationally. Because these brands are commonly accepted, their presence in lyrics, CD covers, and video clips is extremely high. The most successful Polish record label and clothing line, PROSTO, sometimes has its logo and products exposed in video clips from beginning to end. The artists throughout the clip show off the newest designs and collections. Other rap brands use the same method of promotion. Most of these goods are distributed through direct internet sales in the same way as music. The designs often reflect the intertextuality of rap. For instance, a hoodie from Koka Wear intentionally imitates the Nike logo and its slogan. The brand name is replaced by "Koka," written using the same font; instead of a Nike swoosh, there is a line of cocaine powder; and below the logo, the slogan says, "Just do it."

Conclusions

In our view, the analysis of brand presence in Polish hip hop poses a relevant contribution in three respects. First, the study explores the ways in which rap music lyrics explicitly cite name brands. We determined the different character of brand references, encompassing mundane domestic products, Polish luxury brand items, and internationally produced commodities that, while available in Poland and symbolically resonant, remain beyond the reach of a majority of the population. This seems important, as it unravels how brand images, which might be understood as part of a particular consumption context, reproduce and renegotiate broader social values and attitudes when used in rap lyrics. As our study reveals, in Polish rap those values encompass the construction of a new sense of self in reference to Polish neoliberal reality and nurture the idea of classlessness and collective solidarity. The symbiosis of hip hop and consumption is also reflected in the way it is created and performed. Second, the study offers a complex study of hip hop's transnational and local intertextuality. Our study contains a comparative dimension and points at the parallels between the U.S. and Polish contexts as well as their differences. The former include connecting the role of the rap artist with that of a businessperson, employing the language of consumer society, generating culture-specific commodities, or using the same musical tools. The latter, such as rejecting some of the brand meanings or some of the products, prove that global brand identities transmitted through international hip hop engage with local hip hop ideology as well as local brand identities. Third, our methodological approach sheds new light on researching hip hop. After undertaking a quantitative study, we went beyond a basic analysis of lyrics and counting the number of name brand citations toward studying the context. By using interviews, we were able to explore that context in detail, considering multiple contexts and the levels of the sources of brand meaning.

In emphasizing the critical analysis of brand presence, this article has offered limited insight into other elements of the culture, such as the image of brands on the American scene. Further research might be required in order to study that issue in its different cultural contexts in order to understand the whole apparatus involved in generating, transmitting, and negotiating brand meanings in hip hop.

Notes

1. The verb "spitting" is often used as a slang term for rapping.
2. All translations are my own.

References

Alba, Joseph.W., and J. Wesley Hutchinson. 1987. "Dimensions of Consumer Expertise." *Journal of Consumer Research* 13(4):411–454.

Androutsopoulos, Jannis., and Arno Scholz. 2003. "Spaghetti Funk: Appropriations of Hip Hop Culture and Rap Music in Europe." *Popular Music and Society* 26:463–479.

Archer, Louise., Sumi Hollingworth, and Anna Halsall. 2007. "'University's Not for Me—I'm a Nike Person': Urban, Working-Class Young People's Negotiations of 'Style,' Identity and Educational Engagement." *Sociology* 41:219–237.

Baudrillard, Jean. 1998. *The Consumer Society: Myths and Structures*. Thousand Oaks, CA: Sage.

Bauman, Zygmunt. 2007. *Consuming Life*. Malden, MA: Polity.

Belk, Russell W., Kenneth D. Bahn, and Robert N. Mayer. 1982. "Developmental Recognition of Consumption Symbolism." *Journal of Consumer Research* 9:4–17.

Blair, M. Elizabeth 1993. "Commercialization of the Rap Music Youth Subculture." *Journal of Popular Culture* 27:21–33.

Campbell, Margaret C., and Kevin L. Keller. 2003. "Brand Familiarity and Advertising Repetition Effects." *Journal of Consumer Research* 30:292–304.

Charles, Kerwin Kofi, Erik Hurst, and Nikolai Roussanov. 2007. *Conspicuous Consumption and Race*. Cambridge, MA: National Bureau of Economic Research.

Charnas, Don. 2010. *The Big Payback: The History of the Business of Hip Hop*. New York: New American Library.

Charry, Eric S. 2012. *Hip Hop Africa: New African Music in a Globalizing World*. Bloomington: Indiana University Press.

Condry, Ian. 2006. *Hip Hop Japan: Rap and the Paths of Cultural Globalization*. Durham, NC: Duke University Press.

Danesi, Marcel. 2006. *Brands*. New York: Routledge.

Dennis, Christopher. 2012. *Afro-Colombian Hip Hop: Globalization, Transcultural Music, and Ethnic Identities*. Lanham, MD: Lexington Books.

Deshpande, Rohit, Wayne D. Hoyer, and Naveen Donthu. 1986. "The Intensity of Ethnic Affiliation: A Study of the Sociology of Hispanic Consumption." *Journal of Consumer Research* 13(2):214–220.

Friedman, Monroe. 1985. "The Changing Language of a Consumer Society: Brand Name Usage in Popular American Novels in the Postwar Era." *Journal of Consumer Research* 11(4):927–938.

Goldman, Brian. 2007. "Putting Lamborghini Doors on the Escalade: A Legal Analysis of the Unauthorized Use of Brand Names in Rap/Hip Hop." *Texas Review of Entertainment & Sports Law* 8(1).

Guibert, Jérôme, and Emmanuel Parent. 2005. *Sonorités du hip hop: Logiques globales et hexagonales.* Clermont-Ferrand: M. Seteun.

Halkier, Bente, and Iben Jensen. 2011. "Methodological Challenges in Using Practice Theory in Consumption Research. Examples from a Study on Handling Nutritional Contestations of Food Consumption." *Journal of Consumer Culture* 11:101–123.

Howard, Marc Morjé. 2003. *The Weakness of Civil Society in Post-Communist Europe.* Cambridge: Cambridge University Press.

Katz-Gerro, Tally. 2004. "Cultural Consumption Research: Review of Methodology, Theory, and Consequence." *International Review of Sociology* 14(1):11–29.

Kent, Robert J., and Chris T. Allen. 1994. "Competitive Interference Effects in Consumer Memory for Advertising: The Role of Brand Familiarity." *Journal of Marketing* 58:97–105.

Kozinets, Robert 2001. "Utopian Enterprise: Articulating the Meanings of Star Trek's Culture of Consumption." *Journal of Consumer Research* 28:67–88.

Long, Norman, and Magdalena Villarreal. 1998. "Small Product, Big Issues: Value Contestations and Cultural Identities in Cross-Border Commodity Networks." *Development & Change* 29(4):725–750.

Mazzocco, Phillip J., Derek D. Rucker, Adam D. Galinsky, and Eric T. Anderson. 2012. "Direct and Vicarious Conspicuous Consumption: Identification with Low-Status Groups Increases the Desire for High-Status Goods." *Journal of Consumer Psychology* 22(4):520–528.

Mukherjee, Roopali. 2006. "The Ghetto Fabulous Aesthetic in Contemporary Black Culture." *Cultural Studies* 20:599–629.

OLiS. 2013. "Oficjalna Lista Sprzedaży—Archiwum."

Ong, Aihwa, and Stephen J. Collier. 2005. *Global Assemblages: Technology, Politics, and Dthics as Anthropological Problems.* Malden, MA: Blackwell.

Potter, Russell A. 1995. *Spectacular Vernaculars: Hip Hop and the Politics of Postmodernism.* Albany: State University of New York Press.

Prelinger, Ernst 1959. "Extension and Structure of the Self." *Journal of Psychology* 47:13–23.

Roberts, Johnnie L. 2002. "The Rap of Luxury." *Newsweek,* September 2, 42–44.

Rose, Tricia 1994. *Black Noise: Rap Music and Black Culture in Contemporary America.* Hanover, NH: University Press of New England.

Rucker, Derek D., and Adam D. Galinsky. 2008. "Desire to Acquire: Powerlessness and Compensatory Consumption." *Journal of Consumer Research* 35:257–267.

Rucker, Derek D., and Adam D. Galinsky. 2009. "Conspicuous Consumption versus Utilitarian Ideals: How Different Levels of Power Shape Consumer Behavior." *Journal of Experimental Social Psychology* 45:549–555.

Schouten, John W., and James H. McAlexander. 1995. "Subcultures of Consumption: An Ethnography of the New Bikers." *Journal of Consumer Research* 22:43–61.

Serazio, Michael, and Wanda Szarek. 2012. "The Art of Producing Consumers: A Critical Textual Analysis of Post-Communist Polish Advertising." *European Journal of Cultural Studies* 15:753–768.

Solomon, Thomas. 2009. "Berlin-Frankfurt-Istanbul: Turkish Hip Hop in Motion." *European Journal of Cultural Studies* 12:305–327.

Stoute, Steve, and Mim Eichler Rivas. 2011. *The Tanning of America: How Hip Hop Created a Culture That Rewrote the Rules of the New Economy.* New York: Gotham.

Suresh, Sheena, P. Mohanan, and Gopal Naresh. 2012. "Brand Success Redefined: An Analysis of the Interrelationships among Various Brand Dimensions." *Psychology Research* 2:32–39.

Tervo, Mervi. 2013. "From Appropriation to Translation: Localizing Rap Music to Finland." *Popular Music and Society* 37(2):1–18.

Walla, Peter, Gerhard Brenner, and Monika Koller. 2011. "Objective Measures of Emotion Related to Brand Attitude: A New Way to Quantify Emotion-Related Aspects Relevant to Marketing." *PLoS ONE* 6(11):e26782. doi.org/10.1371/journal.pone.0026782.

Zilg, Antje 2011. "That's Amore: Brand Names in the Italian Food Market." *International Journal of Applied Linguistics* 21(1):1–25.

DISCOGRAPHY

Tede. 2001. *S.P.O.R.T.* RRX Desant, Warsaw.

TenTypMes i Lepsze Żbiki. 2013. Alkopoligamia, Warsaw.

PART III

HIP HOP ON THE MARGINS

CHAPTER 9

COSMOPOLITAN INSCRIPTIONS?

Mimicry, Rap, and Rurbanity in Post-Socialist Albania

Nicholas Tochka

ON THE STREETS of Tirana, Albania, hip hop issues from pounding car speakers and teenagers' cell phones jangle forth hooks from recent rap hits.[1] Rows of Albanian-language CDs with cover art modeled closely after the visual aesthetics of American rappers share space on record store walls with illegally dubbed albums of global superstars. Young men in internet cafés stream tracks from hip hop groups based in Albania, Kosova, and the United States, and Tirana-based rappers' clothing, possessions, and love lives provide scintillating copy to local gossip rags. In 2009, a hip hop group even received third prize at the state radio-television's prestigious annual singing competition, and, the following spring, its lyricist penned the Socialist Party's campaign song, "Çohu!" (Stand Up!).

Over the past decade, *hip hop shqip*, Albanian-language rap, has entered the mainstream. This chapter examines the ends to which locally produced hip hop has been employed by young people from Albania since the late 1990s,[2] with a focus on two contrasting trends. On the one hand, hip hop, along with other global genres such as alternative rock, metal, R&B, and dance music, has become a vehicle through which young Albanians experience membership in an imagined global community. A way for rappers and listeners to imagine new, transnational senses of belonging (Appadurai 1996), hip hop style provides a potentially empowering means of self-making to individuals navigating post-socialism at the nation-state's peripheries or in migration. On the other hand, hip hop has become a key signifier within an emerging, Tirana-based entertainment economy focused on fashion, style, and consumption. To underscore its inaugural issue's mission statement in 2004, for example, *Teens*, a "magazine for young people . . . as well as those who still feel a little bit 'teen' inside," employed a stock photo of fashionably dressed young women in front of a DJ. Integrated into Albania's emerging re-cording industry, hip hop here supports recent efforts to reassert Tirana as the post-socialist anchor of an Albanian-language mediascape.

Each project derives from a common motivation held more widely in con-temporary Albania: the deeply felt imperative to define the cosmopolitan contours of belonging in a newly deterritorialized world. Cosmopolitan, in this descrip-tive sense (Perman 2012), denotes the quality of the political, social, and musical projects Albanians today pursue by imagining post-socialist geographies that necessarily stretch beyond Albania's borders. In the music field, the promotion of popular genres coded as "modern" (*modern*), especially hip hop, R&B, and rock, has furnished young Albanians a privileged means with which to access a mo-dernity constructed as existing "outside" the nation-state's borders, whether in Europe, the United States, or simply "the West." Hip hop thus provides a site for examining the politics and aesthetics of recent claims to membership in a global order. Seeking not to "indigenize" global styles, rappers forgo musical hybridiza-tions that might suggest a place-based "identity."[3] Instead, rappers closely emulate or, as some critics would have it, mimic the style of American hip hop artists. Taking this seeming mimicry at face value, I seek to understand rappers' precise reproductions of American hip hop's musical and visual codes as "cosmopolitan inscriptions," a creative means by which individuals mark, or inscribe, them-selves and the spaces they inhabit in imaginative new ways.

My narrative examines two contrasting groups: the first, a cohort of eco-nomic migrants based in Athens, Greece; and the second, participants in Tira-na's emerging entertainment economy. Faced with nested deterritorializations wrought by post-socialism, each group uses hip hop to reterritorialize socially meaningful spaces. A reaction to the social, economic, and political exclusions now restructuring young Albanians' lifeworlds, these strategic projects have de-lineated new spaces of inclusion in one case, even while reinscribing long-standing hierarchies of difference in the other.

Post-Socialist Albania's Deterritorializations

Promoted as the "symbolic achievement of the socialist 'paradise'" (Vullnetari 2012:115), Tirana anchored the musical production of "modern" visions of society and self in the People's Socialist Republic of Albania before 1991. The capital housed the institutional core of a robust national infrastructure that adminis-tered the composition, performance, and broadcast of new musical works, while protectionist media policies secured Tirana-based elites' monopoly over the Albanian-language mediascape. At the same time, Tirana functioned as a center of desire for many Albanians inhabiting the nation-state's peripheries. Accord-ing to one district resident, the capital "ticked all the boxes on our checklist. Art is made here, other activities, the modern life as we saw it in films or read it in books" (Vullnetari 2012:115). Due to strict regulations on internal migration, this "modern life" remained inaccessible to all but the most politically connected citizens until the 1990s (Saltmarshe 2001:170).

Under post-socialism, the center has not held. In the 1990s, the privatization of Tirana's cultural field fragmented symbolic production, giving rise to decentralized networks of recording studios, distribution companies, and private media companies across Albania, the Republic of Kosova, and Macedonia (see Sugarman 2010:18–19). The emergence of an entrepreneurial class in Kosova, until the mid-1990s a significant audience for, but not producer of, Albanian-language media, allowed Prishtina, together with cities in Macedonia, Western Europe, and the United States, to surpass Tirana as the "new musical capitals" of the Albanian-language mediascape (Sugarman 1999:140). At the same time, emigration—comprising 20 percent of Albania's population, or some 800,000 people—has multiplied potential "centers" for economic migrants in Greece, Italy, and the United States (King, Mai, and Schwandner-Sievers 2005). Political instability has further weakened the nation-state's formerly firm borders, facilitating drug and human trafficking (Davies 2009) and initiating disorganized patterns of internal migration from outlying districts to the capital. No longer protected by demographic quotas, Tirana's population has expanded by a factor of three, as rural persons displaced by the collapse of regional economies seek the "modern life."

The deterritorialization of media and national space has occurred in tandem with the promotion of global popular musics. Within Albania's remarkably heterogeneous post-socialist mediascape, global pop, rock, and hip hop genres index "modern" taste. In part, nonlocal media's privileged status derives from urban viewing practices under late socialism. In the 1980s, clandestinely watched Western media began to function as a "periscope," offering viewers "access to radically different ways of being, having, and behaving" (Mai 2001:178, 183). During the 1990s, the Democratic Party–led state media heavily promoted Western music—especially local heavy metal and hard rock groups, as well as Whitney Houston–inspired power ballads—over the local socialist-era *estrada* genre, "light music," which virtually disappeared from broadcasts (Tochka 2013).

Hip hop became popular with listeners in Albania not through state broadcasts, which tended to favor rock and pop styles, but through an influx of inexpensive cassettes of American artists, which entered Albania via young male economic migrants. Rap's initial popularity in the late 1990s gave rise to two trends. First, migrants in Greece began recording under the name Nga Jugu Në Veri (From South to North), a reference to their diverse regional backgrounds. Led by the group 2Die4, these rappers emulated American gangsta rap, and their low-tech productions were popular with fans who perceived them as sounding "hard," creating "rap" (*rrep*), as opposed to "hip hop" (*hip hop*). Second, commercially oriented,

Tirana-based acts were founded. Their smoother, R&B-influenced tracks with humorous, inoffensive lyrics were designed to appeal to young listeners. Several were funded by national telecommunications companies, hotels, or boutiques. By 2010, many these groups' members had entered an emerging entertainment economy based in Tirana as lyricists, producers, or television personalities. Each trend demonstrates the broad and, at times, contradictory ways that young Albanians have sought to reterritorialize the nation-state's post-socialist geography since the late 1990s.

IMAGINING HOME: FROM SOUTH TO NORTH

Composed primarily of Albanian-born friends who met in Greece, the hip hop collective Nga Jugu në Veri (From South to North, hereafter NJNV) initially consisted of rapper G-Bani, from the northeastern district of Dibra; Crazy Girl, from the southeastern district capital of Korça; the group 2Die4, from the central city of Fier; and a handful of collaborators. Members had emigrated to Greece from their district hometowns in the early to mid-1990s, and began recording Albanian-language tracks for distribution in Albania by 2000. Unlike early hip hop acts based in Tirana, these rappers composed their own beats, wrote all their own lyrics, and collaborated with one another on their usually self-financed albums. After securing distribution through a Tirana-based company, and with the 2003 establishment of the private music video channel BBF, NJNV albums and singles began reaching a broad audience in Albania.

Bristling with shout-outs to district towns, NJNV tracks often foregrounded rappers' positionality vis-à-vis "home." In "Në rrugët e lagjës sime" (On My Neighborhood's Streets, 2003), rapper Crazy Girl portrayed the place she held "in [her] heart and mind forever," Korça. Despite having left her childhood behind in Albania for young adulthood in Greece, Crazy Girl rapped, her 'hood (*lagjë*) was where she "was born and was happy," where she "learned the Albanian language." Mixing a personal register focused on friends and family with official historiography—Korça housed the first Albanian-language school, opened on March 7, 1887, commemorated nationally as Teachers' Day—Crazy Girl's homage nested personal feelings of belonging within a national narrative. Other rappers thematized their positions vis-à-vis the nation-state in more general terms. In 2004, G-Bani and rapper MJ-Xhelo, with singer Vassy, began collaborating, in a self-conscious nod to their migrant status, under the name "+355" (Plus Three-Five-Five), Albania's international calling code. The group's first track, "Edhe këtë verë" (This Summer, 2004), depicted the pleasures of returning "home" to Albania during summer vacations.

But tension between rappers' stated affinities for home and their style of expression arise in NJNV members' precise emulation of American hip hop's conventions. Unlike hip hoppers elsewhere, who have drawn on socially conscious exemplars such as Public Enemy in order to express shared political stances (e.g., Perullo 2005; Urla 2001), NJNV rappers modeled their performance personae after more morally ambiguous American gangsta rappers. West Coast gangsta rap, especially as associated with the Los Angeles–based label Death Row Records, has several characteristic features: a medium-tempo, laid-back groove often termed "g-funk" in reference to the 1970s funk from which many artists' beats derived; certain formal properties, such as "intro" tracks with spoken dialogue, or skits interspersed among musical tracks on albums; and lyrics that were often condemned in the mainstream American press as obscene or as glorifying violence. Because West Coast models themselves often concerned marking "place" (Forman 2002), gangsta rap provided a framework for enunciating belonging in ways that complicated NJNV statements about home. In Crazy Girl's homage to Korça, described above, for example, she began with a spoken-word intro explicitly placing herself *outside* the nation-state—referencing the track and the Greek recording studio with the spoken words "Crazy Girl, [here at] Studio Emfasis [in Greece], 2003."

NJNV rappers' fealty to American models encouraged criticism, but also made them popular with young listeners. For their critics, rappers' "imitation" of foreign models evidenced their creative bankruptcy, their mimicry symptomatic of what local commentators more generally decry as the post-socialist "bastardization" of "national culture." Members' use of English-language expressions, especially the casual misogyny of substituting "bitch" for "woman," or the vulgarity of "motherfucker" for "friend," further distanced their productions from any prior Albanian-language modes of expression. For listeners, however, this same "mimicry" functioned differently. Responding to a message posted to an online forum criticizing rappers for "stealing" music (i.e., too closely mimicking global styles or too baldly sampling American artists), one young fan of the NJNV group 2Die4 responded, "[It might] not be good for Albanian music, but for talking about Albanian reality, hip hop or rap is just the thing. Yes, many [rappers] use stolen music, but at least they transmit the things hip hop ought to transmit."[14] This listener felt that close emulation of global examples was warranted because rap was a "natural" medium for commenting on "reality." My sense is that other listeners were attracted to NJNV productions for reasons not subject to such clear articulation: namely, the allure of hearing, seeing, and having a cosmopolitan music culture all of one's own.

The surface nature of rappers' adoptions of global hip hop did not detract from, but rather contributed to most young listeners' attraction to NJNV's music. The obvious cosmetic quality of these cosmopolitan elements marked NJNV's tracks as legitimately modern. Small tattoos, popular since the 1990s, provide a starting point toward situating this phenomenon more broadly in the Albanian context. Indelibly inked by adolescents on themselves and their friends, "token" images became a fad for many young men in the mid-1990s. A way of marking their physical bodies as distinct from those of their forebears, while simultaneously signaling affinity with a global social body of pop and sports stars, these permanent, cosmopolitan inscriptions provided an imaginative point of articulation between their bearer and the outside world.

For three friends from the central Albanian district town of Fier, hip hop style—and especially the sounds and image of American rapper Tupac Shakur (1971–1996)—functioned analogously. Calling themselves 2Die4, after a tattoo on the late rapper's chest, group members figuratively and literally wore the American rapper's influence on their sleeves—when I met rapper Niku in 2005, he pulled up his shirt to reveal a small token tattoo, reading "2Die4." The video clip for the group's track "Më pëlqen" (What I Like, 2003), which contributed to their wider popularity in Albania, depicted the three members rapping with friends on a graffiti-covered basketball court.[5] Wearing backward-turned baseball caps over do-rags, oversized athletic jerseys, and gold jewelry, the rappers postured half-bent, holding with one hand cigarettes between thumb and forefinger, as one would a blunt, and with the other hand, low-riding baggy jeans. A mock-serious litany of the group's likes and dislikes, the track explicitly linked 2Die4 to Tupac Shakur by invoking his name in the final verse ("I like to listen just to rap, Tupac"), which was accompanied visually by a fan lifting his jersey to reveal a 2Pac T-shirt. The clip's outro provided the track's most enduring image. Under a larger mural featuring Shakur and the track's title, one of the rappers scrawled a graffiti message reading "2DIE4 2PAC."

Not simply visual, 2Die4's fidelity to West Coast models could be heard in the rappers' assiduous reproductions of Shakur's very flow. The highly individual rhythmic and micro-rhythmic groove characteristic of a rapper's performance style, flow—like a sonic fingerprint—includes his or her particular inflections, syncopations, or emphases. An innovative, "fresh" flow is, at least for many American listeners, a key element in rappers' reception (Alim 2009:109). Shakur's instantly recognizable rapping employed several features: an easygoing syncopation, accomplished by deemphasizing downbeats and preceding them with a strong upbeat, as well as a handful of typical rhythmic patterns, including long-short-short or short-short-long rhythms. 2Die4's members, like rappers elsewhere (e.g., Condry 2006; Perullo 2011), first learned to rap by imitating American recordings. But rather than seeking to cultivate their own voices, these rappers have remained faithful to his style over time.

2Die4's appropriation of Shakur's flow was particularly audible on their debut album, *Jetës Sonë* (To Our Life, 2000). The album included three numbered tracks titled "Jetës Sonë," each different musically but unified through subject matter dealing with emigration, racism, and urban life in a metropolis. Where

Table 9.1. The opening lines of "Jetës Sonë 3" (2001) performed
by group member Bledi Milioneri.

^	^ / _ ^ ^ / _ ^ ^ / _ ^ ^ / _
Dhe di- / kush të më / thotë sep-se / unë nuk e / di . . .
^ ^ / _ ^ ^ / _ ^ ^ /^ ^ ^ ^ / _
E shi- / kon dhe pra- / non për më / te-për ky vazh- / don
(And somebody tell me because I don't know / . . .
You see it and accept it but it keeps going on)

Shakur often employed and varied his flow to emphasize particular words or to
intensify wordplay, the rappers in 2Die4 adopted his flow as a rhythmic, rather
than a poetic, model. At times, 2Die4's adopted flow sounds stilted, even mechan-
ical, in part the result of the Albanian language. In everyday speech, one-syllable
words or conjunctions are often contracted or omitted, while words of two syl-
lables are usually stressed on the second syllable. While this does not preclude
rapping in Albanian, it made direct emulation of Shakur's flow awkward. Group
members thus employed grammatical conjunctions that would normally be de-
emphasized and stressed two-syllable words in sometimes idiosyncratic ways
in order to fit their lyrics into "long-short-short" (—^ ^) motifs derived from
Shakur's style (see Table 9.1).

Not simply a musical or poetic device, group members' emulation of Shakur's
flow functioned as a borrowed mark of "glocal distinctiveness" (Alim 2009:109),
a means to articulate solidarities beyond, and differences within, a post-socialist
Albanian imaginary. Moreover, this Albanian-language version of an American
rap artist promoted a powerful, attractive means of self-making to young listeners in Albania. Between 2004 and 2010, a large number of low-fi productions,
many inspired by 2Die4 and other NJNV rappers, began appearing on internet
sites, radio, and even compilations in record stores. At the same time, NJNV rappers' promotion of graffiti and tattooing contributed to the popularization of
these practices. As an inexpensive and accessible means to demarcate the physical spaces of a potential "hip hop" nation, the spatial transformations of graffiti
and tattooing enabled fans to literally mark both new youth territories and themselves as "cosmopolitan." On the wall behind my apartment block in 2004, for
example, local high school students had tagged "2Pac 2Die4 Snoop Dogg Dr. Dre,"
expanding the list featured in the outro to the video clip "Më pëlqen" to include
two other Death Row Records rappers. As a multimedia style, hip hop in this way
enabled many individuals to begin reimagining their own neighborhoods as
cosmopolitan nodes in an increasingly connected world. A means to articulate

oneself to trends in global fashion, culture, and music, hip hop thus inspired post-socialist practices of cosmopolitan self-making.

RAP AND RURBANITY IN POST-SOCIALIST "TIRONA"

Hip hop functions differently at the center. In Tirana, as in the examples above, rapping marks local affinities with an imagined global scene. But hip hop has also been employed in recent years within an emerging entertainment economy in ways that reinscribe internal hierarchies of social difference formed during the socialist period. Since the late 2000s, parodies featuring hip hop and other youth genres have powerfully *re*-peripheralized would-be cosmopolitan migrants circulating within Albania. Disarticulated from district homes by economic restructuring, a growing "rurban" class—a group occupying a tenuous position as no longer rural, but not fully accepted as urban—has emerged as a significant demographic category (cf. Simič 1973). Though many young people of rural origin go abroad for work, increasing numbers have migrated to greater Tirana. Living in the capital and aspiring to its "modern life," the rurbanite remains for longtime city dwellers an essentially liminal, symbolic figure indexical of post-socialism's deterritorialization of national space. To urbanites, these individuals' fashion, speech, and aesthetic tastes mark them as embarrassingly nonmodern mimics.

The bumbling rurbanite provides rich fodder for satirists. The comedian Bes Kallaku, an actor and writer on the weekly variety program *Portokalli*, has become especially popular for his rurban character, "Gjini." Speaking in a rapid-fire, sometimes incomprehensible dialect while sprinkling in mispronounced or misused English words, Gjini hails from a northern village and often finds himself in absurd situations in the capital. Employed as an urban planner, for example, Gjini buffoonishly announces a massive 5 million euro investment in tourism for the underdeveloped rurban settlement of Kamza. Sensationalized in the media as "backward," Kamza symbolizes the "chaos" of internal migration for many urban viewers. A small settlement of approximately six thousand in 1990, the community has mushroomed to over one hundred thousand today (Çaro 2012). Elsewhere, Kallaku's characters are mocked through baser stereotypes. In the 2011 internet short "Date with Manushaqe," the rurbanite awakes in a cramped bed in his home village following an erotic dream. His "lover" is revealed to have been a sheep licking his face. Elsewhere in Southeastern Europe, rurban listeners are usually associated with commercialized pop-folk genres (e.g., Beissinger 2007; Archer 2012). In Albania, parodies emphasize rurbanites' consumption of both local pop-folk and global styles, with their taste for the latter serving to mark them as idiotic, foolish, or parochial. During Gjini's "dream date" with Manushaqe, for example, he serenades her with a comically inept, heavily accented rendition of Jamaican American singer Shaggy's "Sexy Lady (Drive Me Crazy)."

Building on the popularity of his Gjini character, Kallaku has recently penned several hip hop songs as rurban rapper "Katunari Gangsta" (Gangsta Hillbilly, hereafter KG), including the eponymous "Katunari gangsta" (2011) and "Eminem i Katunarëve" (The Hillbillies' Eminem, 2012). Wearing stylish clothes, oversized jewelry, and expensive accessories, KG's aspirations to be modern are intended to render him ridiculous to the urban viewer. Video clips produced for each track mock-dramatize KG's transition between his home village and Tirana, emphasizing in particular the rurban protagonist's varying modes of transportation, which include donkey, motorbike, minibus, and the quintessential rurbanite vehicle, the Mercedes-Benz. Ubiquitous on Albanian roads, older models are often stolen in Western Europe and then imported to Southeastern Europe, where they can be bought relatively cheaply. After selling his home and livestock in "Gangsta Hillbilly," KG purchases a Benz. Once in Tirana, he parks it in the central Skanderbeg Square by tying it, as one would a donkey, to a signpost. Dazzled by the capital's tall buildings, KG stares up in the fashionable downtown district housing Tirana's clubs and restaurants. When he tries to enter a café, however, the rube mistakenly walks into its large front window before finding the door.

The rurban rapper's incomplete facility with English, media technology, or women consistently marks him as non-urban, as essentially peripheral to Tirana. KG's lyrics employ stilted, ungrammatical English-language borrowings, whether in addressing listeners with "What is *up*, my nee-gahs?" or pronouncing "motherfucker" as "mah-thore-*fah*-core." Yet KG's rhymes also betray a hubris often associated with the rurban figure, as the hillbilly unabashedly claims the city's space for himself. In "The Hillbillies' Eminem," KG plants a flag in Skanderbeg Square, as an astronaut might on the moon, rapping in northern dialect, "*Tirona metropol / Tirona asht e jona*" (Metropolitan Tirana / Tirana is ours). If the rurbanite does not belong, he does not seem to know it. Yet the same clip also foregrounds the decentralized technologies by which rurbanites today are able to make such cosmopolitan gestures. As KG postures in the dirt square of his home village, a young boy interrupts from the door of an internet café to yell, "Come on, Hillbilly, the internet is back on!" A common event in rural areas that experience frequent interruptions to electricity, the sequence dramatizes how technology's promise in democratizing Albanians' access to a global mediascape remains inflected by their geography.

By framing internal migrants as failed cosmopolitans, elites at the center reassert the social distance between themselves and encroaching rurbanites, even as the physical distance separating them progressively disappears. In parodies, the rurban figure remains always incorrectly cosmopolitan, effectively reperipheralized through the very means by which he seeks to assert his belonging in the modern world. This is not to ascribe agency to such representations, but to note that as socialism's mechanisms for administering physical and representational geographies have been superseded, agents at the once unchallenged center are fashioning musical responses to the somewhat disorienting processes of deterritorialization that they face. The uneasiness inherent in parodies about rurban newcomers perhaps demonstrates the extent to which internal migration and the decentralization of symbolic production have successfully challenged Tirana elites' preeminence. In parody, media and physical deterritorializations intermesh, as the restructuring of symbolic and social life that enables inhabitants from former peripheries to imagine cosmopolitan lives for themselves simultaneously provides elites a means to reassert an unassailable difference.

Parodies' focus on Tirana as a pole of attraction for the rurbanizing masses parallels recent efforts to promote the capital as the center for a modern consumerist "youth culture," the focal point of an emerging middle class. Tirana-born rappers have especially contributed to this project by rebranding "their" city as a site with its own particular style, ethos, and argot. The predominance of a slang version of *tironc*, the capital's urban dialect, in hip hop and R&B productions especially, points to how styles coded as "modern" often come to be conflated with Tirana, or, in current youth argot, *Tirona*. In "Tirona"-based rappers' tracks, the substitution of a long, flat "oh" sound for standard Albanian's warm, open "ah"— *jom*, "I am," as opposed to the standard *jam*—aurally marks for listeners an association with the capital. At the same time, *tironc* dialect shares features with the northern dialect mocked in the previous parodies. Parodies thus selectively employ regionalisms to render explicit the difference between registers, as when the Hillbilly Gangsta refers to "house" with the word *shpaj*, a dialect (from the northern Krujë district) substitute for the standard two-syllable *shtëpi*, but also distinct from the *tironc* word, *shpi*.

Tracks produced by a Tirana-based cohort of lyricists and producers, especially rappers Big Basta, Stine, and Noizy, and producer Flori Mumajesi, reinscribe "Tirona" as a cosmopolitan center in various ways. In the video clip for his 2010 track "Bohu gati" (Get Ready), a diss-rap directed at former collaborators, Big Basta appears in a sweatshirt emblazoned with "Tirona Rap 24," or, "Tirona rap—all day long." In its pronunciation (e.g., *bohu* vs. the standard *bëhu*) and grammar (e.g., *me kthy' lëvizje* vs. *duke kthyer lëvizje*, "turning moves . . ."), the track hews faithfully to the *tironc* argot that now suffuses productions created in Tirana's many recording studios. Moreover, Big Basta's track itself focuses on a contract dispute with a top Tirana pop producer, albeit without mentioning his name. Incessantly reported on in glossy magazines, the dispute (and local media's focus on it) demonstrates how Tirana serves as a center for glamour, gossip, and intrigue, as to be "in the know" about Albanian pop culture necessitates that one follow the lives of Tirana-based elites. In turn, Tirana's entertainment economy now publishes gossip magazines that feature confessional interviews with stars, paparazzi-style ambush photography, "wardrobe malfunctions," and best- or worst-dressed lists, much in the tabloid-style mold of TMZ or *The Sun*.

Hip hop productions especially participate in reframing Tirana as a destination for consumption and luxury. Big Basta's collaboration with model-turned-singer Çiljeta, "Déjà vu" (2009), produced by Flori Mumajesi, opens with a hung-over, heavily made-up, and tattooed Çiljeta awakening at midday to her cell phone's ring. "Hello?" At first, the singer puts off the caller, before he invites her to a club. "And there'll be a DJ?" she asks, immediately perking up. Flashing the English words "24 Hours Ago," the clip enters a flashback. The first part shows the singer in her car, a cherry-red 2009 Pontiac Solstice sports car, the symbolic opposite of a used Mercedes-Benz, driving through Tirana's streets before heading to the club. Intercut with scenes featuring Big Basta rapping in front of the Pontiac, the camera hungrily zooms in on the opulence of Çiljeta's cosmetics, clothing, jewelry, and accessories, implicitly proposing Tirona as anchoring her conspicuous consumption. The flashback structure of the video further implies that Çiljeta's protagonist goes clubbing every night, rendering a cosmopolitan "youth" time-cycle of constant pleasure in the capital. Framed as an imaginative center for partying and shopping, this Tirona is represented as a site to which those young people marked as truly modern—tattooed, fashionably dressed, and expertly coiffed—gravitate.

COSMOPOLITAN INSCRIPTIONS?

As Albanians imaginatively reterritorialize their lives, hip hop provides a plastic repertoire of sounds and images with which the potential contours of identity in a deterritorialized world might be shaped. Hip hop practices are as much visual as they are audible. The nonlocal beats, hooks, and flows emanating from tinny computer speakers in internet cafés throughout Albania and its diaspora are consumed with their images, as it is this "broader sensorium of globalized modernity" that users encounter (Stokes 2007:18; Hall 1993). Hip hop's multimedia "resources for experiments with self-making," or "scripts for possible lives" (Appadurai 1996:3), offer young people one attractive means for rethinking their place in the world. The mere existence of these identity projects is itself a remarkable change. Formerly overseen by professionalized symbol producers at the People's Socialist Republic of Albania's media and culture institutions, identity formation has been radically democratized. Yet this shift has not necessarily resulted in more democratic social imaginaries. Instead, hip hop enables the articulation of both inclusionary and exclusionary acoustemologies of belonging, spaces young people might potentially inhabit as participating members of an imagined transnational order, but also spaces that symbolically exclude would-be claimants to the "modern life" as it is lived in Tirana.

Moreover, the attractiveness of hip hop's cosmopolitan inscriptions stems from a broader reverence for the foreign in post-socialist Albania. Almost uniformly esteemed, nonlocal practices across aesthetic, political, or economic domains are imbricated in wider, hegemonic programs eliding the local assimilation of Western-style reforms with a return to political and economic "normalcy" (cf. Kennedy 1994:4). If some Albanians have explored "Muslim" or "Balkan" identities, the overwhelming majority—whether elite, in migration, or rurban— understand themselves to be aspirants to, if not yet full citizens in, a global order, a powerful social fact shaped in no small part by constant appeals in the public sphere about the "necessity" of the nation-state's political "return to Europe," or the essentially "European" nature of Albanians (e.g., Kajsiu 2010; Nixon 2010). The seemingly commonsense nature of this desire obscures underlying processes of subjectification. If global music styles offer young people a means to reterritorialize post-socialist life, they simultaneously render this life understandable in particular ways (Mazzarella 2004). Even if unwittingly, rappers, producers, and listeners are caught up in a wide-ranging economic assemblage aimed at refashioning young people into consumers, "teens," or "the youth." And here as elsewhere, hip hop functions as "an instrument of normativity" (Eisenberg 2012:559), embedded within a capitalist logic of personhood based on individual taste and consumption, as well as a political project aimed at producing "European" citizens.

It is in relation to wider processes of coming to terms with post-socialism that Albanian-language hip hop's cosmopolitan inscriptions must be situated. As often frustrated others vis-à-vis an imagined global order, all Albanians strategically contend with very real exclusions, both in emigration and "at home." When Albanian speakers go abroad as economic migrants, many pretend to be of another nationality in order to find employment in countries where dominant stereotypes about "the Albanian" revolve around notions of backwardness and criminality. "The need for strategic mimicry and humble disguise in the face of a powerful yet (with regard to Albania) ignorant West, comes as a shock to most Albanian émigrés" (Schwandner-Sievers 2008:51). In national politics, Albania's ongoing exclusion from transnational communities, and especially the European Union, has been understood as the state's key obstacle to modernity. Political mimicry, attempts to demonstrate the nation-state's willingness to adopt any and all reforms demanded by Brussels, are often understood locally as efforts to effect "correct," if superficial, self-representation to "the West." Hip hop's symbolic reterritorializations similarly are cultural responses to pressing questions about how belonging should be constituted after socialism. As young people navigate a telescoping range of potential communities—dwelling "at home," going "to Europe," or representing "Tirona"—they articulate membership for themselves as legitimate participants in a global order.

Coda: Membership, Mimicry, and Post-Socialism

Issues of mimicry and membership have wider implications in post-socialist Eastern Europe, especially in areas where the social reorderings that resulted from local "uncertain transitions" (Burawoy and Verdery 1999) raised and sharpened questions of identity that have yet to be resolved (cf. Buchanan 1996:227). Attitudes toward global popular culture, whether seeking to valorize it or to dismiss it, to assimilate it or to safeguard against it, stem from local subjects' shared understanding of themselves as inhabiting a new epoch. Diverse parties navigating this "new world disorder" (Jowitt 1992) hold stakes in rethinking what membership in a world no longer ordered by the mutually constructed opposites of "East" and "West," or "First World" and "Second World," might entail. How do individuals living under the successors to political-economic orders that structured much "smaller" worlds, as in Albania, or ones that had been significantly oriented by their relationship with Moscow, as in Bulgaria or Central Asia's Soviet Socialist Republics, articulate and claim new forms of belonging, especially ones that cross local, regional, and national boundaries? To what extent—if at all—does the socialist period inflect claims made by contemporary "youth," the majority of whom were born after the triumphant return of "democracy" to the region?

As former and new centers pull and reshape local mediascapes, new aesthetic projects are generated that provide a window onto regional issues of change and continuity. In Southeastern Europe, one significant trend has been toward the self-conscious hybridization of global recording studio aesthetics with local folkloric genres to create commercial "pop-folk" genres (see Buchanan 2007). Often analyzed as promoting a postnational "Balkan" identity (Rice 2002; Apostolov 2010), remixed genres tell the story of how local subjects are creatively reshaping geographically grounded senses of identity in the face of destabilizing social change. Long imagined in Balkanist discourse as irretrievably "Other" (Todorova 1997; Sulstarova 2006), local subjects in this narrative strategically transmute the handicap of their essential alterity into a point from which they might access a vernacular, "Balkan" modernity. This framework does not, however, account for the widespread adoption of global pop styles, and especially rock, metal, dance, or hip hop musics. As former members of Europe's so-called "captive nations," Eastern Europeans have most recently been framed not only as Others within Balkanist discourses, but as objects of alterity within a Cold War–era ordering of the globe into competing and mutually incommensurable "worlds" (Pletsch 1981). The seemingly pressing need to imaginatively exit the Second World animates these young musicians' strategic mimicries, and their faithful reproductions of global styles represent deeply felt claims to membership in a post-socialist order.

And here exists an avenue for putting the "post-" of post-socialism in dialogue with its counterpart in postcolonialism (cf. Chari and Verdery 2009). In an essay that surveys literature on postcolonial practices of mimesis, and which inspires this coda's heading, James Ferguson (2008) examines the uneasiness with which scholars of colonial and postcolonial Africa have approached "the cultural other" who wants to become "like us." Such scholarship, Ferguson writes, has tended to frame mimetic cultural practices as sites of covert resistance and subversion. In seeking to unearth a deeper logic undergirding these mimetic practices, well-intentioned scholars often overlook how these local practices constitute claims to rights in a global order that has excluded and, in many cases, continues to exclude, entire populations in economic, ideological, diplomatic, and political terms (2008:559–561). As in postcolonial Africa, so too in post-socialist Eastern Europe? In forgoing localizing or indigenizing practices, the hip hoppers described in this chapter pursue a musical technique shared more widely by "post-" subjects who refuse engagement with "local" forms they understand to be tainted by association with the recent past—whether socialist, colonialist, or nationalist (cf. Luvaas 2009; Shipley 2012). Rappers' cosmopolitan practices in Eastern Europe thus might be located within a broader range of projects concerned with making sense of the present, as the local adoption of global music style enables young people to negotiate and experience membership within and across newly "post-" worlds.

NOTES

1. Research for this chapter was conducted in 2004–2005 with funding from the IIE Fulbright Program, with subsequent research in 2009–2010 funded by an American Council of Learned Societies East European Dissertation Research Fellowship. Portions of this chapter were previously submitted to Stony Brook University's Department of Music as an MA thesis and presented at the Mid-Atlantic Chapter of the Society for Ethnomusicology meeting at the College of William and Mary in 2007. I gratefully acknowledge the attendees at this conference, thesis readers Jane C. Sugarman and Frederick Moehn, and students in my 2013 Global Pop seminar at Tufts University for helpful comments on this project during its various stages.

2. This chapter focuses on Albanian speakers living in (and moving between) the nation-state of Albania and economic migration, especially in Greece. On the experiences of Albanian speakers in Kosovo and Macedonia, see Sugarman 2007, 2010.

3. Ethnographies of how marginal groups strategically adopt and adapt "global culture"—examined through the keywords "creolization," "domestication," "hybridization," "indigenization," or "localiz[ation]" (Appadurai 1996; Hannerz 1996; Rommen 2007; Slobin 1993; Solomon 2005)—have pointed to the resistance-based politics of hybrid musical practices. My argument, in contrast, is informed by the neologism "delocalization," as described by Luvaas (2009) in regard to Indonesian indie pop, a process by which musicians "use transnational aesthetics to challenge existing constructions of locality," seeking to "shed the old skin of placehood . . . and replace [it] instead with a reconstituted version of the local, constructed out of global pop culture resources" (248–249).

4. See http://www.kavajaonline.com/forumi/topic/2277-hip-hop/page__st__10 (accessed March 22, 2013).

5. Albanian hip hop video clips are widely available online. This video clip and the clips discussed below can be found on YouTube and several Albanian-language sites. In most cases, the musicians or production companies themselves upload this content.

References

Alim, H. Samy. 2009. "Translocal Style Communities: Hip Hop Youth as Cultural Theorists of Style, Language, and Globalization." *Pragmatics* 19(1):103–127.

Apostolov, Apostol. 2010. "The Highs and Lows of Ethno-Cultural Diversity: Young People's Experiences of Chalga Culture in Bulgaria." *Anthropology of East Europe Review* 26(1):85–97.

Appadurai, Arjun. 1996. *Modernity at Large: Cultural Dimensions of Globalization*. Minneapolis: University of Minnesota Press.

Archer, Rory. 2012. "Assessing Turbofolk Controversies: Popular Music between the Nation and the Balkans." *Southeastern Europe* 36(2):178–207.

Beissinger, Margaret. 2007. "Muzica Orientals: Identity and Popular Culture in Postcommunist Romania." In *Balkan Popular Culture and the Ottoman Ecumene: Music, Image, and Regional Political Discourse*, ed. Donna Buchanan (pp. 95–142). Lanham, MD: Scarecrow.

Buchanan, Donna. 1996. "Wedding Musicians, Political Transition, and National Consciousness in Bulgaria." In *Retuning Culture: Musical Changes in Central and Eastern Europe*, ed. Mark Slobin (pp. 200–230). Durham, NC: Duke University Press.

Buchanan, Donna, ed. 2007. *Balkan Popular Culture and the Ottoman Ecumene: Music, Image, and Regional Political Discourse*. Lanham, MD: Scarecrow.

Burawoy, Michael, and Katherine Verdery, eds. 1999. *Uncertain Transition: Ethnographies of Change in the Post-Socialist World*. New York: Rowman & Littlefield.

Çaro, Erka. 2012. "Winners or Losers? The Adjustment Strategies of Rural-to-Urban Migrants in Tirana, Albania. *Journal of Ethnic and Migration Studies* 39(3):501–519.

Chari, Shari, and Katherine Verdery. 2009. "Thinking between the Posts: Postcolonialism, Post-Socialism, and Ethnography after the Cold War. *Comparative Studies in Society and History* 51(1):6–34.

Condry, Ian. 2006. *Hip Hop Japan: Rap and the Paths of Cultural Globalization*. Durham, NC: Duke University Press.

Davies, John. (2009). *"My Name Is Not Natasha": How Albanian Women in France Use Trafficking to Overcome Social Exclusion*. Amsterdam: Amsterdam University Press.

Eisenberg, Andrew J. 2012. "Hip Hop and Cultural Citizenship on Kenya's 'Swahili Coast.'" *Africa* 82(4):556–578.

Ferguson, James. 2008. "Of Mimicry and Membership: Africans and the 'New World Society.'" *Cultural Anthropology* 17(4):551–569.

Forman, Murray. 2002. *The 'Hood Comes First: Race, Space, and Place in Rap and Hip-Hop*. Middletown, CT: Wesleyan University Press.

Hall, Stuart. 1993. "The Local and the Global: Globalization and Ethnicity." In *Culture, Globalization and the World-System: Contemporary Conditions for the Representation of Identity*, ed. Anthony D. King (pp. 19–39). Minneapolis: University of Minnesota Press.

Hannerz, Ulf. 1996. *Transnational Connections: Culture, People, Places*. New York: Routledge.

Jowitt, Kenneth. 1992. *New World Disorder: The Leninist Extinction*. Berkeley: University of California Press.

Kajsiu, Blendi. 2010. "'Down with Politics!' The Crisis of Representation in Post-Communist Albania." *East European Politics & Societies* 24(2):229–253.

Kennedy, Michael. 1994. *Envisioning Eastern Europe: Postcommunist Cultural Studies.* Ann Arbor: University of Michigan Press.

King, Russel, Nicola Mai, and Stephanie Schwandner-Sievers, eds. 2005. *The New Albanian Migration.* Brighton: Sussex Academic Press.

Luvaas, Brent. 2009. "Dislocating Sounds: The Deterritorialization of Indonesian Indie Pop." *Cultural Anthropology* 24(2):246–279.

Mai, Nicola. 2001. "'Italy Is Beautiful': The Role of Italian Television in Albanian Migration to Italy." In *Media and Migration: Constructions of Mobility and Difference,* ed. Russell King and Nancy Wood (pp. 95–109). New York: Routledge.

Mazzarella, William. 2004. "Culture, Globalization, Mediation." *Annual Review of Anthropology* 33:345–367.

Nixon, Nicola. 2010. "Always Already European: The Figure of Skënderbeg in Contemporary Albanian Nationalism." *National Identities* 12(1):1–20.

Perman, Tony. 2012. "Sungura in Zimbabwe and the Limits of Cosmopolitanism." *Ethnomusicology Forum* 21(3):372–401.

Perullo, Alex. 2005. "Hooligans and Heroes: Youth Identity and Hip Hop in Dar Es Salaam, Tanzania." *Africa Today* 51(4):75–101.

Perullo, Alex. 2011. *Live from Dar Es Salaam: Popular Music and Tanzania's Music Economy.* Bloomington: Indiana University Press.

Pletsch, Carl. 1981. "The Three Worlds, or the Division of Social Scientific Labor, circa 1950–1975." *Comparative Studies in Society and History* 23(4):565–590.

Rice, Timothy. 2002. "Bulgaria or Chalgaria? The Attenuation of Bulgarian Nationalism in a Mass-Mediated Popular Music." *Yearbook for Traditional Music* 34:25–46.

Rommen, Timothy. 2007. "'Localize It': Rock, Cosmopolitanism, and the Nation in Trinidad." *Ethnomusicology* 51(3):371–401.

Saltmarshe, David. 2001. *Identity in a Post-Communist Balkan State: An Albanian Village Study.* London: Ashgate.

Schwandner-Sievers, Stephanie. 2008. "Albanians, Albanianism and the Strategic Subversion of Stereotypes." *Anthropological Notebooks* 14(2):47–64.

Shipley, Jesse W. 2012. "The Birth of Ghanaian Hiplife. In *Hip Hop Africa: New African Music in a Globalizing World,* ed. Eric Charry (pp. 29–56). Bloomington: Indiana University Press.

Simić, Andrei. 1973. *The Peasant Urbanites: A Study of Rural-Urban Mobility in Serbia.* New York: Seminar Press.

Slobin, Mark. 1993. *Subcultural Sounds: Micromusics of the West.* Middletown, CT: Wesleyan University Press.

Solomon, Thomas. 2005. "'Listening to Istanbul': Imagining Place in Turkish Rap Music." *Studia Musicologica Norvegica* 31:46–67.

Stokes, Martin. 2007. "On Musical Cosmopolitanism." Macalester International Roundtable, paper 3. http://digitalcommons.macalester.edu/intlrdtable/3.

Sugarman, Jane C. 1999. "Mediated Albanian Musics and the Imagining of Modernity. In *New Countries, Old Sounds? Cultural Identity and Social Changes in Southeastern Europe,* ed. Bruno Reuer (pp. 134–154). Munich: Verlag Südostdeutsches Kulturwerk.

Sugarman, Jane C. 2007. "'The Criminals of Albanian Music': Albanian Commercial Folk Music and Issues of Identity since 1990." In *Balkan Popular Culture and the Ottoman Ecumene: Music, Image, and Regional Political Discourse,* ed. Donna Buchanan (pp. 269–307). Lanham, MD: Scarecrow.

Sugarman, Jane C. 2010. "Kosova Calls for Peace: Song, Myth, and War in an Age of Global Media." In *Music and Conflict,* ed. John Morgan O'Connell and Salwa Castelo-Branco (pp. 17–45). Champaign: University of Illinois Press.

Sulstarova, Enis. 2006. *Arratisje nga Lindja: Orientalizmi Shqiptar nga Naimi te Kadareja* [Escape from the East: Albanian Orientalism from Naim to Kadare]. Chapel Hill, NC: Globic Press.

Tochka, Nicholas. 2013. "Voicing Freedom, Sounding Dissent: Popular Music, Simulation and Citizenship in Democratizing Albania, 1991–1997." *European Journal of Cultural Studies* 17(3):298–315.

Todorova, Maria. 1997. *Imagining the Balkans.* New York: Oxford University Press.

Urla, Jacqueline. 2001. "'We Are All Malcolm X!': Negu Gorriak, Hip Hop, and the Basque Political Imaginary." In *Global Noise: Rap and Hip Hop Outside the U.S.A.,* ed. Tony Mitchell (pp. 171–193). Middletown, CT: Wesleyan University Press.

Vullnetari, Julie. 2012. *Albania on the Move: Links between Internal and International Migration.* Amsterdam: Amsterdam University Press.

FILMOGRAPHY

+355. 2004. "Edhe këtë verë" [video]. Tirana: Max Production.

Big Basta (Lyrics), Stine (Music). 2010. Bohu gati [Music video]. Tirana: Max Production.

Kallaku, B. 2012. "Eminemi i katunar've" [The Hillbillies' Eminem] [video]. Tirana: Loku Production.

Kallaku, B. (writer), and E. Isai (director). 2011. *Gjini: Takimi me Manushaqen* [Gjini: The date with Manushaqe] [internet short]. Tirana: Studio Pro Grishaj.

Kallaku, B. (lyrics and director), Stine (music), and E. Isai (director). 2011. "Katunari gangsta" [Gangsta Hillbilly] [video]. Tirana: Erandistic.

Mumajesi, F. (music), Big Basta (lyrics), and Çiljeta (vocals). 2009. "Déjà vu" [video]. Tirana: Supersonic Production.

DISCOGRAPHY

2Die4. 2001. *Jetës Sonë* [CD]. Tirana: Superstar Records.

2Die4. 2003. "Më pëlqen." *Thjeshtë Kuptojë* [CD]. Tirana: Superstar Records.

Crazy Girl. 2003. "Në rrugët e lagjës sime" [On my neighborhood's streets] [single].

G-Bani. 2004. *Midis meje dhe vet'vetës* [Between me and myself] [CD]. Tirana: BASS Records.

CHAPTER 10

VIOLENCE AS EXISTENTIAL PUNCTUATION

Russian Hip Hop in the Age of Late Capitalism

Alexandre Gontchar

I AM ABOUT to play a few tracks by contemporary Russian hip hop artists. I expect the usual mixture of crime, violence, profanity, and political critique; but what I hear blows my mind. This is nothing short of conceptual poetry.

> Never been to the States, don't really know how to do rap, don't smoke crack, don't wear a zoot suit, haven't sold a single track, haven't signed with anyone, and it looks that Method & Red don't know my body Eugene here. This here is no Backstreet Boy's Band. This here is an underground bang, get down my friend. I'm walking to a night club, snow under my feet. Tonight I am rapping and I have already packed up a few beers. The scene is twenty-first-century Chelyabinsk: nervous people are almost running; time passes slowly, as if it didn't exist.

In Triagrutika's "Big City Life," a voice with a recognizable Ural accent spins a story about carving out an authentic artistic identity by coming to grips with one's historicity and turning the facticity of concrete existence into a source of inspiration and philosophical reflection. But before I have time to ponder globalization and its discontents, or how to stop making love to one's ego-ideal and lead an authentic life, I am stunned by how the classic notion of epiphany is reworked in "Memory" by Krovostok, a contemporary Russian hip hop band.

If memory in this track is likened to "a Disneyland inside an Auschwitz on thin ice," visiting it brings the kind of insight one gets after have been "under the projector lights exploding the darkness," when "the ice is breaking, attractions are in full swing, and everything that happened shows up clearly, without any gaps." I would like to lament the information overload, fatal strategies of the postmodern, hyperreality, or dialectic of enlightenment, but this time it is Oxxximiron's triple rhyme "my fair maiden's saying no out of principle has killed my inner prince like a Gavrilo Princip" in "Gremlin's Song," which catches my attention. In a twenty-first-century reworking of Alexander Pushkin's "Conversation of a Poet with a Bookseller" (1824), the role of money in relation to the authenticity of one's art is now considered, but not in connection with the French Revolution and the onset of the bourgeois industrial age. The song becomes an extended meditation on the ethics of art production, on whether to join the ranks of mainstream hip hop or stay underground. The poet's life follows the plot of "*The Adventures of Neznaika* [Dunno][1] turned inside out like the dead body of a whore from *American Psycho*" as he recognizes himself as one of the aesthetes who "kept making up jargon without realizing that in the meantime they have been walking a Cerberus" and come to live during the time when "Russian rap is finally recognized . . . this subculture is developing like a tumor."

Much has changed since 1984, when DJ Alexander Astrov together with the electronic band Chas Pik (Rush Hour) presented their collective project *RAP* at a local discotheque in Samara, USSR. Throughout its nearly thirty-year history, Russian hip hop, and particularly its underground subgenre, has witnessed, against the backdrop of the increasing commercialization of the music scene, a growing diversification of its musical and performing styles; its social, political, and philosophical agendas; and its audience's demography. That the phenomenon of Russian hip hop has not been given the attention it merits is a fact. In this chapter I first sketch a history of Russian hip hop from its early days (1984–1995), through its formative period (1996–2001), into its "Open Era" (2002–present). Providing, where necessary, a brief overview of contemporary hip hop artists in Russia and the subgenres in which they work, I will focus my discussion of the formal style and thematic preoccupations of conceptual Russian gangsta rap texts, using the examples of Krovostok and N1NT3NDo.

In its early days, Russian hip hop, while by no means a uniform music phenomenon, favored the mode of artistic expression that is best described as "conceptual (re)presentation." Chas Pik, Sergei Minaev, Bogdan Titomir, Van Moo, MC Lika, and their like performed not so much the kind of music that would have been identified as rap music by an American audience, as displaying their *familiarity* with the stylistic and aesthetic principles operant in the records of their American counterparts, the diversity of whose generic membership can only be grasped by a term as broad as "electronic music."

Among the most important principles was a new vocabulary bound up with an imported ethos unknown to the late Soviet audience. Words like "hip hop" (*khip-khop*) and "showbiz" (*shoubiz*) now referred not only to the multidimensional reality of the music scene, but also to the imperatives to dress fashionably (*odevaisia kruto*) and look good (*vygliadi OK*). The type of identity conjured up by the early Russian hip hop artists was based on a consciousness of new cultural commandments, following which allowed a personal freedom, understood as a high degree of individuation made possible by distinguishing oneself from the crowd, an act fully conditioned by the crude "us versus them" binary. And whether the topic of conversation is sex, as in Malchishnik's *Let's Talk about Sex* (1992) and *Miss Large Breasts* (1993); or personal freedom understood in the absolute sense by a mind akin to that of a rebellious teenager, as in D.M.J.'s *This World Is Mine* (1993); or one's awareness of the social chaos residing in virtually every sphere of post-Soviet space, as in Bad Balance's *The Stick-Up Men* (1992), common to these works is what can be called an act of the context-generating "pointing out." While capable of emphasizing the connectedness of various elements comprising the human being-in-the-world and thus successfully reinstating the idea of the human subject as a desiring being, the kind of subjectivity appearing in most of the above texts is one that operates without a notion of the individual world as a unique existential space that reveals itself through unique metaphors and imagery.

The year 1996 marks the beginning of Russian hip hop's formative period, for in addition to the emergence of MC Del'fin (Dolphin), one of the finest poets of the Russian music scene to have ever appeared, D.O.B-Family, a music community came into being with such artists as K.T.L-D.L.L., Bust A.S.!, D.O.B., Raby Lampy (Slaves of the Lamp), and Slingshot. Del'fin's *Out of Focus* (1997) and *Depth* (1998), Mister Maloi's *Will Be Dying Young* (1995) and *Enjoy Your High* (1997), and Raby Lampy's *This Doesn't Hurt* (1998) collectively established the minimal set of existential parameters defining the persona of the lyrical hero in Russian hip hop, still a very young genre. Always self-absorbed, the new lyrical hero, by virtue of his dual nature as street fighter and a disillusioned romantic, finds inspiration in his "sickness unto death" in his incompatibility with the morass of the everyday. Living in a dog-eat-dog world, this new shape of artistic consciousness is doomed to solitude, alienation, and misunderstanding. Driven by the acute realization of its finitude, primarily mortality, it constantly seeks to "break on through to the other side," with suicide and consciousness-altering substances always at its disposal.

The impressive arsenal of artistic skills and devices available to these "riders on the storm" includes masterful creation of moods, exquisite choice of symbols that capture the fundamental structures of the human world, virtuoso use of language, and an unparallel ability to pull an emergency brake of time by losing oneself in a wild celebration of the very possibility of experiencing anything as anything, of being the very dynamic field of possibilities that a human being always is. And while the first two video clips of Russian hip hop have already been produced—Bad Balance's "Urban Ennui" (1996) and Del'fin's "Drug Dealer" (1997)—five more years will have to pass before the unhappy consciousness of the urban dweller becomes an important element of the poetics of life as an existential gamble taking place in one of Basta's texts "under the burden of the lead cupola, in the center of a colorless urban center."

By the time Kasta records the all-time best-selling album in the history of Russian hip hop—*Gromche vody, vyshe travy*[2] (Loud as the Grave, 2002)—two rap festivals (Rap Music, organized by Bad Balance since 1994, and MIKRO, run since 1998) will have become important cultural institutions. Russia will get on the map of the international hip hop community after entering the MTV charts, the tragic pathos percolating through virtually all texts of its hip hop performers giving way to Romantic irony and the flexibility of language games. One thing the Open Era artist will learn to do particularly well is to view their historicity as what gives access to the treasure trove of the Russian musical tradition as a source from which to draw inspiration for the unique creative response to the particular situation. And to this tradition the worldview of a lonely romantic taking a stand on his being according to the street commandments has always been important.

Their opposition to mainstream Russian hip hop is not what distinguishes the alternative dimension in the texts of artists like Krovostok, 2h Company, 25/17, Noganno, Krec, Oxxximiron, Rem Digga, and others. Rather, it is the subtlety with which they capture the complexity of human being-in-the-world and expose the strong spell of our illusive certainty in many aspects of what we are used to referring to as reality. Each in his unique way, these poets explore fundamental categories of human experience; uncover the complexity of relational networks behind the tension between the social and the individual; and offer a penetrating critique of modern society and its capitalist economy, the technology-driven dehumanization of the world, the brutal instrumentalism of science, and the lack of authenticity. And it is language itself that reveals in these texts a certain awareness of their facticity and the invisible presence of background practices that form the conditions of their possibility.

Already in their debut album, *Rivers of Blood* (2004), Krovostok presents its artistic manifesto and defines some of the key themes it will later elaborate in *Like an Exit Wound* (2006), *Dumbbell* (2008), and *Meat Jelly* (2012). Choosing a veteran gangster persona as a receptacle for the divine inspiration necessary to tell a good story, Krovostok builds on the tradition of estranging the political through what Dmitry Likhachev (1935) once dubbed the "tribal primitivism of criminal speech," which as stylistic device was most famously used in the linguistic experiments of Iuz Aleshkovskii in his samizdat novel *Nikolai Nikolaevich* (1970). Doing so allows the artist to foreground the opaqueness of the human subject's basis to itself as an epistemological constraint *necessary* for autonomy and self-creation.

The lyrical hero of "Biography," one of the debut album's tracks, remembers his life during the split second separating him from death, which Martin Heidegger (1962) defines as the "impossibility of any further possibility." His worldview

and life experience appear as lacking the complexity of character and sophistication of nature of the classical tragic hero, for what he remembers belongs to the
realm of the quotidian: "an evening at the riverbank, shish kebabs, Anna's blow-
job, my bros holding beer bottles," and "how nice it was in Havana: all those
sunsets, shorts, and palm trees." This banalization, however, is a conscious gesture, one not stemming from the creating artists' lack of skill or some inherent
limitation that belongs to the genre of Russian conceptual gangsta rap. Krovostok
sees depicting the peripeteia in the existential gamble of a nameless thug, who had
lived during the civil war–like chaos of 1990s Russia, possible only in view of having access to the language he spoke and to the worldview that informed his actions. And this is exactly what allows Krovostok an unprecedented power of character individuation in Russian hip hop. In "Biography," Krovostok tries to grasp
the protagonist's subjectivity by putting him in a liminal situation, when at the
limit of his of field of possibilities, he reveals in a final act of recollection the things
most dear to him.

When the two Makarov pistols pointing at him begin to look like the eyes of
his mother at the time of her burial in church, time slows down, so that before
spitting out three teeth on the concrete floor of the execution room, his blood filling his mouth inviting him to one last voyage, the dying hooligan remembers his
son, his first pair of boxing gloves, and his guardian angel. In this text, a gangsta
soldier does not die because this is what the conventions of the genre require.
Thrown into the melting pot of Russian history, he dies during the period when
the Russian state, already under Vladimir Putin's reign, begins to monopolize
violence, expropriating what was privatized under Boris Yeltsin's presidency. Re-
distributing their loot, yesterday's gangsters become tomorrow's deputies of the
Duma. What further stands out in this text—apart from its circular narrative
structure, virtuoso use of *fenia* (criminal argot), stream of consciousness used to
convey liminal events, and the comic strip vividness with which the story is told—
is the foregrounding of the factor of timeliness as the basis for historicity as a
horizon that always bounds personal identity.

Human identity appears here and in other Krovostok texts as always grounded
in history and networks of social relations. It appears as something more pri-
mordial than self-interpretation, namely something that is ontologically prior to
it, as something always enclosing one's self-conscious mode of self-writing in the
form of narrative. Personal identity thus appears in Krovostok texts as a "flickering
in the enclosed circuits of historical," something that accounts for "why the prejudices of the individual, far more than his judgments, constitute the historical
reality of his being" (Gadamer 1975:245). As human beings, we are pre-reflectively
sensitive to possibilities of action that we see in a polarized perceptual field as in
a field of action, so that a "host of signs which guide action" (Merleau-Ponty
1962:112) is constantly brought into view. In their exploration of the gangster-

self, Krovostok remains mindful of these epistemological scruples throughout their entire investigation.

The worldview of the lyrical hero belongs to the "anti-world" of Russian prison subculture, a culture that had for a long time used visual representation in the form of tattoos—a few of which the protagonist of "Biography" has and to which he refers as "souvenirs from the North"—as a technology of political resistance. Tattoos' vivid imagery and the arcane symbolism involved in the production of meaning both seem to warrant this view, for the extension of the site of struggle at the level of social language to the body of the outcast, and the symbolic repossession of identity possible through the mobility of the sign emphasize transformation via the (re)signification of the convict's body. And yet these objections to the dominant culture, stated as poignant political messages, engage in a struggle of discourses at the level of signs and thus fall short of political action. Far from being an exotic means of carving the inmate's alternative identity, the tattoo appropriates it only to sustain the rigid hierarchy within the criminal world itself, strengthening its structural integrity all the more.

Krovostok's choice of the lyrical persona as a social outcast is particularly successful, because the question becomes not whether political resistance is a valid category within an interpretive framework through which to study tattooing as a mechanism to oppose social, political, and cultural exclusion of the inmates by the state, but whether one's actions are, in principle, capable of ripping oneself out of the fabric of power in a way that can overcome the (inter)subjective character of any identity.

It would seem that as reactionary, not subversive, the body-marking practices aimed at establishing an alternative discursive field that would traverse the dominant discursive power did little besides impeding political action. Despite the rich gallery of visual images at their disposal, the inmates, their hegemonic vision dependent on opposition to the state, acted within the boundaries and via the means of the dominant ideology. Theirs, it seems, was the triumph of the sign. And here is exactly where Krovostok offers another account of history, another model of self-creation.

Krovostok's "fluid bodies" make it clear that insofar as the convicts' bodies were involved as visual sites of dissent, the practice of political resistance took place not through the production of the visual signs seeking to deny the figures of authority through the grotesque subversion of the immutability of some political holy of holies. Rather, essential to their technology of resistance was presentation of the body as a site of an ongoing artistic creation that used hybrid semantic codes to establish meaning. This stressing of the fluidity of the body, of its continual change from crystallized closed entities to a dissolution into the less stabilized experience characteristic of human identity, jarred significantly with the tenets of the positivist platform of Soviet science.

Dmitry Likhachev's pioneering effort to bring to light the peculiarities of the criminal worldview suggests that its key element is a resurrection of the magic attitude toward the word and dependence upon superstition, the remnants of the tribal magic consciousness (1935:60). While more recent accounts of the worldview behind the highly complex and nuanced codes of meaning (Condee 1999; Plutser-Sarno 2003a, 2003b, 2004; Schrader 2000) managed to eschew the shortcomings of Likhachev's "imperial" anthropological method, they did little in the way of conceptualizing the category of political resistance in terms of science's foundational epistemology.

Because science still to a large degree depends on the presupposition that what it approaches is homogeneous and is subject to universal and necessary laws, it also presupposes that the principle or force behind the individual entities comprising the world of appearances simply informs these entities so that they are understood by us as having been created for a particular end. According to Michael B. Foster (1935, 1936), this idea goes back to the double vision of the relationship between God and the world that first originated in Plato and had since then been selectively incorporated into Christian theology and modern science. This confusion between a god that relates to the world as the creating Demiurge and a god that does so as father to son, also sustained by Aristotle in the manufacture/generation distinction in his philosophy of nature, is at the core of how science had for a long time approached nature and living things. Unlike in the case of *artificial production*, in *generation*, the author imparts his productive power to his offspring, but does not supply intelligibility to it in the form of some embodied concept as an artificer does to an artifice.

In view of this move of the modern natural sciences to present nature as a self-generating system, the functioning of whose living entities can be deciphered through observation of different concepts embodied in it as in some multifunctional artifice, the convict's body as a site of a self-creating identity that resurrected the generation element in the disenchanted world of Soviet positivism was a big problem. Linking tattoos and transgression with the creation of a "second skin" by Soviet prisoners, Krovostok sees both as acts of political resistance centered on the reenchantment of the world around them, one that now argued for the existence of God and his presence as a power of self-creation.

Mindful of the fact that the poetics of the self that had originated under the auspices of Russian rock adds the antisocial attitude and heroic pathos of the Russian chanson—*blatnaya pesnia* (prison songs) marketed en masse—and is estranged through a stance of epistemological skepticism, Krovostok has the protagonist of "Biography" risk his life to be free. Having accidentally killed a Gypsy woman during a major drug-trade operation, he gets a 15-year sentence, which he is to serve somewhere in the north. Having escaped from the courtroom with a partner, they hide in the forest, where, according to prison lore, one of the two must taste human flesh and escape, first by boarding a freight train and then by hitchhiking all the way to Moscow, where his "bros" will get him a new identity.

Within the artistic worldview containing this as a folded generic script, the role of suffering is also reassessed, and it now has to do with the Russian soul even less than with the Aristotelian *kairos* (the right moment for total transformation) or Kierkegaardian *Augenblick* (the blink of an eye—a fleeting, epoch-making moment). Krovostok's gangster is never at home in the world because not to be at home in the world is constitutive of what the artists see as being human. Equally essential to being human is embodying a temporal structure whose point of access to reality lies in an absorbed coping with entities in the world, and whose narratives are often punctuated by multiple scenes of graphic violence, many of which serve as a metaphor for the human always being pressed into concrete and limited possibilities.

But if ripping oneself out of the structure of power relations is difficult, even more so is not becoming a prisoner of virtual reality, especially in view of the abundance of mind-altering substances and the countless hours that could be lost at the Play Station. The interpenetration of the real and the imaginary is shown as belonging to the human as it is explored in "Lobster-Pizza." Here, the protagonist, while high on weed and coke and having anal sex with a minor, showers with bullets from the Uzis he is holding in each hand the cops who appear at his door, together with the witnesses, whom the evil neighbors call just to frame him. "White Jaguar," the last track from Krovostok's debut album, takes the exploration of the interaction of how real and imaginary interact in a different direction, away from the solipsistic captivity into which a freely creating consciousness so often falls.

In "White Jaguar," the entire narrative unfolds according to the logic of a 3D first-person shooter like Doom, Duke Nukem 3D, Quake, and others whose popularity peaked during the 1990s, but with nowhere near the intensity of violence that accompanied the statewide redistribution of government property freed after the fall of the USSR in 1991 and the (re)mapping of the terrain of "business" influence within the slumbering economic market. After arriving at the enemy's castle, the protagonist kills each of the villains inside with a different weapon, avenging the death of his close friend, whose head the rival gang delivers to him shortly before his "ascent," together with the money to exchange for the drugs he has.

The bringing to ruin of the citadel of evil functions as a powerful metaphor, not because it thematizes the dematerializing experience of graphic violence that abounds in, among others, Alexei Balabanov's *Brat 2* (2000), Jim Jarmusch's *Ghost Dog: The Way of the Samurai* (1999) and *Limits of Control* (2009), or David Cronenberg's *History of Violence* (2005) *and History of Violence* (2007), but because in centers on the protagonist's *misrecognition* of the world around him as an entity separate from and opposing him. The endless succession of villains threatening to take his life functions here as a symbol of the paralyzing fear of losing the

"mineness" of what is experienced, of being a walking zombie, a blind conform-
ist shaped by the totality of background practices, which, while itself remaining
invisible, serves as basis for the intelligibility of the world.

In "Fuck Ups," it is the authenticity that has to be wrestled away from "the
others" in an uneven street fight among several thugs, whose mutual realization
that they are not and cannot be all reality is the minimal form of self-consciousness
required for the formation of the public realm. Thus the realization of the defeat-
ing nature of the death struggle in which these consciousnesses are interlocked—
there cannot be self-consciousness without life because slaying the other does not
give me what I want (to be recognized)—brings about a triumphant master (our
protagonist who wins the fight) and his slaves (every thug he has vanquished in
the uneven battle in the parking lot). But inasmuch as our protagonist would like
to conceive of himself as the master of his future—that is, someone who by voluntarily embracing the anxiety of death as a condition for having an authentic
identity begins to determine the course of history—his is a position of dominance
in what is essentially an animal kingdom.

Because he sees the limitation of others' freedom as an act preventing them
from limiting his freedom, he too is a slave who, for the most part, is living an
inauthentic life. The interrelation of a plurality of individuals so that they can be
a universal community without losing the possibility of individual existence for
its members requires, at the very least, morality as a self-consciousness that knows
duty to be of its essence, and not the existence of self-consciousness simply aware
of other self-consciousnesses. Insofar as the slave is recognized not as a person
but as a thing, the master is outside the empirical realm of personhood, and thus
becomes a mere slave of death as the ultimate master. The fundamental structure
of self-consciousness that lies in its internal duality, which the (de)centering of
the self by the other brings, appears in "Fuck Ups" as a space for the crudest kind
of differentiation of the "I-self" (a particular individual) from the contingent historical "anybody-self" (a person as a mere embodiment of cultural practices of
his time) that forms via voluntary aberration from the totality of existing normative claims regulating the everyday. The struggle for authenticity measured as a
degree of aberration from the "publicness that primarily controls every way in
which the world and human beings get interpreted and it is always right" (Heidegger 1962:165) is worked out in more detail in Krovostok's second album, *Like
an Exit Wound,* in the tracks "Stool Sample," "Croaking," and "Blue Sky."

The first track celebrates the protagonist's changing understanding of the
meaning of the stool sample he is carrying to the lab at his local hospital. What
he first regards as merely a hunk of matter appears at the end of his mediation as
a symbol of the dehumanized facelessness of the average understanding of human
life, one to which normativity as a totality of existing practices tends to reduce
individuality to sustain itself. The comfort of the inconspicuous familiarity in

which one finds oneself when living out one's life according to some (pre)recorded script turns out to be exactly what precludes every possibility for a self to be individualized down to itself. High on weed, the protagonist reminisces about his past happiness, and then goes through a list of 49 professions that could have been his. But because choosing any one of them would be equivalent to voluntarily accepting a beheading by the homogenizing force of the operant background practices, he pulls the trigger and liberates his "utmost ability to be."

In "Croaking," an equally impressive list of ways to leave the world of human concern is given. Multiple points of human exit seem to chart the domain of the average understanding of being. The inevitable interruption of our involvement with the world that death brings mixes different genres and registers. Official formulations of the cause of death, lifted directly from a death certificate, merge with instances of free indirect speech of someone who, during the funeral, describes the deceased as "having died so unnaturally young," and with comparing the intensity of dying to the grimace of hate that distorts the countenance of a hungry fighting pit bull during its last seconds.[3] Stories of the unremarkable exit of star musicians such as Jimmy Hendrix, John-Paul Jones, and Bon Scott are interspersed with more subtle references, including one to the exiled Russian writer Ivan Alekseevich Bunin, who dies filled with the sour juice of the Antonovka.[4] Death appears here as a kind of limit, as one of the guises of determinate negation that undermines the rigidity of any categorical sets, like that of contemporary literary criticism that still often resorts to the "high art versus mass art" binary. One's freedom of self-creation is possible only in view of the intelligibility and meaning preexisting in the world, both of which are bound up with human finitude that seems to turn the indeterminacy that every human is into a human "capacity" for "existential content," so that a narrative of one's life as a project can be written.

From the opening stanza, starting with a summary of what constitutes human essence borrowed from the now cult apocalyptic *Planet of the Apes* (1968)—"Alone among God's primates, he kills for sport, or lust, or greed"—"Blue Sky" is a comic strip–style narrative of a criminal battle for territorial control that does not go as planned. Its visuality amplified by using only four verbs (attack, die, split, heal) to render climactic scenes, the story, while making references to Quentin Tarantino's *Reservoir Dogs* (1992) and Aleksei Balabanov's *Dead Man's Bluff* (2006), demystifies the romantic aura surrounding the Russian gangsta of the 1990s by stressing the artifice of the imagery each of its individual panels contains.

The protagonist here is not a human person but a contingent discursive formation whose elements come together as in the form of a collage, an assembly of products and actions that have been associated with the Russian gangster starting from the 1990s. "Blue Sky" lacks the individuating power of dialogue of *Reservoir Dogs,* whose Mr. Brown ventures a nuanced psychological interpretation of Madonna's "Like a Virgin" and Mr. Pink expounds his no-tip social philoso-phy. Nowhere to be found is the precision with which Balabanov shows the carnage that followed the redistribution of state property during the turbulent 1990s as a killing frenzy of a total blind fire, in which every man seeking power in Russia was involved. "Blue Sky" suggests simulacrum as gangsta's *only* reality, stressing the void behind the system of meaning-generating symbols of the Russian gangster subculture.

It is also on this track that a ubiquitous Grand Cherokee, the archetypal Rus-sian gangster-mobile of the 1990s, merges with a black Brabus, not unlike the one in which contemporary hip hop artists like UGO, during the late 2000s, drove around to collect what was theirs, into a single gangsta-mobile. Using hybridiza-tion to accentuate the structural importance of the gangsta-mobile, Krovostok posits the Russian gangsta as a mixture of reality and fiction, emphasizing its quality as a repository of associations always already invented by the others. Six years later, in "Boys," the gangsta subject will reappear, not as a totality of cul-tural signs that shape it, but as a selfless heap of physical remains associated with concrete historical individuals. But because each of the body parts comprising the heap seems to capture the essence of the gangsta to whom it belonged before be-ing killed with a rocket launcher, Krovostok stresses an archeology of knowledge that always approaches the question of the meaning of being on the ontic and ontological levels.

Among the more complex and original philosophical intuitions of the band is experimentation with verbs of motion that allows us to ask whether it suffices, in describing the way humans are and what can be thought to constitute experience, to distinguish between differentiation and differentiated, or between consciousness and its object. And whether what mediates between the two realms is "an un-known root of sensibility and reason," "will," "background practices," or "the communicative function of language," this entity, according to Krovostok, al-ways ends up laying a claim to being a center of meaning, some kind of absolute. The phenomenological thematization of the gangsta by Krovostok emphasizes a vision of the world as a *hierarchy of differentiated elements*. Thus, on the one hand, the deconstruction of the props used to create existential space in "Blue Sky" ap-pears as a critique of *intellectualism,* particularly of its tendency to approach the world as a synthetic whole "made" by "the subject" from the surrounding "ob-jects." On the other hand, this kind of deconstruction brings our attention to the fact that we always find ourselves in some polarized space where things already have meaning and significance, and where some things but not others are seen as worth doing.

In *Dumbbell.* the grotesque estrangement of the gangster begins not only to target the existential predicament of man, but also to expose some elements from the ideology of contemporary bourgeois society. The ethos of contemporary nihilism in "S(ex).M(oney).W(eed)" from the album reveals a daring *Übermensch*, a Steppenwolf ready to die just to continue to lead a life in the absence of which pleasure becomes as distant as "a minaret on the North Pole." In "H(allucinogen s).E(uphoriants).S(timulants)," drug use, if prescribed, ceases to be a practice authenticating one's marginality and becomes a way to suggest suppression as one of the principal mechanisms to maintain the stability of Russia's social function, turning people's attention away from the rapid deterioration of traditional values and stigmatization of deviance.

Several lines of criticism directed at the now increasingly popular decision by young people to start a family only after reaching some carrier milestone, at not being able to take proper care of one's parents and not being willing to care for them, and at the paralyzing fear people have of the ostracism they will have to withstand if they reject the product consumption–based model of human equality. The minimalist refrain reminiscent of the crudeness of the punk lyrics that originated in the UK in the 1970s and its naïve political agenda captures the complexity of the real as a list of three things that everyone in society is expected to do blindly to avoid possible inconvenience: "to hell with children, pitch the old folk, and send everybody else to the asylum." A variety of distraction strategies is available, according to Krovostok, to the contemporary individual. One can participate in a new religious movement such as Scientology, or discover one's physical limits through extreme fitness programs, or lose oneself for hours on end in various social networks, or go to BDSM private clubs, or plan another vacation trip, or talk about the meaning of life in blogs, and many more. These socially accepted ways to escape the existential angst are effective, however, only to a degree, as they leave one with only three real answers. Personal freedom is shown here as a freedom to chose among hallucinogens, euphoriants, and stimulants (H.E.S), which are the three proofs that "paradise fits inside a medicine bag."

Virtually all the tracks on their latest album, *Meat Jelly* (2012), use violence and mass art material as a medium for philosophical reflection. "Countryside" tells how one can never fully get away from the past. The protagonist ends up having to face his demons, which appear in the form of a wolf that grows out of the puppy he adopts just after migrating to the village to escape the madness of big-city life. A messenger from the past, the wolf attacks the protagonist in a barn where he is feeding a calf, putting an abrupt end to his idyllic lifestyle. Central to human existence as shown in this track is a succession of various guises of fleeing or activities aimed at not having to confront the indeterminacy of one's being in the world.[5] Of equal importance is the existential predicament of having to always carry the "sediment" of one's past within one's present. And when the darkness subsides and one sees his entire past as an uncanny structure like "a Disneyland inside an Auschwitz on thin ice," as in "Memory," the weight of the existential guilt associated with it is far too heavy a burden to simply equate it with another source of artistic originality. It appears instead as a traumatic event forcing one to seek solace in the endless diffusion of its memory through the signification afforded by the multiple activities drawing our attention to their average everydayness.

In (re)creating the mood of a killer who, before torturing his victims, recites a nursery rhyme, whose line *"pizdosevich, pizdosian, nalik ili smert' ot ran"* cleverly puns on the less than promising future awaiting him who refuses to pay cash, for the spectacle of his end (*pizdets*) will organically comprise the brutality with which the Soviet serial murderer Gennady Mikhasevich disposed of his victims and the brilliance and wit of Soviet standup comedy legend Evgenii Petrosian. And since the gangster-protagonist describes a vase with flowers that he sees in the apartment of his victim, where he is having some tea before the interrogation, the artifice of the text and the narrative it contains both become accentuated. The story of a gangsta who comes "to collect" is created as if by accident; it is an unexpected fruit of some "aberrant" mind wondering on and off about the still life (vase with flowers) it originally sets out to paint. A hymn to violence, the gangster's sadistic rapture contains within it an important question from the field of narrative ethics, one that posits the human subject as an eternal battleground between the self- and other-attributed subject position, which makes every artist, if reluctantly, an ideologue of his worldview, no matter how dogmatic its central tenets are.

In its popular adaptation, the ubiquitous corporate philosophy of the self that hinges on little other than the empty optimism of humanistic psychology, which first originated in the work of Carl Rogers, is lambasted in "Think Positively." Here the protagonist can only recite a series of meaningless "success mantras" that urge equanimity in view of human "life being a dance under the vigilant eye of a solicitous god." Yet when "painkillers don't help anymore," when one has finally "scalped people to get an elite wig," "robbed the elderly," and ventured beyond good and evil, one enters the nightmare of seeing life and all of its ideals as a single "still frame showing a lollypop stuck to a human corpse."

Written in an amphibrachic trimeter, "Vegetable" depicts the modern subject as a dynamic pattern of random reactions to a current of sensory stimuli. Rendered as fragmentary, the subject's experience is confined to the unceasing bombardment of consciousness by mass media with a host of transgressive meanings that infect one's mind like viral organisms do one's body. Its sense of agency denied, the subject now appears as a mere totality of various institutional practices, as a structure lacking the interiority of a human being. The subject becomes instead the very electric current underlying the transmission of the sequence of news and gossip with which human attention is dissipated. Finally, "Stung" describes a train of thought that runs through the head of a 13-year-old who has just captured a massive booty, having double-crossed his partners in crime. Before he is shot to death by the police who have been involved in the operation all alone, the massive sum of money because of which everyone dies is presented as a symbol of the temptation of reason and how it sees intersubjectivity, and also as one of the avatars of the collective id of capitalist society.

The infinite wealth appears as an illusion of an infinite ability-to-be. Here the radical indeterminacy of an existing self has apparently been turned into the radical indeterminacy of an omnipotent being. This dream of existing within the social fabric in an unlimited number of ways now claims to have shaken off the yoke of being radically dependent on the other: it posits money as a symbol of the social in the form of a space of people's radical dependency on one another with the overcoming of the (inter)subjectivity of the self. The face mask the bank robber wears during the act does not so much conceal his true identity as reveal his blindness to the radical dependency on the other as a fundamental feature of himself. His (mis)recognition of the other within himself defaces his human persona. His new facelessness now is the new type of sociality he creates for himself, one that belongs to the mimicry of the social embeddedness to which he is doomed as a fugitive.

In his clip "Giv mi mani," NiNT3NDo, one of the stage personae of Vasilii Vakulenko—also known as Basta or Noggano—estranges money by depicting it not as an invisible adhesive of the social or the weightless smoke of human (inter) subjectivity, but as a narrative center, a master signifier of contemporary hip hop narratives. Making visual references to Konstantin Buslov's *Dough* (2011), itself a fine philosophical study of the old Russian idiom *"Million ne delitsia"* (Can't divide a million),"[6] it strives together with "Mama I'm a Criminal" and "Confiscated" to capture the sequence of the computer-spun algorithms behind the persona of a Russian gangsta. In many Russian criminal fictions there lurks a romantic echo of a self-imposed fate, central to which is the idea of Christian martyrdom, which also resurfaces in the form of amour-propre, a kind of self-love that depends on the opinions of others and often underlies a secret pleasure one gets from watching others recognize one's wretchedness during a confession. This pleasure inhering in one's stoic acceptance of punishment that is invariably brought about because of someone's unexpected betrayal, NiNT3NDo explores as a grand narrative of Russian gangsta and examines as a metastructure of its self-consciousness. Especially important here is that money promises completeness and self-sufficiency, seducing reason to believe in the possibility of an (un)finalizable futural projection within the field of concrete "earthly" possibilities. Expensive cars, beautiful companions, and wealth become symbols of an infinite ability to be which the Russian gangsta worships, of a beyond to which he strives to get in order to be reconciled with his "true essence."

A tongue-in-cheek commentary on the structure of power in contemporary Russia, "Otmeli" (Confiscated) features in its title a neologism consisting of the verbs *otymet'* (to fuck somebody up) and *mesti* (to sweep). NiNT3NDo does not just point to the economic marketplace as a place where the poor are devoured by the rich, but suggests that the true source of the conflict between Mikhail Khodorkovsky[7] (who appears in this track as Mishka the banker) and President Vladimir Putin is not limited to a mere conflict of individual wills. Instead, N1NT3NDo sees two different and clashing visions of Russia's future: one in which the sovereign state is ruled by the council of Russian oligarch-princes and another according to which it is simply turned into a transnational corporation. Using Vladislav Surkov's[8] term "sovereign democracy" (*suverennaia demokratiia*) as justification for any type of coercive measures directed at individuals to weaken the extent to which Russia can be engaged in global economic processes without the control of the state, the government apparatus, stressing how much it values the country's history and tradition, cloaks the present in the mantle of Russia's glorious past. Doing so allows the state to justify its actions, but also recycles some formulas from the past in which to pack the existing state of affairs. The rhetoric of Russia's economic liberation hinges on the memory of dependency from time of the Golden Horde, thus urging every citizen to partake in the collective act of sacrifice and withstand whatever privations may come. Yet Putin himself plays a double role, for he is connected through his name to Tsar Vladimir the Great, under whose rule Rus' entered the Christian world in 988,[9] while acting as Russia's own Chengiz Khan, overseeing the flow of resources in the elaborate system of tribute payment within Russia.

Unlike Vakulenko's first alter ego, Basta, the emotionally estranged street fighter of Russian *urbana* (urban city), whose poetic sensibility organically coexists with the ethical values of Soviet prison, and unlike his second, Noggano, whose criminal background allows him to exchange letters in the form of hip hop tracks with a fellow artist, Siava, as if the two were Russian thieves in law[10] (*vory v zakone*) serving a sentence, the artistic persona of N1NT3NDo is a computer program. Vasilii Vakulenko's third alter ego appears as an elaborately designed shooting module that randomly generates every individual track, while capable of functioning as a computer simulation program in charge of synchronizing the neural activity of the player with the unfolding of the game script. The virtual gangsta self appears here as a random interplay of the discursive means with which the characters in Russian gangsta narratives are constructed and their realities "verified." Like his colleagues in Krovostok, Vakulenko combines elements from Russian gangsta lore with those from mass art in a way that favors pastiche and casts away parody. As a totality of the narrative nodules this construct uses, the Russian gangsta appears as a holographic collage.

The grotesque world of Russian conceptual hip hop offers a vision of a self-deconstructing reality whose algorithms start short-circuiting one another as the text begins to unfold. A variety of stylistic and narrative devices serve this end, including, among others, the mixing of high and low registers of Russian, playing with multiple epistemological frames within a single narrative, and extending the horizon of intelligibility of the text-world beyond the worldview of the lyrical hero. Turning the heritage of Russian and world culture into a spring from which to draw knowledge in order to forge a unique perspective on human being-in-the-world, Russian conceptual hip hop artists put to the test the generic boundaries within which they work and renegotiate what it means to be a creative artist.

NOTES

1. Part 1 of the children's trilogy created by Nikolai Nosov (1908–1976), which includes *The Adventures of Dunno and His Friends* (1954), *Dunno in Sun City* (1958), and *Dunno on the Moon* (1966). The last part was the most popular, as it featured the life of a capitalist society as seen through the eyes of a socialist child.

2. A pun on the original Russian idiom *"tishe vody, nizhe travy,"* which translates as "quiet as the grave."

3. This is a double reference to Jack London's tales of surviving in the white solitude and to Del'fin's "Dog's Fight," in which mutual recognition is not how the sociality of human reason unfolds in the existing structure of human relations.

4. A variety of apples with a strong acidic flavor, also nicknamed "the people's apple," popular in Russia and made by Bunin a symbol of the world of Russian small gentry nobility, largely extinct by the beginning of the twentieth century.

5. Like always being tempted to be distracted by something curious that has little significance in relation to what one sees as essential.

6. In its full form: "It is very easy to divide ten thousand, very difficult one hundred thousand, and you can't divide a million."

7. The oil oligarch imprisoned for 12 years during Putin's reign for his attempt to influence the course of Russian politics. His trial is often referred to as "the show trial," just like those under Stalin during the so-called Great Purge.

8. Vladislav Surkov was the chief of the Russian Presidential Administration from 1999 to 2011. He was also the main ideologist of the Kremlin.

9. I use here the date suggested in the Primary Chronicle and not the years 990 and 991, as suggested by other scholars.

10. Russian mafia bosses.

REFERENCES

Condee, Nancy. 1999. "Body Graphics: Tattooing the Fall of Communism." In *Consuming Russia: Popular Culture, Sex, and Society since Gorbachev,* ed. Adele Marie Barker (pp. 339–361). Durham, NC: Duke University Press.

Foster, Michael B. 1935. "Christian Theology and Modern Science of Nature," Part I. *Mind* 44(176):439–466.

Foster, Michael B. 1936. "Christian Theology and Modern Science of Nature," Part II. *Mind* 45(177):1–27.

Gadamer, Hans-George. 1975. *Truth and Method,* trans. Garrett Barden and John Cumming, New York: Crossroad.

Heidegger Martin. 1962 (1927). *Being and Time*, trans. J. Macquarrie and E. Robinson. New York: Harper & Row.

Likhachev, Dmitrii. 1935. "Cherty pervobytnogo primitivizma vorovskoi rechi" [Primitive features in the speech of thieves]. *Iazyk i Myshlenie* 3–4:47–100.

Merleau-Ponty, Maurice. 1962. *Phenomenology of Perception*, trans. Colin Smith. London: Routledge & Kegan Paul.

Plutser-Sarno, Alexei. 2003a. "The Language of the Body and Politics: The Symbolism of Thieves' Tattoos." In *Russian Criminal Tattoo Encyclopaedia*, eds. Sergej Vasziljev and Aleksei Plutser-Sarno, vol. 1 (pp. 26–53). London: Fuel.

Plutser-Sarno, Alexei. 2003b. "All Power to the Godfathers!" In D. S. Baldaev, *Russian Criminal Tattoo Encyclopaedia*, eds. Sergej Vasziljev and Aleksei Plutser-Sarno, vol. 2 (pp. 32–57). London: Fuel.

Plutser-Sarno, Alexei. 2004. "Russkie Vorovskie Tatu: Ot Teksta k Simvolu." *NLO* 68.

Schrader, Abby M. 2000. "Branding the Other/Tattooing the Self: Bodily Inscription among Convicts in Russia and the Soviet Union." In *Written on the Body: The Tattoo in European and American History*, ed. Jane Caplan (pp. 174–192). Princeton, NJ: Princeton University Press.

CHAPTER 11

UNMASKING EXPRESSIONS IN TURKISH RAP/HIP HOP CULTURE

Contestation and Construction of Alternative Identities through Localization in Arabesk Music

Nuran Erol Işık and Muran Can Basaran

PATTERNS IN VARIATIONS in the characteristics of cultural groups can provide an opportunity to study different dimensions of narratives, musical forms, and identities. Hip hop culture is one such cultural language through which it is possible to decipher a certain formation, which can also be defined as a suitcase carrying hybrid identities as well as musical forms. The hybrid character of Turkish hip hop culture stems from the way in which it has merged with what is called "arabesk music," which combines different musical forms of Anatolian and Middle Eastern influences. This new form of music made an impact on the emergence of a reaction among the populace, whose meaning-making practices involved listening to authentic local music that expressed their own lifestyles. The theme of arabesk lyrics strongly emphasized fatalism, hegemonic masculinity, and love, which combined as a form of cognitive dissonance. It first emerged in the 1990s as a language and indicator of the demand for recognition among the lower classes, but after 2000 it developed into an integral part of the mainstream popular culture, a cultural form that permeated every sphere of society.

The impact of arabesk music on other genres of cultural formation has grown to the extent that hybrid forms of different genres have become widespread, a process facilitated by internet technology. The youth, especially those living on the "other side of the tracks" in big cities, and those who are unable to feel empathy for the majority of the cultural formations around them, appropriated hip hop music into a localized form; that is, they integrated it into arabesk music, borrowing from the lyrics as well as musical character of hip hop. The so-called "arabesk rap/hip hop music" started to become a "vehicle for pride and anger, for asserting the self-worth of the community" (Beadle 1993:85). Young men, especially those without employment or security, started to produce their own music via internet technology, which gave them an opportunity to disseminate arabesk hip hop locally, nationally, and internationally.[1] The question the authors of this chapter ask is as follows: How are the youth of culturally distinct populations able to find a common voice via the appropriation of cultural resources developed to articulate issues that shape the lives of the subculture called "arabesk rap"?

The evolution of Turkish arabesk rap culture into a full-fledged subculture brought increasing visibility to authentic rituals expressed via lyrics and lifestyles. One of these rituals can be defined as a verbal duello, whereby rappers articulate improvised lyrics spontaneously in small-scale concerts for localized audiences. Such artistic duels may be considered as intense competitive displays having the added purpose of serving to construct alternative identities through rhyming practices. Thus, this chapter aims to contribute to the examination of the cultural significance of arabesk rap music by revealing the ways in which meaning-making practices, and their modes of expression and markers, are constructed in this musical style. By doing this, the authors aim at making a contribution to the literature on hip hop/rap music mediated by global and local cultural markers. It is assumed in this chapter that arabesk rap is an outcome more of arabesk culture, rather than of hip hop culture. Thus, first, an evaluation of arabesk music will be presented, followed by an assessment of the sociological and poetic characteristics of the subculture of arabesk rappers. The chapter will also include examples of texts used in artistic duels as well as song lyrics, both of which can be considered as forms/styles that reflect identity markers.[2]

A Short Glance at "Arabesk" Music in Turkey

Various cultural trajectories have been investigated in Turkish society to describe local and global elements of popular culture that come together in interesting forms. When it comes to studies of popular culture, a large majority of studies have been focused on what is produced for the entertainment industry. In a society where the pace of social change is almost unpredictable, it seems inevitable to take a look at "vernacular musico-linguistic practices" (Krims 2002:9) in order to fully grasp the ways in which different narratives have been constructed and delivered in different settings. It is also necessary to assess cultural forms produced and mediated in and through different practices, because the normative statuses of gender, ethnic, and class identities have been embedded in such cultural practices as subcultural styles.

In Turkish society, since the 1950s there seems to have been a unique way of living called "the arabesk culture," which can be sociologically and anthropologically observed in the forms of music people listen to, daily rituals they engage in, and even in political situations. Arabesk music, accompanied by a unique mentality or way of thinking and feeling, became part of Turkish mainstream culture that needs to be investigated, not only as a way of living, but as a way of expressing and signifying the world. An in-depth cultural analysis reveals that the sociological phenomenon called arabesk transcends revealing itself as a "sentimental mood" or as a cultural artifact of a migration process; on the contrary, it should be accepted as a way of signifying the world for many people coming from various different social backgrounds.

> Never have I been free of sufferings,
> As I am the relentless creator of them.
> Each and every line of mine makes a lesson for man.
> "What difference would it make," I am asking you,
> "If one is greeted only once in a blue?"[3]

These words are taken from the lyrics of an arabesk song sung by a very popular performer of the genre in Turkish society, wherein some people signify the world by creating unique expressions related to sufferings and sorrows. Arabesk is not only a cultural form; it is at the same time a condition that refers to a unique mentality, a form of thinking, and "a way of living," all of which are produced and reproduced by the living practices of many people experiencing different lifeworlds. In other words, the arabesk cultural condition is a very significant cultural referent for many people living in different settings, and the ways in which lyrics are formulated depict a tension between cultural forms of Western and non-Western ways of living. The arabesk cultural condition is also related to understanding ambivalent elements in identities of different natures; specifically, people living in urban areas in Turkey have identities that combine both rural/traditional as well as semiurban characteristics. Arabesk is also a cultural artifact stemming from the process of creating an otherness in the lifeworld of Turkish society.

Arabesk cultural symbols are products of a complex sociological transformation marked by a rapid migration from rural areas to many urban settings starting from the 1950s, which brought to the cities migrants who could not identify themselves with the urban culture and its practices or the ways of living they were exposed to. In general, arabesk lyrics include themes such as sorrow, love, passion, separation, love, resignation of fate, and resentment. Arabesk music and performers became quite widespread in popular culture, and there have been various forms of arabesk music consumed not only by new inhabitants of urban settings, but also by people defined as urbanites but coming from different segments of the society.

In order to understand the ways in which such a cultural form affects the process of meaning making, makes people rebel and conform at the same time, and offers them an identity, one needs to look at arabesk as a symbolic form which constructs identities in a society where the project of modernity has been heavily focused on the cultural sphere. At the same time, for those who internalize the arabesk meaning making, "the other," that is, the urban and modern as well as Western, is deconstructed in the construction of their own lifeworld, which needs to be understood at the level of poetics in arabesk music, a special genre employing important themes of its own (e.g., love, beloved, ritualism, rebellion) and other culturally unique attitudes. It is assumed that reading the poetics of arabesk offers an opportunity to decode the process of meaning making via a specific cultural form, to analyze social representations of "love" as a metaphor in society, and to understand the ways in which tensions between identities have been and are resolved in hybrid forms of culture (Isik and Isik 2013).

As is well known, the symbolic modalities of the ear make possible a collective communication where different voices may join simultaneously and form polyphonic webs, and where groups can gather and be united in strong and emotional experiences of communality. Collective musical activities can bind people together and thus restructure social differences. Experiencing arabesk, for that matter, has bound together people who have migrated from the periphery into the central metropolian areas. Orhan Gencebay, one of the most important artists who experimented and developed a syncretic musical genre, argued that arabesk consisted of a synthesis of three kinds of music: Turkish folk, Turkish art, and Oriental—a type of light Turkish classical music that is associated with commercial establishments and belly dancing (Markoff 1994).

In addition, there seems to have been a cultural differentiation and specialization in arabesk music, which was facilitated by major technical advances in the music industry, which made possible the production of arabesk music for the masses. The masses, not only newcomers in *gecekondu*[4] areas, but people from different segments of the society, have been listening to Ferdi Tayfur, Müslüm Gürses, and others, whose music and style consisted of subcultural elements in the construction of identities. According to Özbek (1988:124), arabesk music could be classified as follows: "folk arabesk" (İbrahim Tatlıses, Emrah, Ceylan), "tavern music" (Cengiz Kurtoglu, Nejat Alp), "art music-like arabesk" (fantezi), "oriental arabesk," and "revolutionary arabesk" (Ahmet Kaya). Thus, the arabesk cultural form reveals rather generative and grouping patterns in the cultural field, as a result of which it was becoming its own musical genre.

Clearly, a genre is defined through its relations to neighboring genres. These contextual relations of difference are indeed crucial. Also, genres are not only located among surrounding genres, but are also connected to nonsymbolic phenomena of a material, bodily, economic, political, social, or psychological kind (Fornas 1995). The arabesk genre is also surrounded by Turkish art music as well as folk music. The instruments used for arabesk are heavily influenced by Egyptian mainstream music, which is often referred to as oriental music. The instruments include violins, *qanun* (plucked, trapezoidal zither), *ud* (plucked lute with a short, bent neck), *ney* (end-blown flute), *riqq* (tambourine), and *tabl* (goblet shaped drum). Additionally, accordion, saxophone, clarinet, electric organ, and sometimes synthesizer and bongos are utilized (Markoff 1994).

It can be argued that arabesk is a type of indigeneous cultural form, a type of hybrid culture including themes such as spiritualism à la Islam, a resistance to the configured Western persona, a strong emphasis on tradition, and a tendency to accept collective, masculine, and patrimonial themes embedded in a unique lifeworld and history. It is a cultural form experienced not only by newcomers in urban areas, but by a large segment of the population. A search for maps of meaning based on a quest is symbolized as a mixture of problems, struggle, pain, and a relentless exclusion from society. Therefore, arabesk fans only know what is available and accessible to them, and they define and interpret what they observe in clear terms, among which the theme of love is the most important symbol in making sense of the senselessness among others.

In this context, love does not stem from people's need to love. Individuals who internalize the Arabesk culture prefer love because it is a simple "humane" condition for living and surviving. Thus, relating the theme of love to a humane characteristic brings about an acceptance of a transcendental being, God, above individuals, who owns and shapes everything, including human lives. Thus, love is given by God on an equal basis, and also *love is the only thing which can be shared equally.* For example, the followers of Müslüm Gürses construct the most meaningful reference point or cultural code through the theme of love.

> No wonder I failed to keep my promise
> Even after I confessed and asked for forgiveness.
> You planted love in me.
> Please God, deprive me of laughter.
> And may stones be thrown at me
> As I am so deeply in love (again).

More clearly, on the one hand love is a kind of reaction toward a world that is materially defined and valued; on the other hand, love refers to a sphere of spirituality and a representation of this world. Those who seem to be "haves" compared to the "have-nots" are defined as devoid of love, because love can only be reached as a result of a nonopportunist and a noncalculating attitude, even commitment. It is possible to deny one's own self, if a person loves, whereas persons who are into material possessions and achievement are calculating, self-centered, and selfish, and therefore doomed to be unsuccessful in terms of loving.

ARABESK RAP AS A VOICE FOR MARGINALIZED YOUTH:
WHAT'S LOVE GOT TO DO WITH IT?

In this context, arabesk rap, also known as "love rap," has emerged as a genre created and contextualized within the virtual world made available through technological and societal changes in Turkish society. The privatization of TV channels,
the spread of internet technology, and the mediated nature of popular culture
all transformed musical genres such as arabesk. Arabesk rap, as a hybrid and a
glocalized genre that served as a performative space for marginalized communities,
has become an indicator for voices to be heard. Unlike arabesk music in general,
arabesk rap never became a form appropriated by the entertainment industry. In
order for the rappers to feel a connectivity, they formed virtual communities
where they presented their amateur work and challenged other rappers as part of
their struggle for recognition.

Arabesk rap seems to have been emergent as a cultural form usually associated with particular spaces rather than other elements. As Solomon (2005) notes,
rap music, with its characteristic practice of "representing" place, is a particularly
appropriate genre for investigating the musical imagination of locality and musical relationships between the local and the global. As is well known, the visibility
of rich and poor, reflected in the formation of space, has been increasing in big
cities since the 1980s, which were marked by neoliberal policies in Turkish society. The production of any type of vernacular culture functioned as a symbol of
such a differentiation in space. The impact of rap/hip hop culture in other countries
on Turkish arabesk rappers has been significant in terms of arabesk rap fans' eagerness to adapt themselves to a similar cultural form, in which both preaching
and singing were part of the vernacular poetics reflecting similar themes produced
by arabesk singers: belief in God, honor, resistance, anger, love, gendered identity, and patrimonialism.

As is well known, Turkish migrants in Germany have been one of the transmitters of European culture for many Turks. The ways in which rap music was
introduced in Turkish popular culture have been multidimensional in the sense
that a large majority of children of the first generation of Turks living in Germany have been absorbed into a multicultural environment. While some of
these have been fans of rap music, a minority group, those who experienced
struggles in adopting themselves to German culture, could have been labeled as
arabesk rappers. Arabesk rap was created by internal and external cultural
dynamics that were significant in terms of being a voice of both mediation and
survival. As described above, arabesk rap has been called love rap. There are no
major musical differences between these two, but the term love rap was used
because the lyrics are about emotional subjects. The musical styles of Dutch-
Turkish arabesk rap and made-in-Turkey arabesk rap may be superficially simi-

lar (both using lots of samples from arabesk), but the lyrics are very different (Arıcan, 2011).

In addition, the ways in which rap music and hip hop culture have been appropriated and reworked by the Turkish youth led to the formation of a subculture based on producing a hybrid music via amateur technological tools, which also facilitated the dissemination of arabesk rap thorough internet technology. Arabesk rappers have differentiated themselves from American rappers by committing to values such as blood brotherhood (*kanka*), rebellion against "fate," platonic love, and monogamy. They also reveal characteristics different from arabesk by referring to a certain type of braggadocio, the use of slang, a misogynistic attitude, a certain type of commitment to patriotism, use of drugs, and other types of "deviant behavior." While fans of the original arabesk were recognized by their virility, bravado, and sincerity, the youth of arabesk rap have not embraced some of these values, such as commitment, moral purity, and love of God. While the original arabesk fans have been excluded from the modern settings of urban living and labeled as *kıro* (a racial slur which is usually a label for Kurds, a man descending from a mountain), some arabesk rappers are referred to as *apachi,* which is a term characterizing certain physical looks. Labels for arabesk fans have been replaced by a new type of identity formation based on reproduction of a feeling of superiority of one's in-group versus the inferiority of out-groups. The stylization of arabesk rap culture has been embedded in a lifestyle with features such as a physical look including certain hairstyles, fake jewelry, sunglasses, and a language with distinct phonetic marks. For example, while letters such as *w* or *q* do not exist in the Turkish alphabet, arabesk rappers use these letters in their lyrics. The production of arabesk rap music using amateur tools and settings signifies a will to resist or dissent, which is not based on an organized culture.

The Poetics of Arabesk Rap and the "Culture of Diss"

The process of dissemination of arabesk rap has been accelerated by the abundance of private channels as well as technological advancements in the 1990s. Compared to rappers who have marketed their work through the entertainment industry in different venues, arabesk rappers have not been absorbed into that industry, except for a few representatives such as DJ Akman and Musa, who were not native to Turkey. Unlike other rap musicians and fans, arabesk rappers have remained a closed community using different linguistic tools to express their lack of resources and disconnectedness from so-called advantaged groups.

The major themes of arabesk, namely fatalism and rebellion, have been come to characterize the voices of arabesk fans as well as pop music fans. A more subjective understanding of the world came into the picture, and the theme of resignation (*tevekkul*) was less emphasized by young arabesk rappers, reflecting the social and cultural changes in Turkish society. Arabesk music, which was itself a hybrid music, started losing the authenticating value that was evident in the emergence of arabesk music in 1950s. Instead of struggles related to modernization, young arabesk rappers started to reveal tensions stemming from, for example, identity politics, globalization, and the disempowering practices of social institutions. While arabesk fans have been following a culture and language of authenticity, arabesk rap fans have internalized a poetics which seems to be a "language of survival," characterized by the daily ups and downs of love relationships and efforts to legitimize the use of drugs to ease those daily pains and struggles. The lyrics heavily reflect a language of argot, deviant behavior, an expectation of protection from motherly figures, a protest against being an "other," loneliness, and alienation.

In this regard, İsmail YK and Cankan are important because we can see them as moving toward what we now see as arabesk rap.

> I was ready to give you my life if you wanted it.
> Where are you headed, precious?
> It was I who had always cherished you
> I had always cherished you
> Only to be left alone and forgotten for life.[5]

Or, as in the lyrics by İsmail YK:

> Let me walk on the roads you walked.
> Let me come to you, I beg you.
> I'll give up my life for you if you want it.
> Let me walk on the roads you walked.
> No way! No way, I can do without you[6]

One of the interesting characteristics of arabesk rap is the ritual called "diss," which is an act of verbal duello between rappers. Other rappers have appropriated such contests more often than arabesk rappers, but there seems to be different aspects to the challenge as between arabesk rappers and hip hop artists/rappers.[7]

The etymology of "diss" stems from "disrespect," which was adapted by rappers to express a quarrel as a public confrontation. Such artistic duels have been part of the rap scene at both underground and overground levels. As Kaya notes, the rapper is an intellectual storyteller who has advice for his/her audience and who wishes to mobilize his/her local community against the power of hegemonic and/or coercive groups. The rapper also reminds us of what we are already inclined to forget, namely, the "communicability of experience," which is destined to decrease (Kaya 2001:181). The crosstalking of rappers with music, that is, battling or dueling, has been interpreted as having characteristics similar to the tradition of minstrels (*aşıklık geleneği*) in Turkish culture. However, rappers and arabesk rappers are tougher and more bitter when it comes to expressing their reactions toward established economic and political structures in the homeland (Arıcan 2011).

In traditional rituals, local minstrels participate in such verbal duels by singing traditional songs and playing an instrument called the *saz*. These duels take three forms: The first type of duel remembles an exam in which at least two minstrels are questioned by the audience or a group of people. The minstrels sing traditional songs so as to reply spontenously to the lyrics sung by other minstrels. These lyrics are based on rhymes and ironic semantic structures. The second type of duel takes place beween two minstrels who battle through lyrics that refer to the artistic inabilities of the other minstrel. This way of challenging is considered as having folkloric and artistic quality and significance. The third type of duel is based on judging the ability of a minstrel to answer questions asked by the other minstrel. The questions are embedded in song lyrics, which are supposed to have artistic and aesthetic quality (Oguz 2005).

That such local traditional rituals or poetry traditions have had an impact in the construction of certain rituals in popular culture as well as in arabesk rap music as society struggles for authenticity can be easily observed in the cultural scene. Although the degree and intensity of appropriating verbal duels in rap music is greater than in arabesk rap, which was never integrated into the cultural industry, arabesk rappers have also used such the language of the duel to reflect their bravado and virility. Internet technology and virtual identities have made it easier for them to adopt such local traditions into a glocalized form of rap music. Greater internet access for young rappers brought about the dissemination and different adaptations in their subculture. Their disempowered status is compensated for via their virtual identities, which are marked by an aesthetics of poetics that reflects battles and struggles that are unique in Turkish culture. Arabesk rappers not only criticize the ways in which they have been discriminated against and disempowered; they also complain about the othering processes in society that also racialize them; that is, they are labeled as outsiders in the society in all aspects. Arabesk rappers draw on stereotypes of rich Turks to racialize those who do not have legitimate status in society. They also draw on other arabesk rappers' attitudes in judging one another in harsh terms. Such challenges, expressed through lyrics that include slang and neologisms, are accepted as part of arabesk rap culture, as well as a will to collaborate toward conflict (Alim, Lee, and Carris 2011). In other words, although arabesk rappers seem to express their feelings and wishes through such duels in the virtual world in their lyrics and styles, their efforts to form a rapping session can be accepted as part of a collective imagination which is sustained by a web of traditional and postmodern characteristics.

The battle between rappers and arabesk rappers has been evident in various virtual communities. In general, most rappers do not accept arabesk rap as a genuine musical genre, which creates a problem of artistic legitimacy. Arabesk rappers tend to reply to the rappers by engaging in such artistic duels, as the lyrics by Arsız Bela show in the form of a "diss to rappers":

Howdy, it's me again.
What is this reckless rapper rated?
This rhythm goes off and off by my word
Learn me (right), get to know me (right), get to know your dad (right)
This zombie can make arabesk also
I never talk trash, but act
You cannot tie the blabber's mouth like a slip knot in a bag, brother.

Waiting for you, run after me.
Never been into secrets.
This generation is different, my man, not nice.
Don't you ever say hip hop to me.
You're round like a ball.
Gonna roll you.
Learn me right, get to know me right.
Can't be a foe to you, but myself.
You are probably scared of yourself.
(But) I am not fond of low profile.

The word "diss," which is a neologism, has a connotation of slang nature; that is, the word "diss" also means "to tune," "to calibrate," "to adjust." Arabesk rappers' tendency to use slang in lyrics, combined with the "talking in rhythm" aspect of , can be interpreted as a resistance to modern rules and formal principles. While they are dueling via such rituals, they adjust and readjust the language so as to accommodate themselves to the world of strangers. The use of language with a high degree of "freestyle" articulated with different linguistic games constitutes a feature of a subculture that forms its own language and stylistic features. The act of dissing, in this context, becomes an identity marker which belongs to a community that experiences conflicts and battles of various natures. The verbal duels provide not only a medium for the expression of issues relating to othering and degradation, but also a will to feel part of a community. In this sense, the cultural ritual of diss can be accepted as a trope signifying the verbal duels as challenges compensating for the lack of participation in institutional life. Thus, arabesk rappers diss one another, just as their societal existence is interpreted as having a diss affect.

CONCLUSIONS

As arabesk rap music make inroads into the cultural sphere of disadvantaged urban groups in Turkish society, it is perhaps easy to overlook the intersections between cultural and linguistic manifestations of different popular cultural genres. As is well known, freestyle rap battles have always included linguistic tools that emerge from perceived transgressions, insults, and disses (Alim, Lee, and Carris 2011). Arabesk rappers in Turkey also articulate a freestyle poetics embedded in neologisms of different kinds. In this chapter, an assessment of arabesk rappers has been made by referring to arabesk music, a hybrid form of culture in Turkey, which is still a popular form of music accepted as a unique and authentic signifier of ambivalent nature in regard to Turkish modernity. Future research on manifestations of rap music in Turkey will need to employ an interdisciplinary approach, including musical innovations and structures, audiences' way of appropriating rap music, the anthropological dimensions of rap communities, and ethnographic studies on the reception and formation of similar cultural groups.

When it comes to understanding hybridity in cultural venues, one should note the immediacy of media and technology allowing different cultures to innovate and express their cognitive and affective idiosyncrasies. In a world where contested selves are expressed through various tools, arabesk fans have been appropriating rapidly changing technologies, which foster the reproduction of feelings of shared connectivity along with different cultural axes, some of which represent divisions as well as unifications. Arabesk music has been following a track which functions as both a unifying and a dividing cultural marker in Turkish society. Arabesk rappers have been affected by this role of arabesk culture, which has demanded to be recognized and accepted by other segments of society. After the 2000s, different forms of arabesk markers were sustained and reproduced through different avenues in Turkish society, which has been affected by the rise of Islamism, neoliberal policies, and identity politics. Arabesk rappers emerged out of this complicated and colorful picture, providing a language of survival for those who could not be accommodated in the institutional structure of the society. They created their own styles and subcultural features, which were disseminated through the innovative acts of internet pages. Although a large majority of arabesk rappers could not market their products in the music industry, they reproduced and reformulated a language or channel for those disadvantaged groups who have been exposed to modern and postmodern lifestyles. Thus, their expressions in song lyrics were the outcomes of a coconstruction of a world which included the ambivalences of arabesk culture: fatalism and resistance, resignation and love, and honor and subordination are among the themes characterizing arabesk rappers' subcultural values. Their use of their bodies as places for identity markers, their use of virility as a resource for self-empowerment, and their expressions of vulnerability all depict complex anthropological and sociological puzzles to be solved. Although such a localized form of rap music could not make inroads into the commercial sphere of popular entertainment, it definitely appears to have been situated in a world of vulnerability, fragility, and sensibility. The disses rappers have used are only one type of wording challenging their wordlessness in public sphere. It is time to acknowledge other forms of musical innovations and spheres of normativity as signs of cultural framing in diverse social contexts.

NOTES

1. The genre called "arabesk rap" has emerged as a result of rap and hip hop culture produced in other societies. As Krims (2002) notes, rap describes only a kind of music, whereas there is also hip hop dancing, visual art, and clothing. Since the authors did not investigate subcultural characteristics of hip hop culture, this chapter will only refer to arabesk rap culture with distinctive aesthetic and poetic characteristics.

2. This chapter is written in a period when the role of arabesk music in Turkey is being discussed in the cultural public sphere due to the sudden death of one of the most prominent artists in arabesk music, Muslum Gurses. The arabesk rap which is evaluated in this chapter is accepted as one of the important markers or tropes to understand the nature of hybridity in Turkish culture. The chapter is based on a framework evaluating the major characteristics of arabesk rappers and the poetics of arabesk rap.

3. The authors would like to express their gratitude for all the translations of arabesk lyrics, which were done by Ayla Balcı, instructor at the Department of Foreign Languages, Anadolu University, Eskisehir, Turkey.

4. Turkish version of shantytowns built at the margins of the big cities since 1950s. They were absorbed into the urban dwellings with the impact of government regulations which granted them legality.

5. Canimi istesen hazirdim ben vermeye
   Nereye gülüm söyle nereye
   Canim istesen hazirdim ben vermeye
   Sana Gözbebek gibi ben baktim
   Unutuldum cok yanlizim

6. Yuruduğun yollarda yuruyorum
   Yalvarırım bırak ben geleyim
   Canımı iste feda edeyim
   Yurudugun yollarda yuruyeyim
   Olmaz sensiz olmaz

7. Please see rappers challenging arabesk rappers at: http://www.youtube.com/watch?v=wfAE2DgS4lM; http://www.youtube.com/watch?v=8TWeHXIoRvs; http://www.youtube.com/watch?v=byQBBSJIPlg; Arabesk rappers challenging rappers: http://www.youtube.com/watch?v=1ApQHYNVIDQ; http://www.youtube.com/watch?v=iHhUsTSK6qY.

REFERENCES

Arıcan, Tunca. 2011. "Turkish Rap in the Netherlands: Globalization, Diasporic Identity and Cultural Conservatism." Unpublished dissertation, University of Bergen.

Alim, H. S., J. Lee, and L. M. Carris. 2011. "Moving the Crowd, 'Crowding' the Emcee: The Coproduction and Contestation of Black Normativity in Freestyle Rap Battles. *Discourse and Society* 22(4):422–439.

Beadle, J. 1993. *Will Pop Eat Itself? Pop Music in the Sound Bite Era.* London: Faber and Faber.

Bennett, Andy. 1999. "Hip Hop am Main: The Localization of Rap Music and Hip Hop Culture." *Media, Culture, and Society* 21:77–91.

Elflein, Dietmar. 1998. "From Krauts with Attitudes to Turks with Attitudes: Some Aspects of Hip-Hop History in Germany." *Popular Music* 17:255–265.

Fornas, J. 1995. *Youth Culture in Late Modernity,* London: Sage.

Isik, C., and N. Isik. 2013. *Arabesk ve Muslum Gurses.* Istanbul: Ferfir.

Kaya, A. (2001): *"Sicher in Kreuzberg": Constructing Diasporas: Turkish Hip-Hop Youth in Berlin.* Bielefeld: Transcript Verlag.

Klebe, Dorit. 2004. "Kanak Attak in Germany: A Multiethnic Network of Youths Employing Musical Forms of Expression." In *Manifold Identities: Studies on Music and Minorities,* eds. Ursula Hemetek et al. (pp. 162–180). London: Cambridge Scholars Press.

Krims, Adam. 2002. "Rap, Race, the 'Local,' and Urban Geography in Amsterdam." In *Music, Popular Culture, Identities,* ed. Richard Young (pp. 165–179). New York: Rodopi.

Markoff, Irene, 1994. "Popular Culture, State Ideology, and National Identity in Turkey: The Arabesk Polemic." In *Cultural Transitions in Middle East,* ed. S. Mardin (pp. 225–235). New York: E. J. Brill.

Oğuz, Öcal, et al. 2005. *Türk Halk Edebiyatı El Kitabı.* Ankara: Grafiker Yayıncılık.

Özbek, Meral. 1988. *Popüler Kültür ve Orhan Gencebay Arabeski.* Istanbul: Iletisim.

Solomon, Thomas. 2005. "Living Underground Is Tough: Authenticity and Locality in the Hip Hop Community in Istanbul, Turkey." *Popular Music* 24(1):1–20.

CHAPTER 12

HIP HOP AS A MEANS OF FLIGHT FROM THE "GYPSY GHETTO" IN EASTERN EUROPE

Michal Ruzicka, Alena Kajanová,
Veronika Zvánovcová, and Tomas Mrhalek

THE DEEP STRUCTURAL changes associated with the post-socialist transformation in Eastern and East-Central Europe have most notably been tied to the political transformation, the transition to a market economy, the denationalization of state-owned property, and changes to socio-spatial structures and relations.[1] Economists and political scientists have focused mainly on the macro-level aspects of the post-socialist transformation (Kornai, Haggard, and Kaufman 2001; Milanovic 1998), while sociologists have tended to focus on the experiential and societal level of the transformation (Burawoy and Verdery 1999; Hann 2002; Mandel and Humphrey 2002).

Scholars studying ethnicity and poverty in Eastern European transitional societies have drawn attention to the dramatic decline in socioeconomic status and the general destitution of life for Roma/Gypsy communities since the fall of the state-socialist regimes (e.g., Gabal Analysis & Consulting [GAC] 2006; Ladányi 2001; Barany 2002; Ringold 2000; Stewart 2002; Ladányi and Szelényi 2006; Vašečka, Jurásková, and Nicholson 2003).[2] The Roma have become an "icon" of the adverse aspects of post-socialist transformation in Eastern and Central Europe, "a symbol" of poverty and marginalization (Radičová and Vašečka 2001:179). Their deepening marginality often tends to be explained through reference to the restructuring of labor markets, deindustrialization, and resulting mass unemployment that are seen as the main forces in determining forms of urban marginality.

Existing research on poor Roma families tends to conceptualize its object and analysis in terms of "marginalization" or "social exclusion," both of which direct attention to processes that target "the excluded" from outside (the restructuring of labor and housing markets, the "exclusive society," etc.). In this chapter, we propose to supplement these approaches by also studying the "internal" forms of adaptation and resistance that members of poor Roma communities adopt as a reaction to their disadvantaged position. By means of an epistemological shift away from *object position* (i.e., being a passive object of exclusion) to *subject position* (i.e., being an active actor possessing agency, but also subject to a certain level of external constraint), this chapter aims to show how young Roma employ means of artistic expression to voice their own perspective on their predicament, rather than that studied and analyzed by outside, non-Roma observers.

In this chapter we identify and describe the ways in which young Roma express themselves by means of rap and music to better understand the ways in which these artists reflect on what it means to live on the margins, under conditions of social, economic, and political marginalization. To fulfill this task, we build our research on interviews with select Roma rappers in order to learn more about Roma hip hop, which has to this point been a rather under-researched offshoot of modern "ethnic" music.

Exclusion of Roma (Gypsies) in former Czechoslovakia

Roma, sometimes referred to as "Gypsies," are Europe's largest nonterritorial ethnic minority. In Slovakia, most of the Roma live in rural areas (Hurrle 2006; Filadelfiová, Gerbery, and Školba 2006; Jakoubek and Hirt 2008; Scheffel 2005), while in the Czech Republic they live predominantly in urban settings (Rösnerová 2003; Hirt and Jakoubek 2006; Šimíková and Vašečka 2004). These trends in the geographical location of place of residence can be explained by the specific post–World War II developments. The tragic results of the war included the virtual extermination of the Roma in the Czech lands, as only several hundred survived (Crowe 2007:48–50). Sponsored by the postwar Czechoslovak government, tens of thousands of Roma, mainly from underdeveloped regions of eastern Slovakia, were moved to the (re)industrializing Czech cities and border regions in the Sudetenland in response to a demand for labor to fill unskilled jobs (Baršová 2003; Jurová 1993). This particular postwar development created a situation that provides a unique opportunity for comparative social analyses (cf. Ruzicka 2012a).

Under state socialism, the majority of Roma were employed as unskilled laborers in the construction industry, working as ditch diggers, dustmen, miners, or steelworkers (Davidová 1970:43). Following the demise of the socialist centrally planned economy, with its egalitarian and redistributive approach to employment, the majority of Roma, who had held low-skilled jobs, "were inevitably the first to lose their jobs under the rationalization programmes of new property owners" (Stewart 2002:134). Post-socialist societies had to face not only the effects of the market transition but also the delayed "third industrial revolution" that had been altering Western economies and societies since the late 1960s (Ladányi 2001:73). Stewart (2002) views Roma marginality under post-socialism as an indirect result of market transition, growing rates of unemployment, and racial/ethnic discrimination in the labor market (Stewart 2002:134; European Commission against Racism and Intolerance [ECRI] 2009; European Roma Rights Centre [ERRC] 2010).

As many Roma/Gypsies resided in the decaying city centers under state socialism, they were especially vulnerable to the effects of the post-communist restitution of property, privatization, and capital flows targeting city centers. Given that they were usually unemployed or underemployed, the Roma/Gypsies possessed little economic capital to successfully cope with the capitalist valorization of their housing in the form of rent increases (or other increases in expenses connected with housing). Though rent was still regulated in municipally owned housing stock in the 1990s, the unemployed Roma, like other poor people, had difficulty keeping up with the costs of rent and living expenses in the privatized housing stock, as the level of rent for an average privatized flat grew by 600 percent between 1990 and 1998 (Lux 2003:85).

Post-socialist cities in the Czech Republic have witnessed the exclusion and eviction of poor Roma/Gypsies, labeled as "nonadaptable," in recent years (most visibly by media in the cities of Chomutov and Vsetín). Market forces, discrimination, and a lack of integration policies contributed to these processes. Places of concentrated poverty, inhabited predominantly by people of Roma ethnicity, started to emerge in Czech cities, drawing the attention of academic and other nongovernmental observers, media, and (populist) politicians.

In a recent study of spatial and residential segregation in the Czech Republic, the authors noted about 250 places of exclusion where members of particular social groups have been concentrated (Sýkora, Temelová, and Posová 2007:57). About 55 percent of these segregated places have been predominantly inhabited by Roma (Sýkora, Temelová, and Posová 2007:46). Another study of urban "places endangered by social exclusion" (GAC 2006) identified over 300 places in Czech cities that are inhabited by between 60,000 and 80,000 socially excluded Roma. Debates arose as to how to name and conceptualize this relatively new phenomenon of ethno-racial and socio-spatial segregation. In his comparative analysis of urban marginality in contemporary societies, Loïc Wacquant warned against the unreflective importation of concepts such as "ghetto" from the United States to Europe (Wacquant 2008). American ghettos and European forms of socio-spatial exclusion, according to Wacquant, follow different historical, economic, and spatial logics, and therefore should not be mixed together, and definitely not under the overarching, overpoliticized, and often analytically empty concept of *ghetto* (Wacquant 1993, 2007a). Although ghettos—in an analytically strict sense of the term—do not exist in Europe (Wacquant 2008), there is, according to the author, one exception: Eastern European Roma (Wacquant 2011:18–20). Following Wac-quant to a "Gypsy ghetto" in Czech cities, recent studies have identified the pro-cess of ghettoization, that is, processes and forces leading to the formation of socio-spatial assemblages resembling in their structure and function the U.S. ghetto—enabling us to consider applying the concept of the ghetto to the situa-tion of marginalized Roma families in Eastern Europe (Ruzicka 2012b; Stejskalová 2013).[3] Is it just a coincidence that one of the most notorious Gypsy ghettos in the Czech Republic, located near the city center of Brno, the second largest city of the Czech Republic, bears the publicly recognized label of "Bronx"?

Since 2012, the nickname "Bronx" and its association with the Brno's decayed neighborhood, populated by a large Roma population, has been put to use by Ghettofest, a street festival of ethnic music,[4] an attempt to reduce the ethnic stigma associated with that particular neighborhood. Some Roma hip hop artists have participated in the event, making their voices heard. Most of the performers, however, have come from outside the walls of the "Bronx of Brno." As an attempt to establish a local platform for multicultural communication and exchange, Ghettofest has been a rare yet publicly recognized initiative to transcend the other-wise strong interethnic boundaries dividing Czech society as well as the city of Brno. The lasting impact of Ghettofest on the process of social exclusion and resi-dential segregation, however, remains unclear.

Could the processes of residential segregation and relative deepening of the marginalization of Roma in post-socialist countries support, or stimulate, the "transformative adoption" of cultural forms coming from their analogues in the United States? A comparative analysis of hip hop culture, stemming from—or finding their roots in—marginal places of postindustrial societies, as an au-tonomous form of reflexive artistic expression and a form of social critique, is still lacking. The "new ghettos" of Eastern Europe, slowly forming in the shadow of the cloud raised by the fall of the state-socialist states (Baršová 2003; see also Ruzicka 2012b and Stejskalová 2013), definitely belong among those places where such studies and comparative analyses might be—or perhaps should be—conducted.

Romani Hip Hop: Lost in Translation?

The history of Czech hip hop has not yet been fully "codified" (for a rare study, see Oravcová 2011), but it is generally considered that, as a subculture, it didn't fully form before the mid-1990s. Although the well-known track "Jižák"[5] by Manželé from 1984 is sometimes regarded as the first Czech rap song, it is not regarded as a part of hip hop subculture, as it utilized only the rap style use of vocals without the rest of hip hop culture, such as DJing, break dance, or graffiti. These three elements did not establish themselves as proper hip hop "disciplines" before they could have been imported to the Czech Republic from the West after the rise of the Iron Curtain.

The "import" of hip hop—or perhaps better, the mixing of the local with the global—in the context of post-socialist Czechoslovakia, reflected the local context—social, economic, and political. Czech hip hoppers are not gangsters selling crack on the street corner. Instead, they have been recruited from a whole spectrum of social backgrounds, and only recently has the experience of lower social classes become one of their topics. Czech hip hop never formed along ethnic lines, as it very often did wherever exported outside the United States, especially in Western Europe (Mitchell 2001). Czech hip hop was formed by young white men in a society that was at that time still relatively socially homogeneous, that is, without the significant class differences that have structured the societies of the West. The founding fathers of Czech hip hop were young people coming from various social backgrounds, unlike in Poland (see Pasternak-Mazur 2009); only very rarely were they of Roma ethnicity. A specific branch of Romani hip hop has never formed as a subculture within the larger framework of Czech hip hop. It is true that Romani hip hop has recently gained some popularity through the celebrated performers in the mainstream media like Gipsy CZ,[6] who combines rap and "traditional" Gypsy music, or the rapper called Rytmus.[7] Rytmus became known through the quite successful hip hop project Syndrom Snopp (2000–2005), where lyrics addressed topics such as ethnicity and discrimination or preju- dice; one of his later videos was shot in the Bronx, New York.[8] Roma hip hop projects, individual or collective, usually don't last long enough to "establish" them- selves or gain wider popularity, perhaps reflecting the insecure and unpredictable living conditions of the hip hoppers themselves—as if not only the content (lyrics), but also the form (fleeting in nature and unstable in time and space) reflected what life in a Gypsy ghetto might be about (for a reflection on the currently form- ing Romani hip hop scene, see Radostný 2008).

It is a tricky task to write about a phenomenon that has never truly realized itself—or we should say that it hasn't truly realized itself *yet?* As of today, we must conclude that ethnicity and ethnic boundaries became "lost in translation" (Kolářová 2011:239) within Czech hip hop, when members of the largest ethnic minority remain marginal even among marginal forms of artistic expression.

Our research project, a kind of a pioneering probe into underground music production in the consolidating Gypsy ghettos of the post-socialist world, was not meant to be a complete description or analysis of an established (sub)culture. That's why we did not conduct interviews with well-established and successful hip hop performers. What we were interested in mainly was gaining a better under- standing of the "grassroots conditions" from which Romani hip hop could even- tually realize itself as a form of collective, authentic expression of experience of living on the fringes of the ever-transforming post-socialist society.

METHODOLOGY

With its population of one hundred thousand inhabitants, the city of České Budějovice is located south of Prague, roughly two hours by car. It is one of those towns and cities where the "places of exclusion" and socio-spatial segregation have formed in the last two decades, as identified in the studies discussed above. At least three places (in the political and administrative discourse also referred to as "socially excluded localities") were identified as having spatial concentration of predominantly Roma inhabitants (GAC 2006). We visited one of these sites to find out more about whether music, and particularly Romani hip hop, plays any important role in the lives of young people there.

The site we visited was relatively small: just a few houses in a street where approximately 350 Roma inhabitants moved in together after 1989, amounting to approximately one-tenth of the Roma population living in the whole city.

Although the area of V. Volfa street is relatively small, it holds a prominent position in the symbolic imagination of the dominant, non-Roma population. In the public and media context, as well as in local vernacular and in the hip hop lyrics of our informants, the street is referred to as the "Roma ghetto" or "Gypsy ghetto" and is usually presented as a dangerous place where the majority of crimes committed in the city happen. There has been a significant increase in unemployment (which rose by 40 percent between 2008 and 2009), while crime, especially that committed by juveniles, also rose. "Socially deviant" phenomena, such as drug production and consumption (especially of methamphetamine) or gambling, are alleged to be concentrated in this area (Kozlová and Klufová 2012:25). The flats in V. Volfa street became almost unsalable and are offered for up to 50 percent lower prices than flats in other quarters of the city. This supports the concentration of economically disadvantaged households around this area, further contributing to the already existing territorial stigma (Wacquant 2007b).

One of the few providers of social services in the area of V. Volfa street has been the NGO Salesian Centre for Young People—House of Children and Youth České Budějovice. In addition to providing preventive programs to reduce risky behavior, the organization focuses on social and pedagogical work with Roma children and young people. The center also offers leisure activities and provides premises for a club where young people may get together (Kajanová and Urban 2009). During our field research we observed that there is a fully equipped music room in this "low-threshold club"[9] for local young people, where musicians may both practice and make their records.

The research team members are experienced ethnographers focusing on research among the excluded Roma in Central Europe (e.g., Ruzicka 2009, 2012a, 2012b). In our previous research projects, we noticed an increasing influence of hip hop subculture on the life of young Roma. Based on our previous research, which also concerned the area of V. Volfa street, we conducted a few deep interviews with hip hoppers who had been using the premises of the low-threshold club for their musical production. These were young men living in the neighborhood, who were personally involved in hip hop music production and who considered themselves Roma. The interviews were recorded with the informed consent of the participants. The recordings were then transcribed, repeatedly read through, coded, and analyzed. Our informants also provided us with recordings of their own songs, which were also transcribed and underwent a content analysis. Although, in analyzing interviews and lyrics, we were inspired by grounded theory methodology (Charmaz 2006),[10] our goal was to hermeneutically understand meanings and circumstances that penetrate or, more precisely, frame the experience of young hip hoppers, inhabitants of the local Gypsy ghetto.

WHO ARE THE RAPPERS OF "MÁJ"?

Our informants differed in many respects from the usual stereotype of a young Roma from the Gypsy ghetto.[11] For instance, the average age of Roma parents when their first child is born is 18 years in the Czech Republic (Davidová 2010), whereas our informants were, despite their ages (16 to 21), childless, without long-term partners, and they had not planned to establish their own families. In these respects our informants differed from an "average" Gypsy ghetto inhabitant, as reflected by one of our informants: "Well, especially at my age, the boys have their wives, children" (M, 21).

Our informants also had relatively higher education than is usual in Gypsy ghettos. They usually had a certificate of apprenticeship, although they themselves did not consider this an important factor in finding a suitable job at the labor market. Like other inhabitants of excluded areas, they had experienced discrimination on the grounds of their ethnicity, especially when looking for a job, but even when they find a job, they say:

> When I was working at Tesco, I learned there a bit that they were pitching into me, weren't they? They did not trust me. Nine months of bullying, there. (R2, 21).

Our informants held temporary jobs, worked on an occasional basis, and hunted for jobs through their relatives or employment agencies. They dropped hints that they had other sources of income, so-called "business" or "secret sources" (R4), but they didn't want to talk about them in detail.

Our informants indirectly explained how they had approached hip hop. They talked about their long-term participation in other hip hop forms before engaging with rap (e.g., beat box or graffiti). They also mentioned the influence of motivation by their relatives and peers who recognized and supported their talent. They perceived their talent for rap as something for which they were predestined.

Reflections of Everyday Life in the Ghetto

Living their everyday lives in the stigmatized ghetto, far removed from the social, economic, and cultural infrastructures of the dominant society, young Roma rappers nevertheless perceived their place of residence as "their own"—a situation they could not escape and did not want to deny. Presenting themselves as coming from "the ghetto" was part of the image these young artists had been using to establish their hip hop identity. This residential statement, however, did not mean accepting the social, economic, and political conditions that permeate the everyday life in the ghetto. On the contrary, rap was used by our informants to reflect upon these conditions in a critical manner.

Everyday life in the ghetto was predominantly perceived as "a drag," stemming from two sources: The first was the nature of the place of residence, a housing estate with insufficient leisure activities and an absence of people with whom they might carry out these activities, since their friends had their own families and related worries. Another source of "boredom" was the structural inequalities that prevented the young artists from participating in the dominant culture, inequalities related to the previously mentioned discrimination in the labor market.

> T: "And what're you doing in your leisure time?"
> R2: "Well, we are quite bored."
> M: "Well, we are bored, but there is always something. We always have a pencil, a paper, and when we find a flat, yep, music, we always start to write something. We just figure out something."

Hip hop was thus viewed by its authors as a flight from their ever-present boredom, as a method of reaction to difficult living conditions. Despite their critical objections to its character, the informants accepted their residence in the stigmatized place as their own; they identified with it, and their place of residence was a part of their self-presentation.[12] The Roma communities, socio-spatially and economically excluded from the dominant society, create their own social rules and standards, as well as systems of social control for enforcement thereof. The site is perceived, or more precisely, presented as a ghetto with references to the threats stemming from the (allegedly) high rate of crime. Threats and intimidation, both verbal and physical, are described in the hip hop lyrics being analyzed as a preventive activity to avoid entrance by persons who do not belong to the area, especially those not living therein. This mechanism supports the acceptance of their place of living as "their own."

> *My* quarter is small, but well-known. Look out when you are in the V. Volfa street,
> You can't do what you want here, you can't make decisions for us.

We are the ones who watch it here; those who don't know us yet will know us sometime.
All people in the neighborhood will never confront us (TomyMigel).

Watch out! You don't know what to expect here. . . . Watch your back. *I am your black banshee, I got you.* ("VVV Volfa" [song])

Don't walk here alone, the banshee is waiting for you here, dude. (Respekt 2)

FRUSTRATION AND DISDAIN

The reason and motivation for the active artistic work of our informants within the hip hop genre was the opportunity for the artists to express themselves and to let go of their feelings of frustration stemming from their current predicament in society. Neither the informants' statements nor their lyrics clearly show whether their frustration stems from the problems of young Roma living in the ghetto, or the situation in the society at large. Their lyrics tell of confrontation with everyday life pathologies, but, on the other hand, the larger society's issues, as well. Rap is viewed by our informants as a tool for reflecting *social reality,* not fantasy or fictional stories. Informants rap about their personal experience, opinions, and memories. "We mostly rap about our lives, what we feel, what we see" (R4),

Our informants see the source for calming down their feelings of frustration especially in their musical production, when "their" hip hop brings about "emotions of peace and calming down" (R4).

I write songs 'cause I can let off steam in these lyrics, I can just say anything. I take it as my weapon, my lyrics, my rap. Against the people and against all. And my lyrics, what I most often rap about . . . are . . . just what pisses me off." (R1, 19)

Our informants consider drugs and their abuse and easy availability for the young generation as one of the main sources of negative trends in their society. Although drugs are one of essential topics of our informants' lyrics, they, as they say, do not use them, though some had experience with them in the past:

We don't take meth or crack . . . though I am black, I don't use drugs. . . . I don't steal, I don't take drugs and am proud of that. ("VVV Volfa")
I just hate dope. I also can't stand alcohol, either. I even don't drink as much. I hate dope. . . . Honestly, I never take drugs. . . . It seems as a complete rot for me. Why should I use meth that is often used now to have a good time? I can have a good time without meth, can't I? I think it is totally useless, just . . . I can say that I don't smoke anymore . . . . . . and alcohol is definitely bad, yep, like weed [marijuana]. (R1, 19)

Interestingly, some of our informants perceived "legal" drugs such as alcohol and cigarettes as similar to "illegal" drugs:

> Cigarettes are just the same. When you just don't have them, you go dotty and you go and rob the till in the tobacco shop, for example. (R1, 19)

Our informants identified the easy availability of drugs as one of the greatest problems. Drugs are "weakness" and a "mistake," and the informants make an appeal not to use them as they endanger their values, especially the biggest one—the family:

> You who waste your time on the bench,
> Smoking,
> This is not success, but a big mistake,
> This is not Gangsta, but a weakness,
> Let it be your everyday job.
> It is a mistake.
> Your mother believed in you, gave you money every day,
> Gave you everything.
> And you give her a pain in her heart for her kindness
> You think you got an ace in your pocket,
> And, in fact, the whole world laughs at you. ("Gossip")

Hip hop may serve as a "better" alternative to taking drugs: "This rap, this is our dope" ("VVV Volfa"). Interestingly, our informants believe that information on drugs in their lyrics may have a positive and preventive impact on listeners: "When somebody hears it, he takes a leaf out of this book and that's why he won't be interested in [doing drugs] anymore, I think" (R1, 19).

ETHNICITY

Roma/Gypsy ethnicity is a carrier of heavy social stigma in Czech society. Due to hundreds years of exclusion and marginalization, the Roma have been pushed to marginal spaces in the social imagination, turned into passive "objects"—receivers of the dominant society's prejudice and stereotypical projections, and targets of both exclusion and policies of integration or "assimilation." Being perceived as a Roma/Gypsy in contemporary Czech society means being exposed to the effects of a powerful stigma, being looked down upon, and being excluded in public spaces, schools, housing, and employment. Rabušic demonstrated in 1991 that, shortly after the fall of state socialism in Czechoslovakia, over 75 percent of respondents to a representative survey claimed they would not want to have a Roma/Gypsy as their neighbor (Rabušic 2000:68). Eight years later, a Slovak survey revealed that the number had risen to 94 percent (Barany 2002:192). On measured scales of social distance, the Roma/Gypsies usually rank first, even when other "traditional" outcast categories such as alcoholics, drug addicts, or homosexuals are included in the questionnaire (Vašečka 2003:231). We were aware that issues of ethnicity/race, discrimination, and social justice have been rather rarely reflected upon in Czech hip hop, and so we were looking forward to learning more about what young Roma hip hop performers would tell us about these issues.

We observed that ethnicity appeared in the interviews and lyrics of our informants, and we discovered interesting dichotomies, or more precisely, tensions between the *individual* and the *collective*. Where the informants refer to the Roma from the neighborhood, various means of creating distinctions and distance were apparent: "I am different and better." This emphasis on their own individuality was based on their refusal of the "bad" phenomena such as drugs, gambling, and involvement in crime allegedly omnipresent in the neighborhood. The lyrics contain many references to individualism, as the informants feel lonely in their different opinions and behavior.

> I will always act for myself only. ("VVV Volfa")
> Dude, the Gypsy, a man who finally pisses us off, you wonder what is going on here on Máj.
> Romas are everywhere, the crime is everywhere. ("Respekt new")

If, however, the lyrics and/or interviews contain an element of ethnic difference and distinction, as in the form of racism and stigmatization, our informants fight for all Roma. In this context, all Roma people are understood as an integral community to which our informants also belong.

> Ever since my childhood I have fought and I will fight for, and always represent, my black people. . . . The street is empty, our community is unique and rare. ("VVV Volfa").
> A Gypsy always sticks up for another Gypsy, and if not, it is a mistake. This shouldn't be done, this is not the way. One for all, all for one. We're on one boat together. ("Respekt new")

Roma hip hop—at least as seen through our informants' eyes—seems to be both a performance and a process of negotiating the artists' personal and collective self-conception, yet always in the shadow of identities/identifications imputed from outside. Our informants balance on the borderline between accepting the dominant society's values ("drugs are bad") and their refusal ("we are confronted with the major society's racism"). We asked our informants how they perceived their own ethnic identity. Once one of them identified himself openly as Roma, he continued:

I was normally ashamed of that by the age of 15, I was nervous about it. . . . Rytmus [a Roma hip hopper] helped me a lot in this. The way he became more popular and said it was nothing to be ashamed of, you know. He just said he was an absolutely normal person and the way he showed himself— all of that helped me a bit. I told myself why should I be ashamed of being [a Roma]? (R1)

Roma hip hop helped at least one of our informants to reconcile with his identity carrying such heavy social stigma in the dominant society. The stigmatized identity is something a person spontaneously resists, but hip hop provides a space for negotiating the "content" of such an identity. The Roma hip hoppers we talked to did not merely take in the external elements of their membership in the hip hop subculture (especially in relation to the fashion style, etc.); they also saw a possibility in their production to creatively express their point of view and critically reflect on what was going on around them and to voice principles of internal organization in the Gypsy ghetto.

CONCLUSIONS

Our informants are far from being "typical" Roma, or a representative sample of Roma/Gypsy hip hoppers. We have tried to view them in the same way that they perceive themselves: as young Roma living in an oppressive society, at an undesirable address, having limited access to resources and recognition by the dominant society. But this is what distinguishes them from the rest of young frustrated Roma living in the post-socialist world: their willingness to publicly share their point of view, to express their frustration, to be *heard*—not just *seen* (from afar, as mediated by TV and political propaganda). These young people do not fit the preestablished image of a young Roma, as they refuse to be constructed as passive objects of discrimination or "policies of integration"; instead, they actively produce themselves as self-reflexive agents who don't want to belong to the silenced mass of their peers. Hip hop gave our informants the tools for self-reflection and self-expression, and for social critique. It is becoming, at their relatively young age, one of the supporting pillars of their lives, against which the surge of their unfortunate life circumstances may break. Only time will tell whether (Romani) hip hop will remain an artistic expression of collectively felt frustration, or whether it will eventually turn into a vehicle of change after shared social cognition and political force meet at the right moment sometime in the future.

NOTES

1. This paper has been supported by Czech Science Foundation (project no. P404/12/P024—"Responses to Exclusion: Poor Roma Families under Post-Socialism."

2. According to Kalibová (1993), there are about 8 million to 15 million Roma around the world, of whom 5 million to 6 million reside in Europe. In a population projection made in 1993, she estimated that by 2005 about 495,000 Roma would be living in the Czech Republic and Slovakia combined (Kalibová 1993:256). Liégeois estimates the population of Roma/Gypsies to be somewhat higher: 200,000–250,000 for the Czech Republic (out of a total population of ca. 10 million) and 400,000–450,000 for Slovakia (of total population of ca. 5 million) (Liégeois 2007:31). David Crowe estimates that 300,000 Roma, all of whom pursue a sedentary lifestyle, are living in the Czech Republic (2007:256).

3. The term "Gypsy ghetto" was often used by our informants to denote the place of their residence and to point out the material decay, social ills, and social stigma associated with it. We accept the problematic term "ghetto" (see later in the text for a conceptual clarification), as it has often been used by our rap informants in their lyrics.

4. See http://www.ghettofest.cz/en/about-the-festival/.

5. "Jižák" is a publicly recognized nickname for Jižní Město (South City), Prague's notorious fringe area—nowadays stigmatized as a "communist concrete jungle"—where over 100,000 people live in the high-rise state socialist–style concrete blocks of flats.

6. http://www.gipsy.cz/index_en.php; http://en.wikipedia.org/wiki/Gipsy.cz.

7. http://en.wikipedia.org/wiki/Rytmus; http://www.rytmus-kral.cz/.

8. Rytmus (n.d.), "Cigansky sen [video], https://www.youtube.com/watch?v=0YsEpZKaank.

9. "Low-threshold clubs" are areas where young people "at risk" can enter and pursue leisure activities, sports, music, etc.

10. Analyzing the texts, we created open, axial, and selective coding after we repeatedly went through the transcribed interviews and song lyrics. When we first went through the data, the open coding localized the topics in the text and allocated codes to them. We created a list of topics that helped us to see the research problem as a whole. In the case of axial coding, we put the data together again after open coding, making connections between categories. Individual categories were correlated. During selective coding, a central category was found and later put in relation with other categories, and these relations were further verified (Charmaz 2006). Each author coded the grounded theory individually as per the control requirements, and the created categories were consequently discussed and compared.

11. When referring to the people with whom we have conducted our research, we use the term "informant." Although other denotations can be used, such as "information partners," "interlocutors," etc., we prefer to stick to the term commonly used in sociological and anthropological literature.

12. "V. Volfa, our street." ("VVV Volfa")

REFERENCES

Barany, Zolan. 2002. *The East European Gypsies: Regime change, marginality, and ethnopolitics.* Cambridge: Cambridge University Press.

Baršová, Andrea. 2003. "Housing Problems of Ethnic Minorities and Trends toward Residential Segregation in the Czech Republic." In *Romany in the Town,* ed. Gabriela Rösnerová (pp. 10–32). Prague: Socioklub and UNHCR.

Burawoy, Michael, and Katherine Verdery, eds. 1999. *Uncertain Transition: Ethnographies of Change in the Postsocialist World.* Lanham, MD: Rowman & Littlefield.

Charmaz, Kathy. 2006. *Constructing Grounded Theory.* Los Angeles: Sage.

Crowe, David. 2007. *A History of the Gypsies of Eastern Europe and Russia,* 2nd ed. New York: Palgrave Macmillan.

Davidová, Eva. 1970. "The Gypsies in Czechoslovakia." *Journal of the Gypsy Lore Society* 50(1–2):40–55.

Davidová, Eva, ed. 2010. *Kvalita života a sociální determinanty zdraví u Romů v České a Slovenské republice* [The quality of life and social determinants of health among the Roma in the Czech and Slovak Republics]. Prague: Triton.

European Commission against Racism and Intolerance. 2009. "ECRI Report on the Czech Republic (fourth monitoring cycle)." http://www.coe.int/t/dghl/monitoring/ecri /country-by-country/czech_republic/CZE-CbC-IV-2009-030-ENG.pdf.

European Roma Rights Centre. 2010. "Persistent Segregation of Roma in the Czech Education System." http://www.errc.org/cms/upload/media/03/AC/m000003AC.pdf.

Filadelfiová, Jarmila, Daniel Gerbery, and Daniel Školba. 2006. *Správa o životných podmienkach rómskych domácností na Slovensku* [Report on the living conditions of Roma households in Slovakia]. Bratislava: UNDP.

Gabal Analysis & Consulting. 2006. *Analysis of Socially Excluded Roma Localities in the Czech Republic and Absorption Capacity of Entities Involved in This Field.* Prague: Gabal Analysis & Consulting.

Hann, Chris, ed. 2002. *Postsocialism: Ideals, Ideologies, and Practices in Eurasia.* London: Routledge.

Hirt, Tomas, and Marek Jakoubek, eds. 2006. *Romové v osidlech sociálního vyloučení* [The Roma Ensnared in Social Exclusion). Pilsen: Vydavatelství a nakladatelství Aleš Čeněk.

Hurrle, Jakob. 2006. "The Third World in the First World: Development and Renewal Strategies for Rural Roma Ghettos in Slovakia." In *Spatial Planning and Urban Development in the New EU Member States: From Adjustment to Reinvention,* eds. Uwe Altrock, Simon Günter, Sandra Huning, and Deike Peters (pp. 141–162). Aldershot: Ashgate.

Jakoubek, Marek, and Tomas Hirt, eds. 2008. *Rómske osady na východnom Slovensku z hľadiska terénneho antropologického výskumu* [Romani settlements in Eastern Slovakia from the perspective of anthropological fieldwork]. Bratislava: Open Society Foundation.

Jurová, Anna. 1993. *Vývoj rómskej problematiky na Slovensku po roku 1945* [The development of the Roma question in Slovakia after 1945]. Bratislava: Goldpress.

Kajanová, Alena, and David Urban 2009. "Social Work in Socially Excluded Areas Aimed at the Practical Prevention of Social Pathology—České Budějovice." *Sociální Práce/ Sociálna Práca* 2:62–69.

Kalibová, Květa. 1993. "Gypsies in the Czech Republic and the Slovak Republic: Geographic and Demographic Characteristics." *GeoJournal* 30(3):255–258.

Kolářová, Marta. 2011. "Místo závěru: Hodnoty, struktura a životní styl postsocialistických hudebních subkultur mládeže" [In place of the conclusion: The values, structure, and lifestyle of music youth subcultures under postsocialism] In *Revolta stylem: Hudební subkultury mládeže v české republice* [Revolt through style: Music youth subcultures in the Czech Republic], ed. Marta Kolářová (pp. 201–242). Prague: Sociologické nakladatelství.

Kornai, János, Stephan Haggard, and Robert P. Kaufman, eds. 2001. *Reforming the State: Fiscal and Welfare Reform in Post-Socialist Countries.* Cambridge: Cambridge University Press.

Kozlová, Lucie, and Renata Klufová. 2012. "Sociálně prostorové nerovnosti v ohrožené lokalitě sídliště Máj v Českých Budějovicích." *Fórum Sociální Politiky* 6(3):25–29.

Ladányi, Janos. 2001. "The Hungarian Neoliberal State, Ethnic Classification, and the Creation of a Roma Underclass." In *Poverty, Ethnicity, and Gender in Eastern Europe during the Market Transition,* eds. Rebecca Emigh and Ivan Szelenyi (pp. 67–82). Westport, CT: Praeger.

Ladányi, Janos, and Ivan Szelényi. 2006. *Patterns of Exclusion: Constructing Gypsy Ethnicity and the Making of an Underclass in Transitional Societies of Europe.* New York: Columbia University Press.

Liégeois, Jean-Pierre. 2007. *Roma in Europe.* Strasbourg: Council of Europe Publishing.

Lux, Martin. 2003. "Social Rental Housing in the Czech Republic Now and Tomorrow." In *Housing Change in East and Central Europe: Integration or Fragmentation,* eds. Stuart Lowe and Sasha Tsenkova (pp. 83–94). Burlington: Ashgate.

Mandel, Ruth, and Caroline Humphrey, eds. 2002. *Markets and Moralities: Ethnographies of Postsocialism.* Oxford: Berg Publishers.

Milanovic, Branko. 1998. *Income, Inequality, and Poverty during the Transition from Planned to Market Economy.* Washington, DC: World Bank.

Mitchell, Tony, ed. 2001. *Global Noise: Rap and Hip Hop outside the U.S.A.* Middletown, CT: Wesleyan University Press.

Oravcová, Anna. 2011. "Underground českého hip hopu" [The underground of Czech hip hop]. In *Revolta stylem: Hudební subkultury mládeže v české republice* [Revolt through style: Music youth subcultures in the Czech Republic], ed. Marta Kolářová (pp. 123–157). Prague: Sociologické nakladatelství.

Pasternak-Mazur, Renata. 2009. "The Black Muse: Polish Hip Hop as the Voice of 'New Others' in the Post-Socialist Transition." *Music and Politics* 3(1):1–20.

Rabušic, Ladislav. 2000. "Koho Češi nechtějí? O symbolické sociální exkluzi v české společnosti" [Whom the Czechs do not want? On symbolic exclusion in Czech society]. *Sociální Studia/Social Studies* 5:63–81.

Radičová, Iveta, and Michal Vašečka. 2001. "Redistribution's Role in Leveling Income: The Overgrown Slovak Welfare State." In *Poverty, Ethnicity, and Gender in Eastern Europe during the Market Transition,* eds. Rebecca Emigh and Ivan Szelenyi (pp. 157–189). Westport, CT: Praeger.

Radostný, Lukáš. 2008. *Po stopách romského hip hopu.* A2. http://www.advojka.cz/archiv /2008/27/po-stopach-romskeho-hip-hopu.

Ringold, Dena. 2000. *Roma and the Transition in Central and Eastern Europe: Trends and Challenges.* Washington, DC: World Bank.

Rösnerová, Gabriela, ed. 2003. *Romany in the Town.* Prague: Socioklub and UNHCR.

Ruzicka, Michal. 2009. "Researching and Politicizing Migration: The Case of Roma/Gypsies in Postsocialist Czecho-Slovakia." In *Boundaries in Motion: Rethinking Contemporary Migration Events,* eds. Radka Klvaňová, Ondrej Hofírek, and Michal Nekorjak (pp. 70–103). Brno: Centre for the Study of Democracy and Culture.

Ruzicka, Michal. 2012a. "Continuity or Rupture? Roma/Gypsy Communities in Rural and Urban Environments under Post-Socialism." *Journal of Rural Studies* 28(2):81–88.

Ruzicka, Michal. 2012b. "Wacquant v romském ghettu: Poznámky k procesu ghettoizace v českých městech" [Wacquant in a Roma ghetto: Notes on the process of ghettoization in Czech cities]. In *Nové sociálně prostorové nerovnosti, lokální rozvoj a kvalita života,* eds. Jana Temelová, Lucie Pospíšilová, and Martin Ouředníček (pp. 20–45). Pilsen: Aleš Čeněk.

Scheffel, David. 2005. *Svinia in Black and White: Slovak Roma and Their Neighbors.* New York: Broadview.

Šimíková, Ivana, and Imrich Vašečka, eds. 2004. *Mechanismy sociálního vyčleňování romských komunit na lokální úrovni a nástroje intergrace.* Brno: Barrister & Principal.

Stejskalová, Michaela. 2013. "Can We Speak of Ghettos in Czech Cities?" *Slovo* 25(2):3–17.

Stewart, Michael. 2002. "Deprivation, the Roma and 'the Underclass.'" In *Postsocialism: Ideals, Ideologies and Practices in Eurasia*, ed. Chris Hann (pp. 133–155). London: Routledge.

Sýkora, Luděk, Jana Temelová, and Darina Posová. 2007. "Identifikace lokalit koncentrace sociálních skupin a jejich typologie." In *Segregace v České republice: Stav a vývoj, příčiny a důsledky, prevence a náprava*, ed. Luděk Sýkora (pp. 29–58). Prague: PrF CUNI.

Vašečka, Michal. 2003. "Relationship of the Majority Population to the Roma." In *Čačipen pal o Roma: A Global Report on Roma in Slovakia*, eds. Michal Vašečka, Martina Jurásková, and Tom Nicholson (pp. 227–236). Bratislava: Institute for Public Affairs.

Vašečka, Michal, Martina Jurásková, and Tom Nicholson, eds. 2003. *Čačipen pal o Roma: A Global Report on Roma in Slovakia*. Bratislava: Institute for Public Affairs.

Wacquant, Loïc. 1993. "Urban Outcasts: Stigma and Division in the Black American Ghetto and French Urban Periphery." *International Journal of Urban and Regional Research* 17(3):366–383.

Wacquant, Loïc. 2007a. "French Working-Class Banlieue and Black American Ghetto: From Conflation to Comparison." *Qui Parle* 16(2):1–34.

Wacquant, Loïc. 2007b. "Territorial Stigmatization in the Age of Advanced Marginality." *Thesis Eleven* 91:66–77.

Wacquant, Loïc. 2008. "Ghettos and Anti-Ghettos: An Anatomy of the New Urban Poverty." *Thesis Eleven* 94:113–118.

Wacquant, Loïc. 2011. "A Janus-Faced Institution of Ethnoracial Closure: A Sociological Specification of the Ghetto." In *The Ghetto: Contemporary Global Issues and Controversies*, eds. Ray Hutchison and Bruce Hayes (pp. 1–31). Boulder, CO: Westview.

CHAPTER 13

RAPPING THE CHANGES IN NORTHEAST SIBERIA

Hip Hop, Urbanization, and Sakha Ethnicity

Aimar Ventsel and Eleanor Peers

SINCE LATE 2012, a picture of a foggy winter street in the capital of the Republic of Sakha (Yakutia), Yakutsk, has been circulating on the Internet. The picture carries the caption "There are few rappers in Yakutsk because it is difficult to grow up in the street." People who know Yakutsk and its climate understand the humor of the picture: fog during the winter usually means that the temperature is 48 degrees Celsius or more below freezing. Those acquainted with Sakha will also appreciate the implicit reference to the region's peripheral status within the Russian Federation, which is associated with its extreme climate. Sakha covers an expanse of northeastern Siberia only slightly smaller than the Indian subcontinent, and yet it is populated by just over 950,000 people (Perepis 2010). Half of this population is Sakha, a Turkic-speaking ethnic group that has lived under Russian jurisdiction since the colonization of Sakha began in the early seventeenth century. The Sakha population has experienced massive social transformation over the twentieth and twenty-first centuries, as successive Soviet and post-Soviet states have presided over the dissemination of modern infrastructures, technologies, and cultural forms, ushering in a rapid urbanization of the Sakha population over the 1990s and 2000s. The increasing influence of global cultural, economic, and technological trends is raising questions about the meaning of a Sakha identification: How are urban Sakha people to understand their ethnic identity, divorced as they are from the rural practices and cultural forms that have hitherto defined the Sakha community within Russia? Conversely, how does the emergence of a modern Sakha society sit with the continuing perception within Russia and the wider world of the Sakha people and their republic as remote, backward, and even primitive?

Hip hop is, deservedly or not, often associated in popular perception with "gangstas" from the "ghetto." This image indicates rap's association with the tough guys who know the "real deal" of struggles against oppression. In an allegorical way, the photograph's caption reflects the contradictory nature of Sakha hip hop. Sakha hip hop culture emerged with the growth of the first substantial generation of Sakha town dwellers, and offers them a platform to articulate and manifest their generational and national identity. Yet what is generally absent in Sakha hip hop is precisely the "voice of the street" as resistance or protest. Ironically, Sakha hip hop can be regarded as—to paraphrase Ross Haefner (2007)—"good clean fun," and sometimes even as part of the officially approved youth culture. As this chapter will show, the practice of Sakha hip hop simultaneously reproduces and challenges Sakha social forms, as part of the way in which it expresses the emergence of new incarnations of the Sakha people. Although Sakha rap is conditioned by and therefore reflects power dynamics within Sakha, it nonetheless has the effect of problematizing assumptions about the Sakha people that arise out of a wider and more long-standing racial power dynamic within the Russian Federation as a whole. The nature of Sakha rap's intervention into oppressive power relationships is determined by its positioning among intersecting power hierarchies and authoritative discourses, within both Sakha (Yakutia) and the Russian Federation. Sakha rap asserts the presence of an urbanized Sakha people, ready and willing to engage with global cultural trends. In doing so, it questions the presumption—common in both Russian and Sakha communities—that the dominating Russian state and its cultural and commercial institutions set the standards that the backward Sakha should be following. The emergence of Sakha rap is in fact conditioned by its power to mediate responses to a keenly felt dilemma among contemporary Sakha people: Can a modern Sakha community take shape without the Sakha people becoming absorbed into and indistinguishable from mainstream Russian society?

One of the most popular—if not the most popular—musical genres and youth styles in the world is hip hop. This style and music is literally spread from Greenland in the north to New Zealand in the south, from Chukotka to Alaska. It is no surprise that there also exists a wealth of academic and nonacademic literature on this topic, covering all segments and facets of hip hop. The musical innovation vis-à-vis the social origin of African American hip hop has found keen interest among scholars (Kitwana 2005; Perkins 1996; Poschardt 1997; Toop 1992). Hip hop's unique way of writing songs and using samples is seen as a postmodern use of technology, combined with African American traditions and reflections of African American social status (Rose 1989). Apart from the technical side, hip hop has been discussed as a means to spread messages: the discussion of the meaning of hip hop lyrics is a significant part of the hip hop literature. Due its semi-underground status, it is assumed that early hip hop genres, and even some from the present day, function as alternative channels for information, and as platforms for political and social messages—as "post-literate orality" (Rose 1994). Hip hop is seen by some authors as one form of African American resistance that offers a platform within struggles for civil liberties and against racism (Zips and Kämpfer 2001), or a vernacular voice for the disadvantaged ghetto population (Potter 1995). It is also recognized that hip hop as a youth style did much to give political meaning to dress, and contributed substantially in the development of a global club culture (Ogg and Upshal 1999).

However, despite hip hop's reputation for being a quintessentially African American street music, it is also acknowledged that, from the beginning, US hip hop music was largely initiated by producers from the African American and white middle classes, who intended to market it to white suburban kids (Negus 1999; Ogg and Upshal 1999:21–24, 81). Moreover, it has been proved that the uncompromisingly rebellious images of rap artists were often carefully designed by record labels, and rappers showed little resistance to these kinds of marketing tricks (Kage 2002; Lena 2006). These record labels were never "outside the corporate system" (Negus 1999:96), as is demonstrated by the fact that hip hop labels, for instance, generally obeyed copyright laws, even when these laws strictly limited deliberate sampling (Vaidhyanathan 2001). The countercultural message of American hip hop has ultimately been shaped by the political economy of the American popular music industry, along with its conventions and practices.

However, the contradictions between hip hop's image and message, and the music industry's marketing strategies, did not hinder its rapid growth in global popularity. The rebellious and antiestablishment image of African American hip hop was one reason why this style was picked up by US white and Latino youth to express their own identities (Bucholtz 2011; Kitwana 2005; Perkins 1996). Other research demonstrates that power issues are also addressed with the help of this music in other parts of the world, whether in Colombia (Wade 1999), in the Chinese internet underground (Varis and Wang 2011), in Mongolia (Marsh 2010), in Ghana (Shipley 2009), by young migrants in Germany (Bennett 1999), or among Sami communities (Leppänen and Pietikäinen 2010). As with these examples, rap's rebellious image enables it to articulate the alienation of many young Sakha from the conventional association between Sakha identity and village life, with all its implications—although, as in the American case, Sakha hip hop is conditioned by and therefore also reflects the conventions and power dynamics within Sakha (Yakutia).

The discussion around the political message or commercial nature of hip hop music seems to overlook the fact that hip hop is—among other things—a youthful, energetic, and vivid music, which is easy to make with the help of a microphone and prerecorded beats. Hip hop is a rhythmic music with deep basses; it is generally easy to move one's body to it, and it is extremely suitable for collective entertainment. Keith Negus (1999:94) explains the success of rap as "an emotional performative sound event" that should not be reduced only to race, lyrics, or images. Apart from its militant addressing of social or political issues, hip hop also offers possibilities for expressing less radical—but not necessarily less important—views. Sakha rappers present a reformulation of the Sakha national project, and, in doing so, they project forms of Sakha identification to fit new urban realities.

This chapter starts by presenting a history of Sakha popular music since its emergence during the 1960s, showing how popular music in Sakha (Yakutia) has been shaped by modernizing social and political transformations, which have challenged older forms of association, hierarchy, and identification. These transformations were occurring under the aegis of the stated Soviet-era aim to turn the Soviet Union's "backward" peoples—such as the Sakha—into modern nation-states. At the same time, late-twentieth-century Sakha rock and pop laid the foundations for the later recognition of hip hop as an engaging music which was to become integrated into the changing politics and perceptions of ethnic and national identity. Then we chart the development of a visible Sakha rap scene in Yakutsk, showing how Sakha rap manifests specifically Sakha networks, hierarchies, and identities, even as it challenges and rearticulates them. In doing so, Sakha rap also reflects and responds to the changing power dynamics at work within the wider Russian Federation.

THE SAKHA POP MUSIC TRADITION

Music occupies an important position in Sakha culture, both past and present. However, the development and meaning of music in Sakha culture cannot be divided from social and economic change in the wider Russian Empire. Until the Revolution, the overwhelming majority of Sakha people were rural livestock herders and hunters, while only a tiny segment had received an education, forming the urban intelligentsia (Forsyth 1992). Therefore, Sakha music was associated above all with the rural culture. Singing and dancing accompanied all Sakha festive events, rituals, and celebrations, and in fact had an integral role in the Sakha people's practice of shamanism. The Soviet-era introduction of modern technologies and institutions revolutionized Sakha popular music, as it revolutionized Sakha ways of life.

Sakha popular entertainment music first emerged during the 1960s, after the Soviet administration had succeeded in integrating Sakha populations into the Soviet Union's wider network of industrial, agricultural, educational, and cultural institutions. This was the era of an orchestrated light-entertainment music that in the Soviet Union was called Estrada. Estrada music was for both dancing and listening; it enjoyed a wide popularity among the Soviet population, and was adopted by most of the state's ethnic minorities (MacFadyen 2001, 2002). In Sakha (Yakutia), several artists combined Sakha folk music with Estrada in their recordings, and this music became available on the radio, on cassettes, and also in live performance, thanks to the Soviet Union's network of village performance spaces, the Houses of Culture (Doidu 2001; cf. Donahoe and Habeck 2011; see also Ventsel 2004b). During this era, the majority of the Sakha people remained in the villages, and communicated among themselves principally in their native language. The Sakha people living in cities formed a small but educated group (Yakutia 2007). Homegrown pop music—performed in Sakha—enjoyed a particular popularity among Sakha populations.

A decade later, the migration of Sakha people to the cities had increased, but urban Sakha still formed a minority within the wider Sakha population. Moreover, educated people, due their small numbers and close ties to the Russian-speaking community, increasingly switched to Russian, sometimes even to the extent of not teaching their children Sakha (Yakutia 2007). For many urban Sakha, the Sakha language was associated with an embarrassingly "backward" village lifestyle, whereas Russian was regarded as the language of progress. This view accorded with the assumption that modernization is a universal goal for humanity, which was an integral part of Soviet-era historical materialism.

In the 1970s, the first Sakha rock groups who performed danceable music were established. Following in the footsteps of Sakha-language Estrada, Sakha rock was greeted with great enthusiasm. "People liked it because it was in their language," said a founding member of one of the first Sakha rock bands. As this quotation indicates, popular music from its beginning resonated with Sakha identification, and was recognized by many as part of their cultural tradition.

A new generation of rock groups appeared during the *perestroika* years, merging psychedelic and hard rock with traditional music and instruments. This "ethno-rock" enjoyed great popularity among the Sakha people, but also attracted the attention of the wider Soviet population, and even some foreigners (Troitskii 2007). Groups like Cholbon, Aital, or Serge performed on the central Soviet TV channels, but also participated in various festivals abroad. The rise of ethnic rock took place in tandem with the establishment of the autonomous Republic of Sakha (Yakutia) in 1992. These events corresponded with the non-Russian national revivals that were then occurring throughout the Soviet Union, and, in conformity with this trend, both signaled and encouraged a new pride in Sakha heritage and culture. Shamanic rock drew on the rural Sakha music tradition, fusing it with modern instruments and rock melodies in a genre that demonstrated the strength of the Sakha people's cultural heritage, as well as their modern nationhood. Some intellectuals argued that these rock groups should be seen as a sign of the openness and modernity of Sakha culture (Ventsel 2004a, 2009). And yet the wide popularity of ethno-rock was also related to song lyrics that thematized the rural origins of the Sakha people, since listeners felt they could relate to their sentiments.

Considering that most Sakha rock and Estrada artists were first-generation town dwellers who retained a strong connection with their village roots, the use of traditional melodies and instruments is not surprising. This urban–rural connection was reflected in all major genres of Sakha music as a preoccupation with shamanism, ancient Sakha culture, and the notion of one's home village. The content of pop and rock music also mirrored common ideas about Sakha ethnic identity: the village with all its rituals and traditions was seen as the cradle of Sakha culture, whereas the city was an imported life form—a foreign space. For the majority of Sakha people at this time, the city was indeed a different linguistic and cultural space, where they had to adopt different lifestyles and forms of social relationships. Furthermore, notions of the home village symbolized the right of the Sakha people to inhabit the republic's territory, and therefore also had political connotations. Rural traditions and beliefs embodied the moral superiority of the Sakha population over non-Sakha newcomers. After the collapse of the Soviet Union, all these arguments were used by the more radical Sakha nationalists in their struggle for control over the natural resource extraction industry that had developed during the Soviet period. These arguments subverted Soviet-era stereotypes about the backward Siberian peoples, transforming this alleged backwardness into a virtue. Sakha popular music was taking shape in tandem with other art forms, and reflected these sentiments. It had the effect of reiterating associations between a Sakha identity and a rural lifestyle in close communion with the natural world.

The Post-Soviet Era and the Emergence of Hip Hop

The collapse of the Soviet Union was followed by substantial social and cultural changes. Apart from the appearance of a Sakha nationalist political elite in the newly established republic, a significant increase in migration from villages to Yakutsk in particular became a new reality (Argounova-Low 2007). The declaration of sovereignty brought to the fore questions about the ethnic and national consciousness of the Sakha people. Sakha traditional culture and the Sakha language became prominent symbols of Sakha nationhood (Khazanov 1995; Thumann 2002). Political struggles with the Russian Federation's central government met with success. The republican government gained a substantial level of control over the republic's natural resource extraction; in particular, it secured a third of the yearly profits from Sakha (Yakutia)'s lucrative diamond industry (Duncan 1994; Tichotsky 2000). With these changes, a new and very prominent strand of nationalist discourse was introduced into Sakha (Yakutia)'s public culture, while an increasing number of Sakha people viewed the new republic as *their* state and incomers as intruders (Forsyth 1992).

Sakha music also underwent considerable change. New clubs and record labels were established, in addition to private radio stations that could give airplay to local pop music. The local musical landscape acquired more variety: at the end of the 1990s young artists who performed disco and occasionally techno rap music started to appear. Their style became known as *popsa*, a Russian word for "night-club music" (Ventsel 2004a). In 1998 the Duoraan record label was established, which became crucial in releasing new Sakha pop music. Duoraan's "Best of" sampler series was and is of great importance to the local pop music scene: these samplers include only the latest popular hits, and continue to give a very good overview of the current state of affairs in local youth music.

Like the rock or Estrada artists, *popsa* performers were predominantly first-generation city dwellers. Their music was exclusively in Sakha, and their lyrics were strongly oriented toward praising their home village or district. This period also saw the first attempts to produce Sakha music videos. Notably, visual images from the canon of Sakha folklore were common in all popular musical genres. Singers or bands often wore stylized national costumes; images of horses (holy animals in Sakha culture), village buildings, and forests were prominent (Ventsel 2004a). Hence, these videos and this music invoked and reproduced conventionalized, romanticized images of an emphatically rural Sakha culture and identity. Through visual representation, Sakha cultural roots were placed in the village and not in the town.

The end of the 1990s was also the time when the first hip hoppers appeared in the cities of Sakha (Yakutia). These were small groups of teenagers who—apart from listening to the music—attempted to make it by rapping over computer-generated beats. During the early years hip hoppers were often seen as maverick copycats of MTV music videos. Their reputation in the local music scene was also damaged by what was perceived as their "stupid" and "unstylish" appearance: hip hop clothes were difficult to obtain, and these young kids often just wore oversize jeans, jackets, and women's headscarves. And yet the continued adaptation of hip hop cultural forms by a small circle of young people also became visible through the first works of graffiti. In 2000, a wall in an abandoned construction site in Yakutsk was decorated with a huge portrait of Tupac Shakur.

The year 2001 saw a certain shift in Sakha *popsa* music: more and more Sakha artists started to perform songs in Russian. The newly established youth program *Tynnyk* on the national TV station NVK began to broadcast music videos, and several young and fashionable artists, such as Egor or the girl duo Sardaanalar, made videos in which they sang either in Russian or switching between Sakha and Russian. It is unclear whether the producers of the expanding Sakha pop-music business were aiming at a Russian audience, or whether they could simply not ignore the growing population of young Russian-speaking Sakha (Ventsel 2004a). This group had emerged as a result of the massive Sakha migration to

Yakutsk after the decline of the Soviet Union; this migration was partially stimulated by the closure of Soviet-built industrial settlements, which forced many Russian-speaking Sakha to move to the capital, where their children mixed with Yakutsk's Sakha youngsters.

This was the first time that Sakha hip hop enjoyed some mainstream success. During 2000 and 2001, a techno-rap group called X-Up was performing in the republic's nightclubs, and there were rumors that teenagers were organizing popular hip hop house parties. In 2001, Duoraan released another "Best of" sampler on cassette, and this time a hip hop song was included. The artist, using the stage name Gaudeamus, performed the only song in Russian on this album. The song expresses complex attitudes about the village environment, and ultimately the alienation of the urban youth from village culture. The lyrics tell the story of a city boy who travels to a village to visit his relatives. In the village, he is forced to do all sorts of "dumb" country jobs, like chopping wood, or haymaking. During his stay in the village, he meets several local girls and impresses them with his city cool. The only time the Sakha language can be heard in the song is when the Sakha girls express their enthusiasm and wonder about the protagonist. The song is sung with humor, but the position of the rapper is clear: He does not feel at home in the village, and he finds life there primitive, backward, and boring. One may contend that this song is a moment of reflection on the disjuncture between rural and urban lifestyles and the questions this disjuncture poses for Sakha identification. The fact that this song became a hit demonstrates that a significant number of listeners liked and could relate to the message it expressed. While the sampler's other songs praised village life, Gaudeamus ridiculed it, thus challenging conventional public representations of Sakha culture and values, and in doing so complicating the discourses around Sakha identity.

After 2003, Sakha hip hop's popularity seemed to grow year on year, as new generations of urban-born teenagers came of age. For the first time, Yakutsk was home to a substantial community of young Sakha, who had been brought up in the city—and who, most importantly, had a very weak emotional affiliation with rural lifestyles. This generation's Sakha-language skills were and are varied. While some have poor or even nonexistent Sakha, other "city Sakha" are bilingual. This language barrier is one reason behind the widespread urban alienation from rural life. Several of these youngsters were not only unable to communicate with their village relatives, but were also often subject to derogation by villagers, who have long been known for their sensitivity about the issue of Sakha language and culture. As one of these boys said, shrugging his shoulders, "Yes, we have relatives in Oimiakon [an agricultural region in southern Sakha (Yakutia)], but I visit them maybe once a year. It is always a hassle. The language issue—'Why don't you speak it, how can it be that you do not understand what I say?'"

The first Sakha hip hop sampler—titled in English *Sakha Rap*—was released on CD in 2004, and contains only songs in Sakha. By 2005, Sakha hip hop was becoming an increasingly striking presence, especially in Yakutsk, where there were several artists performing alone or in "crews." Another sampler CD—*Sakha Rap 2*—contained tracks by 18 artists. Most tracks are in Sakha, but a few are in Russian. Not unusual also were collaborations, in which several artists rap in Sakha or Russian in turn.

In the summer of 2006, Yakutsk hosted a hip hop festival, organized by the city council. This event was advertised on a large scale, and local media organs covered the event extensively. At the same time, a short-lived hip hop music journal was founded—a small, glossy publication that informed its readers about new DJs and events in town, but also contained stories and pictures about hip hop fashion and international or Russian artists. This journal contained several advertisements and sponsor logos, and local businesses also sponsored the hip hop festival. This demonstrates that Sakha rap culture followed a pattern widespread in local Estrada or rock music, in that rap artists participated in state-organized music events with commercial sponsors. This toleration of official sponsorship arguably disqualifies any pretentions Sakha rap might have toward being entirely protest or counterculture in its orientation. It is more likely that rappers wanted to stand in the limelight on an equal basis with earlier music generations.

By 2006, Duoraan had recognized hip hop's market potential and released a well-produced sampler with the English title *Sakha Next People,* which, according to the label's tradition, presented the latest and most exciting hip hop hits. The sampler album begins with the song "Eppetekh Tyllarym" (My Untold Words), a love song performed by Sasha Lukin, Fill, and Stas Noev. This song was a huge hit, and in 2007 these artists released a video for the song. The shoot was organized by Stas Noev, who, in addition to being a rapper, was also a DJ working at the most prominent Sakha pop music radio station, Radio Victoria Sakhalyy, where he occasionally played hip hop and club music during late-night broadcasts. Stas's comment on the video was, "We wanted to do our own thing. All Sakha music videos are related to the village. The band stands in an *alaas* [a large forest clearing, where animals can be pastured], and you see lakes or horses. We wanted to have something very different." Despite the fact that not all Sakha pop acts emphasize the rural idyll in their videos, the video for the song "Eppetekh Tyllarym" was radically different from anything that had preceded it. The video starts with the trio entering a dark sports hall, where they sit down around loudspeakers. Then the viewer sees a girl waking up in bed. She is obviously of mixed European-Asian origin, and is wearing only underwear. After she smiles shyly, the video cuts to a group of fashionably dressed break dancers. The rest of the video consists of a constant intercutting between the artists, the girl, and the break dancers. Visually, the video is a celebration of urban fashion and lifestyle. Artists are shown in expensive and fashionable clothes; at least two break dancers demonstrate impressive dance skills. The emphasis is clearly on contemporary youth culture and the independence of young people. In keeping with the sampler's English-language title, the track and its video show their producers to be integrated into global youth culture, and therefore confident about asserting attitudes toward both sexuality and Sakha identity that contravene older norms. The appearance of the mixed-race girl expresses what has become an increasingly common phenomenon—and, in doing so, emphasizes the ambiguities that surround Sakha identification, while problematizing claims about "pure" Sakha culture and identity.

In comparison with 2000 and 2001, Sakha hip hop went through a rapid transformation during the mid-2000s, which continued until 2007. The music moved from a closed minority circuit to radios and mainstream stages. This was also the period of a considerable shrinking of Sakha nationalist mobilization. In 2004, President Vladimir Putin had abolished the election of the Russian Federation's regional heads and presidents as part of his centralizing reforms. The federal government also succeeded in depriving the republic of its control over the diamond and other natural resource industries. President Shtyrov, elected in 2002 and reinstated in 2006, was a Russian unable to speak Sakha. The Sakha language suddenly had less political value as a marker of Sakha identity. And yet the "loss of the diamonds" consolidated a sense of resentment among the republic's various ethnic groups, because all were seen as losers in the reform. Simultaneously, efforts of intellectuals and cultural workers to promote Sakha culture did not stop. On the contrary, activists realized that this was the only sphere where they could influence public opinion. Therefore, new pressure has been generated for Sakha youth to take an active interest in traditional culture, since this is perceived as the only way the Sakha can avoid becoming completely Russified. These tensions are well reflected in the attitudes older cultural activists have expressed toward hip hop. The director of the national Sakha Theatre has criticized hip hop as being an unsuitable, alien music and fashion. Even the owner of Duoraan records, Byokka Byotrop, has described hip hop as "soulless music," contrasting it negatively with ethnic rock bands.

By 2006, Yakutsk and the republic's other industrial cities had changed for the better, thanks to improving economic conditions in the whole of Russia: new shops, bars, and clubs opened, and major international brands were on sale. This transformation meant that the new generation was able to maintain a consumerist urban lifestyle on a scale that had previously been impossible. Sakha hip hop continued to flourish, and new songs and albums appeared. Through their lyrics, rappers emphasized a new desire to align themselves with the rest of Sakha music and people. Apart from a preoccupation with common themes like love and friendship, songs about being proud of one's Sakha identity and hometown were produced and played on the radio. It thus became clear that young rappers did feel part of the Sakha nation, whether their first language was Russian or Sakha. Those who were able to speak Sakha also demonstrated in this way their respect for the Sakha language. The young urban Sakha generation showed through their lyrics that they wanted to be part of their local music tradition, and not outside it.

The recognition hip hop received at this time is illustrated by the success of the artist Jeada, who is currently the republic's most prominent hip hop star, often appearing on stage with *popsa* artists. He has released several successful albums, which have contained at least two patriotic songs. Moreover, in 2009 he was the main protagonist of the film *Dalaha ustun unguor* [Guarding Hope]. Jeada plays a rap star struggling with the local music business. At the same time, he wants to find his mother, who abandoned him during his childhood. Jeada, as the positive protagonist, is in constant conflict with greedy producers, who speak mixed Russian and Sakha. At the end of the film, Jeada travels to a village and finds his mother. The film shows Yakutsk as an urban jungle with nightclubs and wild concerts. By speaking good literary Sakha himself, Jeada represents the contemporary young hip hop fan who is simultaneously proud of his Sakha heritage. He is well aware of his roots and the importance of family ties. Meanwhile, the greedy music producers who have lost their language and identity are shown to be immoral people, who are only interested in money. As a whole, the film asserts that urban Sakha are part of the Sakha nation, despite their use of foreign musical genres and clothing. Notably, in real life Jeada has a "good guy" image, and is known for being conscious of and taking responsibility for his heritage. In 2010, he started the youth project Aiar Aian, in cooperation with the republic's parliament. At the project's public launch, he stated that its aim was to encourage young people to be active, to study, to make music, and to "change things." Jeada's general popularity is similar to Elvis Presley's, in Greil Marcus' (1977) reading: both might be engaged in making controversial music, but through their social engagement—one launches a youth project, the other serves in the army—the artists conform to mainstream values. Meanwhile, the willingness of politicians and journalists to collaborate with Jeada in this youth project reveals an answering recognition of Sakha rap's worth and relevance among members of the Sakha elites.

CONCLUSIONS

Sakha rap's prominence within the negotiation of alternative urban Sakha identifications demonstrates both the impact of global cultural forms around the world and the way in which these cultural forms are assimilated into the warp and weft of local circumstances. Jeada's music claims a new authority for urban Sakha identification, while his social position and activism reflect the changes, contradictions, and pressures currently at work in Sakha society, as they sit with the underlying power dynamics of the wider Russian Federation. Sakha nationalists can no longer aspire to a significant level of political autonomy, as the republic again becomes a provincial part of a wider, Russian-dominated federal state; meanwhile, Sakha traditionalists are unable to counter the power and attraction of global popular culture for the newly urbanized youth. And yet Jeada is claiming simultaneously, first, the right of the urbanized Sakha population to a Sakha identification, and second, the positive value of the Sakha cultural heritage. His delineation of the urban Sakha who is, nonetheless, committed to a traditional cultural heritage expresses perspectives from the growing nationalist-influenced urban Sakha population, while challenging those in the wider Russian Federation who might regard the idea of a modern, urbanized, and yet proudly Sakha person as an oxymoron. Despite its adherence to the stylistic and musical conventions of American hip hop, Sakha rap has emerged as a unique cultural form, which manifests the tensions contemporary Sakha people experience as it mediates possible resolutions.

References

Alim, Salim H. 2009. "Straight outta Compton, Straight outta München: Global Linguistic Flows, Identities, and the Politics of Language in a Global Hip Hop Nation." In *Straight outta Compton, Straight outta München: Global Linguistic Flows, Identities, and the Politics of Language in a Global Hip Hop Nation*, eds. Salim H. Alim, Ibrahim Awad, and Alastair Pennycook (pp. 1–22). New York: Routledge.

Alim, Salim H., Ibrahim Awad, and Alastair Pennycook. 2009. *Global Linguistic Flows: Hip Hop Cultures, Youth Identities, and the Politics of Language*. New York: Routledge.

Argounova-Low, Tatiana. 2007. "Close Relatives and Outsiders: Village People in the City of Yakutsk, Siberia." *Arctic Anthropology* 44(1):51–61.

Bennett, Andy. 1999. "Hip hop am Main: The Localization of Rap Music and Hip Hop Culture." *Media Culture Society* 21(1):7–91.

Bucholtz, Mary. 2011. *White Kids: Language, Race and Styles of Youth Identity*. Cambridge: Cambridge University Press.

Crate, Susie. 2006. "Ohuokhai: Sakhas' Unique Integration of Social Meaning and Movement." *Journal of American Folklore* 119(472):161–183.

Cushman, Thomas. 1995. *Notes from Underground: Rock Music Counterculture in Russia*. Albany: State University of New York.

Doidu, Aisen. 2001. *Khohoon, Sehen, Kiine, Teatr*. D'okuuskai: Bichik.

Donohoe, Brian, and Joachim Otto Habeck. 2011. *Reconstructing the House of Culture: Community, Self, and the Makings of Culture in Russia and Beyond*. New York: Berghahn.

Duncan, Peter J. S. 1994. "The Politics of Siberia in Russia." *Sibirica* 1:13–23.

Forsyth, James. 1992. *A History of the Peoples of Siberia: Russia's North Asian Colony 1581–1990*. Cambridge: Cambridge University Press.

Haefner, Ross. 2007. *Straight Edge. Clean-Living Youth, Hardcore Punk, and Social Change*. New Brunswick, NJ: Rutgers University Press.

Kage, Jan. 2002. *American Rap: Explicit Lyrics, US-HipHop und Identität*. Mainz: Ventil.

Khazanov, Aanatolii M. 1995. *After the USSR: Ethnicity, Nationalism, and Politics in the Commonwealth of Independent States*. Madison: University of Wisconsin Press.

Kitwana, Bakari. 2005. *Why White Kids Love Hip Hop: Wankstas, Wiggers, Wannabes, and the Reality of Race in America*. New York: Basic Books.

Lena, Jennifer C. 2006. "Social Context and Musical Content of Rap Music, 1979–1995." *Social Forces* 85(1):479–495.

Leppänen, Sirpa, and Sari Pietikäinen. 2010. "Urban Rap Goes to Arctic Lapland: Breaking Through and Saving the Endangered Inari Sami Language." In *Urban Rap Goes to Arctic Lapland: Breaking Through and Saving the Endangered Inari Sami Language*, eds. Helen Kelly-Holmes and Gerlinde Mautner (pp. 148–160). Basingstoke: Palgrave Macmillan.

MacFadyen, David. 2001. *Red Stars: Personality and Soviet Popular Song, 1955–1991*. Montreal: McGill-Queen's University Press.

MacFadyen, David. 2002. *Estrada?! Grand Narratives and the Philosophy of the Russian Popular Songs since* Perestroika. Montreal: McGill-Queen's University Press.

Marcus, Greil. 1977. *Mystery Train*. New York: E. P. Dutton.

Marsh, Peter K. 2010. "Our Generation Is Opening Its Eyes: Hip Hop and Youth Identity in Contemporary Mongolia." *Central Asian Survey* 29(3):345–358.

Negus, Keith. 1999. *Music Genres and Corporate Cultures*. London: Routledge.

Ogg, Alex, and D. Upshal. 1999. *The Hip Hop Years: A History of Rap*. London: Channel 4 Books/Macmillan.

Perepis. 2010. http://www.gks.ru/free_doc/new_site/perepis2010/croc/perepis_itogi1612.htm (accessed May 19, 2013).

Perkins, William E., ed. 1996. *Droppin' Science: Critical Essays on Rap Music and Hip Hop Culture*. Philadelphia: Temple University Press.

Poschardt, Ulf. 1997. *DJ Culture: Diskjockeys und Popkultur*. Stuttgart: Tropen.

Potter, R. A. (1995). *Spectacular Vernaculars: Hip Hop and the Politics of Postmodernism*. Albany: State University of New York Press.

Rose, Tricia. 1989. "Orality and Technology: Rap Music and Afro-American Cultural Resistance." *Popular Music and Society* 13(4):45–44.

Rose, Tricia. 1994. *Black Noise: Rap Music and Black Culture in Contemporary America*. Middletown, CT: Wesleyan University Press.

Shipley, Jesse W. 2009. "Aesthetics of the Entrepreneur: Afro-Cosmopolitan Rap and Moral Circulation in Accra, Ghana." *Anthropological Quarterly* 82(3):631–668.

Thumann, Michael. 2002. *Das Lied von der russischen Erde: Moskaus Ringen um Einheit un Grösse*. Stuttgart: DVA.

Tichotsky, John. 2000. *Russia's Diamond Colony: The Republic of Sakha*. Amsterdam: Harwood Academic Publishers.

Toop, David. 1992. *Rap Attack: African Jive bis Global Hip Hop*. Munich: Wilhelm Heyne.

Troitskii, Artemii. 2007. *Back in the USSR*. St. Petersburg: Amfora.

Vaidhyanathan, Siva. 2001. *Copywrights and Copywrongs: The Rise of Intellectual Property and How It Threatens Creativity*. New York: New York University Press.

Varis, Piia, and Xuan Wang. 2011. "Superdiversity on the Internet: A Case from China." *Diversities* 13(2):70–83.

Ventsel, Aimar. 2004a. "Sakha Pop Music and Ethnicity." In *Sakha Pop Music and Ethnicity*, ed. Erich Kasten (pp. 67–86). Berlin: Dietrich Reimer.

Ventsel, Aimar. 2004b. "Stars without Money: Sakha Ethnic Music Business, Upward Mobility and Friendship." *Sibirica* 4(1):88–103.

Ventsel, Aimar. 2009. "Sakha Music Business: Mission, Contracts, and Social Relations in the Developing Post-Socialist Market Economy." *Sibirica* 8(1):1–23.

Wade, Peter. 1999. "Working Culture: Making Cultural Identities in Cali, Colombia." *Current Anthropology* 40(4):449–470.

Yakutia. 2007. *Yakutia: Istoriko-kul'turnyi atlas.* Moscow: Feriia.

Zips, Werner, and Heinz Kämpfer. 2001. *Nation X: Schwarzer Nationalismus, Black Exodus und Hip Hop.* Vienna: Promedia.

PART IV

HIP HOP AND GLOBAL
CIRCULATIONS OF BLACKNESS

CHAPTER 14

LA HAINE ET LES AUTRES CRIMES

Ghettocentric Imagery in Serbian Hip Hop Videos

Irena Šentevska

THIS CHAPTER GIVES an overview of the dominant modes of appropriation of "ghetto" imagery in Serbian hip hop videos and the location-specific modifications of its conventions adopted from African American hip hop culture. The French title of the chapter, however, indicates that the trajectory of these appropriations has not always followed a straight line: They also came from secondary sources, in this case the French "ghetto cinema" and the overall reception of hip hop culture in the Francophone world.

Another important French reference for this article is Loïc Wacquant's problematization of the term ghetto when it describes contexts other than African American disadvantaged neighborhoods. Wacquant basically considers the European perception and contemporary use of the ghetto as a cultural myth, and this myth is sustained on various levels: by governmental structures, academia, and the cultural industry (e.g., cinema and popular music). Adopting and processing this ghettocentric imagery/rhetoric, hip hop became a powerful conduit for these problematic and contested interpretations of social disadvantage. This becomes especially evident in the light of Serbia's recent experiences of political, economic, and cultural isolation during the conflicts in the former Yugoslavia, and the overwhelming feelings of deprivation, hopelessness, and disregard for the official structures of the society. This chapter consequently conceives the notion of the ghetto as a cultural construct with elastic physical borders: from one music video to another, the ghetto may refer to (represent) one (more or less) disadvantaged neighborhood, a whole city (Belgrade, Niš, Novi Sad, etc.), or Serbia as one big, ultimate ghetto.

As a brief introduction, the chapter traces the history of appropriation and local modifications of the various stages in the development of the African American hip hop culture, first in late socialist Yugoslavia (1980s), and then in Serbia as an independent state with a recent history of "ghettoization." We proceed toward questions of "realness" and "authenticity" and various aspects of locally specific understandings and representations of the ghetto in the Serbian context. To describe how ghettocentric imagery works, we jump to Serbia's "ultimate ghetto" and mythical place of origin of the local hip hop culture (Serbia's South Bronx, so to speak)—the "projects" of New Belgrade. We outline the history of New Belgrade's development and its public image in the socialist period (as a "collective dorm," notorious mostly for its boredom), then as the "heart of darkness" of Milošević's isolated and criminalized Serbia (also home to Serbia's major hip hop and graffiti artists), and post-2000 as Belgrade's municipality with the highest GDP and a privileged area for foreign investment and large-scale development. All of these urban and social transformations were reflected in Serbian films and, of course, in music videos (not exclusively) of the hip hop genre. After discussing certain ideological premises in Serbian responses to "gangsta" and "conscious" rap, we proceed to the main substance of our analysis—hip hop videos—and look at how ghettocentric imagery represents and communicates the notions of identity, belonging, and patriotism; how it pays tribute to its African American roots; how it perceives and communicates "blackness"; and which strategies of escape from the ghetto it devises. How, in this escape, hip hop crosses over into new territories (turbo-folk, world music, various dance and club cultures) is another subject of this analysis. We conclude with the observation that with all the escapist imagery borrowed from turbo-folk and other genres of commercial popular music, escape from the ghetto can only be temporary: without the ghetto—at least in Serbia—there is no hip hop.

GETO (I)STORIJA: A BRIEF HISTORY OF SERBIAN HIP HOP

Chuck D of Public Enemy "did not think it was conceivable that there would be such a thing as a hip-hop record" (Chang 2005:130). "Nobody ever thought that this would have a Serbian version," said Dragan Ambrozić, a rock critic from Belgrade, in February 2007 at a roundtable in the National Library of Serbia titled "A New Culture: Hip Hop Epics and Ethics."[1] Dragan was referring to the early socialist 1980s, before then-Yugoslav rock and pop musicians like Goran Bregović with Bijelo dugme, Bora Đorđević with Riblja čorba, Đorđe Balašević, Dušan Kojić Koja with Disciplina kičme, or Rambo Amadeus started to experiment with rapping, acknowledging their awareness of the rising global musical trend with roots in South Bronx. However, hip hop did emerge in Serbia in the early 1980s with the formation of the first b-boy groups,[2] focused on break dancing. The first Yugoslav hip hop release, *Degout EP* (Jugoton, Zagreb, 1984), by Belgrade hip hop pioneers the Master Scratch Band, was recorded free of charge in the Druga maca studio, because the music was appreciated at the time as innovative and radically different. Serbian hip hop tradition has it that in the late 1980s, Branko Bojović (Bane Sanšajn) went to the United States on a student exchange, where he found himself at an N.W.A. gig. Thoroughly impressed with the "Black Beatles"[3] from Compton, he sent some tapes back home, and upon return to Belgrade (1988) formed the band Green Cool Posse, which later (1994) reemerged as Sanšajn (Sunshine). The year 1988 saw the formation of another pioneering hip hop band, Who Is the Best? led by Aleksandar Džankić, a.k.a. MC Best, who played an important role in the rise of hip hop in Serbia with the radio show *Geto* (Radio Politika), which he launched in 1992. Many bloggers opine that in this early phase, rap music was concentrated in a single New Belgrade block, as all the early MCs were neighbors (*komšije*—Balkan term for "homies"). The ensuing wave of demo-bands (Bez kaucije, Crno-bela veza, JSSS [Jedva smo se skupili], etc.) featured Robin Hood (formed in 1988) as the main exponents. However, the 1987 (debut) single of the band Budweiser ("Ponoćna trka") marked a turning point in the local development of hip hop culture. The first hip hop bands started to emerge in other Serbian towns (e.g., 2B4 Time from Smederevo and Sound Control from Niš). The early days of hip hop in Serbia saw the rise to power of the Serbian communist-turned-nationalist leader Slobodan Milošević. When, in 1995, the first official hip hop albums were released, Serbia was already in a deep economic and political crisis—engaged in bloody ethnic conflicts that were raging throughout Bosnia and Croatia, isolated under UN sanctions, and practically excluded from the rest of the world. The first label that would release Serbian hip hop (Gru, CYA, Sunshine, etc.) was, surprisingly, Jugodisk, a recording company mainly concerned with turbo-folk music. Also in 1995, ITMM released Robin Hood's only album, featuring some "gangsta conscious" themes like the popular track "Geto storija." Thus, already in 1995, with the first official releases, Serbian hip hop was powered by two driving forces centering on the notion of the ghetto: (1) "centripetal" (stories about the desolate life within its confines), and (2) "centrifugal" (strategies of escape from it, either through crime, politics, or show business). The first drive gave hip hop a sense of self-containment and pride in "representing" the local area—'hood, city, or country—perceived as a ghetto. The second drive led to innumerable crossovers that set the stage for rapping in any conceivable situation—from "hip hoperas" to reality TV shows and "minstrel" hip hop versions of turbo-folk hits, not to mention the overwhelming presence of DJs, graffiti, hip hop choreography and fashion across every conceivable media form.

OLD SCHOOL, NEW SCHOOL

The first wave of Serbian hip hop peaked in 1997–1998, headed by Voodoo Popeye, Bad Copy (from South Central Kotež[4]), Straight Jackin', Belgrade Ghetto, C-Ya, 187, Sha-Ila,[5] Black in Soul, Rhythm Attack, Feel the Pain, Maddoggz, S.K.I.D.S. (Sima Kosmos Iz Dalekog Svemira), Ding Dong, Full Moon (Shorty and Juice), Rebel Without a Pause, BG, White Niggaz, and the popular Montenigers, natives of Montenegro. The second (and most prominent) wave was associated with the launch of the record label Bassivity Music (2002), dedicated to publishing only Serbian, Bosnian, and Croatian rap acts. The true expansion of hip hop culture in Serbia followed its debut release, *V.I.P.—Ekipa stigla,* featuring the characteristic hit "Ako riba drolja postane" (If a Bitch Becomes a Ho). This wave also brought along the band Beogradski sindikat, whose rap political satire "Govedina" stirred up the Serbian media. Other eminent representatives included Prti Bee Gee, (re-formed) Bad Copy, Juice, Shorty (later Bata Barata), CB4, Suid, X3M, D-Fence, Big Boss or Jan Zoo, along with MC Monogamija, Bauk Squad, FTP! Hain Teny, KG Odred, THC la Familija, Seven, Flow & Empty, Demonio, Bvana, Struka, Lud, Marčelo, DeNiro, Beton Liga, Krang, Blokovski, and so on. The last release of the second wave (marking the end of Bassivity Music in early 2007) was *THC la Familija,* including the track "Za ulicu, ortake." After 2006, the hip hop scene in Serbia had to reform: faster internet connections and ever-new technologies made hip hop available to a wider audience. MySpace began to be used en masse for promoting new releases. The place vacated by Bassivity Music was taken over by the Rap Cartel label of the Take It or Leave It record company, and its first releases, *Tačno u pre podne* (Prti Bee Gee) and *Majmun Idžuo* (THC la Familija), started an avalanche of popularity for Serbian rappers. A new generation came to the fore, featuring Marlon Brutal, Sale Tru, Hartmann, Princip, Sajsi MC (Ivana Rašić), J Cook, Skubi, Gazda Paja, Iskaz, Mlata, and others.

BLOK, BRATE, BRUKLIN: ON THE QUESTIONS OF "REALNESS" AND "AUTHENTICITY"

The way in which a particular culture contextualizes hip hop is shaped in its encounter with local history, ideologies, and social value systems; the resulting forms are, in a sense, hybrids, but characteristic *topoi* like the ghetto, the 'hood, and basketball yard mostly remain in the picture. According to the musicologist Iva Nenić, the notion of the ghetto in the Serbian hip hop context refers to:

1. the ghetto as a part of the city inhabited by members of the middle class[6] with a(n over)developed sense of belonging to their 'hood, and
2. Serbia as a ghetto (Nenić 2006:160–161).

"Serbia is a ghetto" is a hip hop truism, appearing in many forms and manifestations, from graffiti slogans like "Slobodan, thank you for the ghetto" (signed Reperi), to rap lyrics and visual iconography (videos and feature films). However, Loïc Wacquant, who studied contemporary developments in black American ghettos, reminded us that "ghetto" is not simply a topographic entity or an aggregation of poor families and individuals, but an institutional form—a historically determinate concatenation of mechanisms of ethno-racial closure and control. The ghetto is a socio-spatial formation that is culturally uniform and based on: "(1) the forcible relegation of (2) a 'negatively typed' population, such as Jews in medieval Europe and African Americans in the modern United States, to (3) a reserved, 'frontier territory' in which this population (4) develops under duress a set of parallel institutions that serve both as a functional substitute for, and as a protective buffer against, the dominant institutions of the encompassing society" (Wacquant 1997:343). Put differently, what qualifies a place as a "real" ghetto are the four major forms of racial domination found at work—namely categorization, discrimination, segregation, and exclusionary violence. After the 1990 riots in the poor industrial neighborhood of Lyons, Vaux-en-Velin, France (along with other European countries) was submerged by a wave of "moral panics" that saw the postindustrial urban periphery of Europe as transforming into "American-style ghettos." According to Wacquant, this "media legend" was soon adopted by politicians and (largely ignorant) academia—equally unacquainted with the banalities of the French working (or, rather, unemployed) class banlieues or the realities of the black American ghetto. In response to this situation, Wacquant traced how the "communal ghetto" of the mid-twentieth century mutated into a "hyperghetto" on the American side, and "how the working-class territories of the European urban periphery underwent a process of gradual decomposition, but one that, contrary to the dominant discourse, moved them away from the pattern of the ghetto, to the point where one can characterize them as anti-ghettos" (Wacquant 2009:109). He concludes that, on both continents, it is the *state* that is the major determinant of the intensity and forms assumed by urban marginality, through its mediation of struggles over the definition, distribution, and appropriation of public goods. To put it simply, according to Wacquant, what is in Europe (Western and Eastern) perceived as a "ghetto" simply does not qualify. With all their praise of realness, what hip hop narratives of marginality communicate is a metaphor, not the "real thing": hip hop "lives in the ghetto of the white imagination" (Queeley 2003:2). Searching for the "real ghetto" in Serbian hip hop videos is not likely to take us to places that meet Wacquant's criteria (Roma settlements which are "real" and are "ghettos"). They will, rather, take us to places like 36 Cherry Blossom Close in Staines (Surrey), imaginary home of Ali G, the illegitimate king of the *wiggas*.

7, 9, 11: New Belgrade—the "Ultimate Ghetto"

The diagnosis of Serbia as a "closed society," its (rightful or not) isolation from the (rest of) the "world," and life in a "ghetto" have featured as dominant themes in Serbian cinema since the early 1990s.[7] Within Serbia as "the great ghetto," one part of Belgrade had been granted a mythical aura as the ultimate "ghetto within a ghetto": New Belgrade (Novi Beograd), perceived as a paradigmatic *banlieue défavorisée.* Just as *Les HLM (habitation à loyer modéré*—suburban working-class neighborhoods with moderate rents) were transformed in socialist Yugoslavia into urban projects of leveling for the socialist middle class, genre patterns and narratives of European ghettocentric films were adopted by post-Yugoslav filmmakers and, consequently, by music video directors. The main stream of influence came with Mathieu Kassovitz's 1995 "ghetto film" *La Haine:* New Belgrade eventually found its place on international movie screens as a "French-style ghetto" with Luc Besson's productions *Banlieue 13* (2004) and *Banlieue 13—Ultimatum* (2009), featuring David Belle, the "founder of parkour."

"Notorious" New Belgrade blocks were the favorite home for overlapping ghetto and gangsta film narratives (*Ledina, Jedan na jedan, Apsolutnih sto, 7½, Ljubav i drugi zločini,* etc.) With the sinking of New Belgraders down the social ladder, the "ugly concrete blocks" transformed on screen into realms of crime and anxiety—as "scars on the city's body and soul." However, the imaginary ghetto did not reside solely in the blocks of New Belgrade, although Gandijeva and Nehruova happened to be its favorite addresses. When necessary, it moved downtown, or almost anywhere around Belgrade: the ghetto was and still is a mobile metaphor for a "camp" for the victims of transition—those who have failed to find a proper place in the post-socialist economy.

How New Belgrade was exploited in film narratives tells a lot about its "domestication" in hip hop videos. But what is New Belgrade, anyway? Conceived in the late 1940s, immediately after the Second World War, as the representative modern (brand) new capital of the socialist Yugoslavia, New Belgrade surfaced all the political and economic transformations of the country, becoming in its late-socialist period a predominantly residential area—notorious mostly for its boredom. Raised upon a marshy "wasteland" between two rivers (Sava and Danube), with scarce public landmarks and largely lacking in content other than apartment blocks and spacious parks, New Belgrade was perceived both from outside and from within as a "collective dorm." Construction of the "proud New Belgrade" was launched on April 11 (New Belgrade Day), 1948, by brigades consisting of young volunteers and war veterans. The symbolic importance attached to the construction of the new capital had been confirmed on many levels—one of them being Boža Ilić's painting Sounding of the Terrain in New Belgrade (240.5 × 441.5 cm), exhibited at the XXV Venice Biennial in 1950 as the iconic image of

Yugoslav socialist realism. In the 1960s, New Belgrade became the home of the largest modern Yugoslav hotel (Jugoslavija), the seat of the Yugoslav government (Savezno izvršno veće), the Central Committee of the Communist Party (Zgrada društveno-političkih organizacija), and the Museum of Contemporary Art. However, with the decentralization of political power in the Yugoslav federation (1974 Yugoslav Constitution), New Belgrade began to lose its administrative importance, becoming a predominantly residential area. Moreover, highly undifferentiated and inhabited mostly by the socialist middle class (managers, professionals, skilled workers), according to the modernist principles of "equal opportunities" for quality housing in an up-to-date urban environment (with moderate rents). The 1990s saw a general decline in the quality of life in New Belgrade (as indeed everywhere in Serbia): along with the general crisis in the society and the new (proto)capitalist economy, privatization of the apartments brought with it unresolved issues concerning the maintenance of the buildings, façades, elevators, plumbing, and so on. Aging modern buildings of the "proud new Belgrade" began to be perceived as the "heart of darkness" of the isolated and criminalized Serbia. And this is where hip hop enters the picture.

In a rare academic essay on the graffiti art of New Belgrade, Ljiljana Radošević tried to explain "how and why graffiti emerged in New Belgrade" and "what makes that part of the city different from others." Namely, the first New York–style graffiti emerged without a "plausible explanation" in Block 45. "A long, long time ago, the graffiteers' story goes, there existed only three blocks in New Belgrade: the East Block, the West Block and Block 45. Since Block 70 was built, it has been a bone of contention in the area, for in keeping with the good old Serbian tradition, your next-door neighbor is your worst enemy. Despite frequent quarrels, graffiteers from the two blocks drew together" (Radošević 2009:162). Belgrade's first graffiti artist, Miša Jens, wanted to paint the whole block, because "where there is a lot of concrete there should be a lot of graffiti." In the early days everyone came to Block 45 because it provided optimal working conditions:

- a critical mass of graffiteers,
- walls covered with nonabsorbent tiles,
- a cool atmosphere, and
- friendly neighbors[8]

(quite unlike the Transit Authority and mayor's office of New York in the 1970s). However, after the ousting of Slobodan Milošević (October 5, 2000), New Belgrade entered a new era of post-socialist development. Foreign investors (banking, telecommunications, real estate, energy, retail and wholesale trade, etc.) found it particularly attractive for a number of reasons.[9] The socialist collective dorm and the post-socialist ghetto was transformed into the "new business and trade centre of the city and the country," a part of the city experiencing striking trans-formations and high-profile development. This process of transition from ex-socialist to market economy (along with the ensuing conversion of capital) is sometimes called "*from plan to market or from plan to clan*" (Szelenyi 1996). As elsewhere in the Balkans, its wider political context is the transition from an au-tocratic government to a clan-based pseudo-democratic oligarchy (which is Ser-bian hip hop's major concern) and a national/monoethnic state of segregation and exclusion (which is far less often perceived as a problem in the hip hop commu-nity). Surveys of the residents of New Belgrade confirm its rapid transformation into a "shopping centre of Belgrade." Block 45 became a "cool" neighborhood "that has it all" (Backović 2010:140) in the eyes of young mothers and elderly housewives, and its ghetto reputation from the 1990s mostly relies on lousy main-tenance of the apartment blocks. Due to the rapid development of New Belgrade blocks, real estate price ranges from €1,700 to €2,300 per square meter—considerably above the Belgrade average of €1,459/m² (Backović 2010:145). And with the new residential areas affordable only to members of the political, busi-ness, and showbiz elites, New Belgrade went through the transition from a "neigh-bourhood as a community" to a "neighbourhood as a commodity" (Petrović 2007:3). Finally, the question of whether Block 70 really is a ghetto was answered by Stevan Vuković in the following terms: "No, it isn't, except for those whose ghettocentric imagination is running wild." Moreover, "if one sticks to the ghetto-game, one can only choose between fading to black (pro-ghetto, or ghetto-power attitude), or fading to white (getting out of it), which are just two sides of the same coin" (Vuković 2009:220–221).

VELIKI BRAT: ON QUESTIONS OF IDEOLOGY

The dissolution of the Socialist Federal Republic of Yugoslavia (1992) and the for-mation of the new nation-states in the Balkans had a powerful impact on the lo-cal music scenes, providing fertile soil for genres wherein the rediscovery and propagation of respective national cultures played a prominent role. According to the prevailing stereotypes informing both media and academic discourses, particular music genres (such as turbo-folk) represented a paradigm of national-ist speech and right-wing rhetoric, whereas rock and other underground music genres daringly challenged official cultural policies.[10] This is a fairly simplistic picture of the interaction between the music and the politics: artists falling in the same genre compartment often communicate ideological opposites, while respec-tive elements of "the national" and "the global" interact within differing (and often contradictory) ideological frameworks. All this applies to hip hop in Ser-bia. Moreover, according to Iva Nenić, "every serious attempt at grasping this phe-nomenon must confront its basic paradox—propagation of the national identity and 'reaffirmation of authentic Serbian values' combined with global hip-hop's contemporary urban *topoi*" (Nenić 2006:164).

Who Is the Best and Rhythm Attack released their first albums in 1996, and Belgrade Ghetto, Bad Copy, Straight Jackin', and Voodoo Popeye did so in 1997, the years of mass demonstrations of the students and citizens of Serbia against the government's fraud in the local and parliamentary elections. The emerging hip hop scene felt quite detached from the spectacle of local politics that dominated the public sphere, attempting to form its own, "counter-public" sphere, preoccupied with the daily business of surviving the "ghetto" and "getting a break" from it (in imaginary "pimp rides," in swimming pools, high on weed, or simply hanging out around the block with the homies). While the mass demonstrations in Belgrade, which lasted from November 1996 to February 1997, carried around the slogan "Belgrade Is the World," the rappers emphatically claimed "Belgrade Is a Ghetto." "This voice was coming from a particular social setting, which was in a state of desperation because of the political isolation and criminalization of the society:

> "Welcome to Belgrade, it's more black than white,
> Try to rebel and the bullet you will get.
> Bang!, bullet in the head; Whose deed it might
> be, that bloody hicks are all you have met.[11]

"There seemed to be no way out, because the society was structured in a strictly hierarchical and authoritarian manner, and the oligarchies running it seemed to be safeguarded and untouchable" (Vuković 2009:204–205). In accordance with the tongue-in-cheek observation that "Serbia did not have its own mafia, but rather in Serbia the mafia had its own state" (Pavlaković 2005:40), gangsta and conscious rap have reflected the two faces of this coin since the "dark 1990s": the former dissects the criminal underground, the latter the corrupt political elites, which continue to be concerned exclusively with the distribution of political and financial privilege. Yet the former approach ranges from utter fascination with the criminal lifestyle and nostalgia for the wild and uninhibited '90s, to exclamations of "never again" and neat (government-sponsored) campaigning for "gun-free," "drug-free," and "safe sex" Serbia. (Also Serbia as a water polo or tennis superpower.) The latter revolves around the theme of politician-cum-gangster, aligning with different strategies for dealing with corruption in the political sphere—from those self-consciously cosmopolitan and globally aware, to the most radical expressions of chauvinism and hate speech targeting the culprits in a flamboyant or simply plain "talk shit" manner. It communicates political messages "to the population and age group generally uninterested in politics, which speculates on the level of slogans and undifferentiated personal discontent" (as one of the targeted politicians put it in a public debate with Beogradski sindikat[12]), fueling the local counterpart of what Adam Krims calls the "cultural resistance industry."[13] In a social context that leaves the citizens of Serbia (all age groups) constantly exposed to frustration and disappointment, all they are left with is to claim a spot within the system they disrespect. In the wider context of changes the youth cultures underwent throughout post-socialist Europe—augmenting the sense of loss, disorientation, and degeneration[14]—hip hop raises probably the loudest (and more or less unarticulated) voice of this dissin'.

U KABRIOLETU: THE GHETTO AND HOW TO ESCAPE FROM IT—IMAGES OF BELONGING AND STRUGGLE

Non-Western hip-hop scenes often adopt its formal elements in a straightforwardly literal manner, through a process additionally perceived as "domestic Orientalism" (Yousman 2003:386). The same applies to the main thematic concerns—critical reflection of the social reality and representations of the cultural identity (of the ghetto).[15] Typically, we do not "discover music of such violence in places of great misery like Ethiopia or the Congo—unless it's imported American hip-hop."[16] In their conventional imagery, hip hop videos support the major themes of belonging (to the 'hood) and struggle (strategies of survival in a violent local environment). According to Tricia Rose, nothing is more important for the narrative of a hip hop video than situating the MC in his (or her) milieu, among the members of the respective crew or gang. Hip hop videos are typically situated in subway trains, buses, abandoned buildings—almost exclusively in black neighborhoods—with lavish use of shots depicting favorite street corners, crossroads, parking lots, basketball courts, schoolyards, rooftops, and the familiar faces of the local homies. Rappers insisting on homies and their 'hoods turned the spotlights to the black American ghetto (Rose 1994:10–11). However, "where the ghetto has been culturally shackled to a negative symbolic configuration of images and ideas, the 'hood offers a new terminology and discursive frame that can simultaneously address conditions in all 'hoods everywhere" (Forman 2003:65).

In a "school example," the video for "'Round Here" (2003), performed by Memphis Bleek, Trick Daddy, and T.I., renders this invocation of the 'hood as simultaneously local and universal in straightforward visual terms. The video is set in three locations; each setting aligns with the rapper who delivers the verse and represents his 'hood. "'Round Here" opens with an image of Memphis Bleek standing in front of the Marcy Projects in Brooklyn (Bedford-Stuyvesant), where he and his mentor, Jay Z,[17] grew up.[18] To further root himself in New York, Bleek wears items like a Brooklyn Dodgers coat or hat, with words or symbols associated with the city. He claims his spot on the corner, indexing the competitive working world of the street-level drug dealer. The scene then switches to scorching-hot Miami, home of Trick Daddy, who is depicted in his natural habitat, the Miami analog to Bleek's 'hood. Trick is also dressed in clothing that celebrates his hometown—mainly oversized replicas of University of Miami football and basketball jerseys. He is either seated on steps outside low-rise (and presumably low-income) housing or standing in front of a run-down corner store with a sign that reads "Fried Chicken." The director uses the same motifs as in Bleek's verse, but introduces more scantily clad female extras, in accordance with the lyrics. Following the same formula, the third verse is rapped by the Bankhead (Atlanta) native T.I. (wearing an Atlanta Braves cap), in the front yards of small "Southern style" ill-kept houses, occasionally leaning against a Cadillac.

Such formal elements were widely adopted in Serbian hip hop videos addressing 'hood subjects. Nevertheless, the 'hood as a "floating signifier" of universality generally stands for themes of deprivation and struggle in harsh and often violent (criminal) circumstances. On the other hand, the 'hood as a marker of locality notably translates into visual tropes of belonging, loyalty and—patriotism. As we have seen, in the Serbian hip hop discourse, the 'hood and the ghetto are one and the same—metaphorical expressions of life in a closed society with metaphorically elastic geographical borders: at times they refer to a neighborhood of Belgrade or any other Serbian town; at other times they "revisit" the countryside[19] (not necessarily attached to urban environments). Sometimes a whole city is conceived (and depicted) as a "ghetto-hood," and sometimes the whole country is the ghetto in question. Certain visual elements consequently assume the function of anchors that resolve the discrepancies between the metaphorical and the real, the local and the universal. For example:

1. Cars—symbols of wealth, empowerment, and (even more importantly) social and spatial mobility. Cars are the most effective vehicles for crossing the lines and "getting out"—whatever there is to get out of. They are also the safest spots from which to observe and reflect on one's "natural habitat." Also instrumental in impressing the opposite sex.
2. Rooftops—the ghetto observed from a rooftop somehow loses its borders. The sense of restraint is also diminished.
3. Basketball yards—supreme symbols of the universality of the local. Where there is realness, authenticity, and community, someone must be playing street basketball.

The recent (2011) video "Rep i grad" (Rap and the City) by the hip hop quartet Fantastična četvorka (F4) (consisting of Škabo, Marlon Brutal, Žobla, and DJ Iron), exemplifies this dynamic of elusive borders and complex interactions between the local and the universal (conceived as global)—as well as the domestication of the formal conventions of American hip hop videos. The video opens with wide panoramic shots of Belgrade, then swiftly grounds us on the busy highway running through the "posh" area of New Belgrade. The first MC, Škabo (Boško Ćirković, ex-Beogradski sindikat) addresses us with an intertextual nod to Carrie Bradshaw, claiming, however: "This is not America—we are rappin' white." His version of "white rapping" includes (in the following order) the tropes of: (1) the "heart," full of (2) love for his city and his "masterpiece" (baby); (3) threats from the "global village"—namely (4) universal commodification and (5) Jamie Oliver, as opposed to the (6) advantages of the meat-based local cuisine; (7) corrupt politicians; (8) the deprived working class; (9) "genocidal Serbs" and (10) natality rates; (11) VAT; (12) Čeda;[20] (13) the mafia; (14) elections; (15) Hugo Boss; (16) Bensedine Valium as a metaphor for social conformism; (17) pornography; and (18) AIDS. Škabo delivers his verse wearing an Adidas T-shirt featuring a Star Wars stormtrooper. The next MC (Marlon Brutal) introduces new themes of: (1) the loss of Kosovo; (2) justice and (3) God; (4) Borham Tadiqi;[21] (4) Serbian victims in Croatia and Bosnia; (5) Serbia's international reputation; (6) Euroskepticism;[22] (7) homophobia; (8) Dačić;[23] (9) fascism, nazism, patriotism, and nationalism; and (10) "moderate" xenophobia.[24] Marlon is wearing a T-shirt[25] decorated with the Serbian patriotic 4S logo (*Samo sloga Srbina spasava*) arranged around a soccer ball crossing his heart, while the right side of his chest bears the Nike trademark. MC Žobla, wearing an F4 shirt with the song's ("Moj rep i moj grad") logo, addresses his "socially aware" verse to the corrupt politicians—"fucking cattle whose names I don't even care to remember." Though he "rarely watches the news," he knows "how much they steal." He "doesn't need school" and "doesn't have to move from the block" to be positive that his "city is fucked up." The refrain sums up their arguments as follows:

> The democrats want to cheat us
> They say they go to Europe—they lie to the children of Serbia
> Different crooks looted the country
> They treat everything as merchandise and sell out for dollars.
>
> This is my rap and my city
> I won't let you take my rap and my city
> For me, my rap and my city
> For you—"up yours" as always before.[26]

During the raps we see shots of different parts of Belgrade (from New Belgrade blocks to "respectable" public edifices like the Bitef Theatre or Radio Belgrade) featuring notable representatives of the hip hop community or "Belgrade in general." They strike poses, solemn or casual, looking directly into the camera and asserting their loyalty to "rapping and the city."

Representing the ghetto is a major theme of Serbian hip hop videos. Moreover, what qualifies as a ghetto is best defined in visual terms. The ultimate ghetto—blocks of New Belgrade—provides the most familiar imagery, represented by the respective members of the hip hop community, their homies, grocers, elderly neighbors, kids, dogs, cars, motorbikes, architecture, skate parks, graffiti and basketball in innumerable videos (e.g., Sunshine, "1 na 1"[27]; FTP, "Blok, brate, Bruklin"; Bvana, "Rimujem i kradem"; Rasta and Reborn, "Kad ohladi se beton"; Sick Touch and DJ Rokam, "Preuzimanje"; Mlata, "33 Stil"; Ill G, Skubi, and DJ Rokam, "Dobar dan"; Beogradski sindikat, "Zajebi"[28]) Young MCs (Drakula, Neron, and Roman) from the nearby Zemun, the "Austro-Hungarian" part of Belgrade (also home to the notorious criminals from Zemunski klan), assert their attachment to the five white skyscrapers they grew up in, referring to them as "five white angels" in their video "Pet belih anđela." From the other side (the southern outskirts) of Belgrade, EsB (Ekipa sa brda), a crew from Petlovo brdo, sends another message of love for the ghetto in their video "Volim," amid a bunch of "natives," the basketball playground, and a nice graffiti mural (produced in the video) featuring their logo. (J Cook's video "Ispovest na igli" is another notable tribute to graffiti art as a cornerstone of hip- hop culture.[29])

As already noted, the imaginary ghetto does not reside solely in the remote suburbs of Belgrade: in the video "Kraj," Lud describes the "tough life" in the very heart of Belgrade, particularly in the neighborhood of Dorćol, an ambiguous place with a "cozy" and a "wild" side, separated by a single street (Cara Dušana). Sometimes crews from different (remote) parts of the city join hands and produce double-bill videos, each MC representing his 'hood, as in the videos by Brigada, "Deo sam klana" (Dorćol/Fontana), or THC ft. Marlon Brutal, "Bulevar nasilja" (Bulevar Kralja Aleksandra/Block 21).

Belgrade conceived as "one big 'hood" is also an option: in their video "Uvek biću tu," featuring familiar Belgrade cityscapes, rapper duo Sha-Ila (supported by the members of CYA) declare: "I'll always be here—in my city." Đolo (rapper and respectable music video director), RBS, and (again) Sha (sampling Ceca Ražnatović's turbo-folk hit "Beograd") send a message of pride and affection for their hometown in the video "Moj Beograd," featuring many historical landmarks, including modern ones like Beogradska Arena.

In the video "Živela razlika" (Ding Dong), members of the local community in the Serbian town of Niš (including waiters, dentists, and Chinese shopkeepers) are doing an impromptu choreography related to the song's main topic (sex). Marconiero and I Bee, notable MCs from Niš, address their 'hood and local gossip à la Balkan from the basement (as "voices of the underground") in their video "Svi u kraju." Niš graced Serbian hip hop with some of its wittiest raps (often delivered in the local dialect), including one of the rare programmatic socially conscious rap videos, "Centrifuga" (I Bee, Taz, Marconiero, and Joker). The MCs argue for decentralization of political power in the country and claim that official Belgrade bears the responsibility for parceling Serbia into ghettos of underdevelopment. Niš as a "ghetto of bad maintenance" also features in I Bee and Joker's video

"Đubretara." The city's hip hop (graffiti) talent is represented in Zmaj's video "Odoh."

In the biopic video "Ponos," Marčelo (Marko Šelić), the "intellectual of Serbian hip hop," walks the pavements of his hometown of Paraćin. Boasting hip hop veterans 2B4 Time pay a tribute to their town (and its various neighborhoods) in their video "Smederevo." In "Stari grad" (Škola) we discover an LA-style ghetto (organized mainly around trains and basketball) in the heart of the small industrial town of Priboj on the border with Montenegro. On the other end of the spectrum, the hip hop "cosmopolitans" from Novi Sad, Hain Teny, assert their "no allegiance" attitude from a rooftop in the video "Bez pripadnosti."

Serbia as the ultimate super-ghetto features in many raps, but not in many rap videos. The video "Yo! Yugo," shot in what was still called Yugoslavia, asserted that the country was a ghetto. The video combined documentary footage from the "dark nineties," providing social commentary in its own (visual) terms. MCs Dima, Ila, and Hele repeat the familiar post-2000 motif "Serbia is still in a ghetto" in the video "Sve je to Srbija," mainly in settings around the plateau of the National Library of Serbia and (ironically?) the monument to Dimitrije Tucović,[30] set on the busy Slavia square in downtown Belgrade. The video for M.A.X.'s angry rap "Srbija u rizli" is centered on the New Belgrade side[31] of the bridge connecting—or, better, dividing—the old and new Belgrade (Brankov most), and aptly features mock newspaper headlines. Another variation on the theme of Serbia as a ghetto is developed in the video "Ne znam dokle" (Jach ft. LMR), also featuring the bridges across the river Sava. In a characteristically easygoing manner, the young MCs are addressing the major question of their generation: "should I stay or should I go," that is, leave the ghetto (Serbia) in a forced economic migration. I Bee and Taz proclaim Serbia as "the Hollywood of the Balkans"—sarcastically, of course (*Srbija Holivud*). Their video is somewhat conventionally set around an abandoned ex-socialist factory. However, when the ghetto goes "patriotic," all flashes with flags and national symbols, as in Che Duevara's video "Srbin do smrti," which argues for "Serbia to the Serbs."[32]

Hip hop videos sometimes become windows into the world and daily struggles of tough individuals who try to survive in or (unsuccessfully) escape from their hostile environment (Mija, "Sve u kurac"). In the video "Never Walk Alone" by MCs Monogamija and Mikri Maus, Belgrade transforms into a nasty "gangsta ghetto": "Live fast but pray to the Mother of God, *never walk alone* so you don't end up in a hospital" is the moral, accentuated with shots of the cathedral church of Saint Sava. In hip hop videos—for example, "Dal' si ili nisi" (Hartmann ft. BK2)—even dull[33] and cozy Belgrade neighborhoods like Bežanijska kosa[34] transform into wild zones of street crime and thug lifestyle. (In reality, crime operates on completely different levels.) In the videos like "Priče sa ulice," featuring Žuti from Sick Touch, the New Belgrade blocks are trying to keep up with their bad reputation. Gangsta narratives on survival on the violent streets are often backed with images of urban decay generated by abandoned constructions sites or industrial facilities obsolete in the post-socialist economy (90 Naz ft. Ajzi, "Ja sam iz dgra"; Struka, "Svi psi idu u raj").

Serbian hip hop's enchantment with the mythical figure of the outlaw, as well as its contempt for those who "serve, protect, and break a nigga's neck," often translates into prison and police imagery. Prison narratives in hip hop videos play different genre roles, from documentary (Lud ft. VIP, Struka, Borko THC, and LoOney, "Sekund, Minut, Sat") to action (187, "Princeza sa asfalta"[35]) to romance (Carlito, "Miris njen"). The ambivalent role of the police in the society (object of both fascination and contempt) translates into hip hop videos in which rappers play "bad lieutenant" characters like Škabo in the PKS video "Murija."[36] Moreover, Serbian hip hop's association with the epic poetry tradition and asymmetric decasyllabic verse occasionally translates into video sagas of underworld heroes following the code of the street,[37] in the footsteps of epic figures like Kraljević Marko (Škabo, "Mare, batice"), engaged in a constant quest for *respect*.

IMAGES OF SUCCESS

Fascination with Tony Montanish gangsta figures dates back to the early days of Serbian hip hop video (Budweiser, "On je lud"). However, the accompanying imagery of luxury and success (along with a general redefinition of crime) came with the unfettered nineties. If not through crime, the way out from the ghetto (as we all know) is through a successful career in the music business. As in other music genres (primarily turbo-folk), Serbian hip hop videos abound with images of luxury and success. This often brings about ironic raps that display the gap between the sumptuous imagery of the (sponsored) videos and the reality of low (or no) sales and the daily life struggles of the hip hop community. However, the gap between those who seek fame at any price (even by appearing on *Big Brother* and other reality shows like Juice, Ajs Nigrutin, or MC Niggor) and those who proclaim loyalty to the street and the ghetto is often imaginary as well. Both commitments are legitimate concerns in a rapper's career, and they do not seem to contradict each other. Hip hop's elastic definition of "realness" leads to depictions of (social or showbiz) reality, which sometimes (when affordable) extends to the virtual worlds of computer animation. Beogradski sindikat reached Dionysian heights with their satirical video "Alal vera!" focused on the animated characters of Al Pacino (Tony Montana in *Scarface*) and Christopher Walken (Frank White in *King of New York*). Lud and Struka featured as *South Park* characters in the video "Rep Superstar," the ultimate parody of success in the hip hop business. Serbian rappers flaunt their success mostly at parties featuring a swimming pool (alternatively, a river boat or barbecue) and lots of scantily clad, "'hood rich," and "ghetto fabulous" *bitches*. In accordance with Tricia Rose's observation, their "tales of sexual domination falsely relieve [males'] lack of self-worth and limited access to economic and social markers for heterosexual masculine power" (Rose 1994:15), reflecting the deep-seated sexism that pervades the Serbian music business and society in general. In the evolution of the Serbian hip hop video, we might trace the transformation of the party imagery from innocent teenage gatherings (Who Is the Best, "Baby"; Gru ft. Del Arno Band, "Petak"; I Bee and Taz ft. D-Fence, "Ključ") to decadent VIP (Bad Copy, "Žurka") or gangsta-style parties occasionally featuring celebrity "bitches" from the turbo-folk camp (Juice with Mina Kostić, "Priđi mi polako"). In their pursuit of wealth and success, Serbian rappers find themselves in all sorts of ethnic crossovers, from world music (Cvija with Sanja Ilić and Balkanika, "Đipaj") to turbo-folk (MlaDJa and Big Time ft. Jovan Perišić and Aca Olujić, "Harmonika"). Turbo-folk receives influence from hip hop with particular enthusiasm: hip hop imagery pervades turbo-folk videos in all kinds of imaginative combinations. Turbo-folk (or turbo-pop) stars and starlets eagerly assume the roles of black/ghetto bitches (Sandra Afrika, "E pa neću"; Funky G ft. Juice, "U tvojim kolima"; Dragana Mirković, "Mili, mili") or mean thugs (Mile Kitić, "Paklene godine";[38] W-Ice and Mystic, "Vodi me").

The ultimate escape from the ghetto is—a holiday. We often see Serbian rappers on yachts, boats, and beaches (mostly Greek and Montenegrin) (Bad Copy, "Uno Duo Tre"; I Bee, "Draga pesma"; DJ Shone ft. Geo Da Silva and Juice, "You Move"; MlaDJa ft. Sha, MC Yankoo, and Prince Darrell,[39] "Žurka"; Sinovatz, "Leto"), or occasionally engaged in fancy winter sports (Zmaj, "Bela smrt"). This celebration of luxury addresses those who are denied traditional paths to positive self-image, assuming that self and social esteem can only be achieved through an expensive lifestyle as a coping strategy. "Mainstream hip-hop in this context becomes a form of escapism, as commercially successful rappers invite their audience to identify with a ridiculous and largely staged life of luxury that ordinary people will never experience" (Jeffries 2011:71). With all its escapist imagery, however, the *ghetterotopia* of the holiday testifies to the fact that escape from the ghetto can only be temporary: without the ghetto there is no hip hop.

Notes

1. In Germany, after the enormous success of the Fantastischen 4, terms like Neuer deutscher Sprechgesang (new German recitative) and Neue deutsche Reimkultur (new German poetry) began to be used. "Thus an adopted musical style became grafted onto a national identity which de facto locked out many of its participants. Given hip-hop's special attractions for immigrant youngsters as a different, non-German cultural pattern . . . this nationalist move was particularly problematic" (Elflein 1998:258).

2. Many of them with Romani background, which might suggest that Serbian hip hop did, in fact, emerge in the "ghettos."

3. The name "Black Beatles" came from N.W.A.'s (white) manager Jerry Heller. According to Heller, each member of the group was holding down a key role. "Cube was the chief lyricist, Dr was the beat maker, Eazy was the conceptualizer while Heller was the financier." http://mrdaveyd.wordpress.com/tag/black-jewish-relationships/.

4. Remote northerly neighborhood of Belgrade, also home to Prti Bee Gee, Bičarke na travi, and associated solo acts (Ajs Nigrutin, Timjah, Eufrat, etc.)

5. One member of this rapping duet, Vladimir Ilić Ila (son of the celebrity TV host Milovan Ilić Minimaks), was the first MC who released an album (Ila, *Uvek isti*, 1997) for *City Records*, a label owned by the former rock musician and media tycoon Željko Mitrović, notoriously associated with Milošević's regime. In the post-Milošević era (after 2000), City Records continued to (sporadically) publish Sha-Ila, Gru, Ding Dong, Voodoo Popeye, Who Is the Best, Juice, and others.

6. The middle class in the post-Yugoslav, post-socialist terms, described by the sociologist Aljoša Mimica as "not a *class* in the strict sense of the word," but a conglomerate derived from the artificial joining of quite different social strata that lacked any sense of collective identity and, in fact, never embraced a common value system nor ideology (Mimica 1993:20).

7. See Daković 2010a and 2010b.

8. "If it is an unwritten rule that it is quite legal to roast a suckling in the field in front of a building, then it is legal to draw graffiti as well. . . . It is not rare that a neighbor brings out some brandy to treat the 'workers' while they are busy creating works of art, or that a mother sends out her child to take some cakes to the artists who are in the throes of artistic creation" (Radošević 2009:166).

9. Proximity to the city center across the river Sava; good traffic and communal infrastructure; plenty of vacant land for development; resolved issues of property and ownership; neat real estate registry (unlike the most of Belgrade's municipalities, where the ownership registry is rather chaotic as part of the legacy of the communist nationalization and land speculations in the "swinging '90s").

10. See Gordy 1999.

11. Dobro došli u Beograd, mnogo više crno nego belo,
    Probaj da se buniš dobićeš utokom u čelo.
    Bang, utokom u čelo, čije je to delo
    Da moj grad je najveće selo.
    Who Is the Best, "Welcome to Belgrade," from *Welcome to Belgrade*, 1996.

12. "Nenad Čanak preslušava *Govedinu:* Jaka frustracija, dobra muzika." *Vreme*, October 10, 2002, 614. http://www.vreme.com/cms/view.php?id=323427.

13. "I think a healthy skepticism is in order regarding what one might deem the 'cultural resistance industry'" (Krims 2000:1).

14. See Szemere 1996.

15. Plus secondary themes including sex, love, violence, money, official politics, racial and gender issues, parties, prostitution, drugs, police, prisons, show business, comic relief, irony, or boasting.

16. See McWhorter 2003.

17. While Bleek narrates, Jay Z drives up in a Rolls Royce (he's "the boss com[ing] through" who "makes sure everything's good").

18. "During Bleek's verse, three basic settings are used by the director. In the first setting, Bleek appears alone, rapping in front of the apartment buildings, occasionally with a large sports utility vehicle in the background for decoration. The second setting is Bleek with a group of roughly forty extras, all of whom are black and presumably Marcy residents who live in the

neighborhood the video is filmed in. The extras sing and dance along with the song, positioned as a cluster standing around Bleek, who is front and center. The third group of pictures comprise solo and group shots of the extras, a number of whom are children. Bleek does not appear with the extras as they strike stationary poses, looking directly into the camera with indifferent if not solemn expressions on their faces, symbolizing the unfiltered reality of day-to-day life in the ghetto" (Jeffries 2011:65).

19. For example, in the video "Pozorištance," from the rap duo D-Fence (Marconiero and Joker) from Niš. Atheist Rap from Novi Sad introduced the gangsta theme of narco-agriculture in their animated video "Dve žetve godišnje," adopted by other satirical acts, such as Voodoo Popeye and MC Tattoo Locko ("Distributer vutre") and Ajs Nigrutin ("Indo grasa").

20. Čedomir Jovanović, Serbian politician (b. 1971), leader of the student protests in 1996–1997, currently president of the Liberal Democratic Party (LDP).

21. Albanian version of Boris Tadić (president of Serbia, 2004–2012).

22. "Fuck Amsterdam, I smoke skunk on my block."

23. Ivica Dačić, prime minister of Serbia, political successor of Slobodan Milošević.

24. "If you prefer foreign stuff, go away and stay there [mrš !]."

25. Version of the Nike uniform for the soccer representatives of Serbia at the World Championship in South Africa (2010).

26. Za mene, moj rep i moj grad
    A vama kurac k'o do sad.

27. From the soundtrack for the feature film directed by Mladen Matičević (1 na 1, 2002), which included the band's members in the cast.

28. "Activist" antiviolence video featuring only children from New Belgrade blocks.

29. Rap videos sometimes document imaginary histories of the local hip hop scene (like "Repujemo" by Juice and Coyote, set prominently on overground trains, which have a minor significance for Belgrade's traffic system and, consequently, for the local graffiti culture, which is more mural-based).

30. (1881–1914), leader and theorist of the socialist movement in the Kingdom of Serbia.

31. The ghetto is where the "real" rappers are—in this case it is New Belgrade.

32. Srbija Srbima . . . jebaćemo mater svima.

33. I know, I'm from that 'hood.

34. Home to many Serbian media celebrities, including the Yugoslav folk megastar Lepa Brena.

35. A rare example featuring an action hero who is a "bitch"; moreover, the "asphalt princess" is assassinated in a gang shooting on her exit from the Belgrade church of Sveti Marko.

36. That Škabo likes to dress up as a policeman was definitely attested in Beogradski sindikat's video "Divljina."

37. A "set of informal rules governing interpersonal public behavior, particularly violence" (Anderson 1999:33)

38. Cover of Sexion d'Assaut's Désolé (L'école des points vitaux, 2010) and inaugural video for the recently invented "gangsta folk" genre

39. Black MCs, who rarely appear in Serbian music videos, often serve as fashionable and exotic "accessories."

References

Anderson, Elijah. 1999. *Code of the Street: Decency, Violence, and the Moral Life of the Inner City.* New York: Norton.

Backović, Vera. 2010. *Socioprostorni razvoj Novog Beograda*. Belgrade: Institut za sociološka istraživanja Filozofskog fakulteta.

Balaji, Murali. 2009. "Owning Black Masculinity: The Intersection of Cultural Commodification and Self-Construction in Rap Music Videos." *Communication, Culture & Critique* 2(1):21–38.

Chang, Jeff. 2005. *Can't Stop, Won't Stop: A History of the Hip-Hop Generation*. New York: St. Martin's.

Daković, Nevena. 2010a. "Geto Film." In *Istorija umetnosti u Srbiji: XX vek*, vol. 1, ed. Miško Šuvaković (pp. 883–886). Belgrade: Orion Art.

Daković, Nevena. 2010b. "Imagining Belgrade: The Cultural/Cinematic Identity of a City at the Fringes of Europe." In *The Cultural Identities of European Cities*, eds. Katia Pizzi and Godela Weiss-Sussex (pp. 61–77). Oxford: Peter Lang.

Davey D. 2010. "Breakdown FM: Still Ruthless Interview w/Jerry Heller (Eazy E & the Inner Workings of NWA)." Davey D's Archived Essential Hip Hop Articles. http://mrdaveyd .wordpress.com/tag/black-jewish-relationships/.

Elflein, Dietmar. 1998. "From Krauts with Attitudes to Turks with Attitudes: Some Aspects of Hip-Hop History in Germany." *Popular Music* 17(3):255–265.

Forman, Murray. 2002. *The 'Hood Comes First: Race, Space, and Place in Rap and Hip-Hop*. Middletown, CT: Wesleyan University Press.

Gordy, Eric. 1999. *The Culture of Power in Serbia: Nationalism and the Destruction of Alternatives*. University Park: Pennsylvania State University Press.

Jeffries, Michael P. 2011. *Race, Gender, and the Meaning of Hip-Hop*. Chicago: University of Chicago Press.

Keyes, Cheryl L. 2002. *Rap Music and Street Consciousness*. Urbana: University of Illinois Press.

Kitwana, Bakari. 2005. *Why White Kids Love Hip-Hop: Wankstas, Wiggas, Wannabes, and the New Reality of Race in America*. New York: Basic Civitas.

Krims, Adam. 2000. *Rap Music and the Poetics of Identity*. Cambridge: Cambridge University Press.

Kubrin, Charis E. 2005. "Gangstas, Thugs, and Hustlas: Identity and the Code of the Street in Rap Music. *Social Problems* 52(3):360–378.

McWhorter, John H. 2003. "How Hip-Hop Holds Blacks Back." *City Journal*. http://www.city -journal.org/html/13_3_how_hip_hop.html.

Miller-Young, Mireille. 2008. "Hip-Hop Honeys and Da Hustlaz: Black Sexualities in the New Hip-Hop Pornography." *Meridians* 8(1):261–292.

Mimica, Aljoša. 1993. "Rat i propast srednje klase." *Republika* 81:19–21.

Mitchell, Tony. 1996. *Popular Music and Local Identity; Rock, Pop and Rap in Europe and Oceania*. London: Leicester University Press.

Mitchell Tony, ed. 2001. *Global Noise: Rap and Hip Hop outside the U.S.A*. Middletown, CT: Wesleyan University Press.

Nenić, Iva. 2006. "Politika identiteta u srpskom hip-hopu na primeru grupe Beogradski sindikat." *TkH časopis za teoriju izvođačkih umetnosti* 11:159–166.

Pavlaković, Vjeran. 2005. "Serbia Transformed? Political Dynamics in the Milošević Era and After." In *Serbia since 1989: Politics and Society under Milošević and After*, eds. Sabrina P. Ramet and Vjeran Pavlaković (pp. 13–54). Seattle: University of Washington Press.

Perry, Imani. 2004. *Prophets of the Hood: Politics and Poetics in Hip-Hop*. Durham, NC: Duke University Press.

Petrović, Mina. 2007. "Diversification of Urban Neighbourhoods: The Case Study in New Belgrade." Paper presented at the conference Sustainable Urban Areas, Rotterdam. http://www.enhr2007rotterdam.nl/documents/W14_paper_Petrovic.pdf.

Pratt, Ray. 1990. *Rhythm and Resistance: Explorations in the Political Uses of Popular Music.* New York: Praeger.

Queeley, Andrea. 2003. "Hip Hop and the Aesthetics of Criminalization." *Souls* 5:1–15.

Quinn, Eithne. 2005. *Nuthin' but a G Thang: The Culture and Commerce of Gangster Rap.* New York: Columbia University Press.

Radošević, Ljiljana. 2009. "New York Graffiti in a Socialist Ghetto." In *Differentiated Neighbourhoods of New Belgrade,* ed. Zoran Erić (pp. 160–171). Belgrade: Museum of Contemporary Art.

Rose, Tricia. 1994. *Black Noise: Rap Music and Black Culture in Contemporary America.* Middletown, CT: Wesleyan University Press.

Shelton, Maria L. 1997. "Can't Touch This! Representations of the African American Female Body in Urban Rap Videos." *Popular Music & Society* 21(3):107–117.

Szelenyi, Ivan. 1996. "Cities under Socialism and After." In *Cities after Socialism,* eds. Gregory Andrusz, Michael Harloe, and Ivan Szelenyi (pp. 286–317). Oxford: Blackwell.

Szemere, Anna. 1996. "Subcultural Politics and Social Change: Alternative Music in Postcommunist Hungary." *Popular Music and Society* 20(2):19–41.

Thompson, Robert Farris. 1973. "An Aesthetic of the Cool." *African Arts* 7(1):40–43, 64–67, 89–91.

Venkatesh, Sudhir. 2000. *American Project: The Rise and Fall of a Modern Ghetto.* Cambridge, MA: Harvard University Press.

Vuković, Stevan. 2009. "Whose Hood? Identity Wars in New Belgrade: The Case of Block 70." In *Differentiated Neighbourhoods of New Belgrade,* ed. Zoran Erić, 197–221. Belgrade: Museum of Contemporary Art.

Wacquant, Loïc. 1997. "Three Pernicious Premises in the Study of the American Ghetto." *International Journal of Urban and Regional Research* 21(2):341–153.

Wacquant, Loïc. 2009. "The Body, the Ghetto, and the Penal State." *Qualitative Sociology* 32(1):101–129.

Watts, Eric K. 1997. "An Exploration of Spectacular Consumption: Gangsta Rap as Cultural Commodity." *Communication Studies* 48:42–58.

Yousman, Bill. 2003. "Blackophilia and Blackophobia: White Youth, the Consumption of Rap Music, and White Supremacy." *Communication Theory* 13(4):366–391.

VIDEOGRAPHY

187, "Princeza sa asfalta"
2B4 Time, "Smederevo"
90 Naz ft. Ajzi, "Ja sam iz dgra"
Ajs Nigrutin, "Indo grasa"
Atheist Rap, "Dve žetve godišnje"
Bad Copy, "Uno Duo Tre"
Bad Copy, "Žurka"
Belgrade Ghetto, "Yo! Yugo"
Beogradski sindikat, "Alal vera!"
Beogradski sindikat, "Divljina"
Beogradski sindikat, "Zajebi"

Brigada, "Deo sam klana"
Bvana, "Rimujem i kradem"
Budweiser, "On je lud"
Carlito, "Miris njen"
Che Duevara, "Srbin do smrti"
Cvija with Sanja Ilić and Balkanika, "Đipaj"
D-Fence, "Pozorištance"
Dima, Ila, and Hele, "Sve je to Srbija"
Ding Dong, "Živela razlika"
DJ Shone ft. Geo Da Silva and Juice, "You Move"
Dragana Mirković, "Mili, mili"
Drakula, Neron, and Roman, "Pet belih anđela"
Đolo ft. RBS and Sha, "Moj Beograd"
EsB, "Volim"
Fantastična četvorka (F4), "Rep i grad"
FTP, "Blok, brate, Bruklin"
Funky G ft. Juice, "U tvojim kolima"
Gru ft. Del Arno Band, "Petak"
Hain Teny, "Bez pripadnosti"
Hartmann ft. BK2, "Dal' si ili nisi"
I Bee, "Draga pesma"
I Bee and Joker, "Đubretara"
I Bee and Taz, "Srbija Holivud"
I Bee and Taz ft. D-Fence, "Ključ"
I Bee, Taz, Marconiero, and Joker, "Centrifuga"
Ill G, Skubi, and DJ Rokam, "Dobar dan"
Jach ft. LMR, "Ne znam dokle"
J Cook, "Ispovest na igli"
Juice and Coyote, "Repujemo"
Juice and Mina Kostić, "Priđi mi polako"
Lud, "Kraj"
Lud ft. VIP, Struka, Borko THC, and LoOney, "Sekund, Minut, Sat"
Lud and Struka, "Rep Superstar"
Marčelo, "Ponos"
Marconiero and I Bee, "Svi u kraju"
M.A.X., "Srbija u rizli"
Mija, "Sve u kurac"
Mile Kitić, "Paklene godine"
MlaDJa ft. Sha, MC Yankoo, and Prince Darrell, "Žurka"
MlaDJa and Big Time ft. Jovan Perišić and Aca Olujić, "Harmonika"
Mlata, "33 Stil"
Monogamija and Mikri Maus, "Never Walk Alone"
PKS, "Murija"
Rasta and Reborn, "Kad ohladi se beton"
Sandra Afrika, "E pa neću"
Sha-Ila and CYA, "Uvek biću tu"
Sick Touch and DJ Rokam, "Preuzimanje"
Sinovatz, "Leto"

Struka, "Svi psi idu u raj"
Sunshine, "1 na 1"
Škabo, "Mare, batice"
Škola, "Stari grad"
THC ft. Marlon Brutal, "Bulevar nasilja"
Voodoo Popeye and MC Tattoo Locko, "Distributer vutre"
Who Is the Best, "Baby"
W-Ice and Mystic, "Vodi me"
Zmaj, "Bela smrt"
Zmaj, "Odoh"
Žuti, "Priče sa ulice"

CHAPTER 15

THE POWER OF THE WORDS
Discourses of Authenticity in Czech Rap Music

Anna Oravcová

INDICATIONS OF A nascent hip hop subculture in the Czech Republic can be traced back to 1993 when the pioneer graffiti artists started traveling to former West Berlin.[1] Although the first step of adoption and adaptation of American hip hop occurred almost a decade earlier, when a group called Manželé recorded a song called "Jižák, Jižák," a carbon copy of the Grandmaster Flesh /Furious 5 song "New York, New York." In their version, Manželé describes everyday life in one of Prague's largest neighborhoods, Jižní Město (South City). This event became a founding myth for Czech hip hoppers, establishing this part of the capital city as the "birthplace" of Czech hip hop.

By 2014, two decades later, Czech rap music had become one of the most popular music genres among the youth. Czech hip hoppers endorse international hip hop brands, have their own language, and, with independent labels such as Bigg Boss, TyNikdy, and Mafia Records to name a just few, had found their own way of infiltrating the Czech popular music industry. Some of the first rappers gave it up, but some are still around (WWW, PSH); some fans are new, and some came of age with the subculture. With the commercialization and mainstream appeal of some of the artists, the threat of assimilation became real for Czech hip hop subculture, as well.

The aim of this chapter is to examine the ways gender, race, and class influence the discourses of authenticity of Czech rappers and their musical production, and situate them within the global hip hop movement. Looking at the lyrical content of selected rappers, we will see how they relate to American hip hop, how the commercial success of the music genre influences the debates around "real" hip hop, and what the main social issues are that these artists address.

267

My arguments and claims are based on my long-term involvement with the Czech hip hop subculture as a fan,[2] a researcher,[3] and an active member of the subculture.[4] Given my involvement with the subculture and my "insider" position, it is crucial that I pay extra attention to not becoming a spokesperson for "my" community, but remain critically aware of its issues (Hodkinson 2005). My research is based on qualitative methods such as in-depth interviews with rappers, content analysis of their lyrics, and participant observation during various hip hop events. For this chapter I will use examples taken from 10 rap artists and their current music production.

For the purpose of the argument I first provisionally divided the artists into two groups: five "commercially successful" and five so-called underground artists. The first set includes those accepted by the mainstream audience and who were also recognized by the Czech popular music industry by being nominated in the hip hop category at the Anděl Czech music awards:[5] First is Hugo Toxxx, formerly a member of the group KO Kru, which later became known as Supercroo, and whose release of their CD *Toxic Funk* in 2004 is considered a game changer in Czech hip hop because of their use of electronic beats and an approach to lyrics full of vulgarity, controversy, and attacks on mainstream icons of Czech popular culture. The second artist with considerable success among Czech hip hop youth and with an award nomination is Ektor, active on the Czech rap scene since 2008; he is praised for his flow and his assertive and egocentric lyrics. Idea released his first rap demo tape in 2000 with a group from his hometown of Zlín; in the following years he attended numerous freestyle battles, and in 2006 he cofounded and is currently the front man of the independent hip hop label TyNikdy. Prago Union is a group established in 2002 that consists of DJ Maro and Kato, an MC who is considered probably the best that Czech hip hop has to offer, acclaimed not only for his lyrical skills but also for his status as one of the pioneers of Czech rap, as he was a member of Chaozz, one of the first hip hop groups and the most commercially successful; the band was established in 1995 and released five studio albums on the PolyGram label. The fifth spot is occupied by Revolta, who has been labeled the "conscious" rapper, and who has a large fan base at home and abroad, since his music videos often come with English subtitles.[6] His music has a crossover appeal, he is embraced by people outside the hip hop community, and he attracts the attention of the media, especially with his other project, Seberevolta, a fitness program for young people that is presented as an alternative way of spending free time rather than smoking and drinking alcohol.

The second group of artists includes representatives of so-called underground (whether they call themselves underground artists or they are seen as such by the hip hop fans). These were chosen based on their popularity and involvement within the Czech hip hop subculture. A major act from North Moravia is MC and graffiti artist Khomator, a founding member of hip hop collective and major local label Repromanifest. This label is also represented by the group Safari, which in 2011 won the best group category in a nationwide competition called 5 Elements, focusing on every element of hip hop culture and judged by Czech hip hop heads. Rest, representing the TyNikdy label, started rapping in 2003, and is a winner of numerous freestyle battles. Since joining the label in 2006, Rest has released three studio albums. MC Gey, another TyNikdy label MC, stared rapping in 1999 and is known for the irony and satire in his lyrics. Prague's hip hop underground is represented by MC, DJ, and graffiti artist Foggy Fogosh, the founding member of a loose collective of rappers called S.C.U.R. (South City Underground Rappers), and more recently a group called Crewní skupina. Fogosh is the DJ for a monthly event called Old School Rap Attack at Palác Akropolis, and he is involved with several nonprofit organizations providing graffiti workshops for youth.

United States Hip Hop Legacy

Hip hop first came to the Czech Republic in a mediated form, through foreign TV channels including MTV (Waegner, 2004:172), through the graffiti and hip hop scene in Germany, or via personal contact with people who lived abroad. But however it came, as Sifon, the leading member of pioneer hip hop group WWW suggests: "there was no social urge to express ourselves, just the aesthetics."[7] In the Czech Republic, hip hop was first accepted as a sonic experience, as something new and fresh. The message had a secondary role, in part due to lack of English language skills, especially in Czech youths' understanding of English slang and vernacular. In some European countries, especially those that have English language as a second language, such as Holland, local rappers tend to use English (Krims 2001:158); but in the Czech Republic, as well as in Slovakia, there has not been substantial usage of English rap (Barrer, 2009:69). Thus, the first rule of authenticity in Czech rap would be the use of Czech hip hop slang. As one of the rappers I interviewed put it, "there would be no Czech rap without the Czech language."

Rap is understood as a means of self-expression, as a way of articulating the struggles of everyday life without reserve. For the artists chosen in my sample, being a rapper/emcee is a fundamental part of their identity, something they are not willing to give up. Khomator named his album *Terapie* (Therapy), which is what writing rhymes means to him. Idea claims that he has "rap under my skin" in the song "Superhrdina" (Superhero), and Safari compares rap to a kind of drug that makes them "get up from the bed five times at night / to write down my train of thoughts / it's love that I will take with me beyond the grave" ("Zápal mozkových blan" [Meningitis]).

For Czech rappers, knowledge of the history of hip hop culture is of great importance. In their lyrics, they especially reference American MCs who have influenced not only their musical production but also their approach to hip hop. These references then serve as a guideline for the fans, who immediately know with which era the given rapper identifies with and draws on. For example, Rest claims he grew up listening to DJ Premier ("Premiéra" [Premiere]), while in the song "Panáky na zem" (Shots on the Ground) he gives props to the great American rappers who have passed away, just as Toxxx compares his lyrical abilities and personal style to those of Easy E, Biggie, Tupac, or ODB. Revolta is convinced that a rapper should have "the power of words" endorsing other "conscious" rappers such as Vinnie Paz and Lowkey ("Myslím" [I Think]).

Another technique of "horizontal intertextuality" (Androutsopoulos 2009:45) employed by Czech rappers is reference to the American hip hop tradition via samples and scratches in their music. In Khomator's title track "Terapie," we can hear KRS-One and his famous line "Rap is something you do, hip-hop is something you live." Safari uses the line "real hip-hop" in scratch parts of their song "Hip hop," and Rest uses the line "Representing for the real hip-hop" on his record "Premiéra." In the song "Praha" (Prague), S.C.U.R. complain that "nowadays compering dick size and smoking weed is what's in / instead of knowing who Kool Herc is." Khomator goes even further in the track "Onelove," where he raps about the roots of hip hop in New York's Bronx and Brooklyn, and about watching Beat Street and "having a dream, like ML King." These references show that the interest in hip hop culture, at least in Khomator's case, means more than just the well-known icons in the history of rap itself, but suggests his familiarity with the African American struggle. Knowledge of these personalities, events, and places is one way of distinguishing between a mere listener of rap music and a member of the hip hop subculture.

Because of the influence that American rap music and hip hop culture have on the local subculture, certain English words have become an integral part of the Czech hip hop vernacular. Specific words have never even been translated to their Czech equivalents. These include, for example, "flow," "crew," "fellaz," but also curse words like "bitch" and "fuck." When it comes to appropriation of English slang and the frequency of its usage, Hugo Toxxx is the master. On his latest CD, which received the Anděl Czech music award for 2012, called "Bouch Money Mixtape," one can find whole verses that are built on rhymes created with English words. On the other hand, his music brings something new to Czech rap, as he incorporates elements of grime and American "Dirty South" sounds. Toxxx pushes the boundaries of Czech slang a step further, even admitting in his lyrics that people have no idea what he is talking about. I myself did not understand what the word "Bouch" meant until Toxxx explained: "Just as people in Houston pronounce the word 'boss' differently, I took the word 'Bůh' [God] and added a little southern twist to it, to make it sound like 'Bouch.'"[8]

The selected Czech rappers show respect to the pioneers of hip hop culture in their lyrics, through sonic references, and by incorporating specific hip hop words in the Czech language. They also often refer to the history of the local hip hop scene and their ties to neighboring countries like Slovakia, or, in the case of Khomator and Safari, to Polish hip hop.

How About the Message?

The popularity of rap music, and its appeal especially among the youth, has divided the local scene between the so-called mainstream and the underground. In my research, conducted in the course of 2009 and 2010, I oriented on the self-understanding of underground hip hoppers who frequented the now defunct Pantheon club. In the course of my fieldwork, based on participant observation of the regular Monday freestyle open mic and interviews with regular attendees, I noticed that the distinction of where "underground" ends and the presumed corrupting commercial success begins is very subjective and depends on one's opinion of what is or is not "true" hip hop (Oravcová 2011; see also Harrison 2009:9). Rappers' opinions on the state of hip hop, whether local or global, and their definition of authenticity are constant themes of their written lyrics and freestyle rhymes.

The main concern with regard to the idea of "real" hip-hop is commercial success, the degree to which rappers are considered as "selling out" to gain mass appeal and satisfy the broadest audience possible, to the extent that the lyrical content of their songs becomes superficial. Kato, the front man of Prago Union, criticizes the current scene for complaining about its state but at the same time not doing anything about it. Kato encourages what he feels is missing in the Czech hip hop: "You have an opinion? I wanna hear it! / Where you were, what you saw and what does that mean? / And add a little bit of the spice on top of that / you know, risk your neck." The self-proclaimed "Dr. Word with a tongue sharp as a razor" feels that "Most of the emcees interchange bullshit and phrases / the rest of them are just different stages of interphases / so give me the alphabet and watch what I do with it / everything lies between A and Z and this is just a warm up / I suggest you don't leave, aight?" ("Rozcvička" [Warm Up]). Taking into account Kato's long involvement in Czech rap music, his very detail-oriented lyrics, which make one feel like a part of the story, and his use of nuances in the Czech language in his metaphors and juxtapositions put him at the top of Czech rap music and allow him to speak from a position as mentor and critic at the same time. Rest claims that Czech rap is a joke, an empty expression; Safari laments the state where rap is made for money and fame and not the need for self-expression; and Hugo Toxxx compares Czech rap to diarrhea, foot fungus, and hay fever ("Kokot

USA" [Dick USA]). In his own humorous way, MC Gey makes a parody of simplistic rhymes and nonsense rap in the track "Tenhleten" (This One). The overall sentiment is that the art of emceeing is lost, and the scene is dry.

There seems to be a tension between the ideology of underground rappers and their refusal of any commercial success or even the very possibility of making a living through hip hop, securing a livelihood via something that one really loves and enjoys and not having to sacrifice lyrical content or to forfeit the claim to authenticity. Idea describes himself as having "feet on the ground, head in the mainstream cloud / all the while independent, with heart down underground" ("Uhasit oheň" [Extinguish the Fire]). In the song "Superhrdina" (Superhero), he claims that for him rap is not just music but also a business endeavor, and he will not stop counting money. Once one is blessed, doing what one really loves, and is able to make money doing it, there is nothing wrong with it. In the song "Kokot USA," Toxxx raps about how he is living rap, and rap makes his living. His expression "Bauch money" refers to making money off of something that you really love: you do it well and there is no reason for being ashamed of that, because it comes from God, the Universe. At the same time, he has his own record label (Hypno808), he self-distributes his music, and there is no corporate pressure for him to limit himself when it comes to the lyrical content of his songs.

If the hunger for money and fame are the key aspects of what could be called "commercial" hip hop, it is questionable whether any of these artists can be labeled as such. As previously mentioned, none of these artists are signed to a major record label.[9] They all belong to independent labels that, in some cases, may depend on major labels when it comes to distribution deals, but in the age of a growing tendency toward digital downloading, even that might not be a necessity. As Stahl (2003) suggests, what is more important in the definition of authenticity and its boundaries, which are constantly shifting and being redrawn, are power relations and access to commodities (31), or, to use the concept of Sarah Thornton (1995), the subcultural capital. The Bigg Boss label features Toxxx and other artists, including hip hop pioneers WWW and PSH. Vladimír 518 is the front man for the whole label, as well as a graffiti artist, comic book designer, and recently also coauthor of two books, including one on current subcultures and subcultural formations during communism. The visibility of Vladimír 518 in the mainstream media and on the roster of artists of the Bigg Boss label makes the label the commercially most successful entity within Czech hip hop, allows the artists access to better sound, better studios, better video production, and the capacity to invest in marketing strategies, which are elements that most underground rappers cannot afford.

Whether they are rapping about materialism, flaunting their success, or claiming to be "real" because they focus on the quality of expression and on a message with substance, one thing all of these MCs have in common is the expression of their lived reality through rap. They all represent their "true" selves and individual accomplishments as a means of building a sincere relationship with their audience (Jeffries 2011). As one of the rappers puts it, "the worst thing that can happen is when you don't really believe what the rapper is telling you." Foggy Fogosh concurs in his song "Rap Cabaret": "I won't be talking about ghettos and guns, because that is not what's happening here," and thus the audience would not find him credible. This is evident also in the most frequent topics in the body of work of the selected artists, which include definitions of hip hop, everyday struggles (having to live from one paycheck to the next), partying with fellas (with reference to alcohol and weed consumption but strongly against "hard" drug use), diss tracks aimed at anonymous "haters," and representing one's city.

The imperative of understanding "real" rap as the reflection of one's lived reality and point of view means that most of the MCs also speak from a position of privilege. In a public debate on the relationship between subcultures and the mainstream in December 2013,[10] Vladimír 518 pointed out that he doesn't feel there is any crisis to speak of, that we all live pretty well and there is no need for negativity. These remarks are striking, especially in times of numerous anti-Roma demonstrations all over the country. On the other hand, Vladimír 518, representing the white middle class, the front man of the most successful independent hip hop label, surely does not have the same problems and doesn't face the struggles Roma youth do, especially in so-called "socially excluded localities."[11] The fact that Roma hip hop remains on the margins of Czech rap music due to the lack of access to music production equipment and subcultural capital in general, and most importantly the racist stereotype about Roma people, contradicts the romantic notion of hip hop as a platform for the underprivileged youth of ethnic origins to express issues of oppression and discrimination (Mitchell 2001:155). Hip hop and rap music have been recognized as a vehicle for catching the attention on Roma youth, especially by activists and social workers. The question remains to what extent rap is used as a means of integration for Roma youth and, as in the case of the UGC (United Gipsy Crew), a group that formed as an outcome of the hip hop program "Slova místo zbraní" (Words Instead of Weapons) in Žižkov, a high-risk locality due to the increased presence of Roma people, they too just want to have fun and chill.

The notion of authenticity is very much informed by what Czech MCs perceive to be authentic hip hop in the United States, the birthplace of hip hop culture (see McLeod 1999). So the fact that hip hop is first and foremost an African American cultural expression is not lost on them. During my research among the underground MCs, I was told numerous times that no rapper can ever be racist, and that that fact is obvious just by looking at the hip hop artists who support antiracist events and movements. At the same time, when asked about Roma involvement in rap music, the rappers interviewed tended to base their arguments on very racist assumptions such as "they have it in their blood." The beliefs that African American rappers are violent "by nature" and that nobody would invite a Roma person to a studio because they are "all thieves" are examples of some of the prevalent racist imagery.

The reason these issues are not articulated directly in most of Czech rap music production, and why rappers limit themselves in alluding to social problems (Miklódy 2004:169) is that it doesn't reflect their lived reality. In the words of Barrer (2009), who focused on similar situation in Slovak rap, "[t]aking on 'someone else's struggle' could be seen as insincere engagement which is beyond the brief of Slovak rap artists, who have not experienced ethnic discrimination" (72).

Girls × Boys

The general attitude of the audience and of active participants in Czech hip hop subculture alike toward the persona of a rapper can be summed up in the following quotation from one of my interviewees:

> In the Czech Republic, the notion is that if someone wants to rap, he must come from the streets, he must curse a lot, because that is the way it is done, he must be the typical strong man. It has to be a tough man raised by the streets and also selling weed or some other drugs, because that is really dope.

Czech rap music in particular and the hip hop subculture in general is a highly masculine domain. The promotion of masculinity in rap music is shaped by the nature of Czech society, which is still largely patriarchal. With early socialization within families with strictly differentiated gender roles based on the "natural" order of a man being the breadwinner and a woman being the primary caretaker, an educational system that approaches male and female students based on the same binary dichotomies, a language that traditionally uses the generic masculine terms (Kaněčková 2012), and the portrayal of hypermasculinity by American rappers, the emphasis on masculinity in Czech rap music comes as no surprise. The hegemonic masculinity that "valorizes aggression, heterosexuality and capitalist success" (Randolph 2006:205) serves as an ideal for Czech rappers, something they are constantly being compared against, and is considered an agent of socialization not only for men, but for women as well. Thus the masculine identity is based on patriarchal opposition to femininity; in the words of Michael Kimmel (2005), the worst thing imaginable is to be a "sissy": "everything that a man wasn't and a woman was" (47–48).

The notion of rap music as an exclusively masculine domain is supported by subtle and overt mechanisms for the exclusion of women. One such mechanism can be illustrated by pointing out the relative invisibility of women and gender relations in the body of work of the selected rappers. The traditional view among rappers of masculinity and femininity as a binary opposition puts women in the role of a sexual object, the trophy of a successful rapper, the dumb groupie at a concert or the loyal girlfriend who respects the rapper's career (McFarland 2003:93; see also Oware 2009:288). At other times, the perfect loyal girlfriend is embodied in the city, the music itself, or Mary Jane (marijuana). These types of narratives further legitimize the good/bad woman discourse. While the "good" woman obeys the patriarchal system and fulfills the demands of traditional femininity, the "bad" woman, from the standpoint of conservative discourse on gender, engages in morally questionable behavior in order to gain money or power. These arbitrarily created stereotypes of women are often played against each other (Rose 2008; Sharpley-Whitting and Duncan 2007; McFarland 2003:95).

Of the ten artists, perhaps the most traditional view of femininity is represented by Hugo Toxxx, who uses the word "bitch" frequently in referring to men and women alike. In the song "Jedu jako Bauch" (I Roll as a God), Toxxx describes woman's role: shut up, clean and cook, and wait for the "God" to come home. Ektor's second single "Number 1," from his album *Tetris* in collaboration with DJ Wich, expresses his vision of the ideal woman. Ektor warns his current girlfriend that, as the chorus suggests, she has to "give me more, give me more, this is not enough." Some of the directions include: have more fun, cry less, sleep less, wake up earlier, don't be so bitter and boring, show that she uses her brain and go to work, because "your mother was lying when she told you it's all about the beauty." Ektor no longer feels he should support a woman just because she is sexy, sleeps a lot, and on top of that is always nagging.

Visual representation of stories tend to deviate from the narratives expressed in the lyrics, and such is the case with the video to Ektor's "Number 1." The storyline begins with a spoiled young girl being driven to a big mansion, where Ektor and DJ Wich await her arrival. Here the girl is undressed and thrown into a room with just a mattress on the floor. At this boot camp, the girl joins other women in jogging and doing push-ups. As Ektor rhymes about her going to work, he brings her a knife and sends her into the kitchen and the wash room. As the story progresses, we see the girl get in shape and even read a book in her solitary room. This is the right time for DJ Wich to bring her a wedding dress and walk her down to the front door, where the older man who brought the girl in is ready to pick her up. The "remodeled" girl has been turned into the "right" woman, and Ektor and DJ Wich collect the cash. Not only is the song a manual for prospective girlfriends—in the video Ektor and DJ Wich aspire to be the men who are in charge of educating young Czech women: to use their brain, to be in shape, to cook and clean. As Gwendolyn D. Pough (2004) suggests based on her analysis of some of the most famous hip hop songs depicting the male–female relationships, it is fairly common that we get the picture of how rappers see women and how women should behave in order to make relationships work.

Khomator describes the overall attitude toward gender roles in his song "Ony × oni" (Girls × Boys), which relies heavily on traditional notions of masculinity and femininity. Using "boys will be boys" rhetoric, Khomator describes women as always nagging, preoccupied by their appearance, always talking instead of taking action, and as inherently different from men (Weitzer and Kubrin 2009:10). All men can do is try to understand women and explain to them that the nature of men is to pass on their genetic information and go have a beer.

Even when we look at songs by Revolta, the proclaimed "conscious" rapper, we see that his lyrics contain criticism of politics, education, medicine, consumerism, materialism, racism, and xenophobia. But in a line in the song "Myslím" (I Think), he raps: "the real beauty of a woman is more than a body for your dick"; the overall sentiment expressed toward women can be summed up in another line: "as long as bitches have a place to buy purses, the only thing they do best is their make-up" ("Až se naše děti vzbudí" [When Our Children Wake Up]). Pardue (2010), studying Brazilian hip hop, points out: "unlike other social categories such as race, class, and place, gender remains a relatively conservative discursive point" (434). Similarly, Katz (2007) suggests, "the more popular conscious hip-hop becomes, the more likely it is to subscribe to the same sexist and misogynistic themes it critiques in mainstream hip-hop" (15).

However, what turned out to be an issue for these particular Czech rappers is the question of their future fatherhood (most of them are in their mid- to late twenties). As Ektor suggests: "these days a complete family is almost a bad joke" ("Jednou to budem mít" [Once We'll Have It All]). In his song "Kde si byl" (Where Were You), Ektor draws on his experience of growing up without a father and insists that his listeners should never give up their "own blood" and run away from the responsibilities of fatherhood. Similarly, Khomator, in a song called "Smířený" (In Peace), tells the story of having to witness family disputes, ending in a divorce—a situation he wants to avoid: "I know what kind of father I want to be one day."

These excerpts reflect the current state of the Czech society. According to the Czech Statistical Office, in 2012 the divorce rate was 44.5 percent.[12] Furthermore, whereas single mothers under communism were protected as employees, after the Revolution, the rise of competition, higher unemployment rates, and discourses about single mothers abusing the system led to the legislative changes in 2006 that cut the privileges of single mothers and their right to work while collecting maternity benefits to the same amount as women living with a partner. Furthermore, attempts to implement better child support have been unsuccessful, and alimony usually covers only 20 percent of real living expenses (Cidlinská 2010).

The focus on fatherhood and the experience of not growing up with a father figure points to the presumed crisis of fatherhood in particular, and masculinity in general. Fafejta (2012) argues that it is socially easy to resign from any form of fatherhood and suggests that some men are even led to that resignation by their environment. While motherhood is still understood as a "natural" prerogative of women—the caretakers—the role of father is shifting, and it is expected that he will be a breadwinner who is also emotionally involved with the family life, which, according to Fafejta, can lead to a situation where "he is neither provider, nor a caretaker" (245).

These particular MCs are determined to play an active role as responsible fathers. In his song "Střepy z minulosti" (Shreds from the Past), Idea raps about the type of knowledge he wants to pass on to his future son. The group Safari touches on the topic of fatherhood as well in the song "Sousede" (Neighbor), giving props to those fathers who have been able to be good role models for their children without succumbing to alcoholism or drug abuse, which are everyday threats in their city of Ostrava. What makes the group stand out is their song "Zločinec" (Villain), which deals with domestic violence. Although they address this very complex issue superficially when they rap about an alcoholic who just has realized what he has done to his family, and the fact that he has caused permanent damage, the message of the song is clear: "Love those close to you and never hurt them."

While love songs per se have not found a place in the expression of these artists, Prago Union might well come very close in their "Outro." In this song, Kato explains in a string of metaphors his obsession with a woman. The song "Apropó" is a good-bye to an ex-girlfriend in which Kato does not need to use curse words when he realizes it's "time to wrap up the dark times when my whole world was between your tights." MC Gey, with his use of satire and sometimes far-fetched humor, describes his love escapades in songs "Rande" (Date), describing a blind date set up on the internet that he almost missed due to stomach issues, and "Kanály lásky" (Channels of Love), in which he takes us on a journey to Venice, Italy, where he ends up robbed by his one-night stand.

Czech hip hop subculture suffers what is characterized by what Tricia Rose calls a "'What women?' syndrome" (1994:150). When I conduct my interviews with Czech rappers, I frequently ask them about their thoughts on the lack of female MCs. The most frequent answer I get is "I don't know," simply because they have never really given it much thought. Based on my long-term fieldwork with Czech rappers, male and female, I came to the conclusion that the lack of involvement of women in Czech rap music is a matter of both structural barriers (different life cycles, gender stereotypes, lack of mentoring, unequal payment) and overt and subtle mechanisms of exclusion, not only by rappers, but also by other women already active within the Czech hip hop subculture (Oravcová

2011). Once female MCs assume a public role as performers, they have to navigate between two equally restrictive positions: the sexual object or the extraordinary strong woman "with balls" (Piano 2003:258).

One of the first rap groups, WWW, had a female member who holds the status of the first female Czech rapper. Lela stopped rapping after starting a family and was briefly featured on a track with PSH, "Nemám rád" (I Don't Like) in 2006. The first official CD by a female rapper was released in 2009 by Lara303, who has been rapping on local concerts for almost a decade. Currently, only a handful of female MCs enjoy some kind of visibility. These include Sharkass, a young freestyler who has made it to the semifinals of *Czecho-Slovakia Has Talent;*[13] Taktika and BioMasha, who formed a group called DIAkritika and who are also spoken-word artists; and Fakné and Potmě, female artists who frequently express social and feminist issues but prefer to associate with the alternative movement rather than the hip hop subculture.

One of the reasons there are no female MCs who could create the rhetorical space to address the sexist (heteronormative and homophobic) tendencies in Czech rap lyrics is the general patriarchal character of the Czech society and attitudes toward feminism. More often than not, feminism is depicted as a monolithic militant ideology promoting hatred toward men. A media-supported antifeminist discourse has affected the way feminism is explained and defended. The public is assured from the beginning that the discussion is about gender, about men and women, not feminism. And though young women are especially aware of the gender inequalities in the Czech society, they still don't have the courage to identify as feminists (Sokolová 2004:200–201; see also Rose 1994).

The reason for such a backlash against feminism in the Czech Republic (and Slovakia as well) has its background in socialism, under which the model of emancipation for women emphasized employment for all women. The ideal of femininity was constructed as the hardworking woman, good wife, and caring mother, a model that put women under a triple burden (Kiczková 2006:12–13). Feminism was understood as something that Czech women do not need nor want, which was the position of the authorities who shape public discourse rather than the opinion of the women themselves.

The Czech hip hop scene seems to reflect this general attitude. And though it would not be appropriate to place all the blame on rappers, it would be progressive for them to realize that the vocabulary they use has an effect on the men and women who are currently listening, thus contributing to their gender socialization and "reinforcing and perpetuating gender inequality" (Weitzer and Kubrin 2009:4). As Rose (2008) suggests, what we need to do is attack sexism, support artists who are "conscious" to the degree that they promote positive images of women, and at the same time educate youth about sexism (131).

Conclusions

Czech rap music has deep connections to the original American hip hop culture, since it provides most of the same points of reference when it comes to the construction of authenticity, whether it is knowledge of the history of hip hop (American and Czech) or the value placed on the lived experience of the rapper. While most of these rappers focus on everyday life, the struggle to make a living, the time they spend drinking beer and smoking weed with their friends, or disrespecting the anonymous "haters," the so-called "conscious" hip-hop reflecting political issues, racism, and xenophobia still have some growing to do. One of the reasons these issues did not take root in the Czech Republic from the beginning is that hip hop was first and foremost a sonic experience, something new and with an impressionable audience, and the message came second. Hip hop in the Czech Republic is mainly represented by "white" middle-class men talking to their middle-class, mainly male, audience. They do not share the experience of people of Roma ethnicity living in the ghettos, where hip hop took a root as well but remains invisible, within the boundaries that separate Roma from the Czech majority. Czech rappers are almost exclusively men who, on the one hand, having been socialized in a patriarchal society, express traditional values on gender relations (employing sexist language and objectifying women). On the other hand, these particular MCs express the tensions in the role of fatherhood in the current social climate.

There is a call for messages of substance to be addressed in the lyrics of the rappers. It would be helpful not to get lost in the arbitrary labels of "mainstream/commercial" and "underground/conscious" and their respective ideologies. Contrary to the situation in American hip hop, these artists are releasing their material under their own labels, and therefore are not under the pressure of big record labels that "continue to put ethics and morality aside to release violent or sexist rap" (Lena 2006:486). In order to be able to really claim a degree of consciousness in their lyrics, Czech MCs would have to start addressing the issues of sexism and racism in depth, and from an informed position, if they really want to make a change. They have to be held accountable for what they say, precisely because words have power and what is being said has an effect on people (Oware 2009:798; Kroh and Suazo 1995:152–153).

Notes

1. This text was written with the support of the Grant Agency of Charles University, GA UK project number 630012, and the university research project of Charles University SVV ISS 2015 number 260 232.

2. I became a member of the Czech hip hop subculture in 2001 when I moved to Prague to pursue my university studies.

3. I have been involved with the study of hip hop since 2006. In my bachelor's thesis I focused on gender stereotypes; my diploma thesis analyzed the position of female MCs within the Czech hip hop subculture; and this chapter represents some of the findings of my ongoing research on the discourses of authenticity in Czech rap music.

4. Since 2010, I have been involved with the organization of two regular hip hop events: Freestyle Mondays Prague, an open mic jam with a live band, and End of the Weak, the Czech branch of international competition for MCs. That year I also started cohosting a radio show focusing on independent and political hip hop from the United States and the Czech Republic. The *Street Cypher* radio show, of which I am the host and the program director, on the only Czech hip hop radio, Spin 96.2 FM, runs every Tuesday from 8 to 11 P.M.

5. Anděl, established in 1991, represents the awards given by the Czech Popular Music Academy. The category of "hip hop and r'n'b" was introduced in 2003. The Anděl award is considered to be the Czech version of American Grammy Awards.

6. A. Oravcová (interviewer) and Revolta (interviewee), September 6, 2012, "Bringing Conscious Hip-Hop to the Mainstream Audience" [interview transcript]. http://worldhiphopmarket .com/revolta-bringing-conscious-hip-hop-to-the-mainstream-audience-czech-republic/.

7. J. Šprincl (interviewer) and Sifon (interviewee), February 23, 2007. aktualne.cz website: http://aktualne.centrum.cz/kultura/hudba/clanek.phtml?id=363170.

8. MaryC (interviewer) and Hugo Toxxx (interviewee), October 1, 2012. *Kruton* radio show [audio file]. http://www.rozhlas.cz/radiowave/jukebox/.

9. The three most influential record companies in 2013 were Universal Music (31.7 percent), Sony Music (19.1 percent), and Supraphone (16.5 percent). http://www.ifpi.cz/cr-celorocni/.

10. The full discussion is available at https://www.youtube.com/watch?v=CpnOlXWte04.

11. The Ministry of Regional Development of the Czech Republic defines "socially excluded Roma localities" as those where there is a concentration of socially excluded people who define themselves as Roma or are defined as Roma by their environment. These localities are characterized by low employment rates, low education, not enough access to legal forms of livelihood, and a tendency to risky behavior. The official web pages include a map of these localities in the Czech Republic. http://www.mmr.cz/cs/Stavebni-rad-a-bytova-politika/Bytova -politika/Programy-Dotace/Ostatni/Socialne-vyloucena-romska-lokalita.

12. http://www.czso.cz/csu/redakce.nsf/i/rozvodovost.

13. The elements of hip hop culture enjoy a great deal of success on Czech and Slovak talent shows, whether it is rap (H16), beatbox (Johny Typek and Tiny Beat), or street dance/break dance (T-Boss).

References

Androutsopoulos, Jannis. 2009. "Language and the Three Spheres of Hip Hop." In *Global Linguistic Flows: Hip Hop Cultures, Youth Identities, and the Politics of Language*, eds. H. Samy Alim, Awad Ibrahim, and Alastair Pennycook (pp. 43–62). New York: Routledge.

Barrer, Peter. 2009. "'My White, Blue, and Red Heart': Constructing a Slovak Identity in Rap Music." *Popular Music and Society* 32(1):59–75.

Cidlinská, Kateřina. 2010. "Politický a legislativní diskurz náhradního výživného v České Republice" [Political and legislative discourse of supplemental child support in the Czech Republic]. Diploma thesis, Department of Gender Studies, Faculty of Humanities, Charles University, Prague.

Fafejta, Martin. 2012. "Koncepty maskulinity: otcové a nezaměstnaní muži" [Concepts of masculinity: Fathers and unemployed men]. In *Konstrukce maskulinní identity v minulosti a současnosti,* eds. Radmila Švaříčková et al. (pp. 241–258). Prague: Nakladatelství Lidové noviny.

Harrison, Anthony Kwame. 2009. *Hip Hop Underground: The Integrity and Ethics of Racial Identification.* Philadelphia: Temple University Press.

Hodkinson, Paul. 2005. "'Insider Research' in the Study of Youth Cultures." *Journal of Youth Studies* 8(2):131–149.

Jeffries, Michael P. 2011. *Thug Life: Race, Gender, and the Meaning of Hip-Hop.* Chicago: University of Chicago Press.

Kaněčková, Eva. 2012. "Maskulinní identita jako důsledek a problém genderové výchovy" [Masculine identity as a consequence and a problem of gendered education]. In *Konstrukce maskulinní identity v minulosti a současnosti,* eds. Radmila Švaříčková et al. (pp. 276–285). Prague: Nakladatelství Lidové noviny.

Katz, Meredith. 2007. "Conscious Hip-Hop: Are Women Included?" Proceedings of the American Sociological Association Annual Meeting (pp. 1–23).

Kiczková, Zuzana. 2006. *Pamäť žien: O skúsenosti sebeutvárania v biografických rozhovoroch.* Bratislava: Iris.

Kimmel, Michael S. 2005. *The History of Men: Essays in the History of American and British Masculinities.* Albany: State University of New York Press.

Krims, Adam. 2001. *Rap Music and the Poetics of Identity.* Cambridge: Cambridge University Press.

Kroh, Franklin B., and Frances L. Suazo. 1995. "Contemporary Urban Music: Controversial Messages in Hip-Hop and Rap Lyrics." *Et Cetera* 52(2):139–154.

Lena, Jennifer C. 2006. "Social Context and Musical Content of Rap Music, 1979–1995." *Social Forces* 85(1):479–495.

McFarland, Pancho. 2003. "Challenging the Contradictions of Chicanismo in Chicano Rap Music and Male Culture." *Race, Gender and Class* 10(4):92–107.

McLeod, Kembrew. 1999. "Authenticity within Hip-Hop and Other Cultures Threatened with Assimilation." *Journal of Communication* 49(4):134–150.

Miklódy, Éva. 2004. "A.R.T., Klikk, K.A.O.S., and the Rest: Hungarian Youth Rapping." In *Blackening Europe: The African American Presence,* ed. Heike Raphael-Hernandes (pp. 187–200). New York: Routledge.

Mitchell, Tony. 2001. *Global Noise: Rap and Hip-Hop outside the U.S.A.* Middletown, CT: Wesleyan University Press.

Oravcová, Anna. 2011. "Underground českého hip hopu." In *Revolta stylem: Hudební subkultury mládeže v České Republice,* ed. Marta Kolářová (pp. 123–157). Prague: Slon.

Oware, Matthew. 2009. "A 'Man's Woman'? Contradictory Messages in the Songs of Female Rappers, 1992–2000." *Journal of Black Studies* 39(5):786–802.

Pardue, Derek. 2010. "Getting an Attitude: Brazilian Hip Hoppers Design Gender." *Journal of Latin America and Caribbean Anthropology* 15(2):434–456.

Piano, Doreen. 2003. "Resisting Subjects: DIY Feminism and the Politics of Style in Subcultural Production." In *The Post-Subcultures Reader,* eds. David Muggleton and Rupert Weinzierl (pp. 253–265). Oxford: Berg.

Pough, Gwendolyn D. 2004. *Check It While I Wreck It: Black Womanhood, Hip-Hop Culture, and the Public Sphere.* Boston: Northeastern University Press.

Randolph, Antonia. 2006. "Don't Hate Me Because I'm Beautiful: Black Masculinity and Alternative Embodiment in Rap Music." *Race, Gender and Class* 13(3–4):200–217.

Rose, Tricia. 1994. *Black Noise: Rap Music and Black Culture in Contemporary America.* Middletown, CT: Wesleyan University Press.

Rose, Tricia. 2008. *Hip Hop Wars: What We Talk about When We Talk about Hip Hop and Why It Matters.* New York: Basic Civitas Books.

Sharpley-Whitting, T. Denean. 2007. *Pimps Up, Ho's Down: Hip Hop's Hold on Young Black Women.* New York: New York University Press.

Sokolová, Věra. 2004. "Současné trendy feministického myšlení" [Current trends in feminist thought]. In *ABC Feminismu* (pp. 199–212). Brno: Nesehnutí.

Stahl, Geoff. 2003. "Tastefully Renovating Subcultural Theory: Making Space for a New Model." In *The Post-Subcultures Reader,* eds. David Muggleton and Rupert Weinzierl (pp. 27–40). Oxford: Berg.

Thornton, Sarah. 1995. *Club Cultures: Music, Media and Subcultural Capital.* Middletown, CT: Wesleyan University Press.

Waegner, Cathy Covell. 2004. "Rap, Rebounds, and Rocawear: The 'Darkening' of German Youth Culture." In *Blackening Europe: The African American Presence,* ed. Heike Raphael-Hernandes (pp. 171–185). New York: Routledge.

Weitzer, Ronald, and Charis E. Kubrin. 2009. "Misogyny in Rap Music: A Content Analysis of Prevalence and Meanings." *Men and Masculinities* 12(1):3–29.

Discography

Ektor and DJ Wich. 2012. *Tetris.* Monitor EMI.

Hugo Toxxx. 2012. *Bauch Money Mixtape.* Hypno808.

Idea. 2012. *Daleko blíž.* TyNikdy.

Khomator. 2011. *Terapie.* Repromanifest.

Lara303. 2009. *Revolution.* X Production/Rootcat Recordings.

Lesík Hajdovský a Manželé. 1991. "Jižák." *Jižák/Na dně.* Bonton.

MC Gey. 2011. *Imaginárium naprosto běžných podivností.* TyNikdy.

Prago Union. 2010. *Dezorient Express.* EMI.

PSH. 2006. "Nemám rád." *Rap'n'roll.* Big Boss.

Rest and DJ Fatte. 2010. *Premiéra.* TyNikdy.

Revolta. 2012. *Evoluce vědomí.* Mafia Records, 2012.

Safari. 2012. *Flow food.* Repromanifest.

S.C.U.R. 2011. *Periférie.* Self-released.

CHAPTER 16

"KEEP IT 360"

(Re)envisioning the Cultural and Racial Roots of Hip Hop through DJ Rhetoric and Ethnography

Todd Craig

IN HIP HOP, there is an adage that has remained relevant as the language and rhetorical patterns of the culture have changed. That adage is "Keep it real." The focus of the statement truly means to keep things brutally honest, truthful, raw, and uncut. As the rhetorical landscape of hip hop has shifted, so has the scope of the saying "Keep it real." In contemporary times, the saying has changed to "Keep it 100"—as in to keep it 100 percent; but while the slogan has slightly changed, the sensibility remains the same. Now there are many variations of this saying, ranging anywhere from "Keep it one hunnid" to "Keep it one-hundo," as said by Peter Rosenberg, one of the hosts of the *Morning Show* on New York City's FM radio staple for hip hop music, HOT 97. The premise of this statement is very simple: The act of "keeping it 100" is an extension of "keeping it real." Sometimes to "keep it 100" does not fall in line with popular sentiment, but requires one to completely go against the grain of what popular culture defines as "real," "authentic," and "true." However, similar to the Nation of Gods and Earths' idea of "my word is my bond," to "keep it 100" means to stay true to oneself, regardless of what the outcome may be. After all, isn't that the level of unadulterated honesty that we should all strive to attain as scholars, educators, researchers, and lifelong learners? But the fact of the matter remains: to "keep it 100" is a straight hip hop paradigm . . . make NO mistake about it.

With these ideals in mind, this chapter aims to "keep it 100" on a number of different levels. It focuses primarily on the cornerstone of hip hop music and culture: the DJ—who utilizes the 360 degrees of circular vinyl and constantly connects elements of the past, present, and future through music. This idea moves the DJ full circle into hip hop historian, tastemaker, and trendsetter. Because, let's keep it 100: there would be no such thing as hip hop without the DJ. So, with such a heavy focus and fascination on the other elements of hip hop such as the MCs, the graffiti writers, the b-boys and b-girls, "Keep It 360" revolves and spins as the records on the turntables do; it is this specific rotation that became the orbital axis of hip hop culture. Thus, this chapter's main concern is to spin the DJ to the immediate forefront, analyzing the formation of hip hop with the DJ as the focal point. In order to do such work, this writing travels through a number of different moments, similar to a DJ mixing between different records—encompassing each revolution of every record as part of a larger DJ set. As such, this writing also functions with the inherent premise of the existence of a DJ rhetoric and literacy. Understanding that this piece of scholarship has been constructed with these ideas in mind will allow you as readers/listeners/party people "in the place to be" to understand how this piece will move fluidly through breaks labeled as narrative, scholarship, and ethnography. After moving through a brief literature review on the DJ in scholarship, "Keep It 360" will access concerns of the global spread of hip hop by Dr. Elaine Richardson, followed by ethnographic data from DJ cultural events in the United States, which foreground research on the practices of Croatian hip hop DJ Phat Phillie. I argue that we must begin to fully acknowledge the cultural and racial roots of hip hop; this is best done by shifting the focus and perspective from the rap-spitting MC back to the cornerstone of hip hop culture: the DJ. The culmination of this chapter will highlight the homie Filip Ivelia, a.k.a. DJ Phat Phillie: Croatian DJ, mover and shaker within the international hip hop world, and founder of the first chapter of the Zulu Nation in Croatia. This is coupled not only with conversation and scholarship from many hip hop scholars, but also with narrative that helps elucidate the hip hop mantra of "Keep it 100" to truly explore the integral role the DJ plays in this culture and music called hip hop. And whether it be the domestic musings in the epicenter called New York City or across the waters in international locations like Croatia—where the soundtrack to resistance is the soundtrack built by the DJ—we can see hip hop culture at its absolute best when the arbitrators and participants are able to create and cultivate their own international grooves based on the philosophy of "keeping it 100": with the original premises and tenets of hip hop that come from very specific locations that are primarily based on the positionality of the DJ, and no one else. Thus, the goal of "Keep It 360" is for educators, researchers and scholars, avid fans, participants, and cultural tastemakers to recalibrate the ways in which we think about hip hop's global flow and burgeoning motion from the East-Coast epicenter and beyond. Make no mistake about it: The MCs are cool, the dancers are dope, the graf writers are what's up . . . but this culture was built on the backs of the DJs. Let's keep it 100 about that hip hop fun fact.

And with this in mind, take a sonic ride with me as we mix on the page.

"PUT THE NEEDLE ON THE RECORD . . .": HOW ACADEMIA KEEPS IT 360 WITH DJ SCHOLARSHIP

It is unfortunate that a brief sweep of electronic databases will reveal an evident lack of DJ scholarship in hip hop studies, even though the DJ—and *not* the MC—is indeed the catalyst and the cornerstone of hip hop music and culture. While many people reference the DJ when talking about the origins of hip hop music, they quickly move past the DJ to talk about the other cultural elements. While writers and scholars like Paul Miller (a.k.a. DJ Spooky), Jeff Rice, Adam Banks, and Mark Katz have begun this process, our scholarship must push further in utilizing the voices of DJs within the culture who have always been active participants, trendsetters, and tastemakers. Very little work has been produced on the DJ, and much of the work that has been produced tends to home in on the metaphor of the DJ as writer or the DJ as collage artist. These studies tend to stick to metaphoric analyses of what the DJ does and how the DJ does it. For example, Paul Miller (also known as DJ Spooky That Subliminal Kid) pushes the idea of the DJ as writer/writer as DJ in his book *Rhythm Science* (2004). Miller's conception of the hip hop DJ as artist, artist as musician, and musician as writer helps him to create a lineage between himself and the writing world he wanted to enter years before his first book. Because Paul Miller also has a life as DJ Spooky, he is able to comment on this relationship as a practicing DJ, but it becomes difficult for Spooky to separate himself from his work as a DJ from an artistic point of view and as an academic, objectively reviewing the research.

As well, scholars like Jeff Rice (2003) and Mark Katz (2012) have both utilized the DJ in their scholarship, talking about the sampling practices of the hip hop DJ and the historical perspective of the hip hop DJ's rise to prominence within hip hop culture, respectively. However, both of these scholars have a tendency to leave out the important paradigm of race in their conversations. There is no way around acknowledging the most important factor in the formation of hip hop music and culture: the common plight of inner-city African American and Latino youth. Does this idea preclude or ignore the fact that other cultures were present during the formation of the culture we now know today as hip hop? No. But it cannot be ignored that hip hop is grounded, rooted, and formulated in urban environments systematically inhabited primarily by African Americans and Latinos at the time of hip hop's birth. Finally, Joe Schloss's seminal text *Making Beats: The Art of Sample-Based Hip-Hop* is a brilliant ethnographic examination and exploration of the hip hop producer. This important work, however, focuses more on the aspect of hip hop music production—by producers who may or may not be DJs first. While it is a critical addition to hip hop scholarship canon, *Making Beats* does not solely focus on the craft of DJing.

With so few sources of scholarship around the DJ, I felt the best thing I could do for this chapter was to "keep it 100" and go to a foundational source of Eastern European hip hop culture to "keep it 360" with the way this chapter shifts in perspective back around again to the DJ. In doing so, it seemed best to move toward the Croatian source who goes by the name of DJ Phat Phillie.

"To the Hip Hip, the Hop It Don't Stop": Rooted Musings via Dr. E on the Real Hip Hop

A few years ago, I presented a paper at New York University's Show and Prove Hip Hop Studies Conference, and I was able to spend some time with Dr. Elaine Richardson, who is known in the United States among English, literacy, and hip hop scholars as "Dr. E." Richardson is the author of *African American Literacies* (2004) and *Hiphop Literacies* (2006). During a panel on the formation of hip hop overseas, Dr. E presented a concern she had with the idea of hip hop and its "global linguistic flows": Sometimes when hip hop travels abroad, it becomes divorced from its blackness and its original roots in African American culture. As I talked to Dr. E and the panel about this process, she shared her worry that as hip hop moves further away from its African American roots, what tends to be neglected— and sometimes even ignored—is that hip hop's legacy is founded and rooted in African American culture. After talking to Dr. E in detail about this, I also found her thinking etched in stone in a review of the book *Global Linguistic Flows: Hip Hop Cultures, Youth Identities, and the Politics of Language*. In this review, Richardson (2010) states very clearly that:

> [in the authors'] attempts to understand the linguistic and cultural innovations that are taking place globally, there is a tendency to de-emphasize the globalized African American and Afrodiasporic discursive foundations of Hip Hop. . . . [A] related question that lingered in my mind as I read this chapter is how does the co-present origins argument work for White "global Hip Hoppers"? It seems to me that it has the potential to erase the Afrodiasporic contribution . . . from a Black linguistics perspective, I see that these diverse communities have appropriated Afrodiasporic ways of knowing, being and doing and encourage Hip Hoppers from any racial or ethnic group to use their available cultural tools as a means of expression. (267–269)

This is not a concern held solely by Dr. E; we have seen throughout scholarship as well as in contemporary settings that as hip hop music and language are appropriated by popular culture, they are also removed and pushed further from their African American roots. Ironically enough, this is a paradigm we've seen throughout the history of African American music and culture, from the blues and jazz all the way through to rhythm and blues and now even hip hop. What becomes intriguing about this notion, however, is that hip hop truly does serve as a "grand equalizer" of sorts, bringing all races, creeds, colors, and genders together in empowering ways; this is based on hip hop's historical formation in battling against an oppressive system that was seen to be at work in inner-city New York.

This is a fight that Richardson has taken up in other texts. Her work in *Hiphop Literacies* (2006) shines in its deliberate act of placing hip hop literacy squarely in the historical context of African American Vernacular English (AAVE), connecting it to black English and the African diaspora that came before it. This becomes an important idea in that it rejects the idea of hip hop belonging to and emanating from popular culture; this is a phenomenon that has happened in the United States with almost every (if not every) form of African American music and culture. Dr. E brings hip hop "home" specifically; thus, youth from everywhere who engage in hip hop are engaging in ways of knowing, doing, and producing based on AAVE and black culture—whether they are able to make those connections or not. So when Richardson frames "hip hop literacy" as a part of AAVE, such that ways of knowing and doing become specifically "hip hop," this does not predicate that the producers or doers are of African American descent. It merely requires that the connections to these things are "hip hop"; anyone of any race can be producers of modalities, discourse, or pedagogy that is specifically hip hop. Because Dr. E has painstakingly placed hip hop squarely at home in the African diaspora, participants in hip hop culture are inevitably participating in black culture. While the mainstream would not want to admit that the majority of its population is engaging in some form of "blackness," it is truly undeniable.

In addition, in H. Samy Alim's book *Roc the Mic Right* (2006), he strives for and successfully attains a blueprint for a linguistic roadmap called hip hop linguistics (HHLx); this linguistic roadmap sets forth the intricacies as well as the sophisticated nature of hip hop culture's language as more than just "a messy and sloppy form of standard English"; instead, similar to Geneva Smitherman's work in *Talkin and Testifyin* (1977), Alim is able to demonstrate the rules and regulations of HHLx, and discusses its power in terms of poetics, and the fact that those complex poetics demonstrate how hip hop artists stand out as the new contemporary poets. As well, Alim's connection of HHLx to Islamic culture and values positions it as a force that can be used to counteract religious stereotypes. Again, we see an African American cultural product dispelling secular stereotypes and separations. The fight between standard American English—which is losing its hold among youth culture—and HHLx can be equated as the same type of battle. But more specifically, the force of hip hop is being used in this battle, through both cultural production (e.g., music, fashion, poetry, art, and other ways of doing/knowing) and through scholarly research, to combat differences that are constantly posed as a lack of knowledge and values within and among members of hip hop culture.

This thinking can also be found in the writing of Emery Petchauer (2009) and various other hip hop scholars. It is clear that researchers acknowledge that hip hop music brings forth powerful emotions and meanings that cut across ethnic and racial lines. If this is the case, what hip hop is able to do to an extent is take the focus away from racial and/or ethnic identities, and bring meaning full circle—or 360—to all participants who are engaging in hip hop culture. Hip hop music may very well bring listeners to researching and learning about new topics and sources of information just because something is mentioned in the lyrics to various songs. But hip hop also functions in a global context; many people make the argument today that the true epicenters of hip hop now reside outside the United States. This is because the "culture" has been able to venture forth from a solely domestic location; in this movement, imitation begets inclusion into new cultures, languages, and contexts. The outcome is that we begin to see hip hop function on an international level, fulfilling its initial goal: being a mouthpiece and an outlet for generations of disenfranchised urban youth. While the issues may vary from town to town, city to city, province to province, and even country to country, as Smitherman (1997) says, "the chain remains the same": Disenfranchised youth become disenfranchised and rally around the same focal points in youth culture that make them feel isolated and minimized.

With all of these concerns in mind, it is my argument that these things do not need to be mutually exclusive. And I make this argument because I think the perspective should be shifted. It is my contention that as hip hop music and culture move from the shores of the United States and into various locations abroad, there will be a point where the music and culture revolve around whatever local issues are presented in a given location (Pennycook 2007). However, I propose that the idea of keeping it 100 by keeping the culture 360 revolves around an acknowledgment that while, yes, there will be localization of the music and the culture, there must also be an acknowledgment of the roots from which hip hop culture springs. And this practice can be witnessed when the perspective is shifted from the language-driven raps of the MC, and is instead shifted back to the cornerstone of the culture: the DJ.

The example that I use is the practices of Croatian DJ Phat Phillie.

"The Real Hip Hop / Is Ova Here!": A Picture That Sets the DJ in Central Motion

Before we make our way across the water, it is important to think about how we arrive at that location in the first place. Part of my research on the DJ entails connecting with DJs at various hip hop events and focal points within the culture. The methodological goal is to engage with the culture from within, to speak from an informed space. Understanding how DJs "keep it 100" in practice requires seeing and experiencing their practices in action. So in order to make the connection and bridge the gap like Nas, I found it important to conjure an image that will help us to understand the page I'm mixing from; so I give you this wrinkle in hip hop time to allow you to see the inner workings of hip hop DJ culture. . . .

The year is 2012, the season is summer. Any avid hip hop community member knows that every summer in New York City there are two important events that capture what we know as hip hop: the Crotona Park Jams and Digger's Delight. A series of block parties orchestrated by Christie Z-Pabon and Jorge Fabel Pabon's (a.k.a. Popmaster Fabel of the legendary Rock Steady Crew) company Tools of War Grassroots Hip Hop, they are set up primarily to pay tribute and homage to the cornerstone of the culture: the DJ. This was the summer I was frantically focused on my dissertation; I had completed over 80 interviews in my qualitative research study on DJs. I was also a full-time father to my newly turned 1-year-old daughter. Mommy and I had to bring her to the essence of the culture that brought us together, so we were trying to figure out how to get to these jams logistically. Unfortunately, we missed the Park Jam with DJs Ca$h Money and Breakbeat Lou; we made it from New Jersey in 40 minutes through rush hour . . . a driving miracle. We were in Crotona Park and could hear the music. Our daughter is a hip hop head; she got so excited that she projectile-vomited across the back seat of our car. . . . Down went that park jam! We had a family engagement for the ultimate joint with Afrika Bambaataa, The Original Jazzy Jay, and KOOL DJ Red Alert . . . Down went that park jam! At this point, after missing Bam, Jazzy Jay, and Red Alert . . . and after missing Breakbeat Lou and Ca$h Money, there was NO way I was gonna miss DJs Boogie Blind, Lord Finesse, and Chairman Mao.

The scene at Digger's Delight is like a cross between the movies *Beat Street*, *Wild Style*, and *The Usual Suspects*. To define it simply, it's what you'd want to see and hear if you are a fan of what is sometimes called "the real hip hop." Picture this: Right in the middle of the stairway in the park on 135th Street and St. Nicholas Avenue in Harlem, as the gentrified business crowds move to and from the buses and trains, Chairman Mao is spinning breaks on 45s. A couple of OGs are rocking the leather Black Spades motorcycle vests, and another rocks the Mighty Zulu Nation black denim vest. Lord Finesse and Boogie Blind are directly across from me; DJ Mel Starr is here, and The Original Jazzy Jay has already made an appearance to set up his equipment. People sit on the benches, the concrete partition, and the grassy lawn. A Latin dude in all black—black skinny jeans and a black V-neck tee to be specific—is breaking, followed by the black kid in the tan cargo shorts, red tee, and black on aqua blue Campus Adidas with the all black skullie. The culture is here and is undeniably strong . . . so much so that even the gentrified business crowds moving to and from the buses and trains slow down, and sometimes even stop, entranced and enthralled by the rapture our culture has always evoked.

I'ma keep it 100 and say straight-up-and-down: This IS hip hop!

And mind you, initially it may only be about 50 people or so, but hip hop leaks out from the concrete and oozes its way out into the atmosphere via speakers and turntables, microphones and mixers, vinyl, Serato, and 45s. Be clear: at Digger's Delight, you're gonna hear rare grooves . . . the title of the party alone tells you what you're in for. It's your favorite DJs' favorite park jam and summertime event. Because the DJs who are spinning have spent blood, sweat, and tears digging for the perfect beats and breaks that people truly love or haven't heard in a very long time, if at all. And it's in those rare grooves, beats, and breaks, all those locations of soul where hip hop was intertextually conceived, forming the musical landscape of the culture. And you're gonna see mad head-nodding and wild scrunchy-smoosh-faced expressions as folks continue to drop those "where'd he get that record?!?" faces. As always, there's black, white, Spanish, Asian, national, international, and many more. There's also more hip hop icons—so many, in fact, that I can't name them all, but I know I should know them.

I can't help but to think this must resemble what it used to look like in Union Square, deep in the Boogie-Down Bronx at the Zulu Jams in the River Center, at the River Park Jams in Queensbridge, at Rock Steady reunions before the location switched up to New Jersey. Hip hop holds a certain type of home here, and even though it's taken me the whole damn summer to get here, it feels like home, like I've been here all summer long and never left. . . . It truly feels like a conversation with that good friend you don't see in forever, but when y'all catch up years later, it's like you never missed a beat . . . word.

This IS hip hop!

Right after Chairman Mao's slaughter-set, Boogie Blind proceeds to KILL it!!!!

Of course, the imperial Grandmaster Caz just strolls in regular with a strut and a diddy-bop that absolutely does NOT signify lateness in any way, shape, or form. Soon after Boogie Blind tears the set down, I get to see Lord Finesse live; partway into his set, he drops the Fat Albert–born Mud Foot vocal of "lay some treats on us" to let you know you're in for something special. And that's when Finesse begins killing the "one two three four hit it!!!" of a James Brown break. Then Jazzy Jay gets on the mic to let us know hip hop photographer Joe Conzo has arrived. And after Finesse finishes demolishing his set, next up is The Original Jazzy Jay.

And then Biz Markie shows up, literally materializing outta thin air, as he is well-known for; one minute things are moving, and then outta nowhere—Biz has appeared. DJs Ted Smooth, Chuck City, and Forrest Getemgump have all arrived. What was once a cool 50 people has now metastasized to a couple hundred, easily. Natasha Diggs is in the park. And then DJ Alamo from Brand Nubian came through. And the whole time, Tools of War Park Jams lifetime MC Grandmaster Caz keeps dropping history on the mic over the beats.

Then I caught up with the big homie Breakbeat Lou (a.k.a. Ultimate Breaks and Beats cofounder). And for me, the cipher was officially complete during Chairman Mao's second set, when the youth standing next to me pulled out the black book and scribed the "Tools of War" graffiti piece with the character live on the set. And when the young kid runs up on this graf artist to look at what he's doing, you immediately see the power of our culture. . . .

This IS hip hop!

We must be very clear, and we must keep it 100: All of this is rooted in the delight of the diggers: It's always DJs first. At this point, all elements ring forth to the fourth called culture. And all of this stems from the cultural shaman who rocks two turntables. It's always DJs first. That's how hip hop culture started, and that's how it continues to thrive in its most purest form. Believe that.

And it is this culture that migrated across the waters into the heart and soul of Croatian DJ Phat Phillie.

"What Goes Around Comes Back Around Again": The Real-to-Reel of the Croatian Hip Hop Ambassador—DJ Phat Phillie on the Set

DJ Phat Phillie's love of hip hop started in ways very similar to everyone involved in hip hop culture: One day, he heard a record on the radio that changed it all for him. Phat Phillie recalls the moment very well: "I first started listening to hip hop back in '84 when I first heard a group called UTFO on a song named 'Roxanne Roxanne'" (DJ Phat Phillie, personal communication, August 25, 2011). From that point on, Phat Phillie became an avid fan and listener of the *Rap Attack Show* from 1984 to 1991. Phat Phillie has a detailed sense of his Croatian history and can clearly recall that "at this point, Croatia was still a part of Yugoslavia. On the *Rap Attack Show* on Radio 101, [the DJ] announced in '91 that he wanted to have some fans be guests to come into the show." At this point, Phat Phillie had already been drawn into the music and culture of hip hop; he would travel overseas to Long Island, New York, for a summer to learn English. He would have his father, who was also a musician, travel back from various countries and bring Phillie records. As hip hop grew, so did Phillie's record collection. Thus, it was pretty easy for Phillie to sit down and craft a letter stating that he had been a fan of the show, about his travels to the United States, and about his extensive record collection. In 1991, Phat Phillie was chosen as a guest to come to the *Rap Attack Show* on Radio 101. Two years later, Phillie was able to make a different move: "From that guest spot, I was able to get my own radio show called *The Blackout Radio Show* in 1993. It was a steppingstone for the whole Croatian hip hop scene. And not only Croatia, but the regional hip hop scene and countries like Slovenia, Bosnia, Serbia, all the neighboring countries."

In 1996, Phat Phillie and his collective recorded and released a compilation called *The Blackout Project,* amassing all the best Croatian hip hop tracks of the time onto one record. Interestingly enough, during the wartime situation in Croatia during 1996, as the government tried to shut down Radio 101, thousands of people converged on the square to prevent the government's wartime censorship; it was the Blackout Crew's theme track that became the score to this moment in the real-life motion picture of protest against the ills of the government.

Shortly after this event, Phillie moved from Croatia to London for six months to gain more exposure and meet more people in the hip hop industry. In 1996, he recalls how "my host was a Zulu Nation king. So when [Afrika Bambaataa] came to London, we would all hang out. And after talking to Bam and Dapo, they decided I would start running the Zulu Nation chapter in Croatia." It is important to note at this point that Phat Phillie returned to Croatia as a different person; he may have left as DJ Phat Phillie, but he returned as DJ Phat Phillie—Zulu King in the Universal Zulu Nation. This becomes paramount because Phat Phillie found himself ushered into spreading the word and the sounds of hip hop, having been cosigned by Afrika Bambaataa, one of the founding fathers of hip hop music and culture. Thus, while Phat Phillie may not necessarily be African American or belong specifically to the Afrodiasporic collective, it was his innate understanding of how African American culture has cultivated hip hop that allowed him to move into his unofficial role as hip hop ambassador in Croatia. Thus, upon his return home in the winter of 1996, Phillie started working at a Croatian club and invited various DJs to come and spin. By November of 1997, Phat Phillie would bring the first US act to do a show in Croatia: O.C. from the legendary Diggin' in the Crates crew. At this point, he would move forward with promotional work as well as DJing. But again, the DJ work was the cornerstone of Phat Phillie's progression in the hip hop industry, and specifically in regard to connecting with Afrika Bambaataa.

When it comes to the *Blackout Radio Show,* Phillie seems to have taken a purist mentality, as he believes his show and members of his crew to be "the keepers of the funk and the keepers of the real hip hop sound. Where everybody's going pop and everybody's going electro, everybody's going house, we're still tryna represent that real raw sound such as DJ Premier, Pete Rock, Statik Selektah, Tony Touch, and do something like they do in their respective shows in the U.S." The DJs Phat Phillie has named here have a lot in common: not only are all of them hip hop DJ pioneers in many respects, but they are also a multicultural collection of DJs. This testifies to the fact that adhering to the tenets of hip hop music and culture does not necessitate being "African American"; it merely demands that you have a respect for African American culture as the progenitor of hip hop as we know it.

When talking about the work he does currently, Phat Phillie describes his process of DJing as very similar to the ways that certain scholars have labeled the DJ:

I love to start DJing at a slower pace and develop my story and develop the vibe in the club and just gradually build up the whole party. . . . Recently, I started a soundsystem together with a good brother of mine J-Ro from the legendary West Coast hip hop group the Alkaholiks. He's lived in Sweden since 2006, 2007 and we started the Likwid Bumz soundsystem. . . . J-Ro's my emcee throughout my sets. So that's an extra flavor for everybody that's in the club: You have not only a DJ who plays great music, but now you have a dope MC who rocks the crowd throughout the party. He's doing all the hip hop chants, and he's rockin' some of his hits from the '90s. He jumps on stage and rocks the crowd. . . . Some DJs are also dope MCs, dudes like Kid Capri or Tony Touch or DJ Premier. They are DJs that also rock the crowd themselves. But then you also have DJs like Jazzy Jeff and some other kats who are just concentrating on their DJing, and they just have their guys rock the crowd for them. So Jeff has Mad Skillz, Phat Phillie has J-Ro. A couple other guys have other MCs. So that's definitely a great addition to what we do: to have somebody rock the mic and bring that extra energy to the club. (personal communication, August 25, 2011)

This is a sentiment that echoes the work of Adam Banks in his book *Digital Griots: African American Rhetoric in a Multimedia Age* (2011). Banks is able to open the door to the idea of the DJ as griot, as the DJ initially gave the storytelling MC that first opportunity to shine at the microphone. It is here that we can see Phat Phillie taking a very purist hip hop stance: He focuses on his mixing and turntable technique, while giving another emcee—J-Ro—an opportunity to shine at the microphone and get the crowd involved in the music. This is the essence of hip hop culture: the music that started from the focal point called the DJ, who extended light to the MC. This is also a very roots-oriented perspective when it comes to hip hop culture. So again, Phat Phillie demonstrates the fact that it is not necessarily about adhering to a particular form of blackness, but instead, he's paying homage to a very purist form of hip hop music and culture, while understanding the historical context of the DJ and the landscape from which that context emerges. It is this philosophy and business savvy that has allowed Phat Phillie over 20 years of longevity and experience that he's had in the DJ game in order to rock different parties in different markets and countries throughout Eastern Europe. When asked why he thought the DJ was an important element of hip hop culture, Phat Phillie's answer was extensive and thorough:

The DJs created hip hop: Kool Herc, Grandmaster Flash, Afrika Bambaataa, Grand Wizard Theodore—all these guys were DJs and they CREATED hip hop, they put it on the map. Also, DJs are the ones who break all the new records. So if it wasn't for DJs, we wouldn't be able to hear all the new music. . . .

Hip hop is out there where McDonald's isn't, so that tells you something! And why is it out there like that? Because local DJs took that energy and took those records and took the music and spread it around. I am responsible for hip hop being big in Croatia, and I'm not solely responsible. But I was on the radio giving them the records, I was traveling to New York to get the tapes, I would get the music from different record companies and play it here. And I'm a DJ. The DJ is the most important figure in hip hop. (personal communication, August 25, 2011)

Currently, DJ Phat Phillie serves as a conduit between many US artists and Croatian and European artists. Whether connecting producers to MCs or serving as a booking agent for US acts to tour Croatia, other countries in the region, and even the larger market of Europe, or writing articles for *The Source* magazine, none of this work would be a viable option for Phat Phillie without his work as a DJ, and specifically his connection to Afrika Bambaataa as a Zulu King of the Croatian chapter of the Universal Zulu Nation. "When I'm asked to introduce myself, I am DJ Phat Phillie. The title 'DJ' is on my business card. I never would've met Bambaataa or Ice-T if I wasn't a DJ."

In closing, the advice that Phat Phillie gives to aspiring DJs truly reinforces the idea of knowing the historical and cultural context of hip hop and where it comes from; he is quite adamant about understanding the history of the culture. "The first advice I would give to new up and coming DJs is to respect the people that paved the way, respect your elders, give them props. Try to learn from us, be patient . . . be original, try not to copy. I took a lot of influences from different DJs and radio hosts, but I never copied. I was never a copycat. I was using what they gave me, and I added something of my own on top of it . . . and learn about the history."

"This Is How We Chill from '93 'til . . .": Conclusions about the DJ at the Helm of the Culture's Ship

These moments I have documented coalesce to elucidate the infinite possibilities when we (re)orchestrate our thinking to align with that of the DJ-first mentality displayed in this work. By putting the DJ back into the forefront of thinking about hip hop music and culture, we can see a radical shift in the way we begin to talk about and approach issues surrounding and involving hip hop. By specifically looking at the blueprint presented to us by DJ Phat Phillie, we can see the exploration of a DJ who faithfully followed the tenets and Afrodiasporic roots of hip hop, "keeping it 100" all the way around the globe—from his travels to Long Island to learn English, to New York City where he bought the hip hop mixtapes, to London where he connected with Afrika Bambaataa, and back around to Radio 101 in Croatia. Looking at the legacy that DJ Phat Phillie has created in the Croatian hip hop scene, we can see how his efforts exhibited a special type of authenticity based on his knowledge of hip hop history and culture, while still fostering a unique representation of hip hop in his Eastern European homeland. This is not about being "black" or "from the 'hood"; this is about acknowledging and honoring the innately African American roots of hip hop music and culture. It is about consideration for the concerns of Dr. Elaine Richardson, who sees the decentering of the Afrodiasporic tradition embedding in hip hop as it travels abroad. It is about the theoretical breaks presented by Dr. Adam Banks, who captures the notion succinctly as "the foolishness of trying to scratch or sample the practices of the DJ, MC, or hype-wo/man in Hip Hop and drop them into our scholarship without thorough, searching attention to the discursive and rhetorical traditions from which they emerge" (Banks 2011: 13). These things can all be considered and honored in new and fascinating ways, as we see with the example of DJ Phat Phillie. Essentially, it's about "keeping it 100" so the culture can fully evolve and rotate 360, full-circle . . . the way the record does for the DJ . . . who's always first.

References

Alim, H. Samy. 2006. *Roc the Mic Right: The Language of Hip Hop Culture*. New York: Taylor and Francis.

Alim, H. Samy, Awad Ibrahim, and Alastair Pennycook, eds. 2008. *Global Linguistic Flows: Hip Hop Cultures, Youth Identities, and the Politics of Language*. New York: Routledge.

Banks, Adam. 2011. *Digital Griots: African American Rhetoric in a Multimedia Age*. Carbondale: Southern Illinois University Press.

Katz, Mark. 2012. *Groove Music: The Art and Culture of the Hip-Hop DJ*. New York: Oxford University Press.

Miller, Paul. 2004. *Rhythm Science*. Cambridge, MA: MIT Press.

Pennycook, Alastair. 2007. "Language, Localization, and the Real: Hip Hop and the Global Spread of Authenticity."*Journal of Language, Identity, and Education* 6(2):101–115.

Petchauer, Emery. 2009. "Framing and Reviewing Hip Hop Educational Research." *Review of Educational Research* 79(2):946–978.

Petchauer, Emery. 2012. "Sampling Memories: Using Hip Hop Aesthetics to Learn from Urban Schooling Experiences." *Educational Studies* 48(2):137–155.

Rice, Jeff. 2003. "The 1963 Hip Hop Machine: Hip-Hop Pedagogy as Composition." *College Composition and Communication* 54(3):453–471.

Richardson, Elaine. 2004. *African American Literacies*. New York: Routledge.

Richardson, Elaine. 2006. *Hiphop Literacies*. New York: Routledge.

Richardson, Elaine. 2010. "*Global Linguistic Flows: Hip Hop Cultures, Youth Identities, and the Politics of Language*, edited by H. Samy Alim, Awad Ibrahim and Alastair Pennycook" [review]. *Journal of Sociolinguistics* 14(2):266–272.

Schloss, Joseph. 2004. *Making Beats: The Art of Sample-Based Hip-Hop*. Middletown, CT: Wesleyan University Press.

Smitherman, Geneva. 1977. *Talkin and Testifyin: The language of Black America*. Detroit: Wayne State University Press.

Smitherman, Geneva. 1997. "'The Chain Remain the Same': Communicative Practices in the Hip Hop Nation." *Journal of Black Studies* 28(1):3–25.

DISCOGRAPHY

Criminal Element Orchestra. 1987. *Put the Needle to the Record* [LP]. Criminal/Chrysalis Records.

Das EFX. 1995. "The Real Hip Hop." *Hold It Down* [LP]. New York: EastWest Records.

Grand Puba, 1992. "360 Degrees (What Goes Around)." *Reel to Reel* [LP]. New York: Elektra Records.

KRS-One. 2012. "Ova Here." *The Mixtape* [MP3]. New York: Koch Records.

M|A|R|R|S. 1987. "Pump Up the Volume" [LP]. London: 4AD/4th & B'way/Island/PolyGram Records.

Souls of Mischief. 1993. *93 'til Infinity* [LP]. New York: Jive Records.

CONTRIBUTORS

ALEXANDRA BALANDINA is Academic Associate at the Technological Educational Institute of Central Greece, Department of Culture and Tourism. She earned her PhD in ethnomusicology from Goldsmiths College, University of London. Her ethnographic research focuses on Iran, Macedonia (former Yugoslavia), and Ireland.

PETER BARRER teaches in the Department of British and American Studies at the Faculty of Arts of Comenius University in Bratislava, Slovakia. He received his PhD in 2008 from Monash University in Melbourne, Australia, where his doctoral research analyzed expressions of national identity in Slovak media and popular culture. His published work includes articles on Slovak popular music, reality television and ice hockey, and images of New Zealand in Slovak mass media.

MURAN CAN BAŞARAN holds a BA in media and communication from the University of Economics and a BA in international relations and European Union from the University of Economics. He is the author of "Visibility of Woman Killings: From the Third Page to the First Page." His senior thesis focused on hip hop/rappers who use arabesk musical elements in their amateur productions.

TODD CRAIG is Associate Professor of English at Medgar Evers College of the City University of New York, where he also serves as composition coordinator. His research examines the hip hop DJ as twenty-first-century new media reader and writer, and investigates the modes and practices of the DJ as discourse that create DJ rhetoric and literacy. Craig's publications include the multimodal novel "tor'cha; a short story" in Akashic Books' *Staten Island Noir*, essays in *Across Cultures: A Reader for Writers*, and *Lead, Follow, or Move Out of the Way: Global Perspectives in Literature and Films*, as well as articles in *Radical Teacher*, the *Killens Review of Arts and Letters*, and forthcoming publications in *Changing English and Modern Language Studies*.

GENTIAN ELEZI is a PhD candidate in politics at the University of Sussex, UK. He teaches at the University of Tirana and works as the director of an independent think tank in Albania. His primary area of research is EU policymaking and enlargement. Past research has focused on post-communist transition and democratization, with a focus on Central Europe countries and Albania.

NURAN EROL IŞIK is Professor of Sociology at Izmir University of Economics, Izmir, Turkey. Her work in cultural studies, political sociology, and the sociology of media investigates issues at the intersection of culture, society, and media. Her latest publications include articles on popular religion, storytelling, and narrativity. Her research focuses on arabesk music as a popular cultural symbol in Turkish society and culture.

PHILIP EWELL is Assistant Professor of Music at Hunter College of the City University of New York. He holds a joint appointment with the City University's Graduate Center. He received his PhD in music theory from Yale University with a dissertation on the music of Alexander Scriabin. His research focuses on Russian music and music theory, twentieth-century music, twentieth-century modal theory, and rap and hip hop music. His articles have been published in *Music Theory Online*, *Music and Politics*, and *Popular Music*, among other journals.

ALEXANDRE GONTCHAR is a PhD candidate in the Department of Slavic Languages and Literatures at Harvard University. His dissertation "The Grand Nomadic Symphony: A Study of Human Finitude in Four Movements" examines how three Russian authors (Leo Tolstoy, Velimir Khlebnikov, and Andrey Platonov) creatively estranged and challenged various philosophical notions of freedom as self-determination.

ADRIANA HELBIG is Associate Professor of Music and Assistant Dean of Undergraduates at the University of Pittsburgh. She is the author of *Hip Hop Ukraine: Music, Race, and African Migration* (Indiana University Press, 2014) and is coauthor with Oksana Buranbaeva and Vanja Mladineo of *Culture and Customs of Ukraine*.

ALENA KAJANOVÁ holds a Ph.D. from the University of South Bohemia, Faculty of Health and Social Studies. She is head of the Department of Social Work. Her research focuses on Romani minorities, social exclusion, and the culture of poverty.

MILOSZ MISZCZYNSKI is Research Fellow at the Centre for the Digital Economy at the University of Surrey and Research Associate at the University of Oxford's Institute of Social and Cultural Anthropology. His current research focuses on the production, distribution, and consumption of music in the digital economy. His work includes a book in Polish, edited volumes, and journal articles published in the *European Journal of Cultural Studies* and *Critical Sociology*.

TOMAS MRHALEK is Assistant Professor in the Department of Pedagogy and Psychology, Faculty of Pedagogy, South Bohemian University. He studied psychology, sociology, and media studies. He is interested in social and intercultural psychology as well as affective and cognitive neuroscience. His projects include studies of excluded groups and minorities.

JASMIN MUJANOVIĆ is a PhD candidate in political science at York University, Toronto, Canada. His work focuses on the postwar democratization of Bosnia-Herzegovina and the role that social and protest movements play in postauthoritarian transitions to democracy more broadly.

GORAN MUSIĆ is a PhD candidate in the Department of History and Civilization at the European University Institute in Florence, Italy. He works as a researcher at the Centre for Southeast European Studies, University of Graz, on a project supported by the Austrian Science Fund "Between Class and Nation: Working Class Communities in 1980s Serbia and Montenegro." His research focuses on Yugoslav/Serbian hip hop scenes, everyday life under socialism, working-class politics, and youth subcultures.

ANNA ORAVCOVÁ is a PhD candidate in the Department of Sociology at the Faculty of Social Sciences, Charles University in Prague, Czech Republic, where she is writing her dissertation about Czech hip hop, focusing on issues of gender and race/ethnicity, and teaching an undergraduate course on youth music subcultures. She uses her weekly radio show to inform listeners about current social and political issues related to hip hop culture.

ELEANOR PEERS is Post-Doctoral Fellow at the University of Aberdeen. She has recently started work on an AHRC-funded project on narrative objects, museum work, and memory in Sakha (Yakutia). Her research focuses on Sakha shamanic revival and has been supported by the Max Planck Institute of Social Anthropology.

MICHAL RUZICKA has been conducting ethnographic research of marginalized Roma (Gypsy) families in Czech urban areas as well as in "Gypsy settlements" in rural parts of Slovakia. His publications include journal articles in the *Journal of Rural Studies* and *Czech Sociological Review* as well as book chapters.

IRENA ŠENTEVSKA has a PhD in arts and media theory from the University of Arts in Belgrade, Serbia. Her interdisciplinary research focuses on identity (re) construction in post-Yugoslav political and cultural contexts, with a specific focus on contemporary arts, media, and popular and urban culture in Southeastern

Europe. Her first book, *Swinging 90s: Theatre and Social Reality of Serbia in 29 Pictures*, is forthcoming.

NICHOLAS TOCHKA is currently Visiting Assistant Professor of Ethnomusicology at the University of Maryland. Since 2004, he has conducted archival and ethnographic field research on popular and concert music in Albania. He is currently writing a history of the state-subsidized genre "light music" under socialism and capitalism in Tirana.

PRZEMYSLAW TOMASZEWSKI graduated from the Institute of Sociology at the Jagiellonian University in Krakow, Poland. He currently works as a research manager at one of Poland's leading courier firms.

ELONA TOSKA is a PhD candidate in the Department of Social Policy and Intervention, University of Oxford. Her research focuses on youth health and well-being. She also analyzes social movements, societies in transition, and cultures of complaint. She has worked for the OSCE during election observation missions in Albania and has run a local NGO in Albania.

TRIIN VALLASTE completed her PhD in ethnomusicology at Brown University in 2014. Her research focuses on the politics and poetics of sound cultures in Estonia, particularly the history and development of the Estonian-language hip hop scene. She currently works at the Center for Russian Culture at Amherst College.

AIMAR VENTSEL is Senior Researcher in the Department of Ethnology at the University of Tartu, Estonia. His publications include "Reindeer, Rodina and Reciprocity: Kinship and Property Relations in a Siberian Village" in the *Halle Studies in the Anthropology of Eurasia* and "Siberian Movements: How Money and Goods Travel In and Out of Northwestern Sakha" in the *Electronic Journal of Folklore*.

PREDRAG VUKČEVIĆ is an undergraduate in the Department of Philosophy at the Faculty of Philosophy, University of Belgrade, Serbia. He has been working as a DJ and MC since 1996, taking an active role in the development of hip hop, jungle/dnb, and techno scenes in Serbia and former Yugoslavia. He is the author of a number of historical and theoretical articles and essays on hip hop culture published in Serbian magazines and webzines. In 2009, together with Zoran Lojanica, he translated and edited the Serbian edition of Jeff Chang's *Can't Stop Won't Stop: A History of the Hip-Hop Generation*.

VERONIKA ZVÁNOVCOVÁ is Assistant Professor in the Department of Social Work at the Theological Faculty, University of South Bohemia, in České Budějovice. She graduated from the Health and Social Studies Faculty, University of South Bohemia. She has worked in Zambia, participating in educational projects for street children and orphans and coordinating the project Adoption for Children from Zambia. She currently works as a social worker with at-risk children in the Czech Republic and is involved in the Pět P program (Big Brothers Big Sisters), focusing on direct assistance to disabled athletes.

www.ingramcontent.com/pod-product-compliance
Lightning Source LLC
Chambersburg PA
CBHW020727180526
45163CB00001B/146